COMPUTERS AND THE POLICY-MAKING COMMUNITY

Applications to International Relations

Prentice-Hall
Series in Automatic Computation
George Forsythe, editor

BATES AND DOUGLAS, *Programming Language/One*
BAUMANN, FELICIANO, BAUER, AND SAMELSON, *Introduction to ALGOL*
BOBROW AND SCHWARTZ, *Computers and the Policy-Making Community*
BOWLES, *Computers in Humanistic Research*
CESCHINO AND KUNTZMAN, *Numerical Solution of Initial Value Problems*
DESMONDE, *Computers and Their Uses*
DESMONDE, *A Conversational Graphic Data Processing System*
DESMONDE, *Real-Time Data Processing Systems: Introductory Concepts*
EVANS, WALLACE, AND SUTHERLAND, *Simulation Using Digital Computers*
FIKE, *Computer Evaluation of Mathematical Functions*
FORSYTHE AND MOLER, *Computer Solution of Linear Algebraic Systems*
GOLDEN, *FORTRAN IV: Programming and Computing*
GOLDEN AND LEICHUS, *IBM 360: Programming and Computing*
GRUENBERGER, *Computers and Communications—Toward a Computer Utility*
HARTMANIS AND STEARNS, *Algebraic Structure Theory of Sequential Machines*
HULL, *Introduction to Computing*
LOUDEN, *Programming the IBM 1130 and 1180*
MARTIN, *Design of Real-Time Computer Systems*
MARTIN, *Programming Real-Time Computer Systems*
MARTIN, *Telecommunications and the Computer*
MINSKY, *Computation: Finite and Infinite Machines*
MOORE, *Interval Analysis*
SAMMET, *Fundamentals of Basic Computer Languages*
SCHULTZ, *Digital Processing: A System Orientation*
SNYDER, *Chebyshev Methods in Numerical Approximation*
STERLING AND POLLACK, *Introduction to Statistical Data Processing*
STROUD AND SECREST, *Gaussian Quadrature Formulas*
TRAUB, *Iterative Methods for the Solution of Equations*
VARGA, *Matrix Iterative Analysis*
VAZSONYI, *Problem Solving by Digital Computers with PL/I Programming*
WILKINSON, *Rounding Errors in Algebraic Processes*
ZIEGLER, *Time-Sharing Data Processing Systems*

COMPUTERS AND THE POLICY-MAKING COMMUNITY

Applications to International Relations

Davis B. Bobrow

Senior Social Scientist
Oak Ridge National Laboratory

Judah L. Schwartz

Education Research Center
Massachusetts Institute of Technology

Prentice-Hall, Inc., Englewood Cliffs, N.J.

PREFACE

This book grew out of a conference entitled "Computers and The Policy-Making Community" held during the month of April 1966 at the University of California, Lawrence Radiation Laboratory in Livermore, California, and jointly sponsored by the Carnegie Endowment for International Peace and The Division of Nuclear Education and Training of the United States Atomic Energy Commission. The conferees were drawn from those concerned with foreign policy in the Executive branch of the federal government and from those in the academic world engaged in research and teaching in the fields of government and international relations. The primary intention of the program was to ease the difficult communication between the political scientists or political analyst and the computer expert. We have been encouraged to believe that the program was successful in several ways.

We hope that this volume may fruitfully serve the same function. It is not a primer in any strict sense of the term. Its purpose is rather to whittle down to human proportions some of the more popular misconceptions about digital computers and their applications to political analysis and to equip the reader with enough understanding to be constructively critical.

This undertaking would have been impossible without the graciousness and cooperation of the Lawrence Radiation Laboratory in general and of James Hill, William Jenkins, Leonard Marks, Judy Tate, Alice Williams, and Dean Wise in particular. To each of them our continuing gratitude.

Finally, we wish to recognize our debt to our wives, Sue Bobrow and Ellen Schwartz, whose patience and good humor made many barriers passable.

Davis B. Bobrow
Judah L. Schwartz

CONTENTS

1. COMPUTERS AND INTERNATIONAL RELATIONS 1
Davis B. Bobrow (Oak Ridge National Laboratory)
Judah L. Schwartz (Mass. Inst. of Technology)

2. INTRODUCTION TO COMPUTERS 20
S. Fernbach (Lawrence Radiation Laboratory)

3. THE LOGIC OF COMPUTING MACHINERY 35
Robert H. Wyman, Jr. (Digital Equipment Corp.)

4. COMPUTER LANGUAGES 56
Leroy Krider (Control Data Corp.)

5. INFORMATION RETRIEVAL AND COMPUTERS 71
Robert J. Howerton (Lawrence Radiation Laboratory)

6. INTERNATIONAL INTERACTIONS: SURVEYS AND COMPUTERS 81
Davis B. Bobrow (Oak Ridge National Laboratory)

7. CONTENT ANALYSIS IN POLITICAL RESEARCH 111
Ole Holsti (University of British Columbia)

8. INTERNATIONAL PATTERN AND NATIONAL PROFILE
DELINEATION 154
Rudolph Rummel (University of Hawaii)

9. SIMULATIONS AND WAR GAMES 203
N. C. Dalkey (RAND Corp.)

10. NUMERICAL SIMULATION OF THE EARTH'S ATMOSPHERE 215
Cecil E. Leith (Natural Center for Atmospheric Research)

11. BURDENS FOR THE DESIGNER OF A COMPUTER
SIMULATION OF INTERNATIONAL RELATIONS 222
Morton Gorden (University of Pennsylvania)

12. ARTIFICIAL INTELLIGENCE AND INTERNATIONAL RELATIONS 246
James R. Slagle (National Institute of Health)

13. THE MONTE CARLO METHOD 253
Harry Sahlin (Lawrence Radiation Laboratory)

14. PICTURES, COMPUTERS, AND INPUT-OUTPUT 272
G. A. Michael (Haverford College)

15. THE TRANSITION TOWARD MORE SOPHISTICATED
PROCEDURES 307
Harold D. Lasswell (Yale University)

16. AN EDUCATIONAL EXPERIMENT 315
Jeffrey S. Milstein (Stanford University)
Davis B. Bobrow (Oak Ridge National Laboratory)

GLOSSARY 347

INDEX 356

COMPUTERS AND THE POLICY-MAKING COMMUNITY

Applications to International Relations

Chapter 1

COMPUTERS AND INTERNATIONAL RELATIONS

Davis B. Bobrow and Judah L. Schwartz

It seems to us that computers are having important effects on international relations research, teaching, and administration. If we want to take the necessary steps, we can now secure and analyze international relations information to achieve levels of understanding which were previously unattainable. This book is intended to clarify the nature of this new and exciting tool for a broad and nonmathematical audience. Accordingly, the book provides, first, an introduction to the computer itself, which should clarify its requirements and operations, and, second, a survey of the kinds of help which computers can provide for international relations purposes and the rationale which has led a number of us to do the work necessary to secure that help. Although we recognize that administrators, researchers, and teachers each have special objectives and problems, this volume deals with basic information needs which all these groups of international relations users share.[1]

It seems useful to begin by taking note of some alternative prospectives on computers and by indicating what perspective we hold. The latter parts of this introduction and the rest of the volume as a whole follow from our stance on what computers and computer users can and must do.

Like many other major innovations, computers are a focus for beliefs which attribute to them almost magical degrees of potency for both positive and negative ends. These magical beliefs are found among

---

[1] The orientation to international relations distinguishes this volume from those intended for a more general disciplinary community (Borko, 1962; Green, 1963) and its scope distinguishes it from those oriented to a particular family of applications (e.g., Feigenbaum and Feldman, 1963; Naylor, *et al.*, 1966; McPhee, 1965).

both professional (Knight and Miller, 1965) and nonprofessional (Lee, 1966) members of American society, and can be summarized briefly.

— *Computers are Merlins.* We refer to the notions that all we have to do is hand our problems to the computer and that it will then solve them both rapidly and correctly. It is only necessary to buy a sufficiently big and fast machine.

— *Computers are Personal Threats.* We refer to the often heard statement, "computers can never replace me" as if somehow the machines "want" to make man less important and that some people are using computers for this purpose.

— *Computers are Autonomous Social Forces.* Whether seen as Merlins or as Personal Threats, computers are discussed as if they somehow operate totally independent of man to shape their environment in fundamental ways. Accordingly, we read articles on "computer intelligence" and "computer diplomacy" (Sulzberger, 1966), and on "management by computer."

It is important to note that none of the perspectives above agree with the views held by professionals who have made substantial use of computers or by nonprofessional Americans who have had indirect contact with computers through contact with users. A study of M.I.T. computer users found a marked absence of anthropomorphic notions or anxieties about the machine (Neisser, 1964). A study of administrators who used computers in a number of West Coast corporations found a positive association between the extent to which a manager used the machine and the extent to which he felt that his job (a) was not routine, and (b) was innovative, autonomous, and involved in human relations (Knight and Miller, 1965). Finally, Lee (1966, p. 34) found that college-educated but not technically trained Americans "indirectly exposed to the world of data processing and computers through their work or by knowing people who make use of the machines...are less likely to feel uneasy about computers than those of comparable background who have not had this type of exposure." If our three magical beliefs have not been supported in the experience of users, what perspective is fruitful with regard to computer use?

We suggest that effective use of computers should be seen as part of the problem-solving process, the success of which depends on the human execution of other parts. The first, and by far most important, of these parts is problem-definition — precisely what are we trying to learn and how can we cut it into manageable parts. Gruenberger and Jaffray (1965, p. xiv) observe, "The short history of computing is already loaded with sad tales of people who never did get their problem properly defined." Second, we have to develop an analytic scheme which will in principle manipulate these data to arrive at an answer to the defined problem, for example, the cost-effectiveness of U.S. programs aimed at Kenya relative to that of programs aimed at Nigeria. Third, we have to decide on and secure the inputs to the computer analysis of our problem, for example, if our problem is to compare U.S. governmental activities in Kenya and Nigeria, we have to specify, and then obtain, the data we need about American programs in those two countries. Fourth, and only fourth, we have to place our data in a form acceptable to the computer (a machine-readable format) and state our analytic scheme in a clear set of instructions for the computer (a program). Fifth, the computer takes the formated data and the program and executes the requested analysis. Sixth, the machine reports the results of what we have asked it to do according to our preferences: for example, a numerical table or a graph. Seventh, we have to decide what the import of the reported results is for our problem.

The purpose of this lengthy example is to emphasize that the key, initial, and final steps in the use of a computer are taken by people, in this case international relations experts, and that the computer-produced results are a function of what we have given (input) to it. Of course, the computer can in principle assist us with some of the earlier stages in the example. To illustrate, the Kenya and Nigeria data could be retrieved from a computerized data bank. However, the existence and utility of the data bank depends on prior human effort. We believe that computers can powerfully assist international relations professionals, but we also believe that we cannot capitalize on the machines unless we make the major effort involved in steps 1, 2, 3, and 7. The work involved in these steps cannot be delegated to computer specialists because it involves a large number of substantive international relations decisions.

This perspective leads us, in this introduction, to the situation which confronts current and potential international relations users and to the question of how computers relate to that situation. The problems we want to progress with are those of international relations and not of computers *per se*. In particular, we will discuss: (1) objective for international relations analysts, educators, and administrators; (2) characteristics of the context in which these objectives must be pursued; (3) the role of numbers and logical statements in this pursuit; and (4) the place of computers in this framework of objectives, context characteristics, and nonverbal expression.

I.   INTERNATIONAL RELATIONS OBJECTIVES

Since we are talking about computers as tools, it seems useful to state what they are supposed to help us produce. What we want to achieve — whether it be to affect the international system, or to create or disseminate knowledge about international relations — can be summarized as correct descriptions, powerful explanations, valid predictions, and value optimizations. Also, we want to achieve any or all of these in as intellectually efficient a manner as possible. Let us very briefly note what attaining each of these objectives involves and illustrate the types of substantive questions germane to each.

CORRECT DESCRIPTIONS

To realistically describe what has been and what is, to recognize what is similar and what is different, to distinguish what is changing from what is constant — each of these abilities has three requirements. These requirements are (1) data, (2) usefully organized data, and, (3) accessible data. In other words, we have to have information which is both accurate and adequate in its scope, which is categorized in pertinent ways and which we can get at easily. At this time, many arguments about international relations are about matters of description and much information germane to these disagreements goes unused or underused. If the preceding requirements are met, we can expect rapid and valid answers to such descriptive questions as: What are the voting blocs in the United Nations? Are dictatorships more aggressive than democracies? What are the differences and similarities between U.S. programs directed at Nigeria and programs directed at Kenya? The better our descriptions, the greater are our chances to attain our other objectives in a planned rather than a chance fashion.

POWERFUL EXPLANATIONS

Of course, we make most effective use of correct descriptions, such as those illustrated above, once we understand the reasons for the situation described. Explanation, and particularly powerful explanation, is the key element of theory of international relations and effective policy to maintain and achieve wanted international situations and to prevent the unwanted. A first step toward explanation is the search for patterns of association or disassociation, for example, between internal political unrest and warlike external actions by states or between complementarity of foreign policies and the existence of a program budgeting system. A second step is to use answers to the classic questions of the "If we have X, how likely are we to have Y" type to set boundaries within which it pays to search for answers to questions of the type "What does X really have to do with Y?" At present we have a large number of less than compatible associational statements about international relations phenomena, almost all of which rest on *some* fragmentary evidence from a small number of instances. If we are to weed this baggage, and we need to, in order to arrive at a coherent set of explanations for international behavior we have to find some way of providing ourselves with the following capabilities. First, we need to be able to search for relationships among a wide and representative set of data which spans a sizeable number of years and countries. Second, we must be able to subject to interconnected examination the linkages between a large number of statistically associated persons, groups, resources, beliefs, and decisions. Third, we have to be able to do so in ways which allow us to explore the extent to which a number of possible forms and degrees of connection fit the data. Fourth, we need to be able to find out what difference alternative possible relationships would make, that is, how sensitive the outcomes of interest are to different connections. In sum, if we are to arrive at powerful explanations, we need to have large data bases, stored in a large and orderly memory whose contents we can manipulate in numerous, interdependent ways (Glaser and Bisco, 1966).

VALID PREDICTIONS

It is commonplace to observe that it is difficult to make valid predictions about international relations because of the importance of "intangible" factors. Yet it is also true that we gain in our ability to make valid predictions which take these factors into account when we: (1) develop empirically supported explanations of what underlies classes of international phenomena (for example, alliances); (2) distinguish between the importance of different characteristics for the state of these phenomena (for example, for alliances between the importance of common languages, commercial connections, and official consensus on the identity and policy of a common enemy); (3) allow for the effects of the many possible determinants of the future; (4) determine to what extent and in what ways possible future situations are the same as known current or past situations; (5) predict not only a final outcome but intervening steps toward that outcome so that prediction can be checked and modified during the period from prediction to outcome (for example, predictions about nuclear proliferation can be reexamined in the light of the advancing or static state of nuclear technology in a country); and (6) combine known "laws" of international behavior with a number of alternative possibilities on less clear factors to assess the probabilities of particular outcomes (that is, what combination of uncertainties would have to occur to change the result predicted on the basis of known probabilities) (Pool, 1964).

VALUE OPTIMIZATIONS

Knowledge pertinent to international relations policy clearly does not stop with description, explanation, and prediction. Policy is a goal-oriented activity, that is, an effort to achieve some preference. Similarly, research and education in international relations should not and need not ignore what is preferred or valued. From an analytic point of view, this creates two needs. The first is to determine what states of affairs are particularly conducive to some values being realized (for example, peace) and the second is to determine whether the means to realize those situations are feasible and desirable in the sense that they do not violate on balance more important values. Accordingly, our interests in international relations involve value optimization in two senses — effective pursuit (how to get to the valued state), and cognizance of the implications of pursuit (so we really want to try to get there). Our ability to answer these questions involves us in the development of two pictures or "worlds" and in the analysis of the changes necessary to get from one to the other. These worlds are: the present world and the values it affords, and, the hypothetical world in which the desired value is attained. Comparing these two worlds, or models, and determining the extent to which they do or do not optimize our values is difficult to do with any precision either in our heads or with paper and pencil. We need a massive extension of our vision and of our mental capacity, but one which we can interrogate.

INTELLECTUAL EFFICIENCY

Who can be against intellectual efficiency? Yet we are all on occasion preoccupied with trees instead of forests, perhaps, without even checking to see if there is a forest. Most international relations information, whichever of the forms above it takes, is part of a long chain of previously established or assumed conditions. The specifics of international relations can be seen as twigs at the end of branches formed by these conditions. For example, to interpret the significance of an act by a foreign government (for example, Soviet scholarships to African students) we use more general or branch information (for example, whether the general intentions of the Soviet Union toward Africa are primarily to foster Communist Party takeovers, neutralism, or economic development). Accordingly, we are more intellectually efficient when we use tools which, first, channel our attention initially to alternative branches and keep us from becoming twig-centered, and, second, enable us to test for the empirical goodness of fit of different branches (for example, alternative Soviet emphases in the example above). In sum, we are more likely to engage in effective "strong inference" (Platt, 1964) if we use rather formal and explicit logical structures and analytic aids which can synthesize a variety of specific observations.

As we will illustrate subsequently, it seems to us that computers can be powerful assistants in the pursuit of all of these objectives. More strongly, the considerations to which we now turn suggest to us that computers are essential assistants if we are to make substantial progress toward these objectives.[2]

II. CHARACTERISTICS OF THE CONTEXT

Those of us who try to understand and affect international relations are working in a context increasingly marked by three important characteristics: complexity, change, and an abundance of information. Our efforts to attain the objectives noted above tend to succeed only to the extent that they cope with these characteristics.

COMPLEXITY

The elements of the international system are both numerous and highly interdependent. Post-World War II developments have heightened these characteristics. For example, there are now more than 50 additional independent nations over the pre-1943 international system. If one thinks about the multiplier effect this has on the number of possible two-nation relationships, its analytic significance becomes even more striking. Developments in weaponry, communication, and transportation have all worked to increase the interactions between states no matter how geographically and culturally separate countries and their populations

[2]If the reader suspects that this is the personal view of the authors, he is right.

may be. These developments have been supplemented by the emergence
of what are in some ways new variables which link members of different
states (for example, the comparisons denoted by slogans such as the
"brain drain" and the "technology gap").

Accordingly, we need approaches which can handle a complex interconnected system and are not compatible with the use of tools (whether
these be concepts, techniques, or standard operating procedures) which
exclude interdependence. Because we are trying to understand "complex
massive systems that respond to many variables at once" (Pool, 1964,
p. 63), we need to be able to employ in a related fashion ideas and facts
from the jurisdictions of many of the social sciences. For example, if our
problem is the Sino-Soviet split, we will want to put together considerations
about historical patterns, economic connections, political arrangements,
and elite psychology.   That is, we have to work across traditional
intellectual boundaries. We also have to be multivariate. To use the same
example, we cannot adequately understand or cope with the split unless
we consider its connections with a *number* of other governments (for
example, in Africa and Asia), of Communist Parties, of nuclear and
conventional weapons, of agricultural and industrial performance indicators, etc.

CHANGE

In addition to confronting us with complexity, the international
system confronts us with rapidly changing, unstable forms of complexity.
Accordingly, we need to be able to organize our understanding of
international relations in ways that are not made obsolete by change
and in ways which allow us to take account rather quickly of the
ramifications of particular changes in the system, for example, a Greek
coup or a French withdrawal from NATO. These requirements call for
an analytic apparatus with the following attributes: (1) organizing
units which do not apply only to time-specific features of the international
system; (2) a set of sensitivity procedures which estimate when particular
changes are likely to have major effects on other aspects of international
relations; and (3) a monitoring capability which keeps track of and brings
to our attention changes which have occurred and are occurring. To the
extent that we equip ourselves with an apparatus of this sort better than
what we now have, we can, with no new information, extend our ability
to anticipate, recognize, and cope with features of the shifting complex of
international relations.   As researchers, we can expect our findings to
have greater longevity in that they are applicable to more than the current

or past situation and greater accuracy in that they are based on data about the current and not the past world. As educators, we increase the likelihood that our students will emerge with intellectual resources whose utility extends through much of their lives. As policy operators, we lessen surprise from unexpected events, widen our field of vision to include more side-effects of policies, and decrease our dependence on concepts and information based on merely a few past situations.

ABUNDANT INFORMATION

International relations is increasingly characterized by abundant rather than scanty data. However, most international relations training has been geared to the assumption that very little information is available on most pertinent matters. We now face a situation where, unless we change, we have only three unsatisfactory alternatives available — allowing ourselves to be flooded, ignoring the data, or making only occasional and fragmentary use of it. How are we to make use of abundant information in ways which warrant the cost of collecting. maintaining, and duplicating it? These generic questions are the same whether one is asking about an academic international relations expert exploiting the growing number of social science data archives (Bisco, 1967) or a State Department intelligence analyst who with 199 colleagues tries to assess 100,000 documents monthly (Diebold, 1966). In the State Department alone, it has been estimated that "original items and distributed copies of . . . communications" were on the order of 64 million in one year (Fazar, 1966).

It seems to us that satisfactory answers to these questions will involve a mixture of three kinds of capabilities. First, we need to be able to draw selectively on these bulging files, that is, to be able to get at only those contents which are relevant with only a modest amount of time for searching and sifting. Second, if we are to benefit from the full capacity of archives, files, and personal and organizational "memories," we need to be able to pull out answers to our questions and not just the materials needed to arrive at answers. That is, we need to be able to pull out data and information reduced to tell us what we want to know — a trend, a casual connection, a degree of dependence — in easily grasped form. Third, to make worthwhile use of the first two capabilities once they are attained, we need to learn how to ask questions which we have always entertained but which we have tended to set aside because it did not seem feasible to answer them. This intellectual reorientation involves our raising our demands in the following ways: (1) seeking to understand more complex relationships; (2) seeking a greater degree of precision, for example, not only the direction but also the rate of change; (3) seeking more powerful forms of understanding, for example, not only whether a relationship is unlikely to have occurred solely through chance but how much of a phenomenon of interest (such as the tenure of a regime) is explained by the relationship. As we move beyond vague tendency statements which are difficult to confirm or disconform except by hindsight, we can expect positive reinforcement for the effort which phrasing fruitful questions requires. We can also expect to learn about sounder rules to decide what information is worth collecting and keeping — just as business managers learn to stock for minimum duplication, maximum demand, and critical need.

III. THE USE OF NUMBERS AND LOGICAL STATEMENTS

There is a class of issues central to the use of computers for international relations purposes. These issues involve the use of numbers and of explicit logical statements and we deal with them because the use of computers usually requires that we prepare our input and instructions in one or some combination of these forms. As we shall see, the latitude which these forms provide is very broad. Although there are areas of similarity between our discussion and the familiar debate about quantification in international relations, the differences are sufficiently important for us to be careful not to assume that the issues are identical. It seems especially useful to discuss four aspects of the use of numbers and logical statements: feasibility given international relations subject matter; the possibilities of misuse; desirability in terms of precision and manipulability; and finally, the necessary user skills.

FEASIBILITY

Discussions about the susceptability of international relations to treatments which involve the use of numerical and logical statements revolve around two questions. Can one state international relations considerations in these forms? Can such statements capture the nature of the international system to a fruitful extent? Let us consider these in turn.

We have all heard contentions that one cannot treat international relations in numerical or explicitly logical terms, that these ways of treating the "soft" material simply don't work. Although not all mathematical techniques can be applied usefully to international relations, we find the complete denial of feasibility rather without a basis. Moreover, computers do not consume only formal mathematical expressions. As Colby (1963, pp. 178-170) nicely states, a computer program (that is, the instructions of the human user) is a "way of dealing primarily with quality and structure rather than quantity and number." Because international relations discourse is full of descriptors of quality (dependent, independent) and structure (bipolar, multipolar), concepts of these kinds are familiar. Whether or not we think of them as logical statements, we use notions perfectly acceptable to a computer all the time (for example, "together with", "as a result of," "subsequently").

The dispute over the fruitfulness of using numerical and logical statements for international relations has as one central element a concern with complexity. Those who dispute the fruitfulness of these modes of expression often contend that they force gross simplification of international matters, and thus distort them fundamentally. The traditional response to this argument stresses the simplifications in much verbal theory and the power of parsimonious physical and economic theory. Those experienced with the computer often answer in a different fashion. "Let's not argue about whether or not in the past mathematical and logical modes of analysis have oversimplified what we agree is the very complex domain of international relations. The real situation is that if you will use these modes sufficiently to communicate with the computer, you now can retain and handle complexities far beyond the capacity of the unaided human mind." "Indeed," they will continue, "that is the great advantage of the computer."

MISUSE

The arguments pertinent to the possible misuse of numbers and logical statements can be divided into those about its contribution to better international relations information and those about its impact on political values (morality). The first set often involves assertions that the use of numerical and logical modes makes it easier for people to: (1) slip falsehoods and omissions by their colleagues; (2) secure automatic acceptance of their findings and recommendations based on their findings; and (3) concentrate on technical details rather than major problems of international relations. The rejoinder to these assertions consists of the observations that: (1) the responsibility for such negative consequences lies with the international relations user and his audience, not with numbers and logical statements; (2) the possibility that modes of treating a problem can be misused does not warrant a conclusion that they are most likely misused; and (3) the import of any accuracy these assertions may have can only be arrived at through comparison with the shortcomings of traditional verbal approaches.

The assertion that values are excluded if one uses numbers and logical statements, as if these modes of expression are somehow dehumanizing, has all the familiarity of an old shoe — an analogy reinforced by the fact that it has as many holes as do many old shoes. The international relations user expressing himself in primarily numerical and logical form, can, to whatever extent he desires, weigh considerations in arriving at a solution, or he can build into his model powerful value systems. If he does not, it is not because the modes of expression available keep him from doing so.

DESIRABILITY

Of course, even if it is feasible to use numbers and logical statements for international relations purposes without deleterious consequences, we have not offered sufficient reason to use them. The sufficient reason, it seems to us, comes from two probable consequences of their employment. The first is that of clarity and precision. We all know that there is considerable "elusiveness" in our conventional terms, their boundaries are unclear, and their usage less than consistent. The use of logical statement produces a confrontation with these ambiguities and a pressure to resolve them. The second important consequence is that of manipulability. That is, if one's categories and their relationships are clear and consistent, and if one has used symbols which "can be transformed as functions of other symbols" (Uhr, 1963, p. 233), one can then much more fully exploit data and see what the implications of theories are. The reader will note that these advantages which we attribute to the use of numbers and logical statements resemble the classical intellectual virtues of rigor, thorough analysis, and the pursuit of the implications of ideas.

SKILLS

It should be understood that in our context, requirements for the use of computers, the mathematical and logical skills which the international relations profession must possess are not great. Orderly and tight thinking will in most cases bring the international relations person to the point where, with the aid of the programmer and the applied mathematician, he can put the computer to work on his problem. The hurdle is in that modest "orderly and tight" phrase, but this hurdle does not stand or fall (primarily) because of the presence or absence of highly developed mathematical or logical skills.

In sum, we suggest that the use of numbers and logical statements to treat international relations is *prima facie* sufficiently feasible and desirable to merit the attempt. Accordingly, we will want to see what these "languages" can do for us unless we are less concerned with powerful understanding of international relations than we are with resisting innovation. The test lies in the benefits which the use of these modes of expression produce.

IV. THE PLACE OF COMPUTERS

What can computers be made to do within the framework of the previous three sections? As we see it, computers can be usefully applied to international relations and other problem areas in three ways: in information management; in data analysis; and in simulation and modeling. We will discuss each of these applications with international relations examples.

INFORMATION MANAGEMENT

The computer increasingly provides a superlative set of clerks and filing cabinets in three senses; ability to assign information to storage or user locations; ability to retain massive amounts of information in memory; and capacity for rapid and selective retrieval of information. Accordingly, one important sector of computer operations will be to make useful large and interrelated sets of communications (for example, cables from foreign stations), reference items (for example, bibliographies on the personality of African leaders), known findings (whether theoretical propositions such as four-member coalitions are less stable than those with three members; or empirical patterns such as the United States increases its military stockpile when the Soviets increase theirs), or data sets (U.S. balance of payments figures for the period 1957-1967). The usefulness of the computer for information retrieval is not confined to its ability to find and present material from large archives. It is well within the state of the art for machines to lead the user to a focused definition of his information needs, to suggest other information that may be useful, and to warn the user of the volume of material he will receive unless he narrows his request. The machines can be programmed to discriminate and relieve the human user of some of his information sifting burden.

With these capabilities, one can see that computer-based information management systems make it feasible to exploit personal and organizational memories, previous analyses, and information accumulations in ways which previously have simply been too time-consuming to be feasible. However, as John Diebold (1966, p. 125) warns, these gains will not result if all that is done is to mechanize "current inadequate information systems." The potential international relations users need to face explicitly the types of questions they want information about and what they consider to be information germane to these questions. An information management system with or without computers pays off only to the extent that it fits with the problems of its users, a fit established at the time that the system is designed. Of course, the fit should be with the questions that the users should ask and not necessarily with those that they currently ask. In this sense, a computerized information management system can be seen as a device for organizational change and improvement.

DATA ANALYSIS

In our discussion of information management, we noted the retrieval of data. Whether data are retrieved from an information base or freshly collected, they gain value as we can analyze them to answer important questions in a powerful way. Computers enter into this process as an extension of our analytic capabilities just as "engines amplify our muscles" (Miller, 1966, p. 110). Data analysis applications are generically similar across a variety of international relations data (for example, the attitudes of mass publics in the developing nations, the content of communications from foreign governments as crises approach and wane, the personal characteristics of Communist elites, or the pattern of trade flows between Western Europe and Latin America). Many of the analytic operations could in principle be performed by humans, if there were enough of them, if they were sufficiently reliable, and if we had enough time to wait for them to do the job. In essence, none of these requirements is usually present and computers can fill a gap in a way which liberates international relations professionals to make the kinds of decisions which they are trained to make.

Through a variety of statistical manipulations, computers can give us the following sorts of information about the international system. First, they can be made to cut through the detail of a mass of specific observations (for example, export-import transactions) to summarize the net result. Second, they can be asked to compare and report the differences and similarities in international relations behaviors at different points in time (for example, the voting of African and Asian members of the U.N. in different sessions). Third, computers can be programmed in an attempt to establish to what extent a number of international behaviors are related to each other in some patterned fashion (for example, exchange of governmental delegations to foreign aid to public praise for each other's foreign policy, or internal violence to participation in external violence). Fourth, computers can be asked to assess the nature and power of the patterned relationships located between international relations actions (for example, the impact of a change in one variable on the related variable(s) as in the case of the impact of a change in the quality of agricultural landholding on deaths from domestic violence). As we noted earlier, the computer can be given the ability both to make these analyses and report only those above a user-set level of significance or importance and to do so in a variety of forms from a complex numerical table to a quickly absorbed pictorial representation. In sum, the data analysis capabilities of the machine make it extremely feasible for an international relations expert to exploit his data in ways that were previously prohibitively costly in time, money, and human energy.

SIMULATION AND MODELING

For our purposes, we can define a computer simulation or model as a theory about the working of some sector of human behavior as expressed in the idiom of a computer program. The theory is set to work on descriptions of the elements (whether individuals, organizations, or objects) which have been placed in the computer memory. This form of computer application may be prognostic (if you start at A what do you get at the end, B?) or processual (if you start at A what happens on the way to the end which produces B?), and may be expressed in terms of mathematical equations or a series of simple logical statements. When we place international relations elements (real or hypothetical) and social science propositions on a computer, we can gain in the following ways. First, we can take account of the very large number of variables and their interactions which characterize the real world of international relations.   Second, we can "watch" what happens as events unfold, that is, computer simulation possesses "dynamic potentiality because programmed concepts actually generate consequences" (Gullahorn and Gullahorn, 1965, p. 354). Third, we can actually see how, given the model stated in the program, variation in the characteristics of the relevant part of the international system affects outcomes and steps toward outcomes. For example, if we have a model of the relationships between tariffs, international trade, and the American economy, we can see what difference it makes if we set the tariff on a particular commodity at a high or low ad valorem percentage. Fourth, in a similar fashion, we can hold the initial conditions of the international system characteristics constant and vary the theoretical statements expressed in our model to see what difference alternative general assumptions make. For example, we can evaluate the consequences of a specified U.S.-Soviet force posture in terms of alternative theories of deterrence. The reader will recognize benefits three and four as cases of the ability to determine the extent to which outcomes are sensitive to possible variations. This ability to narrow the range of potent uncertainties through sensitivity analysis means that computer-based simulation and models, fifth, help us pinpoint the data gaps and theoretical alternatives which are in most crucial need of further investigation (Browning, 1962). Taken together these benefits, allow us to transpose large sections of international relations from the realm of roulette into the realm of chess (Pool, 1964, p. 64), to transform a can of worms into a set of relatively handleable analytic problems.

V.   ORGANIZATION OF THE VOLUME

The computer user will certainly overhear and probably experience the lack of consensus among computer scientists on the priorities and responsibilities of the computer center to which his work will go, and on the merits and demerits of alternative elements of computer technology. To give the user some understanding of what disagreements in these areas can mean for him, we present the chapter by Fernbach (2). Basic information on what a computer is (its logical anatomy in a sense) can be found in Wyman's chapter (3), and an introductory treatment of computer-speak appears in Krider's chapter (4).

Against this background, the following chapters treat the rationale for, the problems with, and the rewards from the use of computers. Information retrieval is the subject of Chapter 5 by Howerton; succeeding chapters by Bobrow, Holsti, and Rummel deal with the analysis, respectively, of opinion survey, public statement, and national aggregate data. Considerable attention is paid to the use of computers for simulation and modeling. Chapters 9 through 12 present illustrations in the context of war gaming (Dalkey), the weather (Leith), international conflict (Gorden), and artificial intelligence (Slagle). Sahlin (Chapter 13) discusses an important technical approach to simulation and modeling which is only applicable through the computer, Monte Carlo processes.

Each of these papers discusses some basic problems and possibilities in computer modeling and has implications beyond its illustrative subject matter. Obviously, an important element in computer applications of any of the kinds above is the extent to which we can benefit from what the computer has been made to do. This in turn depends in large part on the extent to which we can receive the results of analyses and observe the workings of models in intellectually stimulating and efficiently informative ways. Computer graphics, as discussed by Michael, are a particularly promising route to these benefits, especially in their ability to portray the processes expressed in theoretical propositions — processes which for all practical purposes may have hitherto been unobservable.

As we have perhaps repetitiously indicated, a fundamental constraint on the rewards from computer applications to international relations is our ability to select and formulate problems and make use of computer produced results. The last two chapters of the volume bear on this problem. In his chapter, Lasswell suggests some devices to improve our decision-making process in order to make the most of the opportunities provided by the computer. In the final chapter, Milstein and Bobrow present information on the reactions of one set of international relations professionals to the computer and to the educational experiment in the relations between computers and international relations for which the papers in this volume were prepared. Hopefully, this fragmentary data will help others concerned with the diffusion of knowledge about computer applications and requirements to international relations experts.

The two appendices to the volume are intended to supplement the text chapters. Appendix A contains the summary of a panel discussion of some general aspects of the relationships between computers and society — relationships to the information explosion (Carter), to the empirical treatment of political problems (Pool), to management decision-making (Churchman), and to education (Gerard). Appendix B provides a glossary of key terms which the reader will encounter at various points in the book.

The relationships between computers and international relations are, it seems to us, matters not for complacency or worry but for a spirit of "dogged adventure." We hope that you will agree.

REFERENCES

Bisco, Ralph L. "Social Science Data Archives: Progress and Prospects," *Social Sciences Information,* 6 (Feb. 1967), 39-74.

Borko, Harold (ed.). *Computer Applications in the Behavioral Sciences.* Englewood Cliffs: Prentice-Hall, Inc., 1962.

Browning, Rufus P. "Computer Programs as Theories of Political Processes," *Journal of Politics,* 24 (Aug. 1962), 562-582.

Colby, Kenneth Mark. "Computer Simulation of a Neurotic Process," in Silvan S. Tomkins and Samuel Messick (eds.), *Computer Simulation of Personality.* New York: John Wiley & Sons, Inc., 1963, 165-179.

Diebold, John. "Computers, Program Management and Foreign Affairs," *Foreign Affairs,* 45 (Oct. 1966), 125-134.

Fazar, Willard. "Federal Information Communities: the Systems Approach." Paper prepared for the Annual Meeting of the American Political Science Association, Sept. 1966.

Feigenbaum, Edward A. and Julian Feldman (eds.). *Computers and Thought.* New York: McGraw-Hill Book Co., 1963.

Glaser, William A. and Ralph L. Bisco. "Plans of the Council of Social Science Data Archives," *Social Sciences Information,* 5 (Dec. 1966), 71-96.

Green, Bert F., Jr. *Digital Computers in Research: An Introduction for Behavioral and Social Scientists.* New York: McGraw-Hill Book Co., 1963.

Gruenberger, Fred J. and George Jaffray. *Problems for Computer Solution.* New York: John Wiley & Sons, Inc., 1965.

Gullahorn, John T. and Jeanne E. Gullahorn. "Some Computer Applications in Social Science," *American Sociological Review,* 30 (June 1965), 353-365.

Knight, Kenneth E. and John A. Miller. "Impact of Computers on Management." Paper prepared for the Annual Meeting of the American Association for the Advancement of Science, Dec. 1965.

Lee, Robert S. "The Computer's Public Image," *DATAMATION,* 12 (Dec. 1966), 33-35.

McPhee, William N. *Formal Theories of Mass Behavior.* New York: Free Press of Glencoe, Inc., 1963.

Miller, George A. "Thinking Machines: Myths and Actualities," *The Public Interest,* 2 (Winter 1966), 92-112.

Naylor, Thomas H., Joseph L. Balintfy, Donald S. Burdick, and Kong Chu. *Computer Simulation Techniques.* New York: John Wiley & Sons, Inc., 1966.

Neisser, Ulric. "Computers as Tools and as Metaphors." Address delivered at the Georgetown University Conference on Cybernetics and Society, Nov. 1964.

Platt, John. "On Strong Inference," *Science,* 146 (Oct. 16, 1964), 347-353.

Pool, Ithiel de Sola. "Simulating Social Systems," *International Science and Technology,* 27 (March 1964), 62-70.

Sulzberger, C. L. "Foreign Affairs: The Dim-Witted Machines," *New York Times* (Dec. 1966).

Uhr, Leonard, "The Development of Perception and Language: Simulated Models," in Silvan S. Tomkins and Samuel Messick (eds.). *Computer Simulation of Personality.* New York: John Wiley & Sons, Inc., 1963, 231-266.

Chapter 2

INTRODUCTION TO COMPUTERS

S. Fernbach

A BRIEF HISTORY

There are two kinds of computers, digital computers and analog computers. The digital computation is probably one of the oldest concepts in human history. Each of us has ten fingers and ten toes, thus enabling us to count digitally; we count digits. Analog computers are used in analogy with physical laws and I will explain briefly what that means later. The first counting devices that man used other than his fingers were little pebbles. He would arrange these pebbles in groups to indicate the quantity of something, and in this way keep a count. Later on man developed a system of rods on which he put these pebbles and so introduced the abacus, one of the earliest digital computers. Many people think the abacus originated in China or the East; this is not really so. As a matter of fact, it was found in many geographical spots and probably originated in the Mediterranean area. The abacus was quite widely used; it has gone through many modifications and today we still have the modern abacus, the most elaborate one, with us. One bead in the top section and four beads down below comprise the Japanese version. There are experts who can use these computers so well that they can compete favorably with the modern desk calculator and even beat it in speed. However, the use of the abacus led to certain problems. People who had the use of this instrument never developed arithmetic to a great extent. Since they could always count and calculate with the abacus, it was not necessary to develop written techniques. Thus it turned out that it was in India that the Hindus invented one of the most important notions of arithmetic, namely, the zero.

One of the difficulties with counting is the notation that one uses. If one goes back into one of the older languages he finds that there are different notations for one, ten, 100, and so on, so that he can count up to a certain point, and then can't proceed beyond that point without starting a new column; there is no smooth transition from one to the next. People did eventually come up with the idea of positional notation. Today, for example, we recognize in a three-digit number, one digit as the unit's position, another as the ten's position, and a third as the hundred's position. Further development was hindered until the development of the positional notation of no value, the zero. The abacus does have such a thing; one may have no activity in a particular rod. This was well understood, but to transcribe this to paper seems to have been a tremendous step and nobody did it in these early days. The Hindus did not have an abacus, so they were forced to invent the zero. The moral here is that one should not overuse a computer, because it may keep him from thinking and coming up with some interesting ideas.

One can abuse the computer as well as use it. After the abacus was in wide use, about the year 1000, it took a few hundred years before any great advances were made. The device that succeeded the abacus was a counter, a rotary counter with digits from 0 to 9 which was developed in France by Pascal. It was very much like a hand counter that we use today. The difficult part in counting with such a thing is to have a carry for one wheel to the next when there are several digits to represent. If one digit represented units, as soon as it went through nine and passed through to zero the ten's digit had to add an extra one; this Pascal was able to do very nicely. Thus we had the beginnings of our modern desk calculator back in about the 17th century. Following Pascal, the idea of multiplying with one of these devices was developed and, although the technique was fully complex, it came about just within a few years after Pascal developed his calculator. From then on the computer developed rather rapidly. The modern desk calculator is just a combination of an elaboration of devices developed several hundred years ago. These calculators were used quite heavily until recent years and are still in widespread use.

Analog computers were also developed at about the same time as the digital counter of Pascal in the 17th – 18th century. An analog computer actually translates numbers into physical quantities and then operates on them and measures them. A simple example of an analog computer is a slide rule. A slide rule has two scales whose rulings are logarithmic so that if one adds a length of the slide to a length of the stationary part, the combined length yields the product of the two numbers indicated by the length of separate pieces.[1] The slide rule is thus a very simple analog-type device.

Today most analog devices use electrical principles. For example, in elementary physics one learns that when a current I passes through a resistor of resistance value R, that the product of these two indicates the voltage across the resistor. By providing a device which supplies a known current which can pass through a known resistance, one can obtain the product of these two numbers by simply measuring the voltage across the resistor. This provides us then with an electrical circuit for carrying out multiplication. The analog computer has come into its own rather rapidly, but is not as widely used as the digital computer. The reason for this is that comparable accuracy is very difficult to obtain with the analog computer. It is quite expensive to buy accuracy in an analog computer. If one plots the cost of accuracy one finds that with an analog computer the cost rises steeply as a function of accuracy. With a digital computer it probably is more level, so that there is a crossover point beyond which one would not wish to invest very heavily in analog equipment. On the other hand, analog equipment is used quite often for simulation purposes. We are not going to spend any time on analog computers here because ... basic aim is to study the digital computer and what it can do.

The first digital computer of the form we know today was seen in England in about 1832. Charlges Babbage, one of the geniuses of his time, invented the modern computer over one hundred years ago. Unfortunately, he couldn't build it because the equipment that was available in those days was just not good enough to build a computer, such as he described, with 50 decimal digits of accuracy.

Each digit of Babbage's model was represented by a counter that went from zero to nine. He could store a thousand 50-digit numbers and operate on them. His computer had four sections to it, as most modern computers do. It had a storage section, or memory, an arithmetic unit where arithmetic was performed; a control unit which controlled the operations, and an input-output device to get information into and out of the computer. Very shortly before Babbage designed the machine, a man by the name of Jacquard had developed an automatic weaving system and loom in which he used punched cards to indicate the patterns that he was going to produce in the weaving process. Babbage adopted this idea and

---

[1] Incidentally, logarithms, themselves, were invented in the 17th century. Before their invention, people really didn't do much multiplying, numerically. If one reads Pepys' diary for example, he claims he used to wake up early — at 4 o'clock in the morning — on certain days to take his lessons in multiplication. Here was a very well educated man of his time, and he did not know how to multiply. When Napier invented logarithms, everybody was delighted because now there was a simple way of multiplying by adding; it was soon after Napier invented the logarithm that the slide rule was developed.

used punched cards for the input and output of his computer. (We still use these punched cards today.) He hired a machinist who tried to build this mechanical computer; unfortunately they could not get the accuracy that was needed. His machine shop, because of his attempts to build this machine, produced the most skilled people in Europe at this time. Babbage died a very unhappy man because he never achieved his goal; as a matter of fact, the first machine using all his principles was not built until 1944 — at Harvard by Aiken. If one reads Babbage's works he will find that there hasn't been much change from his original design in the intervening century.[2]

Matters progressed very slowly until Aiken built his electromechanical machine. It was a tremendous machine at the time. It could add, two 23-digit numbers in about $\frac{4}{10}$ of a second and it could multiply these two numbers in about 10 times that — about 4 seconds. There were a few machines built with electromagnetic devices in the 1940's but the first all-electronic computer was built and put into operation in 1945 or 1946. It (the ENIAC) was built at the University of Pennsylvania by Eckert and Mauchly for the government to be used in ballistic trajectory calculations. This machine used vacuum tubes. It was relatively small compared to machines we have today, but it was quite capable for the job that it was supposed to perform. It was about a thousand times faster than Aiken's electromechanical machine, i.e., a multiply took milliseconds rather than seconds. From then on, progress was made rapidly. Eckert and Mauchly started a company of their own and built UNIVAC, the first commercially available electronic computer. Then IBM followed with other computers, and by 1966 we had about 22,000 computers in use.

COMPUTER ORGANIZATION

Normally, one subdivides the computer logically into a number of distinct parts as indicated by their function:

1. Memory unit
2. Control unit
3. Arithmetic unit
4. Input-output device

---

[2] Babbage was also concerned with the programming of the computer. Among those working with him was the Countess of Lovelace, the daughter of Lord Byron; she might be considered the first programmer in history who wrote papers on the use of this computer.

We shall discuss these briefly in an attempt to furnish suitable background for the material in some of the following chapters.

Many devices have been used for storing information. The one suggested by Babbage was a counter that counted from zero to nine. Actually we all use the decimal system and we all like it because it is very simple. It turns out, however, that it is very expensive to build a fast electronic device that has ten levels of storage capability. If one wishes to build a device that represents a decimal system, it should be stable and always be able to indicate a discrete zero, one, two, three or other digit without something happening such that a two becomes a one or a three. Of course, if one had ten switches, and one of them was set, say to four, then one could say that these ten switches were set to indicate a four. Another group of ten switches might indicate a three, and so on. One can represent a large number of decimal digits in this way, but it would take an enormous amount of equipment to do so using ten switches for each digit. This makes the system quite expensive and not even more reliable. It could be less reliable because it has more parts than another system that might represent the digits. For this the binary system with only two symbols, zero and one, is used in digital computers. A string of symbols, each of which can be either zero or one, can then represent the numeric quantities or even characters. To represent the decimal digits between zero and nine, one could have a switch which would represent zero by being off, a one by being on. To get to two since we have already exhausted the use of that switch, we must have two switches, one off and one on representing a two. By continuing in this way we find that we need four different switches to represent the ten digits instead of the ten we needed before. So by the great simplification of representing the decimal digits in this way within the machine, we save on hardware and get reliable operation because it is easy to build switches which will show on and off. The early switches that were built were electromagnetic relays. Later, vacuum tubes were used; they could conduct current, or not conduct current. In other words, they were on or off. Later, other devices were invented. For example, in the UNIVAC there was a storage device that operated by allowing information to flow down a tank of mercury in the form of sonic pulses — sound waves. If there were a pulse at a particular point, that would represent a one, and if it were not there, it would represent a zero. A particular group of these switches could be used to represent a numeric quantity. One could also represent characters. Obviously, a combination of four of these switches will allow one to represent sixteen quantities. In other words, there are more than the ten that are needed for the decimal digits. Hence, other quantities such as plus, minus, and so on can also be represented. If alphabetic characters are devised, one would obviously have to have more switches, and indeed this is what was done. Adding two more positions will allow one to represent 64 characters. Some of the early machines then, like the UNIVAC, had six bits to represent characters. One could operate on six bits, that is, on characters as well as numeric quantities. Today we find that six bits are not enough in that people would like to use more than 64 characters; and indeed, IBM's 360 system uses eight-bit characters allowing for the representation of 256 different quantities or symbols. This is then a binary representation of decimal digits or characters, and in most computers one does operate on these binary numbers to carry out calculations. The computer uses memory cells in which these quantities are stored in this binary representation. The memory consists of quantities of information usually fixed in length. A quantity that is fixed at a certain length is called a *word of information* and is one of the important definitions in the computer world. It can vary from computer to computer, but it is usually a fixed number of bits which can represent a decimal quantity or an alphabetic quantity. In some computers these are fixed at 36 bits, which are roughly equivalent to about eight or nine decimal digits. Some computers such as the LARC, which was built for Lawrence Radiation Laboratory, are decimally oriented computers and use a system similar to this, although not the identical system. LARC has a word length of twelve digits. They are digits, not bits any longer; they are combinations of bits. In actual fact, a single word has 60 bits because each digit here has four bits plus a check bit; a check bit sometimes accompanies these just to make sure that the information is correct, and it serves as a check on the machine as it carries out its calculations. The important definition here is that of the word.   Memory is usually defined as having so many words of information, which determines the memory size. In the Babbage machine we talked about 1000 words, each of which was 50 digits long. The early machines had very few words — a few hundred was considered a large memory then. The UNIVAC itself had a 1000-word memory of twelve decimal digits. Today we are building machines which have one hundred thousand words of memory, and we think that's not sufficient yet. A memory is also characterized in addition to the word size by a quantity and speed — the time it takes to throw one of these switches and how fast can you make one of these create one of these words in that memory. Effectively, the memory consists of a large number of switches and all one is doing is manipulating them — setting them or resetting them.   In the early days of design, a memory was built to operate within seconds or milliseconds. Today we talk about memories operating in millionths of a second or microseconds, which is almost a standard memory speed today.

A digital computer must be able to operate on the information stored in its memory. Information residing in the memory must be transferred to the control and arithmetic unit where operations on it may be performed. The transfer itself is an important function; to understand this let us see how must computers operate. The memory cells where information is stored may be numbered from 000 up through, for example, 999. When a program is put into the computer to be carried out, this program normally appears somewhere in a sequential arrangement. The computer looks at each of these words sequentially in turn and carries out the operation indicated. There are two kinds of computer words in use. One is the instruction word which indicates what function is to be carried out and the reference to some memory location. The other, the operand word or the data word, is the word that contains the particular number being operated on. The location in memory at which the work can be found is called the *address* of the word. A group of these instructions makes up the stored program.

As a very simple illustration, suppose we wish to add two numbers and that these two numbers exist in memory at location numbers 876 and 877. A set of instructions which will enable us to add these two numbers is prepared. In some computers, like a UNIVAC or LARC, a set of characters is used to represent these operations. In other computers one uses a numeric notation. B876, for example may mean *b*ring whatever is in memory location 876 into a register. If A stands for the add function, A877 may mean *a*dd whatever number appears in 877 to this register. Now we say, store it away in memory, and we might use S to represent *s*tore function; S878 will mean store it in location 878. Now we have carried out a sequence of operations involving the addition of two numbers. We haven't indicated how these numbers were placed into the memory originally, but that is not essential for the moment. The instructions for these operations normally appear sequentially somewhere in the memory also, say starting at 000. The operations start there and after we go through them and complete the job, then we go on to another job. There are times when one wishes to be able to shift the control from one of these operations at one sequence of location to another operation somewhere else in memory, that is, to transfer control. This type of instruction allows one to get around in the instruction sequence in memory. Sometimes one wishes to transfer based on the result of an operation that occurred. These are called conditional transfers. At other times one wishes to transfer because he has run out of space or to carry out a special sequence somewhere else. This is called an *unconditional transfer.*

Another kind of operation is the shift operation. A word of information which may consist of n digits can be modified so that the digits appear in the same order but at different positions within the word. For example, let us take some numeric quantity, say 1234, assuming that a word consists of four digits. We might want to shift it to the left and make it look like 2341 where the 1 might actually go end around, or like 2340 where the 1 is lost and a 0 replaces it. There are various types of shifts one can make, and the shift operation is quite important. In standard computers we sometimes do arithmetic in two different ways. Most computers are designed such that the decimal points appear at either the left- or right-hand end of the word. Computers such as these are said to be used for fixed-point arithmetic, that is, arithmetic where the decimal point is fixed. One must organize one's work properly to take care that the decimal point appears in the right place. In cases like this, shifting is quite important. Now to make things simpler, so-called scientific computers have been devised to represent operands or data words a little differently. They actually represent a word by using an exponent, a power of ten, and then the fractional part of the number. For example, the word 123.24 could be represented as a fractional part of 12324 with an exponent of, say two, indicating power of two, meaning a product of 10 x 10 or a hundred. One can write this as 0212324 where the first two digits represent the exponent and the remaining digits represent the fraction. This is called the *floating-point representation.*

This representation makes life for the scientist much simpler since he doesn't have to worry about where the decimal point is. He gets into trouble occasionally because the machine won't handle all ranges of numbers and on occasion he gets out of range, unless he has taken some precautions. But one also gets out of range in using fixed-point numbers. For example, when one adds .8 to .4 he gets 1.2. The result has exceeded the capacity of the word and has been carried past the decimal point. The 1 may be lost unless the computer tells you that this trouble has occurred.

Other instructions that are important are input-output instructions. These enable one to bring information into and out of the memory from some other devices. In this area we haven't progressed very far beyond Jacquard. We still use the punched card as modified by Hollerith who worked for the Census Bureau back in about 1910. This card has been standard through the last 50 years. We use punched cards on which we indicate information and read that information through this processor into the memory. We have to indicate how many cards we wish to read, where we want to put the information, and so on.

This is what the input instructions will do. Similarly, one can punch numbers or results on cards and in this way perform an output function. Early in the 1950's, computer development took two different paths. The first machines developed, like UNIVAC I, were decimal-type computers that had fixed-point arithmetic capabilities oriented to doing commercial problems. This implies manipulation of data and very little arithmetic. The scientist urged changes in these computers by allowing for floating point and insisting on greater speed. The commercial applications don't require this speed because most of their time was spent getting data in and out. This being very slow, one doesn't care how fast the arithmetic unit may be. Scientists, with large problems, put the data in, and then allow the processor to grind and grind until it gets some answers. They want speed, internally, and don't care too much about the input-output. Since the early days matters have been changing so that most machines today will handle either scientific or commercial problems and all one has to do in one case is to add the floating-point capability which comes as a package, and in the other case, the decimal arithmetic type of capability, since commercial people somehow hate to work with binary bits.

The machines that were built fifteen or twenty years ago used devices that were then as fast as possible to store instructions and operands. One device used was a cathode ray tube, a TV-type tube on the face of which spots were stored. They were able to switch this in a matter of microseconds. Today and for the last ten years or so the most stable device that has been used for memory has been what is called a *magnetic core,* a very small cylinder with a hole in it and wires threaded through it. When current flows through these wires, the core material is magnetized in one direction or another depending on the direction of the current. When the core material is magnetized in a particular direction it is said to be switched to, say a one — the other direction would be called zero. There are large arrays of these magnetic cores that make up a memory. Memories of standard computers like the IBM 7094 contain about a million such things. The magnetic cores have been smaller and smaller with time because the smaller they are, the faster one can switch them. Today one can build these devices to switch in about a quarter of a millionth of a second, a quarter of a microsecond.[2] The memory switching time is usually a good indication of how fast a machine is. It turns out that actually the memory switching time is a limiting factor on the speed of the computer because today one can actually

[2] A relatively new unit called the *nanosecond* which is a billionth of a second is now being used for these small times. These cores switch in 250 nanoseconds or 250-billionths of a second.

build transistorized components in the central processor which are faster than the memory devices.

The central processor used vacuum tubes in early electronic computers, then changed to transistors when they became available, and is still in the transistor stage. Soon the transistion will be made to circuits which can be deposited on small ceramic chips. Each chip will incorporate many circuits. One will then be able to build a computer of tremendous speed which will be so small that it will not be noticeable in a room with input-output equipment. The one complication is that the speed of light has to be contended with, which means that wire lengths must be kept very short.

Memories are also getting faster. At the moment we are operating in the nanosecond region and the magnetic cores are pretty standard. There will be some deviations from this in the future, but the speed will be roughly the same. It is hard to envision that within the next five years the speeds will increase by a factor of perhaps one hundred. Memories made up of huge arrays of these magnetic cores are getting larger and larger in capacity. However, it turns out that in very large problems in which one has to store tremendous amounts of data such memories are still not large enough to carry out in a reasonable time the work that has to be done. Most data that people work with easily exceed in number the million bits that a standard-sized core memory contains; consequently one must have storage devices to supplement the main memory. These devices should be capable of storing information which can be transferred in and out of the main memory from which instructions are executed. These devices must also be fast enough so that the computer is not held up while transferring the data. To back up the core memory one uses magnetic disks, drums, tapes, and other similar devices. Let us discuss such magnetic devices for the moment.

In most home recorders, magnetic tapes are used in an analog fashion, that is, the recording head does not generate bits of information, but rather a wave form. In the magnetic tapes used in digital computers, bits of information are created magnetically to provide the binary representation of the character or numeric to be stored horizontally across the tape. Normally, in modern devices, one set of bits represents one character and is followed vertically by large numbers of other such characters. At present one can store roughly a thousand characters per inch of tape. Tape provides a very good storage medium in that a single reel, customarily 2400 feet in length, might store a hundred million characters. The chief trouble with tape is that it is sequential. If one wishes to obtain data at the front end and then at the other end of the tape, it takes quite long because of the slow mechanical handling.

In other words, tape is fine for sequential operations, but not very appropriate for the random-type operation in which one is looking for data scattered throughout the system.

For random search operations, drums and disks are preferable to tape. A drum may be considered to be a cylinder which is wrapped with tape. Unfortunately, it is a fixed cylinder so that one can't take the magnetic surface off and put it away. Once information is stored on it, in a sense it is used up. A tape reel, on the other hand, can be taken off and stored away — another tape reel replacing it on the device that drives it.

The tape reels themselves are inexpensive; the tape drive is expensive. A drum that would store as much information as a single tape on a single tape drive would be roughly comparable in price. Effectively, then, a drive is a more expensive device but it has the advantage that there is random access to its information. A drum cylinder rotates at a specified speed, and like a tape drive has a magnetic head which reads or writes information bits. If there is only one head, one must keep moving it to the various parts of the drum where the desired information is stored and again there is an access problem. If there are a large number of heads one can gain access to any location much more rapidly and transfer the information to or from main memory. The access time is an important parameter. In a drum of this kind, access time is said to be half the rotational time. On the average it will only have to go half way around to get to the point of interest. Random access time on drums then is much better than on tape. Furthermore, drums are usually in a sealed environment whereas tapes are in the open being taken off, put back on, and so on. Tapes are abused and, hence, are not quite as reliable as drums.

Disks are very much like drums except for organization. Disks are mounted on a spindle and the information is searched out by a head which may move in and out on the disk surfaces. Information can be stored on both sides of the disk so that one may have two heads on an arm. One may have a single head which searches up and down and in and out or a large number of heads, one for each surface, or one may even have more than one head on a single surface. The number of heads determines two important items: one, the cost, because the heads are the expensive part of the system, and, two, the access time to the disk file. The chief differences between disks and drums, besides the organization, is the storage capability. One can get more storage per unit volume in a disk file than one can in a drum file. Costs of drums and disks are relatively equal. The magnetic core storage device costs roughly thirty cents for a bit of information.

Cheap ways of providing more core storage at a reasonable cost have been found recently. Supplemental core memory, although it is slower, that is, it doesn't have quite as good access time, can be bought for approximately three cents per bit. This type of "bulk core" memory has a tremendous cost advantage. One could add a million words of storage of this kind as back-up memory and thereby achieve significant improvements in performance for some class of problems. Disks and drums are about two orders of magnitude less than this, that is, hundredths of a cent per bit. There are, then, tremendous cost advantages to be gained by resorting to rotating devices. Tapes are, of course, even less expensive. Their precise cost is hard to figure, because one can always add tape to a tape drive and run through as many tapes as one may wish. They can be moved around very easily. They also provide an input-output medium. Somehow one must be able to get information in and out of the machine. It is clear that if the memory is not big enough to do a particular job, one can temporarily store the information in any one of these devices and then bring it back and forth as needed to run the problem. The devices provide for the intermediate I/O function.

Now there is also the function of getting the information into the computer to start the problem and out to learn the results. The initial job can be performed with tapes. Of course, information must have been put on the tape to begin with. Normally that is done from cards. In any given computer facility, procedures are such that when one has a problem he writes his program on paper, and has the program punched on cards. The cards are then read by a satellite computer and magnetic tapes are prepared to represent the same data on the tape as was once on the cards. Henceforth one can use either the cards or tape to get information into the computer system. Of course, if drum or disk capacity is sufficient, one could permanently store some of this information on such devices, but generally this is not feasible. What is normally stored on disks or drums are those things which are referred to most frequently.

As for output, people like to see the results in the form of printouts or graphs or perhaps they don't want to see them, but wish to store results. In the last case, one can put the final results on tape or cards and store it away. Most computers have printers on line. The standard printers these days run at about a thousand lines per minute, a line consisting of 120 alphabetic characters. There are cathode ray display tubes on which one can actually draw characters which can be photographed so that one can have a record on film. From the film one may go to hard copy or even make movies and other kinds of displays. One can't take very much output from a computer on a printer that runs only a thousand lines a minute. Fast as it may sound, it is much slower than the output one gets on magnetic tapes. If one had to take very large amounts of information out of the computer system by on-line printing, the computer itself would be slowed down. Normally, large installations with large volumes of printing buy one or more small computers which do nothing but the printing or perhaps they also serve as card-to-tape converters, so that tapes rather than cards provide input to the main computer. Similarly, the output tapes are taken from the main computer and printed on the peripheral one. The small computer does nothing but operate as a service device to provide the input on tape and the output on paper.

Let us now turn to the problem of computer language. In the small example that I gave you, I showed that one could use mnemonics to represent operations. The manufacturer, when he builds a machine, indicates what these mnemonics are. This is called *machine language,* the language that one can use to code or write programs. This is the way it was done in the early days when code was written in absolute machine language. The actual address for each of the instruction words, as well as each of the operand words, was defined. Later users started devising new languages which would allow them more flexibility in the use of the machine. One did not define exactly where things were and the mnemonics were such that one could write a program without knowing the details of the machine. Thus so-called *assembly languages* became popular. Not long after, people became a little more concerned about the uses of the computers and the amount one had to learn to use them, so that other higher languages were developed. These languages, called *compilers,* were made as close as possible to the language that the computer user would like. It allowed him to write equations if he were a scientist, or statements in banking, such that when these statements were put into the machine, the machine interpreted them and wrote down the program which then could be followed to carry out the necessary operations. The scientific compilers that are most popular are Fortran, the standard formula translation, and Algol. There's a host of others, perhaps 20 or 30 that are popular in some way or another. For commercial operations there is a language called Cobol. This is widely used throughout the government computer facilities.[3] There are attempts today to try and get these languages

---

[3] As a matter of fact, the government has asked that the Cobol language capability be provided with every computer system. Cobol is not a very good example of higher language, which poses a major problem to the computer industry. The government standardized Cobol before it was really ready to use it. In any case, it exists, and people do use it very heavily in commercial operations.

closer together so that a single language might do for everyone whether he be a commercial user or a scientific user.

I would like to close by stating where we are going, why we are using different kinds of computers and what kinds really do exist.

A relatively common machine is the IBM 1401. This relatively small machine is used primarily in business applications and is mostly what I would call an I/O device. It allows one to get information in and out through a small memory. The important feature of this type of machine is that one can go from cards to tape, or cards to disks, or cards to printer, or tape to printer. It enables one to convert from one medium to another. In actual fact, it has done more than that; it has replaced the tabulating machine, because most commercial operations are very trivial — they require very little arithmetic. For the most part, all it does is move masses of data around. Hence the 1401-type system is used for commercial applications where data is to be manipulated in a trivial way.

IBM has another class of machines which might be called business machines, namely, the 7070, 7080. These are high-trade, expensive systems. They use the same I/O equipment, but one pays more for the central processor and memory because there is more of it, and it operates a little faster. If in any application it becomes more of a data processor than an I/O device, one should trade it in for a 7090 or a 7094. These are the so-called scientific versions and are in the same ballpark insofar as number of elements is concerned — memory words, transistors, and so on. Their cost is roughly the same as the commercial versions.

In the scientific field, there are newer machines; Control Data Corporation built one of the largest that exists today — the 6600. IBM is now coming back with a response to this. There is in the IBM 360 line a model 91 which is to be a very powerful machine, but does not exist yet.

Computers are usually classified by cost. This is a misleading way of looking at computers because the price per unit performance has been dropping over the past ten years. It is far better to represent the capabilities of these computers by operations per unit time. The machines mentioned above are capable of operations at the rate of at least one million operations or instructions per second (mips). I have a pet scheme for classifying machines. One capable of operating at the level of one million instructions per second I call a class 2 computer; one operating at 10 million instructions per second would be class 1, etc. The class 0, being 100 million, is coming within the next ten years. The important classification factor is the number of operations that one can expect per unit time. A large scientific machine formerly cost approximately $3 million. Now one can get a machine in the same class for approximately one-half million dollars. Obviously, putting them in price categor-

54833

ies makes little sense; it is what the machine can do that's really important.

To gain speed, the manufacturers have relied very heavily on building more parallelism into computers. For example, in the very earliest electronic machines, say UNIVAC I, bits were looked at in a serial fashion. They had to flow past a certain point to be recognized, so that one had to wait for the last bit to pass by before the work could be recognized. This type is called a *serial machine,* and obviously is very slow. One can speed this up by looking at all bits at the same time, and in going to the next generation, the manufacturers did just that. In any case the next jump was to a parallel scheme. Modern computers use very high speed components but these alone will not produce the speeds desirable. More and more parallelism is being provided. One way of achieving higher speed is by paralleling the number of processors. This is being done, by leads to programming problems which must be solved to optimize the use of such systems. Basically, however, all machines are the same as Babbage's machine, despite the fact that any slight innovation seems to give rise to a new "generation."

Chapter 3

THE LOGIC
OF COMPUTING
MACHINERY[1]

Robert H. Wyman, Jr.

Typically, a computing machine is constructed of *logic blocks*. One set of blocks — which is more or less fundamental — will be considered in this paper. This set is composed of the AND block, OR block, NOT, and DELAY. The algebra associated with these blocks will be discussed and some examples worked out.

This set of blocks is then used to construct a larger logic unit, the *delayed J-K flip-flop*. A collection of these units — called a *register* — will be considered next, along with the notion of decoding the register contents.

A *binary adder* will be constructed and control will be inserted to add the contents of two registers into one of the registers.

Finally, a *timing generator* will be constructed, a memory unit postulated, and a simple computer with four-instruction set constructed. The execution of the four instructions in sequence is analyzed.

COMBINATORIAL LOGIC

The inner works of computers can be considered to be composed of *logic boxes* or *logic primitives*. Typically, a box, usually called a *gate*, has an output and one or more inputs. The output, naturally, depends on the inputs (see Figure 1).

---

[1] A resume of two lectures that were presented at the LRL Symposium.

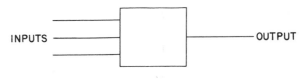

Figure 1

The output and inputs are wires or lines, each of which can take on one of two states, and we can think of these states as "1" or "0", or alternatively "T" or "F."

Figure 2 shows the three fundamental boxes or gates which we will consider:

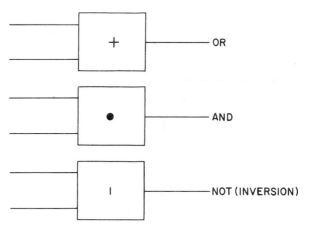

Figure 2

If we give our lines names, the explanations in Figure 3 can be made:

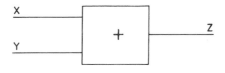

Figure 3

Z will be true $(T, 1)$ if, and only if, X is true $(T, 1)$, or Y is true, or if both X and Y are true.

We can use a shorthand for this which is

$$Z = X + Y$$

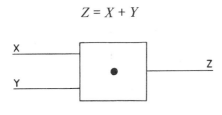

Figure 4

Z will be true if, and only if, X and Y are both true (Figure 4).

$$Z = XY$$

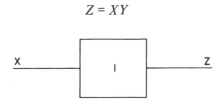

Figure 5

Z is true if, and only if, X is false (Figure 5).

$$Z = \overline{X}$$

NOTE: If a variable (line, wire) is not true, it must be false and vice versa.

An interesting feature of Figures $3 - 5$ is that with I and *one* of the other two, the third one can be constructed. See Figure 6 for an example:

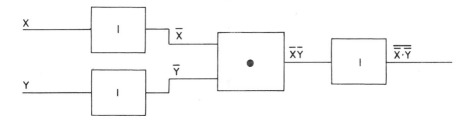

Figure 6

It may not be obvious that $(\overline{\overline{X} \cdot \overline{Y}}) = X + Y$, but Table 1 (a truth table) indicates the equivalence of the two functions.

We construct the truth table by using the rules we previously developed. Thus if $X = 0$ and $Y = 0$, clearly $\overline{X} = 1$ and $\overline{Y} = 1$. Also then

$$X + Y = 0$$
$$\overline{X}\overline{Y} = 1$$
$$\overline{\overline{X}\overline{Y}} = 0$$

Table 1

If				Then		
X	Y	$\overline{X}$	$\overline{Y}$	$X + Y$	$\overline{X}\,\overline{Y}$	$\overline{\overline{X}\,\overline{Y}}$
0	0	1	1	0	1	0
0	1	1	0	1	0	1
1	0	0	1	1	0	1
1	1	0	0	1	0	1

Note that for every possible configuration of X and Y,

$$X + Y = \overline{\overline{X}\,\overline{Y}}$$

If we use ordinary arithmetic, with the exception that $1 + 1 = 1$, and exclude division, we can calculate the output of any sequence of boxes.

Thus, in the case above, if $X = 0$ and $Y = 1$, the calculation shown in Figure 7 can be made.

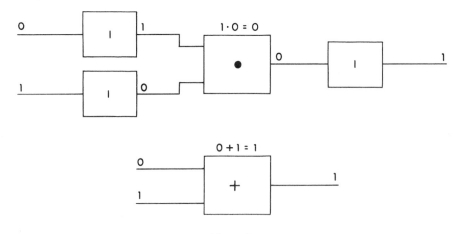

Figure 7

This notation and the rules crudely outlined are known as *Boolean Algebra.* The rules, specifically are

$$0 + 1 = 1 + 0 = 1 + 1 = 1 \cdot 1 = 1$$
$$1 \cdot 1 = 0 \cdot 1 = 0 \cdot 0 = 0 + 0 = 0$$
$$\overline{1} = 0 \quad \overline{0} = 1$$

DELAY

One further box is needed for a computer. This is the time delay box τ of Figure 8.

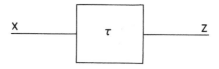

Figure 8

When X changes, Z will change to the same state as X, but will do so τ seconds later.

In many instances in machine design, it is desirable to generate a function using the AND, OR, NOT, boxes and then store the value of this function until some later time.

One kind of storage device is the flip-flop or latch. It can be constructed as shown in Figure 9, using the boxes we have postulated.

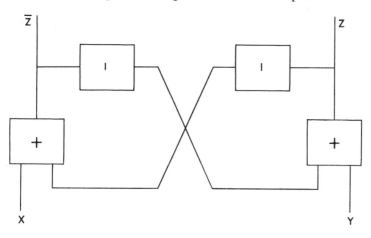

Figure 9

If Y is true, Z will be true. If Z is true and X is false, both inputs to the left OR gate are false; thus $\overline{Z}$ is false. If $\overline{Z}$ is false, both inputs to the right-hand OR gate are true. Thus if Y now goes false, Z will remain true. Now if X becomes true, $\overline{Z}$ will become true and Z will become false.

Problems

1. Using two AND gates and four inverters, construct a flip-flop.
2. Using one AND, one OR and two inverters, construct another flip-flop.
3. Can you construct a flip-flop with two AND's and two inverters?

Answers appear at the end of this section.

A symbol commonly used for the flip-flop is shown in Figure 10,

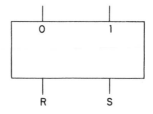

Figure 10

where R and S stand for "Reset" and "Set," respectively. This is the so-called R - S *flip-flop.*

Note that if both the R and S inputs are made true simultaneously, the output of the flip-flop becomes indeterminate; for when R and S go false again, the flip-flop cannot hold both outputs true. Neither can it hold both false. See Figure 9.

The flip-flop shown in Figures 9 and 10 is the most elementary form of flip-flop, and the gate structure which is attached to the inputs is critical.

One very common structure is the cross coupling structure shown in Figure 11.

If the flip-flop is in the "zero" state, $\overline{Z}$ will be true $(1, T)$. If then J is made true, S will become true causing the flop to switch to the "one" state, making S go false.

This leads us directly to the delay problem. It takes energy to make these devices change state. It takes time to couple energy through a gate. And the lower the power levels of the circuits, the more time it takes. If while J is true, $\overline{Z}$ goes false, the amount of energy coupled through the

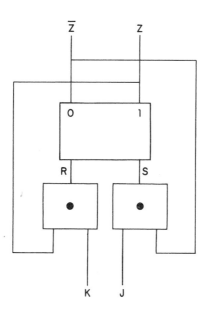

Figure 11

gate may not be enough to guarantee reliable switching of the flip-flop. Thus in many cases, a designer will overtly incorporate delay into his devices.

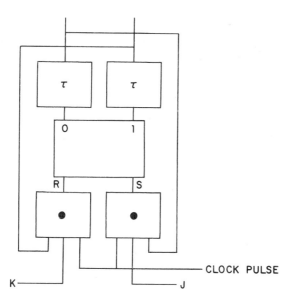

Figure 12

Figure 12 shows an extremely powerful flip-flop. (Powerful in the sense of usefulness). We assume the clock pulse to be a signal which will be true no longer than time τ. We've also shown a three-input AND gate, but this is a simple extension of the two-input AND gate.

If the flip-flop is in the zero state and J is true, when clock pulse occurs, the flop will go to the one state, and τ seconds later (typically, tens of nanoseconds), the right-hand gate will close.

The operation is the same on the K side.

If both J and K are true at clock time, the flip-flop will *change* state. This is extremely important in counting and arithmetic operations.

Note one logical consequence of a flip-flop having two inputs (typically called the "zero" and "one" outputs): Suppose we call a flip-flop by some name which implies (hopefully) its function — say, ADD — so that when it is on (one) we will add two numbers together. We can look at the one output of the flop and equate this to a desire to add if it is true, or not to add if it is false.

On the other hand, if we are not adding, we ought to be doing something else, and the zero side of the flip-flop will now be true. This says we should be doing something else. Which brings us to the notion of decoding.

Answers to Problems, page 40

1.

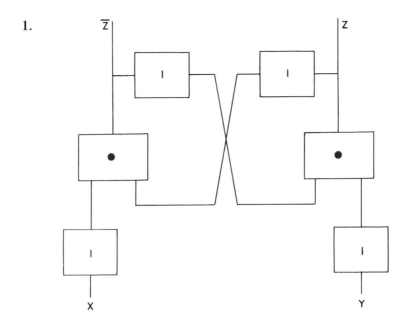

If $X = 1$, $Y = 0$, one input to the left AND gate is false, and $\overline{Z}$ will then be false. Therefore, both inputs to the right gate will be true, and Z will be true. When X goes to 0, one input of the left gate will still be false thus holding $\overline{Z}$ false and Z true.

2.

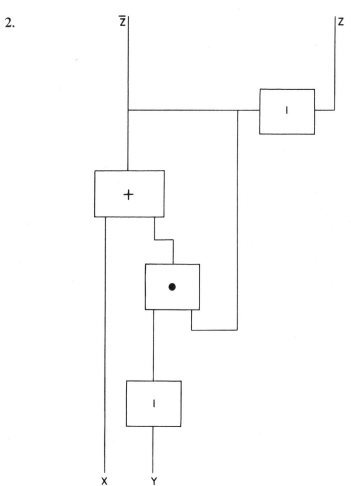

If $X = 0$, $Y = 1$, the output of the AND gate will be false, and so will $\overline{Z}$. Thus Z will be true and $\overline{Z}$ will keep the AND gate off. If $Y = 0$, $X = 1$, $\overline{Z}$ will be true, turning the AND gate on, holding $\overline{Z}$ true when X goes back to 0.

3. No.

DECODING

A *register* is a set of storage devices (e.g., flip-flops) which serve some specific function in the computing machine. The registers are usually given meaningful names such as

> arithmetic register
> multiplier-quotient register,
> instruction register, etc.

A *decoding* of a register tells the computer what to do (instruction) or where to find some data (address).

Suppose we have a three-bit (flip-flop) register. Let us call the flip-flops A_0, A_1, A_2 and let us list exhaustively combinations of the states of these flops. These are listed in Table 2.

Table 2

A_2	A_1	A_0	State
0	0	0	0
0	0	1	1
0	1	0	2
0	1	1	3
1	0	0	4
1	0	1	5
1	1	0	6
1	1	1	7

Our decoding tree could be constructed of eight three-input AND gates as shown in Figure 13.

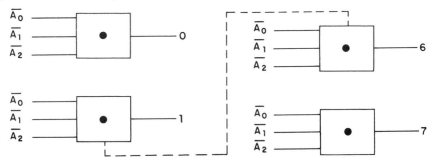

Figure 13

and our three flops will look as shown in Figure 14.

$\overline{A}_2$	A_2	$\overline{A}_1$	A_1	$\overline{A}_0$	A_0
0	1	0	1	0	1

A_2	A_1	A_0

Figure 14

When all three flops are in the zero state, $\overline{A}_0 = 1$, $\overline{A}_1 = 1$ and $\overline{A}_2 = 1$, (it is true that A_0 is false) and the output of gate 0 is true, and all others false. When flip-flop A_2 is one, A_1 is one, and A_0 is zero,

$$A_2 = A_1 = \overline{A}_0 = 1$$

and gate six is true, all others false, etc. Note that with three bits we achieve $2^3 = 8$ states. With n bits we achieve 2^n states.

Another type of tree is that shown in Figure 15. In the tree the decisions regarding the state of a particular flop are made one at a time. This tree offers distinct advantages for large registers in that the number of inputs to a gate are held at two — rather than one — per bit.

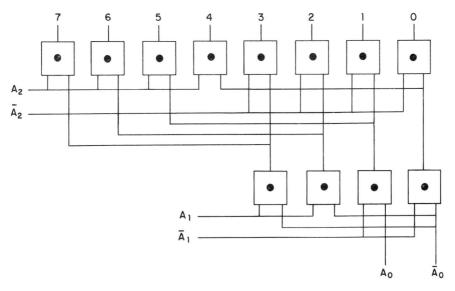

Figure 15

ADDITION

There is one process which is crucial to the operation of these machines and that is addition. And, since the logic we are using is all two-state logic, it is reasonable to suppose we ought to consider binary arithmetic.

Table 2 (page 44) contains the first eight integers and their binary representations. The extension is obvious to more bits. From Table 2 it is also clear that if one (a binary number now) is added to a particular bit position, that particular position changes state. This is nothing new. If you add one to a decimal counter which holds, say, six, it changes state to seven. Further, if we add one to a decimal counter which contains it maximum value, nine, it clearly goes to zero and propagates a carry to the next counter. The same thing occurs in the binary adder.

Furthermore, when people add, typically they start at the least-significant digit, do the addition, write the sum digit and propagate the carry so generated to the next stage. It is clear that if you add only two numbers, the carry can never be greater than one (9 + 9 + carry = 9 + carry). The same is true in binary addition (1 + 1 + carry = 1 + carry).

Let us write the truth table for addition of two bits, a_i and b_i, including the carry c_i. Let us calculate the sum bit s_i and carry out the c_{i+1}, where i represents the bit position, zero being the least-significant bit. See Table 3.

Table 3

c_i	a_i	b_i	s_i	c_{i+1}
0	0	0	0	0
0	0	1	1	0
0	1	0	1	0
0	1	1	0	1
1	0	0	1	0
1	0	1	0	1
1	1	0	0	1
1	1	1	1	1

Using our shorthand logic notation,

$$s_i = a_i b_i c_i + a_i b_i c_i + a_i b_i c_i + a_i b_i c_i$$

(To verify this, take values for a_i, b_i, c_i, and plus them in, remembering that *this is not binary addition* hence $1 + 1 = 1$.

Example:

$$a_i = 0 \qquad \bar{a}_i = 1$$
$$b_i = 1 \qquad \bar{b}_i = 0$$
$$c_i = 1 \qquad \bar{c}_i = 0$$
$$s_i = 0 \cdot 0 \cdot 0 + 1 \cdot 1 \cdot 0 + 1 \cdot 0 \cdot 1 + 0 \cdot 1 \cdot 1$$
$$= 0 + 0 + 0 + 0 = 0$$

Example:

$$a_i = 0 \qquad \bar{a}_i = 1$$
$$b_i = 1 \qquad \bar{b}_i = 0$$
$$c_i = 1 \qquad c_i = 0$$
$$s_i = 0 \cdot 0 \cdot 1 + 1 \cdot 1 \cdot 1 + 1 \cdot 0 \cdot 0 + 0 \cdot 1 \cdot 0$$
$$= 0 + 1 + 0 + 0 = 1)$$

If we assume that we have both flip-flop outputs available, we can construct the network shown in Figure 16.

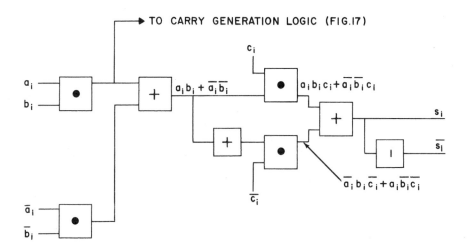

Figure 16

The logic equation for the carry is

$$c_{i+1} = a_i b_i + a_i c_i + b_i c_i$$

and the network is shown in Figure 17.

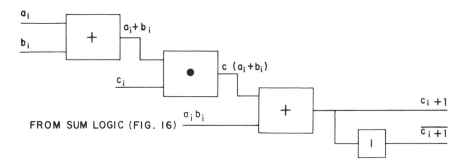

Figure 17

We can represent an adder box for adding two bits and carry by the symbol shown in Figure 18.

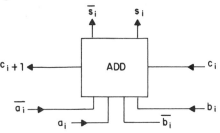

Figure 18

Now, using our delayed *J-K* flip-flop and adder box, let us draw the details of a unit which consists of two four-bit registers and the adder, so that at add time, the sum is placed in one of the registers and its initial contents lost. See Figure 19.

In addition to the ADD pulse, there are Clear A and Clear B pulses, and a Load B pulse. If now we have a storage — or memory — which will fetch a word on command and place it on the input lines, we can see the following sequence:

1. Clear A, Clear B
2. Fetch, Load B
3. ADD
4. Clear B

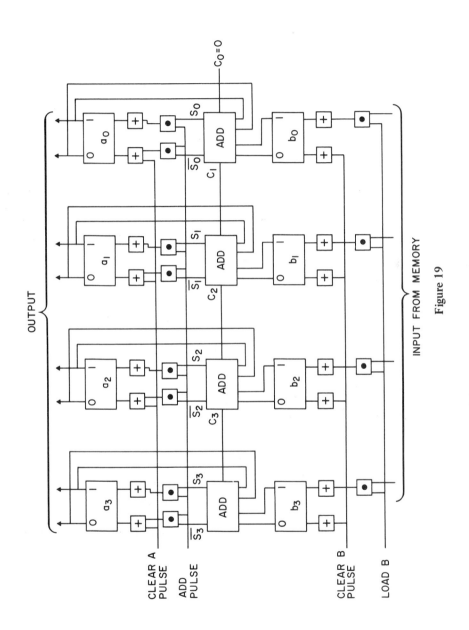

Figure 19

5. Fetch, Load B
6. ADD

The sum of the first word fetched and the second word fetched now appears in the A register.

SYSTEM

Let us now look at the block diagram of the computer shown in Figure 20. Here A, B, Program Counter, Inst., and Address are flip-flop registers.

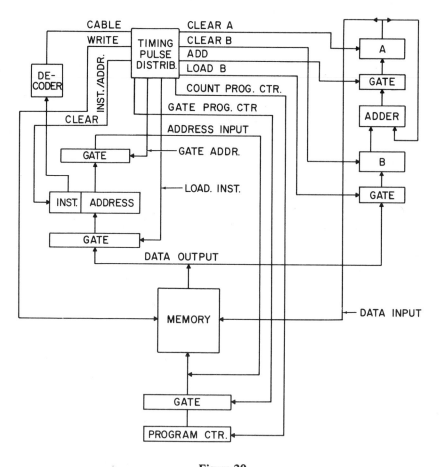

Figure 20

The gates, adder and decoder have been discussed, and we assume that if we give an address to the memory and ask it nicely, it will put the word located at the address on the data-output lines, or store — at the address — the word on the data-input lines. If the memory is given no address, it could do a read cycle from any address since this does not change the contents of the memory. Clearly, if we don't open the gates to the instruction-address register or B register, it is as if we had done nothing. We will make use of this fact.

Let us now look at this timing pulse distributor. Figure 21 shows a subsection of the TPD, called the timing pulse generator.

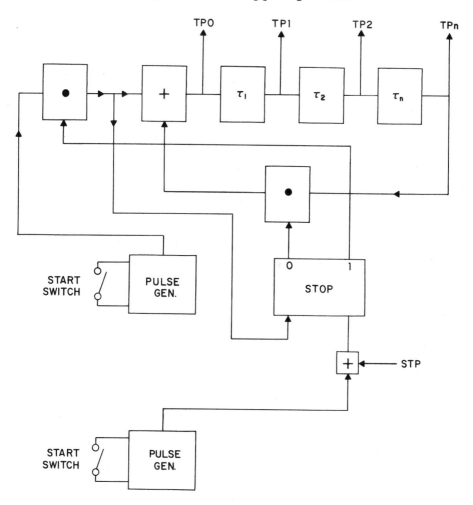

Figure 21

When the Start switch is operated, a short pulse is generated which is called TP0. The Stop flip-flop is now turned off. The pulse TP0 passes through delay τ, and generates TP1, and so on through TPn. We have not specified n since it is not yet clear how many of these pulses we will need. Note that since Stop is off, TPn generates and is coincident with TP0. If we depress the Stop switch, Stop will be turned on — preventing TPn from generating TP0 — effectively stopping the timing-pulse sequence.

The complete timing-pulse sequence typically represents one complete memory cycle, i.e., the time to read the contents of a memory register (which sets that particular register to zero) and then restore the contents. (The contents of the memory register are held in a flip-flop register during the time between Read and Write.) It is clear that we would like to fetch an instruction from the memory, and then execute it.

Let us postulate a flip-flop called Fetch/Execute, which will separate our cycles into the two parts indicated.

The program counter will hold the address of the instruction to be fetched. It will be set initially by switches on the console. Operating the Clear switch on the console will put the Fetch/Execute flop into the Fetch state.

Figure 22 shows the Fetch cycle logic. At TP0 time, if fetching, we turn Gate PC on, which sends the contents of the program counter to the memory as an address. We do not tell the memory to Write, therefore it does a Read cycle which will put a word on the data-output lines. At TP1 time we clear Inst./Address and at TPn time, we sind this word on the data-output lines into Inst./Address by pulsing the appropriate gates. At TPn time, the F/E flop is changed to the Execute state and PC is stepped by 1. Gate PC is turned off just before this.

Suppose now the output of the decoder says that Inst. contains a Load A instruction (LDA).

The logic for this is shown in Figure 23. Three other instructions are shown also:

Add the contents of X to A (ADX),

Store A   (STA),

and

Stop   (STP).

Since we are in Execute, TP0 will turn on gate adder which will send the address register to the memory as its address. Write is off so the memory

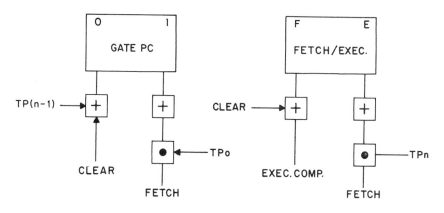

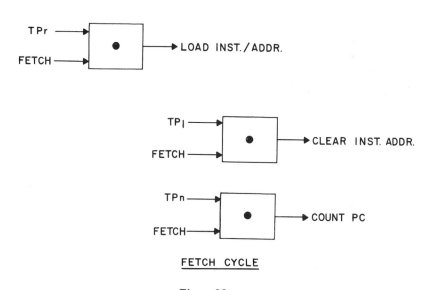

FETCH CYCLE

Figure 22

will read and put the data onto the data-output lines. A and B are cleared at TP1 time, and at TPr time, the contents of the memory data lines are pulsed into B. At TP(r + 1) time, B is added to the cleared A, hence A now contains the word which originally appeared in the location specified by Address.

The ADD pulse also generates the Execution-Complete pulse which switches the F/E flop to the Fetch state.

Remember, the program counter was increased by 1 at the end of the previous Fetch cycle. A new instruction will now be fetched from

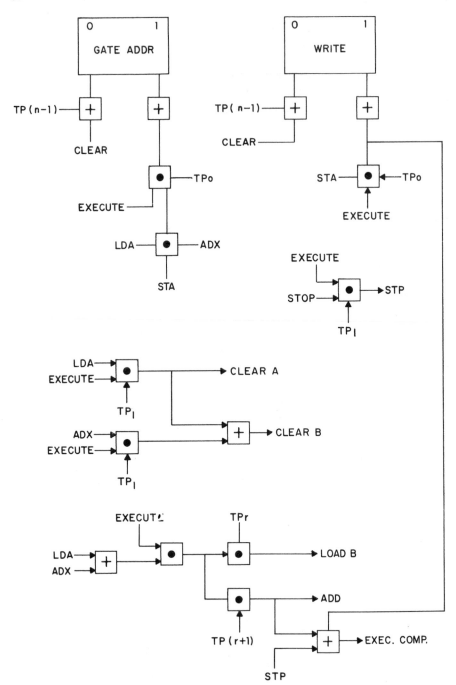

Figure 23

the location just following the location of the LDA instruction. Suppose this instruction is ADX. The execution of this instruction is identical to that for LDA, except A is not cleared.

If the third instruction in the sequence is STA, Write will be turned on at TP0 time. (Exec. Comp. also comes out at this time.) The memory will not put the contents of A into the location specified by the address register.

Another Fetch will naturally be executed. If this brings a Stop, the Stop flop (Figure 21, page 51) will be turned on, thus inhibiting generation of another timing-pulse sequence.

CONCLUSION

We have just designed a very simple computer. It is, however, far from complete. Its instruction set is extremely small. No provision is made for input/output. The operation of the memory is still vague. Nevertheless, we are forced to stop here. The crude outlines of the machine are complete, and that was our aim. To go into more detail will not uncover any further techniques.

Further recommended reading is listed below.

RECOMMENDED READING

1. LOGICAL DESIGN OF DIGITAL COMPUTERS
   Montgomery Phister
   Wiley, 1959

2. THEORY AND DESIGN OF DIGITAL MACHINES
   Bartee, Lebow, and Reed
   McGraw-Hill, 1962

3. THE LOGIC OF COMPUTER ARITHMETIC
   Ivan Flores
   Prentice-Hall, 1963

Chapter 4

COMPUTER LANGUAGES

Leroy Krider

INTRODUCTION

One scarcely begins the study of digital computers before he is confronted with a myriad of languages. There are distinct machine languages associated with each computer. There are assembly languages associated with each machine language. We hear of machine-independent languages, problem-oriented languages, list-processing languages. Of the types of languages above, each has its own name, and hence we hear words like SAP, FAP, COMPAS, FORTRAN, ALGOL, MAD, LISP, and quite literally hundreds of others. It is the purpose of this paper to classify the various types of languages, and to describe their uses.

PROBLEM PREPARATION

The process of preparing a problem for a computer can be divided into various phases. I have chosen to break this into four steps. Step one is definition of the problem. What is it we wish to do? What are the types of information we wish to input to the computer? What processing will these inputs be subjected to? What exceptional cases are there? Perhaps the most important portion of step one (and amazingly often not properly defined), is the question, "What do we wish to accomplish and what question or questions are we asking?" Step two is to reduce the problem to some form of orderly procedure. In step two we do not write out complete details, but rather indicate the general procedure. Flow diagrams are quite satisfactory for this. Step three is to write out in

56

complete detail the procedures to be followed. Step three differs from step two in that everything is completely specified. In step two we may choose to summarize or even omit some portions if their inclusion would tend to confuse general understanding of the problem.

The final step is to translate the language of step three into the language of the computer. This should be a mechanical process. There may be several equivalent ways that the problem may be expressed in machine language, but no new problem specifications should enter at this point.

It should be pointed out that the classification above of steps for problem preparation is quite arbitrary. Indeed they would probably never be followed exactly. Thus, for a simple, well-defined problem one might skip some of the intermediate steps. For a long, ill-defined problem one might expand step two into several levels of flow charts, each more detailed than the previous. In this case it is highly likely that the process of writing out details results in altered problem definition. Hence there may be an iterative procedure between steps one, two, and three. Even step four, the preparation of code, may cause one to re-evaluate step one. Thus, it may be discovered that some aspects of the processing desired are impractical due to machine limitations. On the other hand, one may discover that some useful pieces of information not originally planned for just happen to be available. Nonetheless, the idealized four-step model is a useful concept to bear in mind. In some form or other the steps are gone through, whether recorded or not, whether iterated or not. Further, the model forms a useful basis for description of the major aspects of computer languages. As an example, consider the following trivial problem.

Suppose we have a number X in memory to which we wish to add one if X is greater than or equal to zero, and from which we wish to subtract one if X is less than zero. The previous sentence constitutes step one — the problem is defined. For step two consider the flow chart in Figure 1. The notation used here is more or less standard. Circles indicate control locations, oblongs indicate a decision, and rectangles contain descriptions of computations. The colon is read, "is compared to," and the right-to-left-pointing arrow is read, "replaces the value of." Direction, or flow, of control is indicated by directed arrows outside the circles, oblongs, and rectangles. Note that if we view this properly we have all of the elements necessary to describe a problem; that is, we have a language.[1] Thus flowcharting is our first example of a computer-associated language.

---

[1]The author has intentionally avoided any discussion of the distinction between a language and a notation.

For step two consider Figure 2. Were the computer able to accept this language directly as input we would be done at this point; however, the language in which any given computer operates is quite different from this. As an example, consider the following hypothetical[2] computer. It has a standard length of information (called a *word*) which consists of six decimal digits and either a plus or minus sign. There are 3000 of

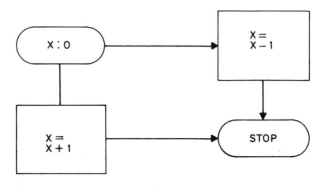

Figure 1

$$\text{IF X LESS THAN } 0; X \leftarrow X - 1;$$
$$\text{OTHERWISE } X \leftarrow X + 1; \text{STOP}$$

Figure 2

these words in the computer memory. They are numbered 0000 to 2999. Computer words are capable of holding either numbers or instructions. If the contents of a computer word is interpreted as an instruction the following applies:

1. Sign position is ignored.
2. The leading two digits specify a code for an operation to be performed.
3. The next four digits refer to a location in memory.

We further assume that there is some method of entering numbers or instructions into specified memory locations, and also that there is a

---

[2]The author has chosen this machine configuration to be typical of a small computer, state-of-the-art circa 1960. The specific choice of memory size, instruction codes, etc. is unlike any computer with which he is familiar.

means of telling the computer from which memory location to obtain its first instruction. From then on the computer is on its own. The instruction set for our computer includes the following commands. In this description XXXX denotes a four-digit number which may have any of the values from 0000 through 2999.

Instruction Description

01 XXXX	The contents of the memory location whose number is XXXX is placed in the accumulator. If this instruction is in memory location YYYY, the next instruction is taken from YYYY + 1; i.e., the next instruction is the next in sequence.
02 XXXX	The contents of the memory location whose number is XXXX is added to the quantity in the accumulator. The next instruction is the next in sequence.
03 XXXX	The contents of the memory location whose number is XXXX is subtracted from the number in the accumulator. The next instruction is the next in sequence.
04 XXXX	If the contents of the accumulator is less than zero, the next instruction is taken from memory location XXXX. Otherwise the next instruction is the next in sequence.
05 XXXX	If the contents of the accumulator is greater than zero, the next instruction is taken from memory location XXXX. Otherwise the next instruction is the next in sequence.
06 XXXX	If the contents of the computer is exactly zero, the next instruction is taken from memory location

	XXXX. Otherwise the next instruction is the next in sequence.
07 XXXX	The next instruction is taken from memory location XXXX.
08 XXXX	The contents of the accumulator is placed in the memory location whose number is XXXX. The next instruction is the next in sequence.
09 XXXX	Stop the computer. The XXXX portion of the instruction is not used.

With this much of our computer defined we can code our sample problem. Let's assume that the number x has been placed in memory location 1500. If the following set of numbers and coded instructions are also in memory and the computer is directed to begin with the instruction in location 0500 our computation will be performed.

LOC in memory	Contents	Meaning
0500	011500	Load the contents of cell 1500 in the accumulator.
0501	060505	If the accumulator contains a zero, execute the instruction in 0505.
0502	050505	If the accumulator contains a positive number, execute the instruction in 0505.
0503	030508	Subtract the contents of 0508 from the number in the accumulator.
0504	070506	Next instruction to be found in 0506.
0505	020508	Add the contents of 0508 to the number in the accumulator.

0506	081500	Store the contents of the accumulator in cell 1500.
0507	090000	Stop.
0508	000001	One.
1500	x	x

The last example was intended to illustrate how even the most trivial problem can give rise to an extremely disagreeable batch of virtually unintelligible numbers inside the computer. The process of going from the reasonably concise notation of step three to the coded instructions in step four was a purely routine one. Since one of the prime functions of a digital computer is to assist the human in the performance of routine clerical tasks, one might ask if the computer can aid in the preparation of codes for its own consumption. The answer to this question is yes, to a surprising degree.

RECOGNITION OF ALPHABETIC CHARACTERS

Before describing how a computer can aid in its own problem preparation, we must say a little about the recognition of alphabetic characters presented to it in the form of, say, punched cards. On most digital computers made today the contents of a punched card can be copied on command into specified memory locations. Each letter is replaced by a unique numeric representation. For example, suppose the name GEORGE SMITH were punched in the first twelve positions of a card. Further, suppose the computer is constructed to make the following letter-to-letter replacement:

G	26	S	38
E	24	M	32
O	34	I	28
R	37	T	39
blank	19	H	27

If the computer is instructed to read the card into words 1000 through 1003, the contents of these words, on completion of the read, would be

262434	372624
193832	283927

With the following code the computer could then ask the question, "Did the card say GEORGE SMITH?"

Location	Contents	Location	Contents
0100	011000		
0101	031200	0111	070066
0102	060104	0112	011003
0103	070066	0113	031203
0104	011001	0114	060555
0105	031201	0115	070066
0106	060108	⋮	
0107	070066	1200	262434
0108	011002	1201	372624
0109	031202	1202	193832
0110	060112	1203	283927

Control will go to location 0555 if the card did say GEORGE SMITH, and to 0066 otherwise.

Thus we will henceforth assume the computer is capable of reading and distinguishing alphabetic, numeric, and special characters (e.g., +, -,*).

ASSEMBLY LANGUAGE

The first artificial languages to be developed in the computer field were assembly languages. Part of their function is to allow the use of alphabetic identifiers for the machine operation codes. Thus, for example, it is much more palatable for a programmer to write F 1000 (F standing for "fetch") than 011000. More specifically, the following definition of an assembly language may be used.

An assembly program is a computer program which operates upon symbolic input to produce machine instructions carrying out some or all of the following functions.

1. Translation of symbolic operation codes.
2. Allocation of storage — to the extent at least of assigning storage locations to successive instructions and of utilizing symbolic addresses so defined.
3. Computation of addresses so defined.

The preceding code, written in an assembly language[3] might read as follows:

```
        DEF     BUF = 1000
        ORG     100
        F       BUF         Fetch the contents of location
                            called BUF.
        SUB     ALF         Subtract from that the contents of
                            the location called ALF.
        TZ      S1          If the answer is zero go to S1.
        T       OUT         Go to the location called OUT.
S1      F       BUF + 1     Fetch the contents of the location
                            BUF + 1 (i.e., location 1001 if
                            BUF is 1000).
        SUB     ALF + 1     Etc.
        TZ      S2
        T       OUT
S2      F       BUF + 2
        SUB     ALF + 2
        TZ      S3
        T       OUT
S3      F       BUF + 3
        SUB     ALF + 3
        TZ      FOUND
        T       OUT
        ALF     262434
                372624
                193832
                283927
```

Ignoring the first two lines for the moment, we have assumed that the assembly program will translate F into 01, SUB into 03, TZ into 06, and T into 07. This is part 1 of the definition of an assembly program. The first instruction (F BUF) will be assigned a memory address and successive instructions will be assigned to successive words. The identifiers S1, S2, etc. will be associated with the addresses which are assigned to the adjacent instructions or data. This satisfies part 2 of the definition. Finally, within the instructions themselves, S1, S2, etc. will be replaced by their assigned addresses. This is part 3 of the definition.

[3]Note we have said *an* assembly language. Since the assembly language is a function of the assembly program, it can be changed by changing the program.

Now consider the first two lines. The price we pay for the convenience of writing symbolically is the introduction into our language of special operators which define the identifiers we have used. These are not instructions to the computer but to the assembly program. Such lines of code are generally called *definition statements or pseudo operations.* The line DEF   BUF = 1000 tells the assembly program to replace any occurrence of the identifier BUF with the value 1000. The line ORG   100 tells the assembly program to assign the location 100 to the first line of true code. With these two pseudo operations all identifiers have been defined. S1, for example, will become 105 and the line which reads TZ S1 will ultimately be translated into 060105.

Note that the assembly language form of the program which tests for GEORGE SMITH has not been executed; it has been translated from the programmer's mnemonics to machine language. This program has been recorded somewhere, possibly on punched cards, and must be reloaded into the computer before it can be executed. This extra step is another price one must pay for the use of artificial languages.

Assembly languages are very helpful in the problem preparation process. Few humans are able to prepare programs in machine language without a large number of blunders. The price we pay, in comparison to the gains, is small indeed.

COMPILERS

Assembly languages assist in the bookkeeping portions of step four and in problem preparation, but do little to alleviate the detailed attention to the machine's operations. Shortly after the first assembly languages were produced, programmers began designing and coding artificial languages which came to be called *compiler languages.* A compiler language differs from an assembly language chiefly in the degree to which the programmer is allowed to symbolize. In assembly language there is a near one-to-one correspondence between lines the coder writes and words in the computer. With a compiler language there tend to be many machine words corresponding to each line written. An assembly language is oriented to the particular computer at hand, while a compiler language tends to be problem oriented and, to a degree, machine independent. An assembly language assists in step four of problem preparation, while a compiler attempts to eliminate step four and invade the realm of step three. The price we pay for using a compiler is increased complexity in the declaration statements and decreased efficiency in the running time of the final machine program. The latter is a direct result of the machine-independent nature of compiler languages. Despite the disadvantages, however, there is, for a large class of problems, considerable gain in terms of programming time, total time, and cost from problem conception to production of answers.

Of the many existent compiler languages we will consider three examples: FORTRAN, ALGOL, and COBOL. Rather than attempt to describe any language in detail we will give examples which indicate the structure of each language.

FORTRAN

FORTRAN, which stands for FORmula TRANslator, was originated by the IBM Corporation in the late 1950's. It is probably the most popular computer language in this country — at least among scientific users. FORTRAN allows the use of statements very similar in appearance to mathematical equations. Operations concerned with input and output are summarized into a short, concise form. Because loops are very common elements in any program, special operations have been included to facilitate loop control.

As an example of a FORTRAN program, consider a sorting problem. Suppose we have 100 alphabetic words, each with maximum length of eight characters, punched beginning in col. 1 on each of 100 cards. It is desired to arrange these in alphabetic order and print them. The following program will accomplish this.

```
        DIMENSION  A(100)
        READ (2, 3) (A (I), I = 1,100)
3       FORMAT (A8)
        DO  4 J = 1, 99
        K = 100 − J
        DO  4 I = 1, K
        IF (A (I) .LE. A (I + 1)  ) TO GO 4
        TEM = A (I)
        A (I) = A (I + 1)
        A (I + 1) = A (I)
4       CONTINUE
        PRINT (3, 3) (A (I), I = 1,100)
        STOP
        END
```

The first line is a declarative line which tells that we will be working with a sequence of values called A(1), A(2), ..., A(100). The second line requests a read from input unit number 2 under the control of format number 3 into the 100 A positions. Format number 3 defines a single input line as having eight characters of useful information. In our case this means the latter 72 columns of the card are ignored. The two statements which start with DO mean to vary J and I from their lower bounds (one) to their upper bounds (99 and 100-J, respectively) and perform all the instructions through and including the line labeled 4. CONTINUE is a special line which forces a check, first to see if I, and then J, has reached its upper bound. Since the statement DO 4 I = 1, K is inside the range of the other DO statement, the I loop will be done each time J takes on a new value. Thus the instructions in the loop will be performed a total of 4,950 times. The actual sorting is accomplished by switching adjacent pairs of items, first for all 99 pairs. This forces the largest value to be on the bottom of the list. The process is then repeated for the 99 values preceding the last. This continues until all items are sorted. The PRINT statement then causes the reordered list to be printed.

The STOP statement causes the computer to halt. The END statement is a sentinel to the compiler that there is nothing more to process.

This method is, incidentally, a very inefficient way of sorting. Nonetheless, the program serves to illustrate several points. First the particular version of FORTRAN employed here is FORTRAN IV. Since it was first introduced, FORTRAN has been modified, extended, and developed for a large variety of computers. Each of these "dialects" of the language differ slightly, although there is a great deal of compatability between them.   FORTRAN is often called a machine-independent language, although some degree of dependency on the computer on which it is implemented does creep in. In the preceding example the assumption is made that a computer word can hold eight alphabetic characters. If this same program is run on a computer whose words can accommodate only six characters, the array A would have to be made 200 words long, and switching would have to be done on pairs of doubles of words.   Further, the assumption is made that the internal numeric representation of letters is such that a numeric sort will produce alphabetic ordering.   This is not the case on many computers. Nonetheless, a FORTRAN program written for one machine can generally be transferred to another machine with a FORTRAN translator in a small fraction of the time that would be required to recode it completely. Experience seems to indicate that coding in a language on the FORTRAN levels reduces problem preparation time by as much as a factor of ten.

ALGOL

By 1957 or 1958, in addition to FORTRAN, there were literally dozens, if not hundreds, of other problem-oriented languages. The programming field at this time began to take a serious look at itself. The result was the formation of an international committee to study languages. In 1960, they published the ALGOL 60 report which specified an ALGOrithmic Language which they proposed for international use. ALGOL is far more precise than FORTRAN. Careful distinction is made between command words and names created by the programmer for his own use. "Level" of a program element is defined with strict rules about referencing between levels. Different levels are set off by special symbols. Recursive coding, that is, the ability for a subroutine to call on itself, is allowed. Because of the large number of symbols needed — more than is provided on most computers — the ALGOL committee published three languages, each called ALGOL. First we have the publication language which takes advantage of the type faces available to a printer — namely upper case, lower case, and italics. The second ALGOL is called reference language. This uses, among other things, underlining to distinguish symbols from coders' names. Finally, we have hardware representation, which, in general, will differ depending on the character set available as input. Typical substitutions are such things as LT for $<$, (/ for [, IF for if (if underlined).

Because of the precise nature of ALGOL, a program probably tends to be more free of subtle errors once it is in a running state. At least in reference notation ALGOL tends to be more readable, again because of its more precise nature. In Europe, where the majority of users were not committed to FORTRAN at the time ALGOL was conceived, ALGOL is quite popular. In this country, it seems to be the general opinion that ALGOL does not offer enough additional advantages to make a change-over worthwhile.

COBOL

Early in 1959, work was begun to establish on a national basis a standard business-oriented language. Reasonably final specifications for this language were published in June of 1961. It is called COBOL. By 1962, most computer manufacturers were producing COBOL translators for their equipment. COBOL, like ALGOL, found the need for many special command words. In the COBOL case this problem was solve by restricting the use of certain words as names available to the programmer. The list of restricted words is quite large. Feeling that in the business field users would not wish to use equations, many optional notations were introduced into the language: $Z = X + Y$ can be written in the following ways:

> COMPUTE Z EQUALS X PLUS Y
> COMPUTE Z = X + Y
> ADD X TO Y GIVING Z

The author personally feels that these options tend to confuse rather than help. One might be tempted, for example, to

> ADD X AND Y TO PRODUCE Z

This is not valid COBOL.

A program written in COBOL consists of four portions called *divisions*. These are the identification, environment, data, and procedure divisions.

The identification division distinguishes this particular program from other programs.

The environment division defines the input and output units available and how they are to be regarded for this program.

The data division allows the description of files of information. The notation used for this is largely tape oriented. The programmer can define files, within which are blocks. A block can be subdivided into data records, which in turn can be subdivided. An example of a payroll file description (FD) follows:

> FD PAYROLL; BLOCK CONTAINS
>   45 CHARACTERS
>
> LABEL RECORDS ARE STANDARD;
>
> SEQUENCED ON NAME;
>
> DATA RECORDS ARE
>
> 01   NAME;   SIZE IS 30
> 02   LAST-NAME; SIZE IS 15
> 02   FIRST-NAME;   SIZE IS 15
> 01   EMPLOYEE-NO; SIZE IS 10
> 02   CLASSIFICATION;   SIZE IS 5
> .03   AREA-CODE; SIZE IS Z
> 03   PLANT-NO;   SIZE IS Z
> 02   HIRE-NO;   SIZE IS 5
> 01   SALARY;   SIZE IS 5

The procedure division contains the operation statements. The coder can, for example, refer to NAME and obtain the 30-character field defined above, or to last name and obtain only the first fifteen characters of the NAME field.

CONTROL ROUTINES

A typical installation running a modern computer will daily process dozens or even hundreds of jobs. Some of these take as little time as a few seconds. Human handling time to mount tapes, place cards in a reader, press start buttons and remove output, however, is measured in minutes. For short jobs, therefore, strictly human operation leads to an intolerable loss of efficiency. One solution to this is to run the computer under the control of a "supervisor" routine. The inevitable consequence of this is the introduction of still another language.

The first of such supervisor routines to be developed were the so-called *batch monitors*. They are still the most commonly used today. These systems accept many jobs submitted by different users and process them one after the other. They take care of loading the appropriate compilers, assemblers, and service routines as needed. They also give advanced warning, where possible, to the human operator for such jobs as mounting and unmounting tapes.

A typical job card deck prepared by a user might consist of the following:

1. A monitor control card which identifies the user.
2. A monitor control card which requests a FORTRAN compilation.
3. The FORTRAN cards to be compiled.
4. A monitor control card which requests an assembly run.
5. The cards to be assembled.
6. A monitor control card which requests the output programs of FORTRAN and the assembler to be combined into one running program.
7. A monitor control card requesting the resultant program to be run.
8. Data cards to be read by the program.

Briefly, a monitor language may be compared to a language like FORTRAN as follows: FORTRAN is a language which employs operators to manipulate data supplied by the programmer; a monitor is a language which employs operators to manipulate programs and other large units of

information. The monitor knows little about a program except that it is
a program, and little about a batch of data except that it is data.

Because of the large difference between the types of operands, the
two classes of languages perform quite different functions. There is a
great tendency for the casual programmer to confuse the two, however.

SPECIALIZED LANGUAGES

The advent of time sharing, computer motion pictures, and on-line
process control, to mention but a few innovations, has led to many
languages designed for special jobs. Another type of language currently
being developed, however, which is worthy of mention, is that which
is designed to assist in the coding of other language translators. There are
two principal advantages to this. First, the time required to prepare a
translator is greatly reduced. Second, and probably more important,
the translator is easier for the experienced user to understand. He is,
therefore, able to modify it if he choses. Doing this on a translator
written in assembly language is almost prohibitively difficult. It is
hoped that developments along this line will be of great aid to users.

Chapter 5

INFORMATION RETRIEVAL AND COMPUTERS

Robert J. Howerton

INTRODUCTION

The use of computers for aiding in the storage and retrieval of information is the subject of this paper. The methodology described is a distillation of experience over the past ten years with our systems as well as those of others. It has been applied successfully to fields as disparate as neutron physics and biologic cell physiology. There is adequate reason to believe that, so long as the ground rules are followed, successful information systems can be developed for the social and behavioral sciences.

Information is defined to be the totality of facts, which belong to unambiguously defined categories, and to which logical order can be assigned. This logical order may be: ranking by ordinal number, alphabetic arrangement, intrinsic numeric value, in short, any reproducible method characterized by the absence of direct recourse to intuition. In this discussion the terms *information* and *data* are used interchangeably. *Information System,* as used here, is a mechanism by which information, as defined above, may be manipulated in a logical fashion to provide lists, graphical displays, and various indexes in accordance with the needs of the users of the system. One of the manipulations, of course, is the retrieval of information appropriate to a specific request. This, however, does not provide an adequate definition of the term *information retrieval* as it is often used. Indeed, it is sometimes regarded as the name of an academic discipline.

The term information retrieval is one of the worst offenders in the language with respect to imprecision and ambiguity. We are stuck with a term which is overly broad and does not describe a discipline or

71

pseudodiscipline but rather a common human activity.

If information retrieval is regarded as a human activity rather than a discipline, three ordered subdivisions follow immediately from a cursory consideration. To retrieve information one first retrieves a reference to the documents which contain the desired information. Next the documents are retrieved and finally the information or data are retrieved by a person reading the documents. It is only at the last step that the desired information is retrieved and then by a specialist who understands the significance of what he reads.

Unless information can be quantified, there is little point in discussing a computerized information system. For example, it is virtually impossible to design a system which could respond to a request such as for "All information which would be useful in making the following decision...." The requestor must know the type of information he requires to make the decision and make his request appropriately. It is true that skilled and inventive persons are working on the problem of creating information systems which can respond to imprecise requests, but this chapter deals with what is currently feasible.

For many fields of science and technology there are certain data which are sought repeatedly by researchers or designers and which can be organized into data files. To eliminate repetitious reference retrieval, document retrieval, and information extraction for the same body of references, compilers organize the data and create information systems for these well-defined fields. For such fields, the researcher or designer need not go back to the general literature of the field, but may direct his request to the specialized information system. Because there are diverse work habits among the practitioners of a field or discipline, it is desirable to provide various means of access to the data of a specialized information system. For example, in addition to the data file, there should be an author index to the references from which the data were extracted, a subject index to the data file, an alphabetized listing of the references, and an accession number list of the references.

It is clear that the discussion above relates to the organization of information into a system which will allow retrieval of quantified data, observations, impressions, historical facts, etc. in accordance with the requestor's need. None of the above necessarily relate to the use of computers. The intellectual effort of organizing information does not require the existence of computers, but if the amount of information is large, preparation of proper indexes and lists by hand manipulation consumes an unnecessarily inordinate amount of time and effort. The role of computers in the development is directed toward manipulation of data to create useful lists or indexes. In other words, the intellectual effort of identification and organization of the data must be expended before the computer can arrange or rearrange the identified and organized information in accordance with anticipated need.

It is often envisioned in popular presentations on this subject, that the ideal situation for retrieval of stored information is by demand search with the user of a system making his request via data-phone or teletype directly to the innermost bowels of a computer, with immediate (*real-time* is, I believe, the magic word) write-out on his console of the answer to his question. There are currently existing systems which operate in this fashion. Indeed there is one operating at LRL which was designed and implemented by the author's group. It is found that such a system is occasionally useful. However, the best-tested, most widely used, and most successful data retrieval system is operated by the Bell Telephone System, and existed long before computers became fashionable. Within a minute or two, the telephone number of any person in the United States can be obtained and no magnetic tapes, disc files, or mass storages need be consulted. It is submitted, therefore, that emulation of this successful system has much in its favor. The use of computers to produce "telephone books" of information is certainly proper and for some fields probably precludes the desirability of having console access to the information system.

It was noted above that information retrieval is logically subdivided into *reference retrieval, document retrieval,* and *data retrieval.* Although work has been done and is continuing on computer manipulation of the free text of documents for the purpose of subject analysis and extraction of factual content, this work is in its infancy and, until much further development, we must assume that analysis and extraction of the contents of a paper are intellectual functions of a subject specialist. Once the data have been extracted from documents by a subject specialist, the manipulation of these data can and should be accomplished by a computer if the number of data is substantial.

Document retrieval is a warehousing problem which has been essentially solved in various ways, some as simple as building larger warehouses or buying roller skates for the runners. The microfilm technique, together with the various sophistications associated with it, forms another solution to the document storage and retrieval problem, although current practice in many installations using microfilm leads to the following, not altogether facetious, definition of microfilm. Microfilming is a technique whereby one may store in a very small volume, a piece of film from which an unlimited number of unreadable copies may be made quickly. So much for *document retrieval.* In the future, when 10^{12} to 10^{14} bit mass storages are common it probably will be feasible to store whole bibiliographies including complete text in the mass storages and to subsequently retrieve selected subsets with a computer but, once again, we are concerned here with what can be done now and, therefore, conclude that computers are not currently of much use in the area of *document retrieval.*

This leaves *reference retrieval* as the subdivision of information retrieval for which computer manipulation of data has been developed and is particularly useful. Clearly, one would hope that through proper programming of a computer much of the intellectual "high priced" effort involved in indexing references with respect to the content could be eliminated. An example of an attempt to create a *reference retrieval system* wholly through word manipulation by a computer is the KWIC (*Key Word In Context*) type index. This method has been tried for the references in a number of fields. In the KWIC index, the substantive words appearing in titles of papers are permuted, alphabetized, and listed with each title presented the number of times a "key word" appears. Unfortunately, titles of papers are not written with KWIC indexing in mind. As a practical example of the problem inherent to KWIC indexes, a bibiliography of 750 references all reporting measurements of neutron cross sections was investigated. It was found that the term *neutron cross section(s)* appeared in 34 per cent of the titles and the terms *neutron(s)* or *cross section(s)* appeared in 77 per cent of the titles. The other 23 per cent of the titles would present a problem.

Another attempt to create a reference system by pure manipulation of terms depends upon the computer's ability to perform simple logical operations, such as requiring more than one term to be present in the title or abstract if reference is to be retireved or to eliminate a reference from retrieval if a certain term is present. This method has not led to notable success, and the reason becomes apparent if one considers that the collection of references being investigated will, for many fields, be made up of papers which use a specialized vocabulary. Further, any requests to the system would likely be couched in the specialized vocabulary of the field. In many areas of the physical sciences, at least, the collection of papers having term A, term B, and term C all present may be burdensomely large. In addition, the likelihood of A operating on B to yield C may be equal to that of C operating on B to yeild A. In such a case, the system would introduce noise into the output by the very nature of its design. One is forced to the conclusion that sone understanding of a field of work is necessary in order to index the papers of the field. The greater the degree of specialization, the more necessary is a detailed understanding if one is to differentiate between papers using the same or similar words but reporting quite different phenomena

Since pure manipulation of characters or words by a computer is not likely to provide a good basis for a reference retrieval system, it remains to examine optimum application of intellectual effort which will result in a reference retrieval system which is adequate for the needs of the users. For many well-defined fields an intrinsic organization of the field exists to the degree that information contained in references in that field will fall into a structured arrangement. Let us assume that there are, for some field, three categories, A, B, and C, such that all references will include data appropriate to one or more of these categories. Furthermore, no reference will include information having a quality associated with it likely to be a criterion for retrieval which is not one of these classes or categories. One may think of these three classes as labels on the axes of a three-dimensional coordinate system. Associated with each class there is a set of terms appropriate to that class. A single term may be appropriate to more than one class but when used a term is tagged to show to which class it is appropriate. As a trivially simple example assume that a corpus of literature exists on the political subdivisions of the world. One of the classes or categories by which the references would be indexed would, of course, be the political subdivision to which it was pertinent. Some of the references might well require more than one entry for political subdivision. In such a case complete indexing entries appropriate to each political subdivision would be executed rather than just a listing of the entries under each class. The point is that a single reference might deal, for example, with a geographic aspect of one country and an economic aspect of another. Unless the formalism of tying all aspects of an index entry is observed, the design of the system will result in intolerable noise. Each concept appearing in the reference must be indexed independently of any other entries for that reference.

In addition to indexing by political subdivision there will be classes or categories corresponding to such things as geographical features, political organization, economic position, weather conditions, military posture. Let us consider one of the more straightforward of these, namely, geographical features. It is conceivable that a user might want references dealing with a certain type of geographical feature of a particular country. In such a case he would like to consult an index which is arranged first by geographical feature, then by country. He could then enter the index under the proper geographical feature with countries listed in a second column and proceed immediately to the second column entries for the country with which he would be concerned. If, on the other hand, his request were for all geographical data of a particular country, he would consult an index in which the country appeared in the first column and geographical features in the second. Such a set of indexes resulting from the permutations of classes or categories has been called a *multicoordinate index*. Clearly, the number of possible permutations may be large if the number of categories is large. In practice, it turns out that an optimum number of permutations is reasonably small and, when the need is shown, it is easy to produce a new index resulting from a permutation not previously used.

The method described for making a multicoordinate index may also be applied to the data themselves after they have been extracted from the pertinent references. Let us assume that it is desirable to classify the coast line according to geographic coordinates, the quality of the ocean bottom for 50 yards seaward of the lowest tide line, the quality between lowest and highest tide lines, and quality of the land for 50 yards landward of the highest tide line. Under each of these there would be a number of *descriptors* or terms which would include, for example, the term "pebbles." This term might occur under any of the three classes but, by its tag (which might be its location on a punched card or magnetic tape) one would know whether the ocean bottom is pebbly, the tidal region is pebbly, or the beach area is pebbly. Of course, all three might be pebbly, in which case the same descriptor would be entered three times with the three different tags.

Since the data are ordered by the intrinsic organization of the field, this data file could be used equally well by an epidemiologist concerned with coastal swamplands, persons seeking an area to place a desalinization plant, or an Under Secretary of State seeking a good bathing beach.

The method by which the permutations are accomplished both for the multicoordinate index and the data file is especially easy and requires little computer time if one has a digital computer available with a large memory and word lengths providing ten to fifteen significant figures. The advantage of the large computer is not trivial. For example, an author index produced on the IBM-7030 (Stretch) in three minutes would have taken eight hours on an IBM-1401. The method used for making the permutations may be of passing interest. Assume there are three categories or classes for a multicoordinate index. Assume also that there are fewer than 1,000 descriptors. Then a descriptor may be characterized inside the computer by a three-digit number. Let us assume that the three categories are A, B, and C and that the descriptors equivalent (three digit) are tagged as $a(i)$, $b(i)$, and $c(i)$ where the i identifies the appropriate entry. If we wish the particular index being made to appear in the order B-A-C, we will multiply $b(i)$ by 10^6, $a(i)$ by 10^3, and $c(i)$ by 1; and add together the results to obtain a nine-digit number. When all the resulting nine-digit numbers are sorted, the machine can then print out the index in the order determined by the sorting procedure. To make the permutation C-A-B, the order of multiplication is $c(i)$ by 10^6, $a(i)$ by 10^3, and $b(i)$ by 1. Obviously, the result of this is an unambiguous identification for the index entry for the pertinent permutation.

This introduction has presented most of the philosophy basic to the scientific information systems which have been developed at LRL. Two information systems will now be described. These two systems, while both scientific, are related to very different fields; one to neutron physics and the other to biologic cell physiology. The similarities in design of the two systems are emphasized rather than the content of either. A background in the disciplines to which the systems are appropriate is not needed.

APPLICATIONS

Each of the two information systems described here is appropriate to a well-defined and strictly delimited field. This point is emphasized because the systems design depends upon the intrinsic organization of the field. The number of pieces of information handled by the system is of far less importance than the degree of organization of the data. Furthermore, if a precoordinated structure is devised for the field, less skilled persons can be used to index the references and extract data than would otherwise be possible.

One of the demonstration systems is for the measured data of the field of neutron physics and the other is for the measurements of the time parameters of biologic cell reproduction in the field of cell physiology. A preliminary step to the design of either system is the determination of the type of requests one can expect will be made to the system. For both systems, author indexes to the references, alphabetic lists of the references, lists of the references arranged by accession number, and various subject indexes are required. Because the fields are disparate, the subject indexes vary in form but the computer methods for producing them are similar. The other lists or "telephone books" are produced by the identical method for both fields since their production is independent of the subject content of the fields.

A single reference may contain many pieces of information, all of which should be included in the system. It would be burdensome to carry along with each datum the entire bibliographic reference. To avoid this, an accession or identification number is assigned to each reference before it (and the data it contains) is entered in the system.

The accession number serves to connect the data and the bibliographic citation. In addition to the complete bibliographic citation, any comments about the reference can be noted when the reference is entered into the system. These comments are free text and are displayed in the reference lists together with the bibliographic material.

The need for author indexes to the literature of a field is common to most fields and no special justification for providing them need be made. Users of the systems being properly inquisitive or perhaps a little distrustful of the systems often wish to find out whether a particular reference has been included. To allow them to do so, an alphabetic list of the references is included as one of the features of the systems. The alphabetic reference list is also a useful in-house tool for those making entries into the systems. The accession number list of the references is, of course, required since the accession number is the link between the data and the references.

Experimental neutron physics is characterized by measurement of some quality of interactions of neutrons with the nucleus of an atom. The kinetic energy of the incident neutron determines the magnitude of the measured quality. The natural organization of this field of physics provides categories or classes of the type described in the hypothetical example but these classes have the labels of target nucleus, particle out, quality measured, neutron energy range, etc. These classes, then, are analogous to geographical classes (features), etc., which were used in the hypothetical example. The data file for neutron physics currently contains about 300,000 individual measurements. Permuted lists analogous to the lists described for the hypothetical example are produced routinely. A full report[1] on the neutron physics system is available.

For the multicoordinate index associated with the field of cell physiology, the natural organization provides classes such as species, type of cell, phase of cell growth measured, etc. The data file is organized similarly.

The steps through which the subject specialist proceeds for this program are as follows:

1. A document pertaining to biologic cell replication is obtained and an accession number is assigned to it.
2. The complete bibliographic citation, the accession number, and any comments are written up on input sheets from which punched cards are prepared. The accession number and bibliographic information are entered in accordance with simple rules with

[1]UCRL-50132 (1966) "A Computer-Oriented Neutron Data Storage and Retrieval System," W. J. Cahill, D. W. Thompson, S. T. Perkins, R. J. Howerton.

respect to the cards and regions of cards into which certain parts of these data are put. The comments are not structured and can therefore be written according to the tastes of the specialist. Once this information has been punched onto cards for a reference, computer codes incorporate the information from the cards into the reference information file from which an author index, an alphabetical reference list, and an accession number reference list are made periodically.

3.   The reference is read and pertinent data are entered on an input sheet for punching onto 80-column cards. These data include the species of mammal studied, organ, cell type, whether normal or abnormal, conditions under which the measurement was made, method used, what was measured, results of the measurement, error reported, time of day, intrinsic special conditions of the measurement which the specialist felt were important, date of the article, an in-house value judgment with respect to the worth of the measurement. Of course, the accession number for the reference must be encoded on the same card to connect the data to the reference. Experience has shown an advantage to encoding all these data on a single card. This is not necessary, since continuation cards can be used, but it is desirable. We have chosen for this system to devise a dictionary of numerical equivalents to the concepts or descriptors of the discipline. Using these numerical equivalents, the pertinent data for a single measurement can be entered on a single card. If more than one measurement is reported, one card is used for each measurement. Some papers report as many as 250 measurements.

4.   The data file is organized and permuted to produce "telephone books," to supply data on demand if a "telephone book" arrangement is not satisfactory for a particular request, or to be used as a data source for mathematical manipulations. For example, a subject specialist has wished to see a tabulation of the measured times required for the genetic code to reproduce in mammalian cells. A demand search produced a list of 102 such measurements identified by the appropriate cell type and DNA (genetic code) replication time. The average of these was calculated at the same time and the value of the average (11.8 hours) printed out with the list. The same basic corpus of data can provide specialized lists such as all genetic code measurements accomplished at midnight versus those done at noon, or the time it takes a cancerous cell to reproduce itself compared to the homologous normal cell. The potential for the

system to produce specialized lists of information appropriate to the field is limited by the types of data produced by the experimentalists and by the skill of the user in prescribing the specific data lists and comparisons he needs. The system itself can accept new concepts as they are measured by a simple and straightforward extension of dictionaries.

SUMMARY

For any collection of information which can be quantified, the methods described here can be used to design a useful information storage and retrieval system. The quantified information may be in the realm of physical or biologic science, as described here, or in the behavioral sciences. The methods are independent of the field so long as the information can be quantified and has an intrinsic organization associated with it.

Chapter 6

INTERNATIONAL INTERACTIONS: SURVEYS AND COMPUTERS

Davis B. Bobrow

This paper deals with the contents of and realtions between three corners of a triangle. The respective corners are: (1) questions we want to answer about international interactions, (2) data supplied by means of surveys, and (3) computer applications to such data. We examine these corners and their relationships to establish certain criteria for those concerned with one or more of these corners. The purpose of these criteria is to enable us to make research and management choices efficiently which will yield powerful answers to powerful questions about international interactions.

Our attempt to inform possible research and management users means that we have to decide what we want (i.e., what are fruitful ways of looking at international interactions, what are useful questions about these, and thus, what kinds of answers are we looking for), and how we should get there (i.e., are survey data and computers fruitful ways to get the answers we want and if so, when). These questions are no different than the ones which *should* be asked in any goal-directed activity. Let us suppose that I decide that my heat bills are too high and that I want to cut them down. Operationally, this may mean that I decide to weatherstrip the doors, or windows, or buy storm windows. Until I make decisions about my goals, based on analyses of my problem, I cannot meaningfully assign probable utilities to alternative materials and tools. We are all familiar with analogies to the instance where someone buys storm windows when what he needed was weatherstripping for the front door. However, we are also familiar with instances where even though we know what we want, we don't know enough about alternative ways to get there to monitor experts of various kinds.

For example, to do what we want, we may need aluminum, but the supplier sells us wood because he thinks metals are sort of cold and austere and wood is warm. Similarly, to use the material we may only need a hand drill, but the supplier sells us a power drill because he sort of loves fancier, more powerful gadgets and we don't know enough to say, "To hell with you, all I need is a hand drill." The purpose of this paper is to establish criteria to reduce the frequency of such errors in our area of concern. Few specific criteria are new. However, they are integrated into a system and assessed for their problem-solving implications. Thus, they should gain considerably in power.

INTERNATIONAL INTERACTIONS:

Since questions about international interactions provide the criterion to assess the utility of survey data as handled by computer capabilities, this corner of our triangle should be examined first. We use the term *international interactions* to refer to behaviors by actors in one state which are intended to be, and/or are in fact, used by actors in at least one other state in selecting their future behaviors. Whether a behavior is "international" or only "domestic" is an empirical question, not one of convenience or custom. We limit the international interactions of concern to us in this paper by means of four parameters: level of generalization, classes of interactions, classes of actors, and analytic aspects. The set of interactions thus defined to be of concern to us represents one of several possible perspectives on international interactions.

The first parameter, level of generalization, involves us immediately in the customary dichotomy between the interests (goals or desired product) of the "policy operator" and the "academic." Since the fruitfulness of the dichotomy is questionable in an important class of problems, it is useful to cope with it in terms of the level of generalization parameter. Let us first discard those classes of products for both groups which are not fundamentally intended to answer questions about international interactions. These include research conducted to justify, by means of more or less scientific papers, beliefs already held, research for career advancement, and research primarily for ritual or monetary purposes. Whether or not such products are legitimate, they do not concern us here, even though such extraneous ends are partly responsible for the salience of the policy operator-academic distinction. What does concern us is the more intellectually relevant dichotomy between "current intelligence" and "nonapplied research." As my choice of the word *dichotomy* implies, these research enterprises are considered to be completely distinct from each other and to encompass all research on international interactions. Customarily, "current intelligence" pertains to work germane to the immediate effects of specific actions within the competence and authority of policy actors on the immediate problems which these actors confront. It is believed to have eminent, operational value for "real-world" problems. Usually, "nonapplied research," held to be in the domain of the academic, pertains to work of immense scope or intense rigor devoid of action implications but directly additive to the storehouse of knowledge. Without deprecating the value for policy actors of analyses of particular point events or the value for academics of grand theory, case studies, and technical rigor, this paper will proceed on the following premise. There is a third class of questions about international interactions for research and analysis, and until significant progress is made with the questions in that class, it is doubtful whether current intelligence can be more accurate or more accurately evaluated, doubtful whether grand theories can be reduced to testable statements, and doubtful whether rigorous but narrow studies can generate findings of significance. The academic tag for this class is "middle-range theory;" it is usually assumed to be empirical rather than metaphysical, and to involve questions not so general that answers to them cannot explain difference or be more than heuristic, and not so specific that answers have no power beyond the specific, epiphenomenal case. Our academic, middle-range problems seem no different in kind than those phrased recently by a senior intelligence analyst: "We're fine with the specific battles and all right with the grand secular trends, but how do we handle or even divide up everything in between?" Obviously, concern with the "middle-range" and with the "in between" involves the abused and powerful concept of appropriate level of generalization.

This congruence of goal exists for a subset of the members of three groups. The groups can be referred to as *external researchers, government analysts,* and *policy makers.* The respective subsets are: (1) researchers who work toward empirically based results, derived from real-world behaviors or from simulations tested against these, and preferably capable of symbolic manipulation; (2) analysts who try to prevent that narrowing of perspective which the demands of specific current events encourage; and (3) policy makers who want to reduce their dependence on private "models" and intuitive assumptions and inferences. Persons who are not members of at least one of these subsets will not be attracted by middle-range or in-between research, although they may support or conduct it for reasons other than answering questions about international interactions.

The second parameter is classes of interactions of interest to us. Obviously, it is beyond the scope of this paper to construct a fruitful typology of international interactions, but it is within the scope to indicate a dimension in terms of which such a typology might be developed. Classifications can derive from numerous alternative dimensions, available or imaginable. For example, these may be in terms of: means employed (e.g., weapons, money, goods, mass media); analytic concepts (e.g., communication, deference, integration, power); or normative values (e.g., aggression, appeasement, exploitation, peaceful, democratic). For our purposes, it seems useful to classify international interactions in terms of problems to be managed or phenomena to be explained. When this criterion of classification is manipulated at the assumed level of generalization, it gives us categories of international interactions such as: assisted national development, nonmilitary exchanges, and political-military bargaining. Categories such as these seem to: (1) name actions, i.e., international interactions, without having to use those concepts which *explain* them; (2) include sufficiently large, but sufficiently bounded, sets of interactions to warrant the kinds of research programs associated with working toward middle-range explanation; and (3) be not agency-or discipline-specific. Germane to the next section of the paper is the fact that surveys can be and have been used to answer questions about each of the example phenomena.

The third parameter in the analysis of international interactions is that of classes of actors, i.e., initiators of and responders to behavior. These classes determine whose behaviors and reasons for behavior are included in the analysis. These initiator/responder categories seem useful: central policy makers, government officials, subelites, and problem-relevant general publics. In any given international interaction, members of these groups may initiate or respond to the behavior. Usually, the first three groups are accepted as germane to international interactions. Central policy makers obviously authorize the behavior; government officials select information, formulate alternatives, and implement decisions; and subelites (e.g., scientists, corporate and interest group leaders, communicators) formulate issues and solutions, attract attention to and disseminate information about these. However, the relevance of the general public has been repeatedly questioned, especially in terms of problems of political-military bargaining. The grounds for excluding the group are that: (1) there is no public opinion about most international behavior alternatives; (2) central policy makers are not influenced in their decisions by public opinion or any image thereof; and (3) except for active and massive dissent, general publics do not significantly affect the consequences of international behaviors (Yarmolinsky, 1963; Lippmann, 1925). For the following reasons, these arguments seem highly questionable. First, certain international behaviors cannot be implemented without public cooperation. Second, central policy makers clearly consider the domestic political costs and rewards of alternative national security policies and defense announcement policies, both in democratic (e.g., U. S. aid policy toward the Soviet Union early in World War II – Dawson, 1959 – and current U. S. policy in Southeast Asia) and totalitarian political systems (e.g., Soviet and Chinese elite efforts to control their publics — e.g., Inkeles, 1959; Yu, 1964). Third, governments frequently consider relevant publics abroad both in assessing the international behaviors of other nations and in selecting their own, as evidenced in Chinese, Soviet, and Nazi publications and in German communications prior to World War I (e.g., Bobrow, 1966; Fagen, 1960).

We have now restricted our goal (product) to middle-range questions, about certain types of interaction classes, as these involve any of four groups of actors. Before we give examples of the kinds of questions which can be asked of international interactions as thus defined, we discuss the fourth and last parameter, which restricts the analysis to what Lasswell (1942) defined as "ideological" as opposed to "material" aspects of international interactions. The "ideological" analytic aspect involves those concepts of concern to the behavioral sciences. Thus, it includes the beliefs and emotions of human beings, the stimuli as these impinge on them, and individual and group conduct which this impingement generates. Obviously, any "complete consideration of goals or alternatives" must involve both Lasswell's aspects. However, we restrict ourselves to the ideological aspect for the following reasons: (1) international interactions cannot be adequately understood or manipulated in terms of technological and economic variables alone; (2) "ideological" variables are inadequately conceptualized, and their operation is least understood; (3) the development of strong multivariate statistical techniques, particularly within this century, and the advent of computers vastly improve the probabilities of fruitful isolation and exploration of ideological variables; and (4) survey data are most powerful in relation to these variables.

We conclude this section with a few examples of the kinds of questions which have answers that are and are not appropriate to our definition of the desired product. In each example, the first question should not lead to appropriate answers; the second should.

Example A

1.   Is aggression a function of frustration?
2.   To what extent will perceived economic improvements decrease the perceived appeals of internal and external violence?

Example B

1.   What percentage of the American public is in favor of civil defense?
2.   To what extent are publics' endorsements of defense policies a function of the positions of salient officials and experts on these policies?

Example C

1.   Will the present government of Ecuador be in office next month?
2.   To what extent and on what bases do significant population elements in the class of nations of which Ecuador is a member feel that it is legitimate and feasible to replace their government?

These examples are not important in themselves. The second member in each pair of examples should lead to middle-range explanations of the behavioral phenomena in question, but it does not replace the kind of explanation which should derive from the first member of each pair. Also, the second member in each pair is only one example of the kinds of questions which would have to be asked about the phenomena which the first member of the pair seeks to understand. However, these examples should suggest the differences between: (1) questions addressed to point-events or to grand universals, rather than to middle-range inquiries; (2) questions addressed to a single behavior and those addressed to several elements of an international interaction sequence; and (3) questions which are concerned only with output (response) and those which clarify the determinants of the output.

Obviously, the desired product defined in this section is immense. However, the issue is not whether or not it can be produced tomorrow. The issue is whether we can devise and implement a strategy to meet a persistent intellectual and policy-making need more powerfully than it is now being met, with a reasonable investment of resources. The remaining sections of this paper discuss the potential role of surveys and of computer capabilities germane to surveys in such a strategy.

SURVEYS

The purpose of this section is to determine the capabilities of a subclass of survey techniques to handle certain questions about international interactions. Survey data refer to self-reports, elicited in person-to-person interview situations, in which the same questions are asked of a sufficiently large number of respondents to produce aggregative data appropriate to certain statistical assumptions. As thus defined, surveys are inappropriate instruments for eliciting information from central policy makers, one of the four groups of actors defined in the last section as germane to international interactions. Aside from the practical problem of access, this group is by definition too small in number to meet the survey statistical assumptions. The other three groups of actors — general publics, subelites, and government officials — are not logically excluded, since in some situations they are accessible and are sufficiently large to meet the statistical assumptions (e.g., Free, 1959; Speier, 1957).

We restrict our attention to that subclass of surveys oriented to certain kinds of questions. As the "ideological" parameter of the last section implies, we are primarily interested in self-reports germane to receiving and processing stimuli and selecting responses. Self-reports of economic and demographic attributes, collected by surveys such as the census, are relevant not for themselves but to anchor respondents in the economic and social systems. For example, data about the race of respondents is not interesting to us *per se,* but differences in attitudes of Negroes and Caucasians toward the police may be.

As noted above, this section tries to determine the capability of our subclass of surveys to make four contributions to questions about international interactions. These contributions have been selected on the basis of two considerations: (1) they require information which it is not obviously impossible for survey techniques to provide, and (2) they represent fruitful means for answering kinds of questions about international interactions which interest us. The contributions are:

1. predicting classes of international behaviors, i.e., actions;
2. describing the nature and distribution of beliefs, emotions, and actions at different points in time;
3. locating predictors of dispositions toward different classes of international behaviors;
4. clarifying the process by which international behavior stimuli are received and handled and responses selected.

The first and third contributions are clearly prognostic, i.e., they state what will be the case at Time$_2$ (T$_2$) and do not involve variables which might intervene between the time when the prediction data are collected (T$_1$) and T$_2$. The second contribution is descriptions of states at several points in time and assumes a monitoring function of the effects of intervening behaviors. The fourth contribution is processual in that it explicates the path between stimulus and response. Although prognostic statements do not require processual ones, process statements can be most germane if one wants to alter, or understand the reasons for, the situation expected to exist at T$_2$ (Abelson and Bernstein, 1963).

In assessing the capability of surveys to make these contributions, we are *not* using two kinds of criteria frequently applied to survey data. The first criteria are those which can be applied to data regardless of the method of collection. These include criteria about the extent to which the data:

1. provide all necessary information for a policy decision or theory validation;
2. can be understood by laymen;
3. allow contradictory interpretations, as distinct from showing the presence of contradictory opinions;
4. are known to all potential users (points 1-4:   Carter, 1963);
5. accord their owners special political powers over others.

The second criteria involve assessing the *user* of survey techniques, not the techniques themselves: for example, problems with a sampling frame or biased questions. Obviously, the criteria we will use in assessing the appropriateness of surveys for these four contributions will derive from attributes of the technique itself.

We now proceed to examine the extent to which our subclass of survey data can reasonably be expected to (1) predict future international actions; (2) record changes in states over time; (3) predict positions on variables which affect the relative probabilities of future international actions; and (4) explicate how actions are perceived, handled, and selected.

Before we examine the capabilities of surveys to predict international behaviors, it should be realized that all four contributions obviously depend partly on the ability of surveys to describe accurately. In other words, all four require that surveys be capable of eliciting self-reports which are fairly congruent at least with the respondent's conscious perception of his relationship to the question. Each contribution involves descriptive requirements specific to it, but all four share two: (1) the survey has to be able to elicit information about states *relevant to the respondent,* as well as the researcher; and (2) the survey has to be able to elicit accurate information about positions on these states.

An example of the relevance requirement is when a sharecropper is asked whether he prefers red or black caviar. If he has never eaten caviar and doesn't even know what it is, he essentially has no relationship to the question, i.e., it is irrelevant to him. If he is forced into choosing red or black, the description of his relationship is not accurate. When face-saving opportunities for respondents to say the question didn't mean anything to them were built into a 1956 national cross-section survey, Converse (1964a) reports that the usual 2% of "no opinions" increased to between 10 and 35%. The sharecropper example and Converse's data refer to the relevance problem of when the respondent has no relationship to the question. Samples of government officials, subelites, and cross-cultural populations present another kind of relevance problem: these respondents may well have a relationship to the question, but it is not among those from which they are being asked to choose. In other words, samples such as these need to be able to structure their own responses, by adding to the interviewer's list of responses or by altering it in some way. Particularly since communication studies (e.g., Davison, 1959; Hovland, 1959; Bauer, 1964) are revealing the extent to which individuals categorize messages in terms of their own "problem-solving," surveys need to incorporate the various self-reporting techniques developed for this purpose (e.g. Hartley, in press; Sherif, Sherif, and Nebergall, 1965; Rosenberg, 1965).

An example of the accurate position requirement is when a northern middle-class housewife is asked how she feels about Negroes. She may be intensely afraid of and dislike them. However, she recognizes that this is not a socially approved response among all groups. Since she doesn't know how the interviewer feels about Negroes, she just says, "Well, I don't know, I guess they're all right." Distortions of position on a state can result from distortion by the respondent (the example) or by the survey design (interview schedule and codebook). In the first case, the problem is to eliminate the respondent's incentives to distort his position (e.g., those for a POW who thinks his interviewer is an enemy intelligence officer or for a government official who thinks his interviewer is some kind of a "spy" for his superior). For these reasons the interview situation and interviewer biasing have been carefully studied (e.g., Hyman, 1954). In the second case, the problems are to preserve the position implication of the response and to use the position category in the same way across respondents. For example, recording the following response as an instance of "anti-Chamberlain sentiment" does not preserve the intensity of the antagonism:

"The dirty so and so, that's what he is, selling 'em like that. He's done the same to all the others now. Only a ruddy Englishman could act like that. He flies to see Hitler, then he comes back and tells the papers that peace is near. He thinks he's going to keep England out of a war. Let the other fellers fight and he'll sell them the arms to do it, is that the big idea? I'll bet he goes to church like his wife does. They'll never be any use to the working class. It's money they're after or something. I'd join up in any Foreign Legion the Czechs start now." (Madge and Harrisson, 1939, p. 73)

Similarly, let us assume that the question is: "How many conversations about politics did you have yesterday?"; that the code categories are actual numbers; and that two respondents are recorded as responding "one." In one case the respondent is a political scientist who spent three hours consulting on a policy project, and in the other he is a plumber's apprentice who was involved in this "political conversation:"

> "There's nowt in t'bloody paper."
> "How's Hitler going on?"
> "Oh, Austria's buggered now."
> "It seemed liked it on Saturday."
>
> (Madge and Harrisson, 1939, p. 42)

These last two quotations are not a plea for that hobgoblin of "flavor" but to demonstrate cases of distortive coding which can affect the descriptive accuracy of surveys.

We now turn to assessing the capabilities of surveys for the four contributions.

PREDICTING FUTURE INTERNATIONAL ACTIONS

The most salient paradigm of survey applications is predicting voting preferences of the general public. These predictions have been exceedingly accurate. For example, the Gallup Poll prediction of the division of the vote deviated only 2.9%, on average, from the actual division in fourteen national elections from 1936 to 1962 (Deutsch and Merritt, 1965). This success has had three unhappy results. First, it is often assumed (frequently when it is to someone's advantage to do so) that the predictive power of surveys for voting preferences can be extrapolated to public survey responses about other kinds of international behavior preferences. Second, it is frequently assumed that public behavior preferences can be extrapolated to subelites, government officials, and central policy makers. Third, it is often assumed that the standard general cross-section election poll is the model for all surveys — specifically for surveys designed to elicit responses about public policy (Pool, 1963). Since the voting preference poll, its forms and its predictive power, is so salient for most of us, it is useful to: (1) describe the voting preference situation, (2) state, criteria for determining the power of opinions to predict actions, (3) relate these criteria to the voting preference situation and to the situation involved in most other kinds of international behavior preferences.

The voting preference situation has six attributes and is relatively unique in the sense that all these six are present at the same time. Respondents in this survey situation:

1. are asked to predict actions which they usually believe they, themselves, can carry out and are encouraged to carry out;
2. include representatives of all the major groups which directly affect the predicted outcome;
3. have vicariously or actually participated repetitively in the identical behavior situation and thus have a good image of its nature;
4. have been exposed to a great deal of information about their action alternatives;
5. are choosing between an explicit and very small set of action alternatives; and
6. are interviewed, i.e., predictions are revised, up to the time just before the behavior situation.

In other words, respondents in the voting preference situation are asked about actions with which they are very familiar, know they can do, which present few alternatives, and on which their private decision making is in an "advanced state of organization" (Lasswell, 1942).

Let us now turn to John Dollard's (1949) and two other criteria for predicting international behaviors from survey responses. Dollard states his criteria in terms of three social situations: origin, test, and criterion. The origin situation is the context in which the verbalized opinion was formed. If no opinion existed prior to the interview and one is expressed, the origin and test (i.e., the interview) situations are congruent. The criterion situation is the one in which the action of interest occurs.

I. Prediction is favored if in the test situation no relevant response element is disconnected from thought and speech. If some relevant elements are thus disconnected...these elements will remain at play in the criterion situation though not registered in the test situation.

II.   Prediction is favored if the sentences of the respondent cover all response elements relevant to the criterion situation. Even where an automatic repression process does not exist, some respondents may have poor skills at verbalizing their feelings and wishes. If the sentence apparatus of the respondent does not stretch over all relevant responses, he will hardly be able to make accurate verbal predictions about his actions in the criterion situation.

III.   Prediction from test to criterion is likely to be favored if the connection between sentences responses and overt action responses has been strongly rewarded in previous learning. Thoughts and opinions are characteristically used to guide and orient behavior. But in some persons a split occurs between thought and action. Such people have not been rewarded for thinking first and then acting.

IV.   Prediction is favored if the test situation provides stimuli only to the verbal response relevant to the criterion dilemma.

V.   Prediction from test to criterion is favored if the origin situation corresponds closely to the criterion situation. Otherwise the respondent is predicting what he would do in a situation different from the criterion dilemma.... Once in it he is likely to say, "I didn't know it was going to be like this."

VI.   Prediction is favored providing that no new origin dilemma intervenes between the test and criterion situation. If such a new origin occurs, it may generate an opinion competing with the test opinion.

VII.   Prediction is favored if the test question explicitly presents the conflict, i.e., anticipations of rewards and punishments, of the criterion dilemma.

We add two other criteria, suggested by the success of the voting preference situation:

VIII.   Prediction from the test to criterion situation is favored if the respondent is asked about action preferences which he himself can take and is encouraged to take.

IX.   Prediction is favored if all groups directly germane to taking the action are represented in the sample.

When we relate attributes of the national cross-section voting preference survey to the criteria above, we observe that the situation meets criteria I, II, III, IV, V, VI, VIII, and IX fairly well. We can see that criterion I partly explains the classic Dewey-Truman prediction error: the "Don't know" response category simply did not include all relevant response elements, such as "Are you leaning toward one candidate more than another, and if so, which one?" We can also see that the accuracy of survey predictions depends partly on the analysts' turnout adjustments. These make allowance for dilemmas of the criterion situation (e.g., bad weather on election day) which are not incorporated directly into the test situation (criterion VII).

When we relate surveys about most other types of international behavior preferences to the criteria above, the probabilities of being able to predict international behaviors from survey responses become exceedingly small. First, questions about international behavior preferences, e.g., use of military force in certain classes of situations, are often asked of respondents, e.g., general public, who cannot directly take actions of that sort (criterion VIII). We may be able to say something about the public reaction to American involvement in these wars, but we cannot directly predict on the basis of these responses whether or not the United States will declare them. Second, even if we are able to interview respondents (e.g., Defense Department officials) who have a direct effect on whether or not the United States will get involved in certain kinds of wars, we may not be able to include representatives (e.g., State Department officials) of *all* groups who directly affect the behavior in question (criterion IX). Defense Department preferences are only one input to the actual behavior decision. Third, even if these sampling problems can be solved, meeting Dollard's criteria presents serious problems. The principal problems are: the rapidity of change on variables pertinent to international behaviors, the response set of the respondent, and the skills of the respondent. The attributes of the international system change rapidly, which means that the criterion situation changes rapidly and that very probably the respondent will receive new inputs before the criterion situation occurs. Thus, it is extremely difficult for a survey to describe the criterion situation validly for the respondent. These problems mean that criteria V and VII will usually not be satisfied, and they exaggerate the effects of time gaps between test and criterion situations (criterion VI). With regard to the response set, it seems difficult to construct an understandable survey question which includes all elements relevant to the response of even a moderately well-informed government official or subelite. If they can all be included, one can reasonably expect them to trigger images of criterion situations or action contexts in addition to the relevant one. These points imply that it is difficult to meet either criterion I or IV singly and very difficult to meet them simultaneously. The final problem, respondent ability, refers to the common observation that lower income and lower education level respondents: (1) have few incentives — rewards or opportunity — to think through their responses to international action criterion situations; and (b) often have difficulty in verbalizing what preferences they do have. For this population group, survey data probably do not meet criteria II and III.

There are two implications of the paragraph above. First, it is not appropriate to use surveys to predict many classes of international behaviors of interest to us. Second, the general cross-section voting preference model of surveys, which is successful in predicting that particular class of behaviors, is thus not the appropriate model of surveys for us to use in assessing the potential contributions of surveys to middle-range international behavior questions.

MONITORING CHANGES IN BELIEFS, EMOTIONS, AND ACTIONS
OVER TIME

If an instrument can monitor changes in "ideological" aspects over time, it can then handle questions about stability and change. Questions of this type are particularly involved in middle-range or in-between analyses, and are thus desirable kinds of questions for an instrument to be able to handle. Particular types of survey stability/change analyses all depend on the basic ability of surveys to record changes in ideological aspects accurately, and therefore the requirements for this capability are our first concern.

Requirements for recording changes and stability in beliefs, emotions, and actions over time are the following:

1.   The instrument has to be able to describe these aspects accurately at single points in time. The requirements for this ability were discussed earlier in this section.
2.   The instrument has to use data categories which maximize the chances of locating change. Obviously, this sensitivity requirement depends on the response variations which the code can accommodate. B ten-level, self-anchoring scale (Catril and Free, 1962), for example, can be expected to bury fewer changes than a trichotomy of "yes," "no," and "don't know."
3.   Observations of change or stability derive from observations of the same or new responses along certain constant (i.e., comparable) dimensions. In the case of surveys, the instrument has to ask the same questions of and use the same code categories for

comparable samples at different points in time.
4. The investigator has to be able to retrieve and manipulate the comparable data.

It is clear that surveys can be constructed to meet these requirements to some extent for certain kinds of belief, emotion, and action questions. How satisfactorily they can be met and for how many types of questions involves a series of empirical questions which have not been systematically explored. However, to the extent that surveys can be constructed to meet these requirements, they make possible several types of change/stability analyses. The following examples of analysis types are not exclusive. The first involves the extent to which beliefs, emotions, and actions have changed during a period characterized by significant events. This type of analysis really measures the insensitivity of respondents to events, i.e., which individuals and groups have not changed the position they held before the event (e.g., Almond, 1960; Deutsch and Merritt, 1965). If respondents have changed their positions, this change cannot necessarily be attributed to the intervening event. This type of analysis is easily performed on slices of a more extended trend analysis (e.g., Cantril, 1947). The second type involves certain questions about long-term social changes by means of cohort analysis (Evan, 1959), which tracks age groups through their life cycle. A third type of analysis involves evaluating the effects of action programs quasi-experimentally (Hyman, Wright, and Hopkins, 1962) by applying the survey instrument several times before, during, and after the program.

LOCATING PREDICTORS OF DISPOSITIONS TO CLASSES OF
INTERNATIONAL BEHAVIORS

The third possible contribution of surveys is to locate predictors, i.e., variables which have the power to predict positions on a large number of other variables and thus explain a great deal of variance in behavior. To understand the power of these predictors, it is useful to review the relationships between descriptions of belief and action states and predictions of future actions.

We have argued that it is unrealistic to expect surveys to predict international behaviors in the way they predict voting patterns. However, we can distinguish between such predictions and locating probabilities of (degrees of disposition toward) classes of action, e.g., succoring *versus* expansionist foreign policies, preserving *versus* modernizing rural lifeways. Surveys can be designed to yield positions on a group of questions which are assumed to indicate broad dispositions. They can also be designed to scale the responses of individuals in terms of intensity of the disposition. However, it is not efficient to collect data on a number of unweighted specific measures every time one is interested in dispositions. First, only a small number of specific measure possibilities can be included in any one survey. Second, the data must be collected for each respondent group at each point in time. Third, the extent to which changes in the attributes of the respondent affect his behavior dispositions are unknown. Thus, it is fruitful to locate a small number of powerful predictors of dispositions toward classes of international behaviors. If we can locate predictors, we can: (1) select those survey questions of greatest explanatory power; (2) anticipate the dispositions of actors interviewed at other points in time and not asked the specific cluster questions, in terms of their positions on predictors; and (3) anticipate if, and if so, how, alterations in the external environment might affect the disposition of respondents.

The process of locating predictors from survey data involves trying to find patterns of responses across questions, but within respondents (either particular individuals or groups), and to isolate variables or dimensions of which these patterns are a function. Promising predictors can be checked against other survey data. The ability of surveys to meet the requirements for deriving predictors depends on their ability to meet the requirements cf two methods which differ operationally but are similar conceptually.

The first, and more traditional, way to locate predictors in survey data is by a moderately simple "breakdown" analysis (Cantril, 1947). Essentially, responses to two or more questions are cross-tabulated to find the degree of correlation between the responses to each. A typical cross-tabulation produces data which can be arranged in cells that reveal the frequency of cross-question response combinations. For example, if we wanted to cross-tabulate membership in Pooh Perplex clubs against political party preference, viewing membership and party preference as dichotomous variables, we would have a table with four cells: Democratic members, Republican members, Democratic non-members, and Republican nonmembers. To continue the example, if party preference were a potential predictor, it would be cross-tabulated with many specific self-reports about social group memberships and attachments, cognitive sets, and basic psychological traits (Scott, 1958).

The requirements for this type of search are simple. First, the survey instrument must have elicited reports of positions on the possible predictors. Second, the number of respondents must be large enough to support multivariate cross-tabulations without running into cells which violate statistical size assumptions. The content and sample size of any one survey is limited. Thus, the first and second requirements are met more adequately if the data and sample size base are enlarged by other surveys. These other surveys (usually old) do not have to have asked identical questions, nor have any particular temporal relationship to each other, nor have questioned the same individuals. Since the investigator is concerned with aggregate, not individual, findings, surveys have to be comparable only in terms of the disposition which a question taps, and the demographic traits of respondents (e.g., Scott, 1965; Pool, Abelson, and Popkin, 1964).

The second way to isolate predictors relies on relatively powerful computations which may or may not locate predictors elicited directly by the questionnaire. Examples of these methods are latent structure analysis, factor analysis, and regression analysis (e.g., Lerner, 1958; Rummel, forthcoming). These methods are particularly promising for evaluating the interaction effects of numerous variables and the relative weighting of predictors. However, their requirements go beyond those stated for standard cross-tabulation. Specifically, application of this class of techniques requires that the data be collected and coded or recoded to facilitate numerical manipulation. To illustrate, in some cases, the data should be expressed as ranks on an equal interval scale; in others, as ranks on an ordinal scale in which the intervals are uneven or unknown; and in still others, as positions on a dichotomous variable, e.g., "yes" or "no," "present" or "absent." Obviously, in terms of the interval or ordinal scaling requirements, the analyst is largely a prisoner of the initial coding categories or conversion possibilities. Recoding responses into dichotomous form, i.e., making each response category, in effect, a yes-no question, involves dubious assumptions about the set of the respondent in the test situation. To the extent that the analyst tries to salvage or otherwise secure ordinal or dichotomous data, he must be able to record the nature of the alterations he has made if he is to know from where his "new" data came.

CLARIFYING PROCESS

The fourth contribution of which surveys may be capable is: clarifying the process by which international behavior stimuli are received and handled and responses selected. This clarification is not designed to predict classes of responses or dispositions toward classes of responses although it may improve our abilities to make these predictions. It is designed to help us understand where an aggregate or group of individuals goes in traversing the analytic space between a stimulus and whatever response it makes and why it goes the way it goes. To the extent that we understand the motion and influence patterns in types of spaces we can improve our ability to understand the dynamics of international interactions and locate at what points what variables affect their coarse. The two basic procedures for process analysis, reconstructing and simulating, impose essentially the same requirements on surveys. As the reader will see, many of these have already been considered in the relation to the previous three contributions.

The reconstruction use of surveys refers to analyses which manipulate question responses to piece together the steps through which an aggregate or group of individuals went to arrive at its response and the nature and import of the influences to which it was exposed during this process. Generalizations are frequently extrapolated from the reconstruction for a particular sample (e.g., Katz and Lazarsfeld, 1955; Coleman, Menzel, and Katz, 1959). The requirements for this approach are the following. First, the survey has to include questions about how the individual received and handled the stimulus and selected his response and about what factors impinged on his thinking during the process. Second, to keep processual reports in perspective, the respondent must also be asked to report his positions on relevant belief and action variables at the beginning of the process, i.e., at entry, or before he received the stimulus. Third, to the extent that the data are gathered retrospectively or pertain to social values, the survey has to build in controls for false self-reports. For example, it should compensate for the tendency to align retrospectively with the winner, e.g., having voted for the winning candidate or held the validated preference, and to distort reports about what are perceived to be unacceptable beliefs and actions/nonactions, e.g., having read only the sports page during the last ten years. Fourth, it is helpful, if not essential, to monitor the same individuals during the course of a particular interaction, i.e., the panel technique (Lazarsfeld, Berelson, and Gaudet, 1944). Technically, these requirements can all be met, but they have to be met by the interview design.

The simulation use of surveys refers to dynamic modeling, which manipulates survey data directly and indirectly. Directly, processual simulations can use survey data to establish the beliefs and actions of relevant actors at the beginning of an interaction and to learn to what influences they will probably be exposed during its course (Abelson and Bernstein, 1963). As we have seen, reconstruction analyses require similar data. Indirectly, the design of the simulation program in terms of variables introduced and the functions assigned to them can rely heavily on the empirically based generalizations generated by reconstructions. Processual simulations are a very different technique than reconstructions, but they do not differ from reconstructions in their requirements of survey data.

We have noted that survey data cannot predict many classes of international behaviors. To a certain, in many cases unknown, extent surveys can generate data appropriate to: (1) monitoring states of action, belief, and emotion; (2) isolating predictors of dispositions toward large classes of behaviors; and (3) constructing processual histories and models. In reaching these conclusions, we have found that the theoretical capabilities of surveys can be limited operationally by problems which occur before the data are subjected to numerical manipulations, i.e., problems during the stages of design, interview situation, and response coding. Many of these problems cannot be resolved by using any data-processing tool, e.g., computers.

However, we have also noted that the capabilities of survey data depend partly on the availability of powerful tools. We will note these dependencies here and examine their implications for computers in the next section. First, the capabilities of surveys for all three contributions increase as the survey data base is expanded in time, number of variables, number of respondents, and types of respondents (Riley, 1962). Second, the ability of surveys to isolate predictors increases as cross-tabulations and more sophisticated analytic operations can be calculated rapidly and reliably. Third, the ability of surveys to simulate processes increases as the survey data base can be manipulated efficiently, the effects of variables can be measured and recorded, and attributes of the actors in the simulation can be updated to reflect the effects of the variables.

COMPUTERS

In the previous sections we tried to clarify what classes of products we wanted and the extent to which surveys are capable of producing them. In this section we clarify the possibilities of using computers to manipulate survey data and what realizing this potential involves. We are primarily interested in using computers to: (1) enlarge the data, (2) facilitate analysis, and (3) simulate, i.e., for dynamic modeling. The discussion of each of these presumes the perspective: "What can computers do with survey data which would or could not be done without them?"

At this point, we cannot estimate the rewards of computer-survey relationships. However, for two reasons we suggest that the costs of using computers to manipulate survey data are greater now than we can anticipate them to be in a few years. First, any period of rapid innovation is characterized by trial and error procedures. Second, partly because computer technology is developing rapidly and competitively, many programs designed at one institution either cannot be used at another or have to be drastically revised before they can be used. We are beginning to see the design of general function programs which will run easily on relatively common machines, e.g., the IBM-7090 (Dixon, 1964; Tyrol, 1966), and of more basic programs which are not machine-dependent.

We now discuss the three possible uses of computers for survey data manipulation.

ENLARGING THE DATA BASE

Using more than one survey to answer a research question is not new, but the advent of modern computing capabilities allows the investigator to handle large numbers of surveys for the first time. Since surveys are relatively expensive to conduct, it is difficult and inefficient to reinterview certain respondent groups, and a large data base has certain analytic advantages mentioned in the last section, the recent development of survey archives is not surprising (Bisco, 1966; Converse, 1964b; Hastings, 1963; and Hastings, 1964).

However, an enlarged data base is more than a physically proximate collection of survey schedules, codebooks, punched cards, and magnetic tapes. We are concerned below with, first, criteria which measure the extent to which one has a working survey data base, rather than "giant morgues for IBM cards" (Scheuch and Stone, 1964, p. 23), and, second, with the tasks which these criteria imply. Carrying out these tasks involves massive problems of data management, in contrast to the more traditional use of computers to perform large numbers of computations on a small body of data. Thus, they require innovation, and will continue to require innovation if we are to keep up with even the current and anticipated survey data, let alone the masses of data accumulated in the past years. The fact that some eight million interviews were performed by 245 research centers in the United States and Europe in 1963 alone (Ruttenberg, 1965) illustrates the dimensions of the data-management problem.

The extent to which a survey collection has been transformed into a working data base is a function of the extent to which the following criteria are met:

1. accuracy (unedited representation of survey content);
2. routinized input and output (standard, economical, and rapid setup of survey data for the system);
3. manipulability (input and output formats which the analyst can use with ease);
4. flexibility (multiple use of the data);
5. efficiency of search and retrieval (ready location and extraction of all, and only, relevant material).

Individuals at MIT, the Inter-University Consortium for Political Research at the University of Michigan, and the Oak Ridge National Laboratory have been particularly active in developing systems which meet these criteria. The work at the first institution is primarily oriented to a time-sharing context in which the user interacts directly with the computer; the latter institutions are primarily working in a "batch" context in which there is no direct interaction.

To demonstrate the kind of effort involved in meeting these criteria, it is useful to discuss the experience of developing system SESAR (Survey Edit, Storage and Retrieval) at Oak Ridge.[1] The problem at Oak Ridge was to develop a system to manage 121 national cross-section surveys germane to American national security attitudes. This meant that we confronted over 7,500 question-answer universes involving well over 100,000 respondents. The work to make this mass usable can be divided into the following five steps. These steps are not specific to our surveys.

1. *The Question Package.* The question package (Type 2 cards) consists of:
   a. descriptive information about the question (techniques of eliciting the response and dependence of the question on other questions);
   b. literal text of the question;
   c. literal text of its response category code.

To produce the package, first, we had to prepare the over 7,500 questions and response codes for typists and keypunchers and, second, we had to place the keypunched material in our magnetic tape data base. This involved searching questionnaires and codebooks and clarifying coding unclarities.

[1]For a partial Technical Summary, see Wilcox, Bobrow, and Bwy (1967).

2.   *The Data Package.* The data package (Type 4 cards) consists of:
a. numerical values of the responses given by interviewees;
b. response frequencies and percentages for different answers to a particular question;
c. a set of statistical measures of the distribution and significance of the responses;
d. the size of the sample used for these statistical calculations;
e. the size and percentage of the total survey sample which is known to have answered the question.

To produce the desired package, new nominal statistics were developed and programs prepared to apply existing statistics for ordinal and interval data. Designed to measure the distribution of response frequencies, the nominal statistics are applicable to response codes unsuitable for scaling. For example, these statistics can be applied to the question: "What country most threatens American national security?" with the response code of "U.S.S.R., China, Cuba."

3.   *The Support Package.* The support package (Type 1 cards) consists of the following information for each question-data universe:
a. date of the survey;
b. name of survey organization;
c. survey identification number;
d. scope of the sample;
e. number of the question;
f. card and column location of the data for the question.

Procedures were developed and applied to automate most of the preparation of this package.

4.   *Integrating Question, Data, and Support Packages.* This merge step is crucial. A number of efficient control and checking devices were developed and applied to insure that the correct question, data, and support packages were integrated.
5.   *Master Output.* The master output consists of:
a. survey volumes which integrate all the information in the question, data, and support packages survey item by survey item;
b. Key-Word-In-Context (KWIC) indexes of the material in the question package.

N37013 0017 C01 1 21 000
N37013 0017 C02 1 21 000
N37013 0017 C03 1 21 000
N37013 0017 C01 2 21 000
N37013 0017 C02 2 21 000
N37013 0017 C03 2 21 000
N37013 0017 C04 2 21 000
N37013 0017 C05 2 21 000
N37013 0017 C06 2 21 000
N37013 0017 C07 2 21 000
N37013 0017 C08 2 21 000
N37013 0017 C09 2 21 000
N37013 0017 C10 2 21 000
N37013 0017 C11 2 21 000
N37013 0017 C01 3 21 000
N37013 0017 C01 4 21 000
N37013 0017 C02 4 21 000
N37013 0017 C03 4 21 000
N37013 0017 C04 4 21 000
N37013 0017 C05 4 21 000
N37013 0017 C06 4 21 000
N37013 0017 C07 4 21 000
N37013 0017 C08 4 21 000
N37013 0017 C09 4 21 000
N37013 0017 C10 4 21 000
N37013 0017 C11 4 21 000
N37013 0017 C12 4 21 000
N37013 0017 C13 4 21 000
N37013 0017 C14 4 21 000
N37013 0017 C15 4 21 000
N37013 0017 C16 4 21 000
N37013 0017 C17 4 21 000
N37013 0017 C18 4 21 000
N37013 0017 C19 4 21 000
N37013 0017 C20 4 21 000
N37013 0017 C21 4 21 000

N37001 7C MR1955   NORC370   QUES017C   CARD 1   COLS 30
NATIONAL SAMPLE

(F)   (IF THINK GOOD POLICY FOR US TO HELP BACKWARD COUNTRIES
RAISE LIVING STANDARDS--QUES. 17A) DO YOU THINK THE MONEY
WE PUT UP FOR SUCH A PROGRAM SHOULD BE HANDLED ENTIRELY BY
OUR OWN GOVERNMENT, OR SHOULD SOME OF IT BE SPENT THROUGH
THE UNITED NATIONS ORGANIZATION, OR SHOULD ALL OF IT BE
SPENT THROUGH THE UNITED NATIONS.
1.   OUR OWN GOVERNMENT.
2.   SOME THROUGH UN.
3.   ALL THROUGH UN.
4.   DON'T KNOW.
5.   NO ANSWER.   55

RESPONSE	FREQ	CUM FREQ	PER CENT	CUM PER CENT
1	524	524	54.0	54.0
2	246	770	25.3	79.3
3	133	903	13.7	93.0
4	65	968	6.7	99.7
5	3	971	.3	100.0
TOTAL	971		100.0	

NOR VAR	56.70	WIL VAR	62.96	QUAR DEV	.60
MODE	1	QUAL VAR	85.10	AVER DEV	.76
MEDIAN	1.36	INDX VAR	.56	STAN DEV	.73
MEAN	1.57	COEF VAR	.47	KURTOSIS	-.63
SE MEAN	.02	SKEWNESS	.88		

STATISTICS CALCULATED FOR N OF   903

TOTAL N (971) IS 79.3 PER CENT OF GRAND N (1225)

Figure 1. A sample entry of data book master output.

The survey volumes allow a number of analyses to be carried out without further recourse to computer data-processing. Figure 1 presents a sample survey volume entry. The KWIC indexes (Janda, 1964) represent a rapid and efficient search and retrieval capability for a large variety of user needs, particularly when they are combined with a TRIAL program to retrieve work packages (Milbrath and Janda, 1964; Janda and Tetzlaff, n.d.). The KWIC indexes can be replaced with more conceptual terms without degrading other parts of the system (Bisco, 1964; Scheuch and Stone, 1964). The index can be used to exploit the data books more efficiently or to formulate requests for data books compiled for specified problems. The frequency and statistical information on each merged package can be used to select data fields to be subjected to analytic computer programs and control the accuracy of the user's input instructions.

The survey data often have to be improved as much as managed. If the surveys to be transformed into a working data base are recorded on cards in formats other than the conventional BCD, single punch per card column, they have to be subjected to another set of operations. Basically, all these operations involve recoding, i.e., moving the data so that they lie in a uniform, conventional format (e.g., Popkin and Shanks, 1964). Until this step is completed, analytic programs have to be individually tailored to each unique format in which the data are expressed. Beyond these minimal steps, the data base is improved if an investment is made to accomplish the following: (1) remove punching errors and unknowns, (2) order disorganized surveys, (3) standardize the number of respondents in the survey, (4) condense "data poor" questions into richer variables, (5) group questions of similar relevance, and (6) integrate filter questions whose codes and respondents are a function of the response to a preceding question (Griffel, 1965).

FACILITATING ANALYSIS

We have devoted relatively detailed attention to the development of an enlarged working data base because it presents the bottleneck to the simple, rapid, and powerful analysis of survey data by computers. After the data have been managed and improved by means of the operations described above, many analyses can be performed immediately if they are within the memory capacity of the computer available and compatible with the mathematical attributes of the data. The reasons for this, of course, are that many of the analytic programs which can be used are common to the natural and biological sciences, and their development has not depended on requirements for survey analysis. Progress is being made in developing computer programs to handle analytic problems fairly specific to surveys, e.g., for locating predictors of dispositions and specific responses (Sonquist and Morgan, 1964), and in input and output systems which require little work or statistical competence of the user (e.g., Morris and Van Vleck, 1965).

SIMULATION

The ability of computers to perform simulations is clear. It is also clear that they can perform simulations far more ambitious than could be conducted without them. For this application, as for many under our analysis heading, they become valuable to the extent that the calculations to be performed are "so numerous as to make a pencil and paper solution an onerous chore. One uses computers when the transformations which the program makes on the data are tediously iterative" (Pool, Abelson, and Popkin, 1964, p. 5). The boundaries on the computer employment of survey data for simulation are boundaries of theory and of data quality and management, not of the computer. If we assume that the initial survey material meets the requirements for processual simulation we stated in the last section, the data base problem discussed above again emerges as the principal bottleneck to the conduct of survey-based computer simulations.

CONCLUSION

It seems to me that these are the basic results of our tour of the triangle. The limits on using computers to analyze survey data to answer middle-range international interaction questions are not a function of computers. They partly derive from limitations inherent in surveys, particularly their dependence on self-reports, and from having to rely essentially on other people's surveys, i.e., on their questions, codes, and samples. These limits are not all logical, i.e., necessary, and many can be removed by extensive working data bases whcih are controlled and developed through computers.

However, quantum improvements require a basic departure from the national cross-section voting preference survey as model and innovative survey methodology. These improvements are clearly possible; their shape has been indicated in prototype studies. Two developments are requisite before the prototype study will be routinely made and before the method can provide powerful middle-range findings about international interactions.   First, fruitful and testable questions about international interactions, compatible with what surveys can do, will have to be formulated and given some priority.   Second, resources for survey research will have to be allocated to the investigation of such questions, either by means of new data collection or by establishing enlarged working data bases to realize the analytic potential of old surveys.

REFERENCES

Abelson, Robert P. and Bernstein, Alex. "A Computer Simulation Model of Community Referendum Controversies," *Public Opinion Quarterly*, 27 (1963), 93-122.

Almond, Gabriel A. "Public Opinion and Space Technology," *Public Opinion Quarterly*, 24 (1960), 553-572.

Bauer, Raymond A. "The Obstinate Audience," *American Psychologist*, 19 (1964), 319-328.

Bisco, Ralph L "Information Retrieval from Data Archives: The ICPR System," *American Behavioral Scientist*, 7 (1964), 45-48.

Bisco, Ralph L. "Social Science Data Archives: A Review of Developments," *American Political Science Review*, LX (1966), 93-109.

Bobrow, Davis B. "The Chinese Communist Conflict System," *Orbis*, 9 (1966), 930-952.

Cantril, Hadley. *Gauging Public Opinion*. Princeton, N.J.: Princeton University Press, 1947.

Cantril, Hadley and Free, Lloyd. "Hopes and Fears for Self and Country," *American Behavioral Scientist* (Supplement), 6 (1962).

Carter, Launor F. "Survey Results and Public Policy Decisions," *Public Opinion Quarterly*, 27 (1963), 549-557.

Christiansen, Bjorn. *Attitudes Towards Foreign Affairs as a Function of Personality*. Oslo: Oslo University Press, 1959.

Coleman, J., Menzel, H., and Katz, E. "Social Processes in Physician's Adoption of a New Drug," *Journal of Chronic Disease*, 9 (1959), 1-19.

Converse, Philip E. "A Network of Data Archives for the Behavioral Sciences," *Public Opinion Quarterly*, 28 (1964b), 273-286.

Converse, Philip E. "New Dimensions of Meaning for Cross-Section Sample Surveys in Politics," *International Social Science Journal*, XVI (1964a), 19-34.

Davison, W. Phillips. "On the Effects of Communication," *Public Opinion Quarterly*, 23 (1959), 343-360.

Dawson, R. H. *The Decision to Aid Russia, 1941: Foreign Policy and Domestic Politics*. Chapel Hill: University of North Carolina Press, 1959.

Deutsch, Karl W. and Merritt, Richard L. "Effects of Events on National and International Images," in Herbert C. Kelman (ed.). *International Behavior*. New York: Holt, Rinehart and Winston, 1965, 130-187.

Dexter, Lewis Anthony. "Impressions About Utility and Wastefulness in Applied

Social Science Studies,"*American Behavioral Scientist,* 9 (1966), 9-10.

Dixon, W. J. (ed.). *Biomedical Computer Programs.* Los Angeles: School of Medicine, University of California, January 1964.

Dollard, John. "Under What Conditions Do Opinions Predict Behavior?" *Public Opinion Quarterly,* 12 (1948-1949), 623-632.

Evan, William M. "Cohort Analysis of Survey Data: A Procedure for Studying Long-term Opinion Change," *Public Opinion Quarterly,* 23 (1959), 63-72.

Fagen, Robert R. "Some Assessments and Uses of Public Opinion in Diplomacy," *Public Opinion Quarterly,* 24 (1960), 448-457.

Free, Lloyd A. *Six Allies and a Neutral.* New York: Free Press of Glencoe, 1959.

Griffel, David. *The Editing Routine.* Cambridge, Mass.: COMCOM Simulation Memo No. 24 (revised), March 1965, mimeod.

Guetzkow,Harold. "Conversion Barriers in Using the Social Sciences," *Administrative Science Quarterly,* 4 (1959), 68-81.

Hartley, Eugene L. "Prediction of American Responses to a Damage Limiting Program," in Davis B. Bobrow (ed.). *Weapons System Decisions.* New York: Frederick A. Praeger, in press

Hastings, Philip K. "International Survey Library Association of the Roper Public Opinion Research Center," *Public Opinion Quarterly,* 28 (1964), 331-333.

Hastings, Philip K. "The Roper Center: An International Archive of Sample Survey Data," *Public Opinion Quarterly,* 27 (1963), 591-598.

Hovland, Carl I. "Reconciling Conflicting Results Derived from Experimental Survey Studies of Attitude Change," *American Psychologist,* 14 (1959), 8-17.

Hughes, Thomas L. "Scholars and Foreign Policy: Varieties of Research Experience," *Background,* 9 (1965), 199-214.

Hyman, Herbert. *Interviewing in Social Research.* Chicago: University of Chicago Press, 1954.

Hyman, Herbert H., Wright, Charles R., and Hopkins, Terence K. *Applications of Methods of Evaluation.* Berkeley: University of California Publications in Culture and Society, Vol. VII (1962).

Inkeles, Alex. *Public Opinion in Soviet Russia.* Cambridge, Mass.: Harvard University Press, 1959.

Janda, Kenneth. "Keyword Indexes for the Behavioral Sciences," *American Behavorial Scientist,* 7 (1964), 55-58.

Janda, Kenneth and Tetzlaff, William H. *TRIAL: A Computer Technique for Retrieving Information from Abstracts of Literature.* Evanston, Ill.: Northwestern University Computing Center, n.d., mimeod.

Katz, Elihu and Lazarsfeld, Paul F. *Personal Influence.* New York: Free Press of Glencoe, 1955.

Lasswell, Harold D. "The Relation of Ideological Intelligence to Public Policy," *Ethics,* 53 (1942), 25-34.

Lazarsfeld, Paul F., Berelson, Bernard, and Gaudet, Hazel. *The People's Choice.* New York: Duell, Sloan and Pierce, 1944.

Lerner, Daniel. *The Passing of Traditional Society.* New York: Free Press of Glencoe, 1958.

Lippmann, Walter. *The Phantom Public and Public Opinion.* New York: Harcourt, Brace and Company, 1925.

Madge, Charles and Harrisson, Tom. *Britain by Mass-Observation.* Hammondsworth: Penguin Books, 1939.

McPhee, William. "Notes on a Campaign Simulator," *Public Opinion Quarterly,* 25 (1961), 184-193.

Milbrath, Lester W. and Janda, Kenneth. *Computer Applications to Abstraction, Storage, and Recovery of Propositions from Political Science Literature.* Paper delivered at the Annual Meeting of the American Political Science Association, Chicago, Ill., September 1964, mimeod.

Morgan, George Allen. "Planning in Foreign Affairs: The State of the Art," *Foreign Affairs,* 39 (1961), 271-278.

Morris, Noel I. and Van Vleck, Thomas H. *A General Cross Tabulation System.* Cambridge, Mass. Memorandum MAC-M-228-1 (revised), August 1965, mimeod.

Polk, William. "Problems of Government Utilization of Scholarly Research in International Affairs," *Background,* 9 (1965), 237-259.

Pool, Ithiel de Sola. "Comment," *Public Opinion Quarterly,* 27 (1963), 558-561.

Pool, Ithiel de Sola and Abelson, Robert P. "The Simulmatics Project," *Public Opinion Quarterly,* 25 (1961), 167-183.

Pool, Ithiel de Sola, Abelson, Robert P., and Popkin, Samuel L. *Candidates, Issues, and Strategies.* Cambridge, Mass.: M.I.T. Press, 1964.

Popkin, Samuel and Shanks, Merrill. *7090 Program Write-Up: MPRCDE (Multiple-Punch Recode).* Ann Arbor, Mich.:   Inter-University Consortium for Political Research, September 1964, mimeod.

Riley, John W. Jr. "Reflections on Data Sources in Opinion Research," *Public Opinion Quarterly,* 26 (1962), 313-322.

Rosenau, James N. *Foreign Policy as an Issue Area.* Paper presented at the Conference on Public Opinion and Foreign Policy, Princeton, N.J., March 1965, mimeod.

Rosenberg, Milton J. "Images in Relation to the Policy Process: American Public

Opinion on Cold-War Issues," in Herbert C. Kelman (ed.). *International Behavior.* New York: Holt, Rinehart and Winston, 1965, 277-334.

Rummel, R. J. *Applied Factor Analysis.* Evanston, Ill.: Northwestern University Press, forthcoming.

Ruttenberg, Charles L. "Report on Data Archives in the Social Sciences," *American Behavioral Scientist,* 8 (1965), 33-34.

Scheuch, Erwin K. and Stone, Philip J. "The General Inquirer Approach to an International Retrieval System for Survey Archives," *American Behavioral Scientist,* 7 (1964), 23-28.

Scott, William A. "Correlates of International Attitudes," *Public Opinion Quarterly,* 22 (1958), 464-472.

Scott, William A. "Psychological and Social Correlates of International Images," in Herbert C. Kelman (ed.). *International Behavior.* New York: Holt, Rinehart and Winston, 1965, 70-103.

Sherif, Carolyn, Sherif, Muzafer, and Nebergall, Roger. *Attitude and Attitude Change.* Philadelphia: W. B. Saunders, 1965.

Sonquist, John A. and Morgan, James N. *The Detection of Interaction Effects.* Ann Arbor, Mich.: Survey Research Center, University of Michigan. Monograph No. 35, 1964.

Speier, Hans. *German Rearmament and Atomic War: The View of German Military and Political Leaders.* Evanston, Ill.: Row, Peterson, 1957.

Tyron, Robert C. and Bailey, Daniel E. "The BC TRY Computer System of Cluster and Factor Analysis," *Multivariate Behavioral Research,* Vol. 1 (January 1966), 95-111.

Wilcox, Allen R., Bobrow, Davis B., and Bwy, Douglas P. "System SESAR = Automating an Intermediate Stage of Survey Research." *American Behavioral Scientist,* 10 (January , 1967), 8-11.

Yarmolinsky, Adam. "Confessions of a Non-User," *Public Opinion Quarterly,* 28 (1963), 543-548.

Yu, Frederick, T.C. *Mass Persuasion in Communist China.* New York: Praeger, 1964.

Chapter 7

CONTENT ANALYSIS
IN POLITICAL RESEARCH[1]

Ole R. Holsti

I. INTRODUCTION

The communication process is an intrinsic part of all social interaction from the interpersonal to the international level. It is no exaggeration to assert that "communication is at the heart of civilization" (Kuhn, 1963, 151). Groups, institutions, or organizations — from the family to the nation — exist by virtue of communication, and cease to exist once communication becomes totally disrupted. It is thus axiomatic that the study of the processes and content of communication is basic to all social sciences. The study of communication content has been approached from a variety of different starting points and undertaken with the tools and conceptual frameworks of several disciplines. Content analysis is a multipurpose research method developed specifically for investigating a broad spectrum of problems in which the content of communication serves as the basis of inference.

This chapter is divided into five parts. The first four sections define content analysis, outline types of content analysis research designs, and survey some political research in which content analysis has been employed. Content analysis by means of electronic computer, and the advantages and limitations of using computers are discussed in the fifth section.

Nearly all basic and applied research in the social sciences depends

[1]Copyright by Ole Holsti. Some parts of this chapter are from a longer paper which will appear in the *Handbook of Social Psychology* (2nd edition), edited by G. Lindzey and E. Aronson; Belmont, Massachusetts: Addison-Wesley.

in one way or another on careful reading of written materials. Given the ubiquity of this process in research, what characteristics distinguish content analysis from any careful reading of documents? Definitions of content analysis have tended to change over time with developments in technique and with the application of the tool itself to new problems and types of materials, and there has been a marked tendency to broaden the boundaries of content analysis through less restrictive definitions. (See, for example, the definitions offered by Kaplan, 1943, 230; Janis, 1949, 55; Berelson, 1952, 18; Cartwright, 1953, 424; and Stone, 1964.)

Among the characteristics of content analysis on which there is wide agreement are those of *objectivity, system, and generality. Objectivity* stipulates that the analysis must be carried out on the basis of explicitly formulated rules which will enable two or more persons to obtain the same results from the same documents. *Systematic* means that the inclusion and exclusion of content or categories is done according to consistently applied criteria of selection. This requirement eliminates analyses in which only materials supporting the investigator's hypotheses are examined. *Generality* requires that the findings must have theoretical relevance. Purely descriptive information about content, which is related neither to other attributes of content nor to the characteristics of the sender or recipient of the message, is of little value.

These three requirements are not unique to content analysis, being necessary conditions for all scientific inquiry. But they serve to indicate that, in general terms, content analysis can be considered as the application of the canons of scientific research to the analysis of communication content. In line with the recent trend toward use of content analysis across a broad spectrum of disciplines, problems, and materials, a broad definition of content analysis will be adopted here: *Content analysis is any technique for making inferences by systematically and objectively identifying specified characteristics within text.*

WHEN TO USE CONTENT ANALYSIS

When should one use content analysis? The wide range of possibilities is suggested by reference to a few of the diverse problems which have been subjected to content analysis techniques in recent years:

What differences among cultures are reflected in the songs and literature of various nations (Sebald, 1961-62; Lewin, 1947)?

To what extent have the political symbols of the New Deal been adopted by American conservatives (Prothro, 1956)?

Is editorial support of a political candidate also reflected in biased news sections (Kobre, 1953; Klein and Maccoby, 1954)?

What has been the Soviet reaction to Voice of America broadcasts (Inkeles, 1952)?

How do outgroup pressures relate to ingroup cohension within the Soviet system (Holsti, 1965b; Hopmann, 1966)?

How are expressions of the "need for achievement" related to stages in the development of a civilization (McClelland, 1961; de Charms and Moeller, 1962)?

Who was the author of the Federalist Papers, Nos. 49-58, 62 and 63 (Mosteller and Wallace, 1964)?

Content analysis is not relevant to all documentary research, however. It can rarely be used to determine the truth of an assertion made in the text, or to evaluate the aesthetic qualities of language. Moreoever, if the social scientist uses documents to settle limited issues of fact, such as to determine which newspapers supported Kennedy and Nixon in 1960, methods other than content analysis could be used more efficiently. But the investigator's questions and the content of documents are rarely coterminous (Dibble, 1963, 216). One approach to documentary research is exemplified by a recent manual, which suggests dependence upon "a sort of sixth sense that will alert you to tell-tale signs" (quoted in Dibble, 1963, 204). The limitation of depending solely upon ordinary reading of documents for purposes of scientific research are illustrated in a study of Richard Wright's autobiography, *Black Boy* (White, 1947). Although the investigator was a trained psychologist, his preliminary appraisal of the book failed to uncover a number of major themes. Systematic content analysis, however, revealed Wright's emphasis on personal safety (18 per cent of all value judgments), failure to identify with other Negroes, and lack of interest in social goals. In general, then, content analysis will be useful whenever the problem requires precise and standardized method for analyzing those aspects of symbolic behavior which may escape casual scrutiny. As such, it may be considered as a supplement to — not a substitute for — subjective examination of documents.

More specifically, content analysis is likely to prove especially useful for at least three general classes of research problems:

1. When there are technical advantages because the volume of material to be examined is such that the investigator must either:

    (a) confine his study to some sample of the total universe of communication; (b) use a team of assistants, each with his own subjective predispositions; or (c) do both. For example, the analysis of key political symbols appearing in "elite" newspapers over a sixty-year period (Lasswell *et al.*, 1952), could not be undertaken on a nonsystematic basis; nor could every issue of each newspaper for the entire period be examined. Such a study would clearly require the use of both sampling and many research assistants. Unless rigorous and explicitly formulated rules for systematic sampling and reliable coding were used, inferences drawn from these data would be of questionable value. Content analysis is a technique for meeting these requirements.

2. When data accessibility is a problem and the investigator's data are limited to the messages produced by individuals. Restrictions of time or space often do not permit the analyst to gain direct access to his subject. In such cases the subject must be studied "at a distance," with the consequence that other social science research techniques (interview, questionnaire, observation) are not applicable. If the subject is no longer alive, he can be studied only through the record of his activities; through what his contemporaries set down about him; or through whatever writings he has left. In some instances the third category constitutes the most revealing, and occasionally the only surviving, source. Identification of unknown authors (Yule, 1944; Paisley, 1964), inferences from enemy propaganda (George, 1959; Lasswell *et al.*, 1949; Whiting, 1960), or analysis of decision-makers' attitudes toward enemies (Holsti, 1967) illustrate this use of content analysis. In short, content analysis can serve as a method of "last resort" when more direct techniques of analysis are ruled out by circumstances.

3. When, given certain theoretical components of the data themselves, the subject's own language is crucial to the research problem. The analyst often requires information of a subtlety or complexity which renders casual scrutiny inadequate, even if undertaken by a skilled and sensitive reader. For example, regardless of the investigator's skill or training one would have little confidence in a comparative analysis of "need achievement" in literary materials of various nations if inferences were based on rough estimates.

CONTENT ANALYSIS RESEARCH DESIGNS

All communication is composed of six basic elements: a *source* or senders; an *encoding* process which results in a *message;* a *channel* of transmission; a detector or *recipient* of the message; and a *decoding* process. Although content analysis is always performed on the message, it may be used to answer questions about each of the other elements of communication. The classical formulation of these questions is, "Who says what, to whom, how, and with what effect" (Lasswell *et al.*, 1952, 12) — to which one more question, "why," may be added.

Each of these questions may be subsumed under research designed for three different purposes. The investigator may analyze messages to test hypotheses and make inferences about: *characteristics of the text; causes or antecedents of the message;* or *effects of the communication.* These three categories differ with respect to the questions which will be asked of the data, the dimension of communication analyzed, and the research design. These differences are summarized in Table 1.

II.   INFERENCES ABOUT CHARACTERISTICS OF DOCUMENTS

The most frequent application of content analysis has been for research problems which can be answered *directly* from a *description of the attributes of the message,* without inference to either the intentions (encoding process) of the sender or the effect of the message upon those to whom it is directed (decoding process). In such studies the investigator is in large part freed from problems of validity, except to the extent that validity is related to sampling and reliability; the content data serve as a direct answer to the research question, rather than as an indicator from which other characteristics are to be inferred.

Much of the research has addressed itself to some variety of the "what" question, testing hypotheses about such matters as focus of attention, trends in communication, or cross-media differences. In studies of this type, the investigator may also want to answer the question "to whom," as when testing hypotheses about the way in which the content of messages will differ according to audience, or to answer questions about "how"; for example, in studies of style or of techniques of persuasion.

The type of research design will depend on the questions which the investigator seeks to answer and on his data. In order to state meaningful conclusions, however, *all* content data must be compared to some other data. To determine that an editorial used the term "freedom" X number of times is a meaningless finding by itself.

Table 1

Purpose	Branch of Semiotics	Type of Comparisons	Questions	Research Problems
To describe characteristics of communication	Semantics (sign/referent) Syntactics (sign/sign)	Messages source A 1. Variable X across time 2. Variable X across situations 3. Variable X across audience 4. Variable X and Y within same universe of document	What?	To describe trends in communication content To relate known characteristics of sources to the messages they produce To audit communication content against standards
		Messages source type A/Messages source type B Messages/standard: 1. A priori 2. Content 3. Noncontent	How? To whom?	To analyze techniques of persuasion To analyze style To relate known character-istics of audience to messages produced for them To describe patterns of communication
To make inferences as to the antece-dents of communi-cation (the encod-ing process)	Pragmatics (user/sign)	Messages/nonsymbolic behavioral data 1. Direct 2. Indirect	Why? Who?	To secure political and military intelligence To analyze psychological traits of individuals To infer aspects of culture and cultural change To provide legal evidence To answer questions of disputed authorship
To make inferences as to the effects of communication (the decoding process)	Pragmatics (sign/receiver)	Sender messages/recipient messages Sender messages/recipient behavioral data	With what effect?	To measure readability To analyze the flow of information To assess responses to communication

When content analysis is used to describe text, there are three basic types of comparisons which may be made.

1. The analyst may compare documents derived from a *single source.* One application of this method is the comparison of the message over *time.* Such studies have been undertaken to analyze trends in usage of political symbols in party platforms (Lasswell and Namenwirth, 1966), presidential addresses (Prothro, 1956), campaign literature (Brown, 1960), and the like. The investigator may also compare messages from a single source in differing *situations,* as in a study of international communication under conditions of low and high stress (Holsti, 1965a). Another, less widely used, approach using content data from a single source involves comparisons across *audience.* Comparisons of communication attributes across time, situation, or audience are intermessage analyses. Inferences may also be based upon the *covariation of two or more variables,* within a single document, or set of documents.

2. Hypotheses may be tested by comparing the messages of *two or more different sources.* Usually the purpose is to relate theoretically significant attributes of communication sources to differences in the messages they produce. For example, this design has been used to identify differences in propaganda appeals of two or more orators (Schneidman, 1963), political parties (Almond, 1954), or nations (Lasswell, 1927).

3. Finally, the text may be compared with an external standard. Unlike the first two research designs, this comparison is with data independent of the content under analysis.

These research designs, as well as some major areas of substantive interest, can be illustrated by a brief review of some studies in which content analysis was applied to answer questions of a political nature.

TO DESCRIBE TRENDS IN COMMUNICATION CONTENT

Interest in measuring trends in national attitudes relevant to international politics has stimulated considerable analysis of the printed media. An early study applied scaling techniques developed by Thurstone to Chinese and Japanese materials during the Far Eastern crisis of 1930-32 (Russell and Wright, 1933). The same techniques were used to examine trends in American attitudes toward Japan and China along a favorable — hostile continuum (Wright and Nelson, 1939).

The most extensive survey of political symbols was undertaken by Lasswell, Lerner, Pool, and associates as one aspect of research on

Revolution and Development of International Relations (RADIR). The studies were designed to identify and map trends in the usage of those symbols expressing major goal values of modern politics. Editorials from one "prestige" newspaper representing each of five countries — the United States, Great Britain, France, Germany and the Soviet Union — were analyzed for the period 1890-1949 (Pool, 1952a). Data from the 19,553 editorials were used to trace changing foci of attention and attitude, as indexed by key symbols, for the sixty-year period.

Editorials appearing on the first and fifteenth day of each month were coded for the presence of 416 key symbols. These included 206 geographical terms, such as names of countries, international organizations, and minority groups, and 210 major ideological and doctrinal symbols – democracy, equality, proletariat, communism, nazism, nationalism, fatherland, and the like — relating to world politics in the first half of the twentieth century. Each time a symbol appeared it was scored as present, and further, the valence of the expressed attitude toward the symbol — approval, disapproval, or neutrality — was recorded. The frequency counts derived were based on the *number of editorials* in which the symbols appeared, not the frequency with which the symbol itself appeared.

Among the many findings were the following:

Symbols of representative government are used where the practice is under dispute, not where it is an accepted part of the tradition (Pool, 1952b, 72).

Hostility to the outside world . . . seems to be very much a function of insecurity. Those nations which have at any given moment dominated the word scene have generally said little that was adverse to "prestige papers" in the other power. The insecure or unsatisifed powers, on the other hand, have generally had editorials full of hostile judgments of foreign states (Pool, 1951, 62).

Two main trends in the modern world are: (1) a shift in the center of attention, in which traditional liberalism is being replaced by proletarian doctrines, and (2) a growing threat of war and a corresponding increase of nationalism and militarism (Pool, 1952a, 84).

One important area of inquiry left relatively untouched by the RADIR studies is that of different and changing meanings beyond approval or disapproval, attached to such symbols as "democracy." This is an area in which a variety of content analysis methods might usefully be applied to supplement the more traditional approach of textual exegesis.

Other somewhat similar studies of political symbols have examined trends in Soviet May Day slogans (Yakobson and Lasswell, 1949), symbols used by the Communist International (Leites, 1949), and the response of Communist propaganda to defeat in elections and strikes (Leites and Pool, 1949).

Trend inventories have varied widely in purpose and quality. Such studies can be useful for identifying major trends across long periods of time, and are relatively easy to undertake; on the other hand, surveys depending on gross categories often conceal more information of interest than they reveal. According to one source, "The most valuable use of studies of content . . . is in noting trends and changes in content. Systems of classification may be inadequate and unstandardized; nevertheless, if a system is used consistently over a time period valuable facts may appear" (quoted in Berelson, 1952, 29). This seems a dubious premise upon which to stake very much research effort. Certainly little is to be gained by precise measurement if the system of categories is inadequate.

TO RELATE KNOWN ATTRIBUTES OF SOURCES
TO THE MESSAGES THEY PRODUCE

Important aspects of social research test hypotheses of the form: "sources with characteristic A are likely to produce messages with attributes w and x, whereas those with characteristic B are likely to produce messages of types y and z." This formulation covers a broad spectrum of studies. The sources may be two individual authors of newspapers; or different media, such as radio and magazines; or communication sources in two or more countries.

The relationship between the editorial orientation of mass media and the nature of their news reporting has been an area of considerable research in the United States, particularly since the Presidential elections of 1936 and 1940, in which the vast majority of the press supported Landon and Willkie. Gerbner has been among the most articulate proponents of the position that all analysis of the mass media must proceed with a sensitivity to the ideological framework of the media. The general proposition that "all news are views" was tested through an examination of nine French newspapers of the political left, the right, and the commercial press. Reporting of a nonpolitical incident — the shooting of a schoolboy by a teacher — was subjected to a propositional analysis. On the basis of significant differences among newspaper types the author concluded that "There is no fundamentally non-ideological, apolitical, non-partisan news gathering and reporting system" (Gerbner, 1964, 508).

Several studies have examined the role of newspapers in electoral campaigns to determine whether editorial support is systematically related to the other aspects of campaign coverage, such as the amount of space devoted to stories of each candidate. The evidence from such studies is mixed, depending largely on the newspaper and election investigated. Blumberg (1954) examined 35 dailies across the United States during the 1952 campaign and found little evidence of bias in news coverage. This finding was supported by Markham and Stempel (1957). A study of fifteen "prestige" dailies during the 1960 campaign indicated that "as a group they gave the Democratic and Republican campaigns virtually equal amount of space in their news columns" (Stempel, 1961, 157). Other studies have found that the political candidate supported by dailies in Florida and California received better news coverage (Kobre, 1953; Batlin, 1954).

A serious limitation of investigations based on space measures is that they tap only a single dimension of bias. Some rough equality of space allocation may be a necessary condition of unbiased coverage, but probably it is not sufficient. During the 1940 campaign the press and radio *focused* on Roosevelt by a margin of 3-2, but *favored* Willkie by better than 2-1 (Lazarsfeld *et al.,* 1944, 117). The more subtle — and probably more important — methods of slanting the news have received less attention than measures of space. One exception is an analysis of eight major daily newspapers during the 1952 campaign. Newspapers were rated on eighteen indices, including size and tone of headline, placement of stories, number of biased remarks, number of pictures, and total column inches of stories on various pages. These measurements gave strong indication of systematic bias in favor of the candidate supported by the newspaper (Klein and Maccoby, 1954).

A similar finding emerged from a study of the British press, which concluded that, with the exception of *The Times,* "There could be no doubt in the reader's mind as to which side the different newspapers supported. News and comment were inextricably mixed in the 'news' reports and special articles" (Royal Commission on the Press, 1949, 359).

Differential coverage of "civil rights" stories has also been related to various characteristics of newspapers, including geographical location, ownership (Negro, white), and political orientation. The findings have generally supported hypotheses of systematic qualitative and quantitative differences in news coverage (Broom and Reece, 1955; Carter, 1957; Breed, 1958).

The hypothesis that the presence of local newspaper competition is related to more adequate news coverage has received some attention. A comparison of 97 newspapers revealed no significant difference in allocation of nonadvertising space in relation to the presence or absence of competition. A second test of 260 newspapers matched for circulation and other characteristics replicated the analysis, and the data again rejected the hypothesis that competitive status has any significant bearing on the allocation of news space (Nixon and Jones, 1956). Similar conclusions were reached by Willoughby (1955, 204). The adequacy of news coverage during the 1960 presidential campaign was related to various characteristics of the newspapers in a survey of 90 dailies (Danielson and Adams, 1961). From this research a "news potential index" was developed which, on the basis of five characteristics of the newspaper, can predict the adequacy of news coverage.

Considerable content analysis research has focused on documents produced by political action groups. Comparative analysis of Communist publications was used to develop a model against which the perceptions and experiences of former party members (determined by interviews) could be compared. Categories incorporating qualitities of the "ideal Communist" were used to code a Communist classic, and the publications of a party in power (Soviet Union) and a weak party (United States) (Almond, 1954, 77). Right-wing organizations (Wilcox, 1962; McEvoy, 1966) and various groups of lobbyists (McPherson, 1964) are among the other political groups whose communications have been analyzed.

Content analysis has also been used on a variety of materials to discover international differences in the content of communication. A comparative study of newspapers in seventeen countries during a seven-day period in March 1951 was conducted under the auspices of UNESCO (Kayser, 1953). The morning newspaper with the largest circulation in each country was analyzed for a period of time selected in advance of actual publication. Comparisons were made of both format and content: the front page, space allocation, origin of news, and coverage of specific events during the week. A supplementary analysis compared four "prestige" papers published in Moscow, Paris, London and New York.

An examination of fifteen "prestige" newspapers published on November 2, 1956, during the dual crises in Hungary and Suez, revealed differences in coverage of these events which were ascribed to the degree of involvement in one or the other event, or to instrumental handling of the news. News of the events in Suez crowded Hungary out of these newspapers; even in the West, "attention was so overwhelmingly on Suez that the full significance of what was happening in Hungary was never made clear" (Schramm, 1959, 138).

Cross-national content analysis has not been confined to printed media. Two studies compared the literature and songs of youth groups in Nazi Germany and the United States. The youth literature in the two countries yielded nearly one thousand expressions of various organizational goals (Lewin, 1947). By frequency count, the German literature placed significantly greater stress on national loyalty, national identification, and determination, whereas American Boy Scout materials emphasized altruism, religion, and creativity. A parallel study of children's songbooks yielded similar results (Sebald,1961-1962). The German sources stressed national loyalty, obedience, and heroic death, and paid less attention to the beauty of nature, play, and Christianity. Content analysis of such materials can reveal important international differences at a specified point in time, but further inferences, unsupported by independent data, are often open to question. A case in point is Sebald's generalization, based solely on Nazi songbooks issued in 1940, that the model character of the German is basically authoritarian.

Content analysis has also been used to examine cross-national or cross-cultural differences in media as diverse as movies, television programming, magazines, textbooks, folktales, sermons, and magazine photographs.

TO AUDIT COMMUNICATION CONTENT AGAINST STANDARDS

When content analysis is used to evaluate the adequacy of communication, the content data are compared to an a priori standard. Much of the early content analysis research in the United States was stimulated by concern over the spread of yellow journalism; studies of New York newspapers by Speed (1893) and Matthews (1910) are examples. This early research was almost wholly devoted to measuring space allocation for various subject matter categories, and much of it has been justly criticized for subjective and arbitrary procedures; Matthews, for instance, aggregated his categories into four major classes — "demoralizing," "unwholesome," "trivial," and "worthwhile." Interest in standards of the mass media has been sustained, however, and many serious technical problems of the early studies have been resolved. In a more recent study, content analysis was used to determine whether the Associated Press and United Press International, each of which had full-time bureaus in Havana, were responsible for charges of inadequate public information about the Cuban revolution. All stories about the Cuban revolution filed during December 1958 were analyzed. Tables summarizing AP and UPI reports were compared to coverage of events in Cuba by major newspapers published in Washington, Cleveland, and Louisville. Scores were computed for percentage of available AP and UPI information used, and the prominence (headlines, placement) with which it was displayed. On the basis of the comparison, the author absolved the news services from charges of inadequate coverage: "The newspapers received enough wire copy to tell the long, continuing story of the Cuban revolution. They made little use of this material, however, until the last six days"(Lewis, 1960, 646).

TO ANALYZE TECHNIQUES OF PERSUASION

Content analysis usually focuses on the substance (the "what" question) of messages. It has also been used to analyze the form or style (the "how" question). For the last three decades, and particularly during World War II, considerable research has focused on propaganda, "the manipulation of symbols as a means of influencing attitudes on controversial matters" (Lasswell, 1942, 106). Often the purpose has been to infer the intentions of communicators from the content of the propaganda, a type of research to be discussed later. The remainder of the research has aimed at developing a theory of form, style, and structure of persuasive communication.

A pioneering study in this area was Lasswell's analysis of propaganda techniques during World War I, in which four major objectives of propaganda, and appropriate techniques of appeal for each goal were identified.

1. To mobilize hatred against the enemy;
2. To preserve the friendship of allies;
3. To preserve the friendship and, if possible,
   to procure the cooperation of neutrals;
4. To demoralize the enemy.

Lasswell concluded that while all four themes were present in the propaganda of every nation, they were applied with varying degrees of success; much of German propaganda turned out to "boomerang," in part owing to the lasting impression that they were the aggressor, in part because of the ineptness of their appeals. On the other hand, British propagandists were successful in picturing humanitarian war aims, and the French were able to portray the Germans in Satanic terms, such as "Hun," and " Boche" (Lasswell, 1927, 195-99). More quantitative methods were used to examine the organization, media, techniques, and symbols of Communist propaganda in Chicago during the depression of the 1930's (Lasswell and Blumenstock, 1939). The Lasswellian influence in propaganda studies has persisted, as is evident in two recent books (Douring, 1959: Barghoorn, 1954).

Several sets of categories for describing and analyzing various aspects of propaganda have been proposed.   One such scheme, developed at the Institute of Propaganda Analysis, enumerates content (name calling, testimonial, bandwagon, etc.) and strategic (stalling, scapegoating, etc.) techniques which have been identified in propaganda (Lee, 1952, 42-79, 210-34).

A somewhat different set of categories emerged from a comparative study of British and German radio broadcasts to the United States during 1940 (Bruner, 1941).   A tentative list identified nine dimensions for describing propaganda: dissolvent-unifying; negative-positive; temporal; personal-impersonal; stratified-homogeneous; authoritative-casual; colloquiality; immediate-remote; and repetitiousness.

Finally, "value analysis," a set of categories for studying personality from written materials, was used to examine the propaganda style of Hitler and Roosevelt (White, 1949).   A number of similarities were found: both stressed traditional moral values, including nonaggression, peace, and national grandeur, and both often used black-white dichotomies.   Hitler also appears to have used an indirect approach to the preparation of the German people for war, by emphasizing the theme of persecution by outsiders.

A study of the picture magazines *USSR* and *American Illustrated,* which are produced by the Soviet Union and the United States for readers of the other country, revealed how persuasive literature is often framed in the value context of the audience.   Both the American and Soviet magazines put greater emphasis on values often attributed to the other nation; that is, the Russian publication emphasized such aspects of Soviet life as industrial growth and a high standard of living, whereas the American magazine stressed cultural and aesthetic interests of its citizens (Garver, 1961).

Research has not been limited to official governmental propaganda. For example, campaign biographies, a form of persuasive literature which appears on the American political scene quadrennially, have been analyzed.   Since 1824, the basic campaign biography theme, to fashion an image of the ideal citizen of the Republic, has remained the same. Moreoever, "rival candidates appear in campaign biographies to be as alike as Tweedledum and Tweedledee" (Brown, 1960).   Considerable content analysis research has also focused on public letters, such as those written to Congressmen, or to various newspapers in the United States, the Soviet Union, and Communist China.

The most evident weakness of propaganda analysis has been the absence of systematic research to relate categories of appeal, techniques, and dimensions (and combinations of these), to effects. What types of appeals are most effective? Under what circumstances? For which subject matter categories? One exception is a detailed investigation of Kate Smith's war bond drive. Content analysis was used to identify characteristics of her appeals which might be expected to elicit particular responses from the audience, and the validity of inferences based on the content data was then checked by interviewing the audience (Merton, 1946). But in the main, questions about how technique and content of appeals are related to effects have remained unanswered.

TO DESCRIBE PATTERNS OF COMMUNICATION

How are patterns of communication affected by situational or systematic changes? In such inquiries, the investigators seek answers to the question "to whom?" An analysis of messages produced by leaders of the Dual Alliance and Triple Entente nations during the summer of 1914 indicated that as war approached, there was a significant increase in messages exchanged within alliances, with a concomitant decrease in intercoalition communication (Holsti, 1965a). The messages produced in seventeen "Inter-Nation Simulations" revealed that after all members of an alliance had obtained nuclear weapons, the modal pattern of communication changed from a "wheel" configuration to an "all channels" pattern (Brody, 1963).

TO ANALYZE STYLE

Studies of style have differed widely in method and have ranged from investigations of the single author to analyses of an entire language. Political rhetoric, especially that of American presidents or presidential candidates, has been a favorite subject for study. One approach is illustrated by a study of Woodrow Wilson's speeches (Runion, 1936). The analysis focused on grammatical aspects of discourse: sentence length, sentence structures, and figures of speech. A more revealing examination of political rhetoric, a study of broadcast addresses by Eisenhower and Stevenson during the 1956 campaign, related substantive and stylistic categories (Knepprath, 1962). The style of the two candidates was compared for subject matter, the form of reasoned discourse, the use of "loaded terms," and types of motive appeals.

III. INFERENCES ABOUT ANTECEDENTS OF MESSAGES

The second major classification of studies is that in which the text is analyzed in order to make inferences about the causes or antecedents of the message, and more specifically, about the sender. Thus content analysis is employed to discover "lawful relations *between* events in messages and processes transpiring in the individuals who produce . . . them" (Osgood, 1959, 36). Within the communication paradigm, messages are examined for the purpose of answering the questions "who" and "why?" Who was the author of a given document? What are the meanings, associations, values, motives, or intentions of the communicator which can be inferred from his messages? Whereas the descriptions of text can be classified under semantics or syntactics, this use of content analysis is a problem in pragmatics — the relationship of signs to those who produce them.

Many early definitions of content analysis explicitly excluded its use for the purpose of inferring the antecedents or causes of content. Nevertheless, such inferences often have been drawn from content data. One major goal of propaganda analysis has been to make inferences about the values, intentions, and strategy of communicators. More recently research on the pragmatic dimension of communication has become a major aspect of content analysis studies; for example, nearly the entire volume of papers from the Work Conference on Content Analysis of the Social Science Research Council was addressed to using messages for purposes of answering questions about the causes or effects of communication (Pool, 1959). The problem, then, is no longer whether content analysts *should* make inferences concerning the cause of communication, but rather — given the trend of research — what steps the investigators can take to enhance confidence in the validity of their inferences.

In order to draw valid inferences about sources from the messages they send, the content data must be compared, *directly,* or *indirectly,* with independent behavioral indices. Owing to possible differences in coding habits — words may have different semantic meaning for different sources — inferences as to the antecedent causes of messages drawn solely from content data cannot be considered self-validating.

The relationship of symbolic behavior and its causes may be established by comparing content analysis data *directly* with some other indices of behavior, such as a study of the 1914 crises in which the degree of hostility in documents written by European decision-makers was compared to the level of violence in their military actions (North *et al.,* 1968).

Inferences based on an *indirect* relationship between symbolic and other forms of behavior are much more frequent in the content analysis literature. The logic of such inferences can be stated as a syllogism: In a given situation, individuals whose behavior patterns are known to be a, b, and c produce messages with characteristics r-s-t, u-v-w, and x-y-z, respectively. Thus, if in similar circumstances a source produces messages with attributes x-y-z, the inference is that it was related to behavior pattern c. A classic example of this research design is the comparison between Nazi propaganda themes with the books, periodicals, and transoceanic cables of certain domestic organizations suspected of sedition, in which content analysis revealed significant similarities on a number of dimensions (Lasswell, 1949). The data obtained by content analysis were admitted by the court as legal evidence supporting the charge of sedition. In this case, the likenesses in the messages of *two separate sources* served as the basis for inferences about the similarity of motives — support for the German war effort.

The research design may also focus on the relationship of events to symbols for a *single source*. The intelligence analyst may examine enemy documents for attributes that have in the past provided a clue to some aspect of the enemy's behavior. In general, the investigator bases his inferences on some demonstrated relationship between events and symbols for the same or for comparable communicators. A weakness of many studies employing content analysis is that such a relationship between symbolic behavior and other forms of behavior has not been established.

TO SECURE POLITICAL AND MILITARY INTELLIGENCE

A most important impetus to the development of content analysis was the large-scale propaganda research during World War II. Numerous social scientists were engaged by the Federal Communications Commission, the Library of Congress, and the Justice Department to study these materials.

The most difficult problem, owing to constraints within which the propaganda analyst operates, was to establish criteria for inference. The FCC used both *direct* and *indirect* techniques (George, 1959). The first method operates from a "representational" model of communication; that is, the investigator assumes that words in the message are valid indicators, irrespective of circumstances. Thus inferences regarding intentions, expectations, and situational factors are drawn *directly* from the characteristics of propaganda content, based on a past correlation of conditions or events and content characteristics. The direct method is illustrated by a study to determine the degree of collaboration between German and Italian propaganda agencies. From consistent differences in broadcasts from Rome and Berlin, analysts concluded that there were no collaboration. Evidence gathered after the end of the war validated the inference (Berelson and de Grazia, 1947).

The single step approach has been criticized for two deficiencies: past regularities are often based on a very few cases, and the method is insensitive to changes in propaganda strategy, which may render past correlations invalid.

An "instrumental" model of communication, in which it is assumed that the important aspect of the message consists in what it conveys, given context and circumstances, underlies the indirect method of inference (the representational and instrumental models are further described in Pool, 1959).

The initial step in the indirect method is to establish the propaganda goal or strategy underlying the characteristics of content. A series of interconnected causal imputations are derived from this point (George, 1959, 41).

| Situa-
tional ← Esti- ←
Factor mate | Elite
Expec- ←
tation
Policy | Elite
Inten- ←
tion or | Propa-
ganda ← Content
Strategy |

In the indirect method, then, the process of inference is broken up into a number of smaller steps.

Despite many difficulties, documentary material on the Nazi conduct of the war indicated that FCC inferences were accurate in an impressive number of cases. For a two-month period (March-April 1943), 101 out of 119 inferences made by the German section were scored as correct. Of methodological interest is the finding that frequency and nonfrequency indicators were about equally successful (George, 1959, 264-66).

TO ANALYZE TRAITS OF INDIVIDUALS

It is a widely held belief among social scientists that the symbolic behavior of the individual can provide important data about the personality, values, intentions, and other attributes of the communicator. Personal documents — defined as "any self-revealing record that intentionally or unintentionally yields information regarding the structure, dynamics and functioning of the author's mental life" — may take many forms, ranging from a diary or intimate letters to autobiographies and speeches addressed to a wide audience (Allport, 1942, xii). The motives for producing personal documents may vary from psychotherapy to hopes of literary fame. Finally, the investigator's purposes in analyzing personal documents have differed, despite the common goal of making inference about the communicator.

Political rhetoric has been analyzed to infer personality traits of the speaker from the logical and cognitive characteristics of his verbal production (Schneidman, 1963). The text was first coded into two category sets.

1. *The idiosyncracies of reasoning:*   32 categories consisting of: (a) idiosyncracies of relevance; (b) idiosyncracies of meaning; (c) arguments containing suppressed premises or conclusions; (d) idiosyncracies of logical structure; and (e) idiosyncracies of logical interrelations.

2. *Cognitive maneuvers:* Consisting of 65 styles of thought development; for example, to switch from normative to descriptive mode, or, to render another's argument weaker or stronger by paraphrase.

The second step in the analysis is to construct, for each idiosyncracy of thinking, the logical conditions under which idiosyncracy is controverted or cancelled out — to use the author's term, *contralogic.* Inferences regarding psychological characteristics of the communicator are then drawn from the contralogic.

To illustrate the method, Schneidman (1961; 1963) examined the logical styles of Kennedy and Nixon in their first two television debates, and that of Khrushchev in speeches delivered after the collapse of the Paris "Summit" Conference and at the United Nations. Inference regarding the personalities of Kennedy, Nixon, and Khrushchev appears to have considerable face validity. For example, Khrushchev is characterized in these terms.

> He feels that others are prone to misunderstand his position and yet he desires acceptance and will even sacrifice other needs or ends to achieve it. He is moody and needful of approval. But with his pessimism about resolving differences, he enjoys conflict and struggle, as much for its own sake as a means to an end . . . He trusts his own instinct, his "natural feel" for things. He is painstaking in certain areas, but in general is impatient and suspicious of detail or subtlety (1961, 61-62).

Pending considerable further research, the psychological correlates of logical styles are only working hypotheses. Nevertheless, as a method of studying style, this technique represents a considerably more sophisticated method than earlier attempts to analyze political discourse through content analysis.

Content analysis is increasingly being used to assess psychological variables in the context of political decision-making, particularly in the area of foreign policy. One approach, a continuation of the Lasswellian tradition, has emphasized elite values and ideology. In the absence of direct measures, Soviet and American publications representing political, economic, labor, military, scientific, and cultural elites were examined to identify major values. Themes regarding the economy, social, and internal political affairs, and external relations were coded into more than forty category sets. An investigation of elite foreign policy attitudes for the same period focused on perceptions of the international system, power relationships, and operational codes. Although Soviet and American value preferences were found to be symmetrical in some respects, and incompatible in others, the data also revealed that elites in both nations displayed "a powerful tendency to act and speak in such a way as to exacerbate [the] differences" (Angell *et al.*, 1964, 473).

A second approach to foreign policy studies has focused on the systematic analysis of documents written by officials holding key decision-making roles. The basic assumption is that foreign policy decisions, like all decisions, are in part a product of the policy-maker's psychological state, that if men define situations as real, they are real in their consequences. Again, the choice of content analysis is based largely on the inability to use more direct methods by which to assess the perceptions, attitudes, and values of foreign policy leaders at the time of decision; systematic analysis of diplomatic documents provides an indirect method to bridge gaps in time and space.

An initial study tested two basic hypotheses about the relationship between perceptions of threat and perceptions of capability during an international crisis (Zinnes *et al.*, 1961). During the crisis leading to war in 1914, perceptions of capability appeared much less frequently in decision-makers' documents as perceptions of threat increased. This study also revealed the limitations, for many purposes, of using frequency as the sole basis of inference. After the 1914 data were recoded to permit analysis on the basis of *intensity* as well as *frequency,* the hypotheses relating to perceptions of capability and injury were re-examined. Decision-makers of each nation most strongly felt themselves to be victims of persecution and rejection precisely at the time when they were making policy decisions of the most crucial nature (Holsti and North, 1965).

Other analyses of the 1914 data, within the framework of a model linking actions and perceptions, have consistently shown that the more intense the interaction between the parties, the more important it is to incorporate perceptual variables (as indexed by content data) into the analyses (North *et al.,* 1966). This strong relationship between perceptions of hostility, feelings of involvement, and policy decisions has also been found in a study of Soviet and Chinese leaders during three crises (Zaninovich, 1964). Another analysis of the 1914 documents, using different variables, tested a number of hypotheses prominent in the decision-making literature. The data revealed that as decision-makers came under increasing stress, they perceived time to become an increasingly salient factor in the formulation of policy, and they became preoccupied with the short-term, rather than the long-range, implications of their actions. Leaders in the various capitals of Europe also perceived adversaries to increase as they came under more intense stress (Holsti, 1965a).

In a study comparing events during the Cuban missile crisis of 1962 with those in the summer of 1914, some important differences emerged. During the Cuban crisis both sides tended to perceive rather accurately the nature of the adversary's actions, and then proceeded to act at an "appropriate" level. Thus, unlike the situation in 1914, efforts by either party to delay or reverse the escalation were generally perceived as such, and responded to in a like manner (Holsti *et al.,* 1965).

TO INFER ASPECTS OF CULTURE AND CULTURAL CHANGE

Anthropologists, sociologists, and students of political culture have traditionally examined societal artifacts to infer constant and variable attributes of culture. Content analysis for this purpose can be illustrated by a series of studies centering on hypotheses relating "need of achievement" to major stages in cultural development.

A person with a high *n* Achievement is someone who wants to succeed, who is energetic and nonconforming, and who enjoys tasks which involve elements of risk. *n* Achievement has been defined operationally as "a sum of the number of instances of achievement 'ideas' or images" (McClelland, 1958, 520). The hypothesis that, "a society with a relatively high percentage of individuals with high *n* Achievement should contain a strong entrepreneurial class which will tend to be active and successful particularly in business enterprises so that *the society will grow in power and influence,"* was tested by scoring samples of literature from the period of growth (900-475 B.C.), climax (475-362 B.C.), and decline (362-100 B.C.) of Greek civilization (McClelland, 1958). When contact data were compared to the area of Greek trade during the sixth, fifth, and fourth centuries B.C., the findings supported the hypothesis that expressions of *n* Achievement index stages in the development of a civilization.

An independent check on these results was made by analyzing inscriptions on vases from various eras of Greek civilization. Aronson (1958) found that "doodling" styles can be used to discriminate persons with high *n* Achievement from those with low *n* Achievement. An objective scoring system for the lines, shapes, and spaces of spontaneous "doodles" had been cross-validated against several groups of subjects. Without serious modification, the same scoring system was applied to the inscriptions on Greek vases. The results substantiated the other findings; the signs of high *n* Achievement were significantly more frequent in the period of growth and less frequent in the period of climax. Other studies centering on need of achievement are reported in McClelland and Friedman, 1952; and McClelland, 1961.

These studies illustrate some of the many possible ways in which content analysis of social and historical documents can be used to test hypotheses. At the same time it should be pointed out that there are many pitfalls, aside from such technical problems as coding reliability. A most important problem, one rarely resolved beyond doubt, is the selection of materials which do in fact represent the culture, or at least some significant segment of it. Does the drama or literature of a period, taken collectively, represent merely a manifestation of the authors' personalities, or does it reflect the more general milieu? One partial solution is to rely on materials which meet the criterion of popularity, as was done in the study of achievement motivation in Greek literature. The rationale has been spelled out in a cross-cultural study of themes in popular drama:

> Our first assumption in this study is that popular drama can be regarded as a case of "social fantasy" — that the psychological constellations in a dramatic work indicate sensitive areas in the personalities of those for whom the work has appeal; their needs, assumptions and values are expressed ("projected") in the drama. The successful play must be attuned to the audience (McGranahan and Wayne, 1948, 430).

A second approach involves examining those materials which explicitly perform the function of transmitting and instilling social norms. Such materials, which may take very different forms across culture and time, have been widely used in content analysis research — for example, Indian folk tales (McClelland and Friedman, 1952); American children's readers (de Charms and Moeller, 1962); and Nazi and American youth manuals (Lewin, 1947) and songs (Sebald, 1961-62).

A third method is to use one or more independent indices against which to correlate content data. In their comparative study of German and American drama during the 1927 season, McGranahan and Wayne used six separate sets of data, both content and noncontent, to support their conclusion that there are real and persistent differences in the psychology of Germans and Americans (1948). A sample of plays from the 1909-10 season was analyzed to determine whether differences could be attributed to Germany's defeat in World War I. Another test compared German audience reactions to movies which had been successful or unsuccessful in the United States. Each of the supplementary tests supported findings based on content analysis, thereby increasing confidence in them.

TO SECURE LEGAL EVIDENCE

During World War II the government asked Harold Lasswell to analyze certain materials and to testify about their content in four cases of suspected criminal sedition. The purpose was to demonstrate that statements by the accused publishers conformed to propaganda themes of the enemy. The materials ranged from over two hundred books in English and Russian in the *Bookniga* case to eleven issues of the periodicals *The Galilean* published by William Dudley Pelley. Eight tests were developed to analyze the materials, the results of which were accepted in evidence by the court (Lasswell, 1949, 177-78).

A more limited form of content analysis has been used by the Federal Communications Commission to determine whether radio station owners conform to prescribed standards. In its annual survey, the FCC compares station logs with ideal rations between commercial and local live, sustaining, and public issue programs. In one case the American Jewish Congress sought to deny an application by the *New York Daily News* for an FM broadcasting license on grounds of unfavorable bias against minority groups. In a split opinion the Commission ruled that both qualitative and quantitative data contained "technical deficiencies . . . so serious as to vitiate any real value the analysis might otherwise have had." At the same time, the Commission ruled in unambiguous terms that content analysis is an acceptable evidential technique if the data are deemed to be of adequate quality (*Content Analysis*, 1948, 914).

On the whole, the use of content analysis for legal evidence has been quite limited. Despite some claims made for content analysis, a posture of skepticism is warranted toward its uses for other than descriptive purposes. Literary infringement cases are perhaps the legal area in which it might be used most suitably. Existing tests suffer from precisely those deficiencies which can be remedied through careful content analysis. The tests developed in the sedition cases, as well as those developed by "literary detectives," might well provide better data than impressionistic scanning.

TO ANSWER QUESTIONS OF DISPUTED AUTHORSHIP

Was James Madison or Alexander Hamilton the author of *The Federalist Papers* Nos. 49-58, 62, and 63? This is one of many problems of literary detection which have been investigated by content analysis. The belief that each person's style contains certain unique characteristics is an old one; methods of inference from statistical description of content attributes go back at least to the nineteenth century (Mendenhall, 1887). But, because there are so many possible characteristics of style which might be used for discrimination, the major task is selecting proper indicators. The problem must often be tackled in a "fishing expedition" manner, as reliable discriminators in one case may fail in another. For example, sentence length, often a useful index, proved useless in the case of the *Federalist Papers* — the undisputed writings of Madison and Hamilton averaged 34.59 and 34.55 words per sentence, respectively.

The frequency of 265 words in the known writings of Madison and Hamilton served as the test for twelve *Federalist Papers* whose authorship was disputed. The data strongly supported the claim of Madison's authorship. The weakest odds in Madison's case were 80 to 1 on *Paper* No. 55; No. 56 was the next weakest at odds of 800 to 1 for Madison. Politically important words turned out to be far less effective discriminators than the high-frequency "function words." This finding is consistent with one generalization which has emerged from other studies of the "unknown communicator" in painting, literature, and music; it is the "minor encoding habits," the apparently trivial details of style, which vary systematically within and between communicators' work (Paisley, 1964).

The pitfalls of authorship studies can be illustrated by the controversy over the assertion that Paul wrote only five of the Epistles (Morton, 1963). The claim was based on an analysis of seven indicators assumed to be reliable as "fingerprints of the mind" for discriminating style:

sentence length, and the frequency of the *definite article,* the *singular pronouns,* the aggregate of all parts of the verb *to be,* and the words *and, but,* and *in.* Using these tests, Morton concluded that six authors wrote the fourteen Pauline Epistles. However, subsequent tests have at least disproved the generality of the seven indicators; the same tests showed that James Joyce's *Ulysses* was written by six authors, none of whom wrote *Portrait of the Artist as a Young Man* (Ellison, 1965). While not resolving the question of who wrote the Epistles, such results clearly cast doubt on Morton's findings.

IV. INFERENCES ABOUT THE EFFECTS OF COMMUNICATION

The third major calssification of content analysis studies is that in which inferences are made about the effects of messages (the decoding process) upon the recepient. The question "with what effect" is a crucial aspect of the communication paradigm; nevertheless, relatively few studies have attempted to answer this question by content analysis. Probably the most systematic research on the decoding process has focused on research to measure the readability of text.

The basic format of content analysis research designed to study the effects of communication is: If messages have attributes A, B, and C, then the prediction is that the effect on the recipient will be X, Y, and Z. Content analysis serves to describe the relevant attributes of the independent variables (A, B, and C). But, as indicated earlier, any direct inference as to effects from content is at best tenuous.

The evidence indicating that the effects of communication are related not only to attributes of content but also to the predispositions of the audience is too voluminous to review here (cf. Klapper, 1960; Bauer, 1964). A single example will suffice. Major themes of political appeals during the 1940 Presidential campaign were identified by content analysis of both public and private media. The reactions of the public to the content of the arguments were then measured by interview. The interaction between content and other factors is summarized by Berelson (1952, 63):

Why do people come across arguments and why do they accept them? Briefly, our answers are these. Mainly, people come across the arguments which the mediums of communication emphasize; they also tend to see the arguments they want to see and other arguments whose statement is appealing. Mainly (within a given time), people accept the arguments which support their own general position; they also tend to accept the arguments which they see in the public communications and those whose statement is persuasive.

To restate Berelson's conclusion in the framework of content analysis research, owing to the variety of audience predispositions and decoding habits, the effects of communication cannot be inferred directly from the attributes of content (what) or style (how) without independent validation. As indicated in Figure 1, measures of the effects may be derived by two methods: (1) Analysis of subsequent messages produced by the recipient to determine if they are consistent with predicted effect; and (2) analysis of other indices of the recipient's behavior.

TO ANALYZE THE FLOW OF INFORMATION

The flow of news to the United States from the outbreak of World War I to America's entry in April 1917 was analyzed by Foster (1937). Over eleven thousand items appearing on the front page of the *New York Times* and in the Chicago press were coded according to origin of the news, and to type of appeal contained within it which might make the reader favor American participation. The data revealed that American readers were almost wholly dependent upon news directly from, or dispatched through, the Entente powers. Thus, events such as the German invasion of Belgium were reported almost exclusively by news received from Germany's enemies. As the United States grew more involved, the proportion of news from American sources increased sharply, as did news containing some appeal favoring American participation.

TO ASSESS RESPONSES TO COMMUNICATION

One aspect of the effects of a communication is the degree to which its symbols become assimilated by the audience. Prothro tested the hypothesis that political symbols of the New Deal have become a "permanent increment to the main body of the American tradition," and that not even successful spokesmen for conservatism reject them (1956, 727). The first Acceptance, Inaugural, and State of the Union addresses of Presidents Hoover, Roosevelt, Truman, and Eisenhower were coded for relative frequencies of "political appeals" (government aid, government regulation, national power, etc.) and "demand symbols" (peace, freedom, faith, controls, initiative, etc.). While demand symbols distinguished Hoover and Eisenhower from Roosevelt and Truman, Eisenhower's political appeals were free from any repudiation of the New Deal, thereby supporting the hypothesis.

Soviet newspapers and domestic and foreign broadcasts were analyzed to assess the effects of Voice of America broadcasts. For a four-year period beginning in 1947, mass communication materials were examined for all references to the Voice of America. A number of content analysis techniques were used to answer different questions. Frequency counts were used to determine the focus of attention and distribution of Soviet references to VOA. Most foreign attacks on VOA were directed to Eastern and Western Europe, with little attention to Latin American audiences. During the four-year period there was a relative increase in attention directed to domestic audiences, especially in those publications read predominantly by the Soviet intelligentsia.

Thematic analysis was used to code more than 2500 references to VOA. These data revealed that the Soviets responded by counteracting the image they assumed VOA had created of the United States, rather than by posing a counterimage of Soviet virtues (Inkeles, 1952).

These, then, are a few of the ways in which content analysis methods have been applied to political materials. It should be understood that the purpose of this summary has been to illustrate approaches to political data by selective examples rather than to review the entire relevant literature.[2]

V.   COMPUTER CONTENT ANALYSIS

The most significant recent development in content analysis is the programming of electronic computers to handle a variety of routine clerical operations involved in textual analysis.

Manual methods of content analysis suffer in varying degrees from a number of limitations. Even elementary forms of the method are expensive and time-consuming. Moreover, most techniques lack flexibility and have a limited ability to deal with complex units of analysis. Finally, content analysis usually requires skilled and sensitive coders, the very type of persons who soon become bored and frustrated by the tedious and repetitive nature of the task. These difficulties lend considerable

[2] Because this paper focuses on political research, some important areas of content analysis research have been ignored; for example, analyses of readability, and studies of the verbal correlates of various psychiatric disorders. These and other applications as well as technical problems − units of analysis, sampling, reliability, etc − are reviewed in my chapter for the forthcoming edition of the *Handbook of Social Psychology*.

validity to Berelson's warning that "Unless there is a sensible, or clever, or sound, or revealing, or unusual, or important notion underlying the analysis, it is not worth going through the rigor of the procedure, especially when it is so arduous and so costly of effort" (1952, 198).

Many of these problems can be minimized or overcome by the use of computers, but computers are not currently able to undertake all of the repetitive and routine chores associated with content analysis. Nor is the use of computers warranted for every type of research. For example, the analyst wishing to determine the space allotted in newspapers to various types of news would find computers of little use; the research could be completed more efficiently using traditional methods of measurement. In general, content analysis problems which are most appropriately analyzed by space/time or item measures will profit little from computers. On the other hand, computers can be of significant help in research when the symbol or the theme are suitable units.

At present most computer content analysis programs fall into one of two categories. Those of the first type are essentially word count programs, the output consisting of the frequency with which each word in the text appears. The second type of computer program is characterized by a dictionary system in which text words are looked up in the dictionary and automatically coded with information representing the investigator's frame of reference and assumptions. The coded text may then be manipulated, categorized, tallied, and retrieved according to analysts' data requirements.

WORD COUNT PROGRAMS

Word or symbol counting is one of the most widely used forms of content analysis. Although considerably less complex than some other method — notably theme analysis — symbol counting can nevertheless present serious problems of reliability. In the RADIR studies, for example, although categories were defined exhaustively, reliability tests on inclusion and exclusion indicated only 66, 68, and 70 per cent agreement (Lasswell *et al.,* 1952, 62). This is one of the operations for which the computer is ideally suited. The computer will perform frequency counts at high speeds with perfect reliability, assuming no error in punching the data onto IBM cards. Moreover, the computer can pick up all symbols, not only those believed, a priori, to be of interest or significance. Thus examination of the output may well reveal the appearance of theoretically important symbols which might not have been considered in the original research design.

There are currently several word counting programs being used across a broad spectrum of research problems. Content analysis based on word counting has been used extensively in psychotherapy. A program for building specialized dictionaries within the vocabulary usage of individual patients has been developed. The computer prints out, in rank-order of frequency, the patient's vocabulary, as well as tabulating a type—token ratio — the number of different words in text of a given length (Starkweather and Decker, 1964). A somewhat similar set of programs are being used for content analysis of psychotherapeutic interviews which orders and lists all words with exact frequencies. The frequency of occurrence of each different word within a segment of text is correlated with every other word across all segments, and the resulting matrix can be factor analyzed (Harway and Iker, 1964).

One limitation of word count analyses is the problem of context, which may lend a given word a considerably different meaning. This problem is partially solved in a program which searches the text for concepts of importance to the investigator and prints them out together with up to 120 words appearing before and after the key concept. The program may be operated with two search options: exact matching of key and content words, or the matching of initial letters in the key and content words (Danielson and Jackson, 1963). Variations of computerized word frequency programs are described in Danielson and Bryan (1963), Carstenson and Stolz (1964), Sebeok and Zeps (1961), and Parrish and Painter (1963).

THE "GENERAL INQUIRER"

Probably the computer content analysis programs currently in widest use are those which have been developed as part of the "General Inquirer" system, "a set of computer procedures for processing 'natural text . . .' that locates, counts, and tabulates text characteristics" (Stone, 1964). Originally developed at the Laboratory for Social Relations at Harvard University for studying psychological and sociological materials (Stone *et al.,* 1962), this system now encompasses a family of dictionaries, data preparation systems, and data analysis programs being used in nearly all social sciences.

Dictionaries. The core of each General Inquirer system of content analysis is a dictionary in which each entry word is defined with one or more "tags" representing categories in the investigator's theory. Entry words may be listed in the dictionary in root form, without frequently appearing suffix endings such as *e, s, es, ed, ing, ion,* and *ly.* If a word in the text with such a suffix is not found in the dictionary, the computer will automatically remove the suffix and look up the word root. A single dictionary form (attack) can pick up all forms (attack, attacks, attacked, attacking) appearing in the text. Thus dictionaries of moderate size, in the range of four thousand words, have a much larger effective capacity. Users of the various General Inquirer dictionaries report analysis of 92 to 98 per cent of the text, excluding proper nouns. A dictionary entry may also specify that the computer check whether specified neighboring words are present in the text; the tags then assigned will thus depend on the idiom found. Words appearing in the text but not in the dictionary are printed out separately on a "leftover" list, and may later be added to the dictionary if deemed important.

More than a dozen General Inquirer dictionaries have been developed to date. The Harvard psycho-sociological dictionary of 3450 words uses 83 tag categories, many of which are relevant for political research. Two sets of tags are incorporated into the dictionary. Each word is assigned a single "first-order" tag which represents the common or manifest meaning of the word. These are discrete, independent variables and can be treated as such statistically. Fifty-five first-order tags are grouped under eleven major headings: persons, groups, physical objects, physical qualifiers, environments, culture, emotion, thought, evaluation, social-emotional actions, and impersonal actions.

Entry words may also be assigned "second-order" tags which represent the connotative meanings of the words. The second-order tags are not independent variables; the meaning of an entry word may be defined by using as many of the 28 second-order tags — which refer to institutional contexts, status connotations, and psychological themes — as appear necessary to give a satisfactory definition. For example, the word *influential* is tagged with three meanings: ideal-value, political, and strong — one first-order tag followed by two second-order tags.

The Harvard dictionary has been used in a number of political applications, including analysis of American presidential nomination acceptance speeches (Smith *et al.,* 1965). These and other studies, as well as detailed descriptions of all General Inquirer dictionaries and programs, are described in more detail in a book edited by Philip J. Stone and associates (1966).

The Stanford political dictionary incorporates considerable theoretical work on semantic differentiation (Osgood, 1962). Thirty-five hundred words are tagged along three dimensions — positive-negative, strong-weak, and active-passive. These dimensions correspond to the *evaluative, potency,* and *activity* dimensions which have been found to be primary in human cognition in a variety of cultures. Each tag is further defined for three levels of intensity. Sample entries in the dictionary include the following:

ABANDON = NEGATIVE 2 WEAK 3 PASSIVE 3
ABET = POSITIVE 2 ACTIVE 3
ABSURD = NEGATIVE 2

In addition to the main dictionary, a dictionary of proper names has been written. The names of persons and places serve as the entry words which are tagged with as much information as desired for identification. Examples of current entries are:

GROMYKO = SOVIET-UNION FOREIGN-MINISTER EXECUTIVE
          COMMUNIST
WASHINGTON = UNITED-STATES CAPITAL
SOVIET-UNION = NATION EUROPE COMMUNIST
RUSSIA = NATION EUROPE COMMUNIST SOVIET-UNION

The proper name dictionary insures the uniformity of identification, and serves to cross-reference proper names, as with Gromyko, Soviet Union, and Russia in the example above. In addition, this dictionary is useful for analyses which depend on discriminating between units and subunits, or for aggregating subunits.

This version of the General Inquirer is being used to develop and test hypotheses relevant to decision-making in crises (Holsti *et al.,* 1965); cohesion within the Soviet bloc (Holsti, 1965b; Hopmann, 1966); the attitudinal components of neutralism (Choucri, in progress); and attitudes toward United Nations intervention in conflict situations (research in progress).

Among many other dictionaries, those relevant for politics include dictionaries for: (1) analysis of lobbying testimony (McPherson, 1964); (2) Lasswell's scheme of value analysis (Peterson and Brewer, n.d.); and (3) studying weapons systems characteristics (Weinland, 1966).

One of the many advantages of the General Inquirer system is that the dictionaries are basically interchangeable; thus the investigator may run his data on another dictionary tagged for different variables. For example, the data in a study of presidential nomination acceptance speeches were analyzed on several different dictionaries (Smith *et al.,* 1965). In interpreting the results it is, of course, important to be cognizant of the theoretical assumptions underlying the dictionary, including the premise that it will be used with populations similar to those for which it was constructed.

Data Preparation.   The text to be analyzed is punched on IBM cards with as little or as much pre-editing as required by the analysts' problem. Most investigations use text directly transcribed onto IBM cards without any coding.   Minimal coding normally involves the separation of complex sentences into one or more themes or "thought sequences," and the identification of indefinite terms such as pronouns.   More elaborate coding systems include the identification of syntactical position of key *words* in the text, and the addition of certain other codes for the *theme* as a whole (Stone *et al.,* 1962; Holsti, 1964).   For example, a sentence might be coded as follows:

CV   A free/3 American/3 people/3 must/4 reject/4 all fatalistic/7 philosophies/7 of history/7.

These codes identify the subject-verb-object (3-4-7) relationship, links between modifiers and referents, time (C = current), and mode of expression (V = imperative).   While such operations add to the time and effort required to prepare the text, they also permit the use of more elaborate analysis programs which may be important to the investigator's research problem.   During the next few years, the General Inquirer group intends to take advantage of recent advances in automatic syntax analysis and add appropriate routines to automatically handle such coding.

Data Analysis Programs.   The General Inquirer system includes a broad spectrum of programs for analyzing text.   A *text and tag* list program prints out the text and tags assigned by sentence in the form of a bilingual book.   A *tag tally* program counts the words in the text which have been tagged in the dictionary.   In addition to raw scores, an index based on the ratio of occurrence of tag words to total words in the text is computed.   For rapid visual interpretation of the results, tag tallies can be printed in graph form.   A separate list of all words in the document not found in the dictionary is also printed out.

A *question and search program* retrieves, tallies, and prints out all sentences in the text meeting any desired specification. The analyst may wish to search the text for all sentences containing a certain *text word* or *cluster of words* — for example, all sentences in which "Soviet Union" occurs as the subject and which also contain the words "nuclear" and "weapons." Questions may also retrieve themes in terms of *tags,* with or without specification of intensity or syntax position.   The *theme codes* may also be used for retrieval. Any of the question specifications may be used singly or in any desired combination, and several retrieval questions can be processed at once.

A *direct table* program, which operates on text with syntax codes, prints out in table form any required information (Armour, 1964). An added feature of this program is that the intensity level of words in the dictionary may be adjusted according to the mode of expression; for example, the score of the word "aid" in the sentence "The United States may aid India" can be reduced by a constant to reflect the probabilistic nature of the assertion. If the analysts wished to determine Chinese attitudes, as expressed in any given document or set of documents, toward itself, the Test-Ban Treaty, and the original signators of that treaty, the information would be printed out — using the Stanford dictionary — in the following format.

0331   KUO MO JO   CHINA   7-26-63   PEKING DOMESTIC
                                                       SERVICE BROADCAST

	U.S.	SOV. UN.	GT. BRIT.	CHINA	TEST BAN
POSITIVE AFFECT	10.00	18.88	4.00	54.20	26.00
NEGATIVE AFFECT	260.00	26.00	28.00	33.00	57.00
STRONG	163.40	55.00	12.00	117.00	77.00
WEAK	2.00	10.00	6.00	5.40	26.00
ACTIVE	129.50	26.00	6.00	71.40	57.00
PASSIVE	8.00	6.00	7.00	21.00	31.00

Information at the top of the table identifies the document number (0331), author (Kuo Mo Jo of China), date (July 26, 1963), and the source. The figures in the table indicate a summary score (frequency × intensity) of expressed attitudes toward each nation and toward the treaty along three dimensions. Other scores such as frequency counts are also computed. Separate tables are produced to exhaust all possible relationships defined by syntax codes. Thus in the document cited above, one table would distinguish the nature of Soviet (or American, British, etc.) actions toward all targets. Another table would score Chinese attitudes toward all nations within sentences in which these countries appear as agents of action, and a third would present the figures on Chinese attitudes about the same nations when they are targets of others' actions. Scores for up to a dozen attitude objects (that is, the column headings) may be analyzed in each pass through the data. Column headings can be changed simply by inserting different control cards; hence the data may be rerun as often as is necessary to satisfy requirements of the research problem. A recent revision[3] of this program permits its use with any dictionary prepared in a standard format; also, tables are punched out in card form for direct statistical analysis by computer.

Users of content analysis often require psychological indexes that will discriminate between two sources. The General Inquirer program has been combined with the Hunt-Hovland "Concept Learner" to produce a program for identifying discriminate functions. The strategy on which the program is based is to search the text for a single concept, or a combination of concepts, which can discriminate the sentences in document A from those in document B. Failing this, the program will continue the process of subdivision until a subgroup is found where a test does apply, or until one of the document sources runs out of sentences (Hunt *et al.,* 1965).

Another variation of the General Inquirer approach to content analysis involves the attempt to duplicate manual scoring methods by constructing rules that enable *the computer* to analyze its own tag applications and to make decisions about the nature of a document on the basis of the tag profiles. McClelland's system for scoring the level of "need achievement" in documents has been programmed for computer analysis by Woodhead and Ogilvie. Among the most complex forms of content analysis, this variant of contingency analysis presages techniques which should prove particularly useful for investigation of many types of political materials.

OTHER COMPUTER CONTENT ANALYSIS PROGRAMS

One by-product of recent interest in machine translation of text has been computer programs for syntactical, as distinct from semantic, discriminations. These may be used for a variety of content analysis problems focusing on the question "how is it said." One of the difficulties of these programs is that there may be more than one possible translation from a given sentence. This defect for the purposes of translation can be turned into an advantage for the content analyst. Two studies have demonstrated the ability of the computer, unencumbered by any preconceptions, or "cognitive set," to produce all possible interpretations of legal literature (Allen, 1963; Langevin and Owens,

[3] By Mr. Kuan Lee of Stanford University.

1963). In each case, the text of the Nuclear Test Ban Treaty was analyzed. While not all interpretations were meaningful, several of the sentences yielded more than one reasonable — and substantively significant — interpretation. Such programs appear to have wide potential application, not only on legal materials, but also in many aspects of communication research.

GENERAL IMPLICATIONS OF USING COMPUTERS
IN CONTENT ANALYSIS

The most apparent characteristic of computers — the ability to analyze text reliably at almost unbelievable speed — requires no further elaboration. Less obvious, but perhaps of greater importance, are the following points.

First, computers impose rigor and discipline on the formulation of research. The investigator using computers for content analysis is forced to make every step of his research design explicit. For example, the dictionary requires an explicit and unambiguous definition of each variable. Because every step in data analysis by computer must be specified with precision, it is not wholly facetious to suggest that all content analysis should be designed *as if* it were to be done by computer. Every analyst approaches his data with assumptions and a theory, however crude. At minimum, making these premises and rules of inference public permits an informed evaluation and discussion of the results.

Second, when data are punched on IBM cards they are amenable to reanalysis as often and for as many different purposes as desired. Traditional methods of content analysis rarely permit the degree of flexibility necessary to exhaust the potential information in one's data. Even the most meticulously coded data can rarely be used later for answering questions that were not incorporated in the original research design. In conventional content analysis research, the investigator almost of necessity instructs the coders to prepare the data to yield answers only for the initial theoretical problems. When content analysis is done manually, if a new hypothesis suggests itself after the data have been coded, the investigator often must choose between recoding the data and dropping the new idea because he is "locked in" by his research design. Data on IBM cards, on the other hand, may be rerun to test hypotheses that had not even been considered at the time of data preparation; the investigator's theory and assumptions are built into the dictionary, and into the data, and the dictionary can be expanded in response to new questions. For example, a set of documents was originally prepared to analyze Sino-Soviet-American interaction during a number of recent crisis periods.   Later the same materials were rerun for the purpose of testing quite a different hypothesis about the rift between Moscow and Peking.

Third, the use of computers enables the investigator to undertake very complex data manipulations, such as contingency analyses involving numerous variables which often cannot be done reliably or economically by hand. When computers are used, the problem of scoring reliability is completely resolved; this does not mean, of course, that the investigator can assume the validity of his results.

Fourth, documents on IBM cards can readily be reproduced and exchanged between scholars. At the time of this writing, General Inquirer users have prepared some fifty different studies, comprising over four million words on IBM cards.   These have been shared informally and will be formally stored and available at the Survey Research Center Archive, University of Michigan.

Fifth, the use of computers frees the scholar from many of the most laborious chores associated with content analysis research. The computer, like any tool properly used, can enhance the creativity of the scholar by freeing more of his time for those indispensable ingredients of significant research — the original idea, the creative hunch, the insight which is necessary to make "facts" meaningful.

Despite this optimistic appraisal of the implications of computers it may be well to conclude on a more cautious note. Just as all research does not lend itself to content analysis, not all content analysis should be done by computer. It is important to remain aware of the dangers in what Kaplan (1964, 28) calls the "law of the instrument," exemplified by the child who, when given a hammer, suddenly discovers that everything needs pounding.   Nor should the limitations of computers be overlooked.   Bad data are not better for having been analyzed by a computer.   Perhaps the single greatest danger in the use of computers is that the investigator may be lulled into accepting the validity of findings without a critical consideration of the steps preceding and following machine processing. Computers cannot save a sloppy research design, nor will they transform a trivial research problem into an important one.   The machine output only reflects the skill and insight — or lack thereof — with which the investigator constructed his dictionary and formulated his research design.   Some years ago, Bernard Berelson (1952, 198) wrote, "Content analysis, as a method, has no magical qualities — you rarely get out of it more than you put in, and sometimes you get less. In the last analysis, there is no substitute for a good idea."   The advent of computer content analysis detracts nothing from the wisdom of that assertion.

REFERENCES

Allen, L. F. Automation: Substitute and supplement in legal practice. *The American Behavioral Scientist,* 1963, 7, 39-44.

Allport, G. W. The use of personal documents in psychological science. Social Science Research Council, 1942. Bulletin No. 49.

Almond, G. A. *The appeals of communism.* Princeton, N.J.: Princeton University Press, 1954.

Angell, R. C., Dunham, Vera S., and Singer, J. D. Social values and foreign policy attitudes of Soviet and American elites. *The Journal of Conflict Resolution,* 1964, 8, 330 - 491.

Armour, Anne. A Balgol program for quantitative format in automated content analysis. Stanford: mimeo., 1964.

Aronson, E. The need for achievement as measured by graphic expression. In J. W. Atkinson (ed.), *Motives in fantasy, action and society.* Princeton, N. J.: Van Nostrand Co., Inc., 1958, pp. 249 - 265.

Barghoorn, F. C. *Soviet foreign propaganda.* Princeton, N. J.: Princeton University Press, 1964.

Batlin, R. San Francisco newspapers' campaign coverage: 1896, 1952. *Journalism Quarterly,* 1954, 31, 297-303.

Bauer, R. A. "The obstinate audience: the influence process from the point of view of social communication." *American Psychologist,* 1964, 19, 319 - 328.

Berelson, B. *Content analysis in communication research.* Glencoe, Ill.: The Free Press, 1952.

Berelson, B. and de Grazia, S. Detecting collaboration in propaganda. *Public Opinion Quarterly,* 1947, 9, 244-253.

Blumberg, N. B. *One party press? Coverage of the 1952 presidential campaign in 35 daily newspapers.* Lincoln, Neb.: University of Nebraska Press, 1954.

Breed, W. Comparative newspaper handling of the Emmett Till case. *Journalism Quarterly,* 1958, 35, 291-298.

Brody, R. A. Some systematic effects of the spread of nuclear weapons technology: A study through simulation of a multi-nuclear future. *Journal of Conflict Resolution,* 1963, 7, 663-753.

Broom, L. and Reece, Shirley. Political and racial interest: A study in content analysis. *Public Opinion Quarterly,* 1955, 19, 5-19.

Brown, W. B. *The people's choice.* Baton Rouge, La.: Louisiana State University Press, 1960.

Bruner, J. S. The dimensions of propaganda: German shortwave broadcasts to

America. *Journal of Abnormal and Social Psychology,* 1941, 41, 311-337.

Carstenson, F. W. and Stolz, W. S. Close procedure analysis programs. *Computer Newsletter,* April 1964, 3, 5-6.

Carter, R. E., Jr. Segregation and the news: A regional content study. *Journalism Quarterly,* 1957, 34, 3-18.

Cartwright, D. P. Analysis of qualitative material. In L. Festinger and D. Katz (eds.), *Research methods in the behavioral sciences.* New York: The Dryden Press, 1953, pp. 421-470.

Content analysis — a new evidentiary technique. *University of Chicago Law Review,* 1948, 15, 910-925.

Danielson, W. A. and Adams, J. B. Completeness of press coverage of the 1960 campaign. *Journalism Quarterly,* 1961, 38, 441-452.

Danielson, W. A. and Jackson, H. A. A computer program for scanning tape for key concepts and their immediate contexts. *Computer Newsletter,* July 1963, No. 1, 1-2.

de Charms, R. and Moeller, G. H. Values expressed in American children's readers: 1900-1950. *Journal of Abnormal and Social Psychology,* 1962, 64, 136-142.

Dibble, V. K. Four types of inference from documents to events. *History and Theory,* 1963, 3, 203-221.

Douring, Karin. Quantitative semantics in 18th century Sweden. *Public Opinion Quarterly,* 1959, 18, 389-394.

Ellison, J. W. Computers and the Testament. *Computers for the Humanities?* New Haven, Conn.: Yale University Press, 1965.

Foster, H. S. Charting America's news of the world war. *Foreign Affairs,* 1937, 15, 311-319.

Foster, H. S. and Friedrich, C. J. Letters to the editor as a means of measuring the effectiveness of propaganda. *American Political Science Review,* 1937, 31, 71-79.

Garver, R. A. Polite propaganda: "USSR" and "American Illustrated." *Journalism Quarterly,* 1961, 38, 480-484.

George, A. L. *Propaganda analysis.* White Plains, N.Y.: Row, Peterson and Company, 1959.

Gerbner, G. Ideological perspectives and political tendencies in news reporting. *Journalism Quarterly,* 1964, 41, 495-508.

Harway, N. I. and Iker, H. P. Computer analysis of content in psychotherapy. *Psychological Reports,* 1964, 14, 720-722.

Holsti, O. R. An adaptation of the "General Inquirer" for the systematic analysis of political documents. *Behavioral Science,* 1964, 9, 382-388.

Holsti, O. R. Cognitive dynamics and images of the enemy. In D. J. Finlay, O. R. Holsti, and R. R. Fagen, *Enemies in politics.* Chicago: Rand McNally, 1967.

Holsti, O. R. The 1914 case. *American Political Science Review,* 1965a, 59, 365-378.

Holsti, O. R. East-West conflict and Sino-Soviet relations. *Journal of Applied Behavioral Science,* 1965b, 1, 115-130.

Holsti, O. R., Brody, R. A., and North, R. C. Measuring effect and action in international reaction models. Empirical materials from the 1962 Cuban crisis. *Peace Research Society, Papers, II,* 1965, 170-190.

Holsti, O. R. and North, R. C. History of human conflict. In E. B. McNeil (ed.), *Social science and human conflict.* Englewood Cliffs, N.J.: Prentice-Hall, Inc., 1965, pp. 155-171.

Hopmann, P. T. International conflict and cohesion in the Communist system. Stanford: mimeo., 1966.

Hunt, E. B., Kreuter, J., and Stone, P. J. *Experiments in induction.* New York: Academic Press, 1965.

Inkeles, A. Soviet reactions to the Voice of America. *Public Opinion Quarterly,* 1952, 16, 612-617.

Janis, I. L. The problem of validating content analysis. In H. D. Lasswell, N. Leites, and associates (eds.), *Language of politics: Studies in quantitative semantics.* New York: George Stewart, Inc., 1949, pp. 55-82.

Kaplan, A. *The conduct of inquiry.* San Francisco: Chandler Publishing Co., 1964.

Kaplan, A. Content analysis and the theory of signs. *Philosophy of Science,* 1943, 10, 230-247.

Kayser, J. *One week's news: Comparative study of seventeen major dailies for a seven-day period.* Paris: Paul Dupont, for UNESCO, 1953.

Klapper, J. *The Effects of Mass Communication.* Glencoe, Ill.: The Free Press, 1960.

Klein, M. W., and Maccoby, N. Newspaper objectivity in the 1952 campaign. *Journalism Quarterly,* 1954, 31, 285-296.

Knepprath, H. E. The elements of persuasion in the nationally broadcast speeches of Eisenhower and Stevenson during the 1956 presidential campaign. Unpublished doctor's dissertation, University of Wisconsin, 1962.

Kobre, S. How Florida dailies handled the 1952 presidential campaign. *Journalism Quarterly,* 1953, 30, 163-169.

Kuhn, A. *The study of society: A unified approach.* Homewood, Ill.: The Dorsey Press, Inc., 1963.

Langevin, R. A. and Owens, M. Application of automatic syntactic analysis to the Nuclear Test Ban Treaty. Burlington, Mass.: Technical Operations Research, 1963, mimeo.

Lasswell, H. D.   Communications research and politics.   In D. Waples (ed.), *Print, radio, and film in a democracy*.   Chicago: University of Chicago Press, 1942, pp. 101-117.

Lasswell, H. D.   Detection: Propaganda detection and the courts.   In H. D. Lasswell, N. Leites, and associates (ed.), *Language of politics: Studies in quantitative semantics*.   New York: George Stewart, Inc., 1949, pp. 173-232.

Lasswell, H. D.   *Propaganda technique in the world war*.   New York: A. A. Knopf, Inc., 1927.

Lasswell, H. D. and Blumenstock, Dorothy.   *World revolutionary propaganda: A Chicago study*.   New York: A. A. Knopf, Inc., 1939.

Lasswell, H. D., Leites, N., and associates.   *Language of politics: Studies in quantitative semantics*.   New York: George Stewart, Inc., 1949.

Lasswell, H. D., Lerner, D., and Pool, I. de S.   *The comparative study of symbols*.   Stanford, Calif.: Stanford University Press, 1962.

Lasswell, H. D. and Namenwirth, J. Z.   Changing values in American party platforms: A preliminary study.   New Haven, Conn.: Yale University: 1966, mimeo.

Lazarsfeld, P. F., Berelson, B., and Gaudet, Hazel.   *The people's choice: How the voter makes up his mind in a presidential campaign*.   New York: Duell, Sloan and Pearce, 1944.

Lee, A. McC.   *How to understand propaganda*.   New York: Rinehart Co., 1952.

Leites, N. D.   Interaction: The Third International on its change of policy.   In H. D. Lasswell, N. Leites, and associates (eds.), *The language of politics: Studies in quantitative semantics*.   New York: George W. Stewart, Inc., 1949, pp. 298-333.

Leites, N. and Pool, I. de S.   Interaction: The response of communist propaganda to frustration.   In H. D. Lasswell, N. Leites, and associates (eds.), *Language of politics: Studies in quantitative semantics*.   New York: George W. Stewart, Inc., 1949, pp. 334-381.

Lewin, H. S.   Hitler youth and the Boy Scouts of America: A comparison of aims.   *Human Relations*, 1947, 1, 206-227.

Lewis, H. L.   The Cuban revolt story: AP, UPI and 3 papers.   *Journalism Quarterly*, 1960, 37, 573-578, 646.

Markham, J. W. and Stempel, G. H., III.   Analysis of techniques in measuring press performance. *Journalism Quarterly*, 1957, 34, 187-190.

Matthews, B. C.   A study of a New York daily.   *Independent*, 1910, 68, 82-86.

McClelland, D. C.   *The achieving society*.   Princeton, N.J.: Van Nostrand & Co., 1961.

McClelland, D. C.   The use of measures of human motivation in the study of society.   In J. W. Atkinson (eds.), *Motives in fantasy, action and society*.   Princeton, N.J.: Van Nostrand & Co., 1958, pp. 518-552.

McClelland, D. C. and Friedman, G. A. A cross-cultural study of the relationship between child-rearing practices and achievement motivation appearing in folk tales. In G. E. Swanson, T. M. Newcomb, and E. L. Hartley (eds.), *Readings in social psychology* (2nd ed.). New York: Henry Holt and Co., 1952, pp. 243-249.

McEvoy, J. Letters from the Right: Content analysis of a letter writing campaign. Ann Arbor, Mich.: Institute for Social Research, 1966.

McGranahan, D. V. and Wayne, I. German and American traits reflected in popular drama. *Human Relations,* 1948, 1, 429-455.

Mendenhall, T. C. The characteristic curves of composition. Science, 1887, 9, 237-246.

Merton, R. K. *Mass persuasion: The social psychology of a war bond drive.* New York and London: Harper & Brothers, 1946.

Morton, A. Q. A computer challenges the church. *The Observer,* Nov. 3, 1963.

Mosteller, F. and Wallace, D. L. *Inference and disputed authorship: The Federalist.* Reading, Mass.: Addison-Wesley, 1964.

Nixon, R. B. and Jones, R. R. The content of non-competitive newspapers. *Journalism Quarterly,* 1956, 33, 299-314.

North, R. C., Holsti, O. R., and Brody, R. A. Preception and action in the study of international relations: The 1914 crisis. In J. D. Singer (ed.), *Quantitative international policis: Insights and evidence.* New York: The Free Press, 1968.

Osgood, C. E. The representational model and relevant research methods. In I. de S. Pool (ed.), *Trends in content analysis,* Urbana, Ill.: University of Illinois Press, 1959, pp. 33-88.

Osgood, C. E. Studies on the generality of affective meaning systems. *American Psychologist,* 1962, 17, 10-28.

Paisley, W. J. Identifying the unknown communicator in painting, literature and music: The significance of minor encoding habits. *The Journal of Communication,* 1964, 14, 219-237.

Parrish, S. M. (ed.). *A concordance to the poems of Matthew Arnold.* Ithaca, N.Y.: Cornell University Press, 1959.

Peterson, R. L. and Brewer, T. L. *The Lasswell value dictionary.* New Haven, Conn.: Yale University: mimeo., n.d.

Pool, I. de S. *The "prestige papers," a survey of their editorials.* Stanford, Calif.: Stanford University Press, 1952a.

Pool, I. de S. *Symbols of democracy.* Stanford, Calif.: Stanford University Press, 1952b.

Pool, I. de S. *Symbols of internationalism.* Stanford, Calif.: Stanford University Press, 1951.

Pool, I. de S. (ed.). *Trends in content analysis.* Urbana, Ill.: University of Illinois Press, 1959.

Prothro, J. W. Verbal shifts in the American presidency: A content analysis. *American Political Science Review,* 1956, 50, 726-739.

Royal Commission on the Press 1947-1949, Report, Appendix VII. London: His Majesty's Stationery Office, 1949.

Runion, H. L. An objective study of the speech style of Woodrow Wilson. *Speech Monographs,* 1936, 3, 75-94.

Russell, J. T. and Wright, Q. National attitudes on the Far Eastern controversy. *American Political Science Review,* 1933, 27, 555-576.

Schramm, W. (ed.). *One Day in the World's Press.* Stanford, Calif.: Stanford University Press, 1959.

Schneidman, E. S. Plan 11. The logic of politics. In L. Arons and M. A. May (eds.), *Television and human behavior.* New York: Appleton-Century-Crofts, 1963, pp. 177-199.

Schneidman, E. S. A psychological analysis of politcal thinking: The Kennedy-Nixon "Great Debates" and the Kennedy-Khrushchev "Grim Debates." Cambridge, Mass.: Harvard University, 1961, mimeo.

Sebald, H. Studying national character through comparative content analysis. *Social Forces,* 1961-1962, 40, 318-322.

Sebeok, T. A. and Zeps, V. J. Computer research in psycholinguistics: Toward an analysis of poetic language. *Behavioral Science,* 1961, 6, 365-369.

Smith, M. S., Stone, P. J., and Glenn, Evelyn. A content analysis of twenty presidential nomination acceptance speeches. Department of Social Relations, Harvard University, February 1965, mimeo.

Speed, J. G. Do newspapers now give the news? *The Forum,* 1893, 15, 705-711.

Starkweather, J. A. and Decker, J. B. Computer analysis of interview content. *Psychological Reports,* 1964, 15, 875-882.

Stempel, G. H., III. The prestige press covers the 1960 presidential campaign. *Journalism Quarterly,* 1961, 38, 157-163.

Stone, P. J. An introduction to the General Inquirer: A computer system for the study of spoken or written material. Harvard University and The Simulmatics Corp., 1964, mimeo.

Stone, P. J. and associates. *The General Inquirer: A computer approach to content analysis in the behavioral sciences.* Cambridge, Mass.: M. I. T. Press, 1966.

Stone, P. J., Bales, R. F., Namenwirth, J. Z., and Ogilvie, D. M. The General Inquirer: A computer system for content analysis and retrieval based on the sentence as a unit of information. *Behavioral Science,* 1962, 7, 484-494.

Weinland, R. G. Methodological problems involved in quantitative content analysis of open Soviet military and political literature. Stanford, Calif., December 1966, mimeo. Prepared under Navy Contract No. N123(60530)51666A.

White, R. K. *Black-Boy:* A value-analysis. *Journal of Abnormal and Social Psychology*, 1947, 42, 440-461.

White, R. K. Hitler, Roosevelt and the nature of war propaganda. *Journal of Abnormal and Social Psychology*, 1949, 44, 157-174.

Whiting, A.S. *China crosses the Yalu.* New York: The Macmillan Co., 1960.

Wilcox, W. The press of the radical right: An exploratory analysis. *Journalism Quarterly*, 1962, 39, 152-160.

Willoughby, W. F. Are two competing dailies necessarily better than one? *Journalism Quarterly*, 1955, 32, 197-204.

Wolfenstein, Martha and Leites, N. *Movies: A psychological study.* Glencoe, Ill.: The Free Press, 1950.

Wright, Q. and Nelson, C. J. American attitudes toward Japan and China. *Public Opinion Quarterly*, 1939, 3, 46-62.

Yakobson, S. and Lasswell, H. D. Trend: May Day slogans in Soviet Russia. H. D. Lasswell, N. Leites, and associates (eds.), *Language of politics; Studies in quantitative semantics.* New York: George W. Stewart, Inc., 1949, pp. 232-297.

Yule, G. U. *The statistical study of literary vocabulary.* London: Cambridge University Press, 1944.

Zaninovich, M. G. An empirical theory of state response: The Sino-Soviet case. Unpublished doctor's dissertation, Stanford University, 1964.

Zinnes, Dina A., North, R. C., and Koch, H. E., Jr. Capability, threat and the outbreak of war. In J. N. Rosenau (ed.), *International politics and foreign policy.* New York: Free Press, 1961, pp. 469-482.

Chapter 8

INTERNATIONAL PATTERN AND NATION PROFILE DELINEATION[1]

R. J. Rummel

When I was asked whether I would like to make a presentation to a conference of this type, I was more than happy to say yes. The interests and backgrounds of the participants at this conference challenge me to communicate to a wide academic and policy audience a momentous revolution that is going on in research on international relations. The computer, in conjunction with a number of other elements, has substantially enabled us to move in this area. Studies that have been completed and that reflect this movement have only now begun to appear. These, in conjunction with those yet to be concluded or published, will in their entirety place into question much of the folklore of the field and its established methodologies.

THE RESEARCH REVOLUTION

This research revolution in international relations is a resultant of developments over the last decade in data, methodology, computer technology training, and funding. Since World War II there has been an increasing flood of published data on the social, political, and economic attributes of nations and their relations with each other. Sources such as *The Statistical Yearbook, Demographic Yearbook, Directions of International Trade, Yearbook of National Account Statistics,* to mention

[1]Prepared in connection with research supported by the National Science Foundation under Grant No. GS-1230.

only a few of the many annual United Nations statistical series, present data on thousands of aspects of all nations. Outside of the data pouring from official international sources, numerous individual publications — like Russett *et al.* (1964), *World Handbook of Political and Social Indicators;* Studensky (1961),*Income of Nations;* Woytinsky and Woytinsky (1955), *World Commerce and Government;* and the *Worldmark Encyclopedia of Nations* (1964) — have contributed to what is turning out to be an embarrassment of data riches. Concomitantly, there has been a growth in "soft" data sources to contribute to this wealth. I have in mind such event data sources as *Facts on File, Deadline Data on World Affairs, The Annual Register of World Events;* such data on international institutions as the *United Nations Yearbook* and *Yearbook of International Organizations;* such sample survey data on national and international opinions and attitudes available to researchers through data archives like the University of Michigan Political Data Consortium; and such data as found in the burgeoning descriptive literature on international institutions, law, and politics.

Along with this growth of data available to the student of international relations, there has been a development of research methodologies. Data generation techniques like content analysis have become increasingly sophisticated with the aid of such studies as Osgood's *Measurement of Meaning* and increasingly automated through the computer by developments such as the *General Inquirer Program* of Phillip Stone and colleagues (1962). With the aid of methodological studies discussing the selection of samples, the prerequisites of good questionnaire of polling items, and the analysis of results, and with the examples of numerous published applications, national attitudinal and opinion surveys are becoming quite rigorous.

As we have grown more sophisticated in data generation techniques, our understanding of data measurement has also increased. Knowledge of what measurement entails[2] enables the researcher to exploit the abundance of hard or soft data by coding it for mathematical and statistical analysis, as well as computer storage and retrieval. Indeed, the development of sophistication in measurement has turned the traditional qualitative distinctions of students of the field, such as nationalism, international

---

[2] At its simplest, measurement involves the assignment of numbers to data such that the arithmetical relationships between the numbers *assumed by the method of analysis* reflects the relationship between the data. For example, U. N. membership can be measured as 0 = not a member and 1 = member. This is a measurement of U.N. data allowing us to apply techniques that require only that one number consistently measure the presence of something (U.N. membership) and the other number measure the absence.

organizations, law, and imperialism, into measured data capable of computer analysis.[3]

Mathematical and statistical developments have increased the ability of students of international relations to handle large numbers of variables, disentangle complex interrelationships, and cope with the qualitative data that often relate to the most important substantive interests of the field. While extending the range and versatility of data analysis, these developments have also drawn together the *analytic* field of mathematics and the *empirical techniques* applied to data. This has extended our ability to develop rigorous mathematical or statistical theories of international relations and to test them with techniques consonant with the theory. The developments I have in mind are those enabling the researcher to determine the best equation to predict the national variation in foreign behavior on the basis of a number of independently acting influences (multiple regression), to determine the patterns of interrelationships in the relations of nations or in their attributes (factor analysis), or to determine the pattern similarity of nations in their interactions (multidimensional scaling; dimensional analysis).

Congenial with the greater availability of data and growing methodological sophistication are developments in the computer itself. Technological improvements have again and again increased the speed, data handling, and analysis capacity of the machine. And each generation of improvements have been made available at a phenomenal pace. To have moved in my own data analyses from the now ancient IBM 650 of 1961 through the 709 and 7094 to the new IBM 360 series of 1966, makes the rapidity of this change awesome to me. In spite of this growth, the computer would perhaps have had little effect on academic international relations research in the United States were it not for the concomitant expansion of university computing centers. The ready availability through such computer centers of "potted" computer programs already written and tested for most standard analyses (except for some easy-to-punch instruction cards, the budding computer user only need submit to the machine operators his data along with the "potted" programs — he does not need to know how to operate the computer nor do computer programming), the computer centers' willingness to help users prepare their data, and the accessibility of the computer to researchers and students, placed the university computer

---

[3]I would go so far as to say that if man has carved out a concept for any phenomenon such that he can denote it verbally, then it can be measured and analyzed through the computer. The traditional quantitative-qualitative distinction no longer should imply that these data are necessarily different. Qualitative data are only data that have not (rather than cannot) been coded into quantitative data.

center on a par with the university library in terms of ease of use and accessibility and as an invaluable research facility for the student of international relations.

So far we have discussed data, methodology, and the computer as separate components in the revolution in international relations research. A fourth component is training. Without researchers who are willing and able to exploit newer methodologies through the computer to use our wealth of data, the current developments in research could not have taken place. Much of the systematic research in international relations has been or is being done by researchers who developed their methodological sophistication outside of the traditional international relations or political science curriculum. Spurred on by their concern over the problem of war, psychologists, social psychologists, sociologists, economists, natural scientists, and mathematicians have turned their attention to international relations and in so doing have imported their methodologies and techniques into the field. Perhaps more important for the long range development of international relations research, some students whose undergraduate training was in the more systematic disciplines, have taken their graduate degrees in international relations (usually in political science with international relations as the major subfield), thus marrying methodological training to a formal substantive grounding. A few of these young researchers, such as Hayward Alker and Bruce Russett at Yale University, already have made notable contributions[4] to the field and have been contributors to the revolution of which I speak. As students of such researchers also become trained in both methodology and substance and themselves go on to teach and contribute to our knowledge of international relations, we can anticipate an intensification of the current revolution and an accelerated convergence on some precisely defined laws of international behavior.

Friction retarding a faster development of systematic research on international relations is no longer due to shortage of data, inapplicable methodologies, or inaccessible computers, but rather to a relatively small number of systematically trained researchers. As within-house training and co-optation from other disciplines increases the number of researchers at work, funding of research will become crucial. Grants by public and private agencies have already played a large role in current research. They support the Center for Conflict Resolution and the Institute of Mental Health at the University of Michigan and the Peace Research Institute at Oslo, Norway. Grants also support such international relations oriented projects as the Stanford Studies in Conflict

[4]For example, see the aforementioned Russett, *et al.* (1964) and Alker and Russett (1965).

and Integration,[5] the Yale Political Data Program (Russett, 1966), the Northwestern Simulated International Processes Project under Harold Guetzkow, and the Dimensionality of Nations Project (now at the University of Hawaii). The programs and results from institutes, centers, and projects of this kind have formed much of the substance of the current revolution in the field.

Generous funding enables the full capability of the computer and newer methodologies to be exploited with large arrays of data, collected and processed by research assistants. Computer programmers can be hired to adjust available programs to peculiar needs or to write new programs to reflect the latest methodological developments. Drafts or tables of findings or research bulletins can be prepared and mailed out to other researchers. And most importantly, researchers themselves can be brought together for conferences or consultation. As our trained researchers increase in number, funding of systematic research in international relations will itself have to increase to keep pace with our expanding research capabilities. Although our current research potential in international relations may be decades from a Manhattan Project type capability, newer developments in computers, data, and methodologies will bring ever closer the ability to absorb this kind of funding and produce policy-relevant knowledge of international relations.

ROLE OF THE COMPUTER

Since this is a discussion of computers as they relate to international relations research and policy making, let me focus a little more on the computer by asking the question "What does the computer enable the student of international relations to do better?" High in importance is that it provides the means for the mass data storage and rapid retrieval spoken of by others at this conference and that we need not dwell on here. But having an efficient warehouse for the data answers only part of the research problem. Data must be related to each other, compared and contrasted, and observed from a number of methodological and theoretical perspectives. In brief, they must be analyzed.

One type of analysis is *data screening.* Data can be sorted, frequencies counted, and frequency charts or histograms computed. Descriptive statistics on the data distributions can be easily generated to inform the investigator of the averages, ranges, and extreme values. Although

---

[5] A description of the project, their methodology, and samples of their results are given in North, *et al.* (1963).

elementary, these operations done by hand on large arrays of data can easily undermine the motivation and exhaust the resources normally available to the researcher. Yet, descriptive statistics are fundamental to understanding the character of the data, and this understanding is prerequisite to more advanced analyses that may be done.

Secondly, the computer enables *data comparison.* Tables can be produced that cross-tabulate the data according to selected categories or ranges. The degree and probability of relationships thus discerned can be assessed through various statistical coefficients like the chi square, coefficient of concordance, or phi coefficient. For what can be done in this regard on nations, I refer you to Bank and Textor (1963), *Cross Polity Survey,* whose approximately 1,400 pages consist almost entirely of this sort of computer output.

Rather than cross-tabulate, the researcher may prefer to assess the intercorrelations between the variables — the attributes or behavior of nations being measured — for which the data were collected. Computer programs generally available will give either plots or coefficients of correlation between all possible pairs of variables for which the investigator inputs data. For correlation coefficients the result will be printed out in a table known as a *correlation matrix.* Often correlation programs are so written as to handle variables for which data are missing for some members of the sample — a blessing for students of international relations who must consider nations for which censorship, secrecy, or undeveloped statistical bureaus often means lack of data. The correlations between national attributes given in Russett, *et al.* (1964), pp. 264-287 is an example of computer capability in this regard.

Fourthly, the computer enables *data dependencies* to be assessed. Often the researcher's interest does not end with correlations, but begins there. Using correlations generated by the computer, he may calculate through the computer (using a multiple regression program) how one variable, say the involvement or noninvolvement of nations in war, is dependent on (predicted, explained, or generated by) a group of independent variables, like economic development, size, population density, and political instability. Moreover, the computer program will weight each independent variable in terms of its contribution to accounting for or predicting the dependent variable and will yield an explicit equation relating the variables. This equation may then be used as a summary description of the dependency found and as an explicit formulation to be tested on other sets of data. For this kind of application the study of Deutsch, Bliss, and Eckstein (1962), is a good example. The authors show the dependency of the ratio of trade to GNP of a nation on its level of GNP per capita, size of population, and sovereignty.

Fifthly, the computer empowers *data interdependencies* to be measured. The patterns or clusters of relationships in the data can be determined and the precise profile of each nation on the patterns can be evaluated. For example, if a large number of attributes for nations yields an economic development pattern of interrelationships then the value of nations as to whether they are high, middle, or low in economic development and by how much can be assessed.

By measuring data interdependencies (by use of factor analysis, multi-dimensional scaling, or analysis of variance programs) the computer can distill the data and reduce them to a small set of indicators that retain almost all the information contained in the larger sample. This, of course, the human mind does continually. Our concepts of inter-national relations, such as negotiation, diplomacy, international organiza-tion, war, nationalism, trade, and the like are concepts each embodying a large number of interdependent activities or attributes of nations. Inter-national relations scholars, policy makers, and journalists have mentally sifted through their multifaceted and complex experiences and knowledge consisting of uncountable bits of data to distill these bits into intuitively based concepts of international relations. These concepts presently organize our textbooks in the field. The computer now gives us the capacity to determine and measure these empirical concepts in a more systematic and testable fashion. This capability of the computer will be exemplified in the next section through a number of concrete examples.

And sixthly, the computer enables *simulation* of the international relations system or its components. By building models of international relations, perhaps with parameters based in part on the results of the kinds of empirical computer analysis mentioned above, the student of international relations can investigate the ripple-like effects of con-temporary international processes like the spread of nuclear weapons, the growth in the number of newly independent economically under-developed nations in the United Nations, the increase of functionally oriented international organizations, or the gradual breakdown in the monolithic bipolar political structure of the post-World War II world.

With regard to the six types of analysis mentioned — data screening, comparison, assessing relationships, dependencies, and interdependencies in the data, and simulation — the computer increases the *scope* and *generality* of analysis. The researcher is able to employ a larger number of variables and cases than otherwise possible. Where previously limited to five or six variables on a hundred or so cases, the investigator can now analyze through generally available programs up to around a hundred variables on tens of thousands of cases; some programs can handle over 200 variables with no limit on the number of cases. The computer has thus helped the student of international relations to free himself from the often repeated limit on behavioralism in international relations — that "there are too many variables to contend with."

Regardless of the kind of analysis done, the computer also makes possible complex error analysis. Rather than be at the mercy of error in his data, whether random or biasing type error, the student can employ the computer to gauge the effect of error on his analysis. He can determine whether his results are invariant of error, and if they are not, he can make them invariant by manipulating the data through grouping procedures to squeeze out the reliable information suffusing the data. Error assessment and control techniques that were formerly much too expensive in computing time to consider can now be applied to data and analysis as a matter of course. Thus, another kind of limit on quantitative studies in international relations — that "the data of international relations are too unreliable to use" — is skirted by the computer.

In addition to increasing the scope and generality of international studies and permitting complex error analyses to be done, the computer also enables what I will term as *branching*. Whenever we carry out analysis on data, regardless of the method, we are always faced with the question "What would happen if . . . ?" We are confronted with alternative research designs that reflect different ways of looking at the data and may yield different answers. Moreover, within any given research design there are always a number of minor methodological decisions to make[6] whose character can give a different emphasis to the substantive conclusions or alter them altogether.

With the branching capability of a computer the investigator need no longer be at the mercy of a specific research design and methodological alternatives selected in ignorance of their effect on the results. He can now try the options to see, indeed, what would happen if he did this, or tried that. Branching enables the student of international relations to get to know his data in a very intimate way. It enables him to check out alternative analyses and various possibilities within a research design. And it allows various error checks to be made. In short, branching allows the investigator to play with his data much like the chemist in a laboratory manipulating an unknown compound through various analyses as he strives to understand its ingredients. Through having tried different analyses and having developed a feel — a gestalt — for the nature of the data, the student can arrive at substantive conclusions

[6] Any social scientist delivering a data analysis paper before a conference will usually be reminded by the discussant of his paper or by the audience of the alternative decisions he could have made.

about international relations that are far more reliable in terms of alternative hypotheses than was true several years ago. The one-shot studies that reflect a linear process of data collection, single analysis interpretations of results, and publication are hangovers from pre-computer traditions.

APPLICATIONS

Rather than elaborate any further on what the computer can do in international relations, it might be helpful to lead you through a concrete set of analysis to show you some of what the computer has done. Two sets of analyses have been selected to display (1) the extent to which the computer has been applied to international relations data and the useful-ness of the results, (2) the possible scope and generality of analysis, (3) the ability to analyze separately and together quantitative and qualitative data, (4) error analysis, (5) coding of international relations data, (6) possible research designs, and (7) use of the computer for pattern and profile identification, and grouping of nations on the basis of similar profiles.

Both sets of analyses are from the Dimensionality of Nations Project (DON).[7] Funded since 1962 by the National Science Foundation, DON is attempting to delineate the major patterns of variation in national attributes and behavior and to determine the dependency of inter-national behavior on socio-economic, political, cultural, and geographic distances between nations. The project is divided into two phases. Phase I is concerned with defining the patterns of variation in the attributes of nations and the profile of each nation on these patterns. Displays 1-5 are from this phase and show the regularities found in the 1955 data on 236 characteristics of 82 nations. The purpose of these displays from Phase I of DON is to illustrate the role of computer analysis in reducing a large mass of interrelated data to a small number of basic patterns.

The remaining displays, 6-15, are from Phase II of DON, in which the focus was shifted from national attributes to international behavior. Phase II is concerned with defining the interaction of patterns of nations and socio-economic, political, and geographic distances between nations and explain-ing the patterns. Shown here are the displays of one of the substudies that delineated the major conflict interaction patterns between nations for

---

[7]The project's research design and results as of 1964 are described in Rummel (1966). A proposal updating the description to 1966 is available from the project, Social Science Research Institute, University of Hawaii.

1955. These displays exemplify the intensity of computer analysis possible on what are traditionally considered qualitative data.

DISPLAYS 1-5

Many students unfamiliar with computer analyses have difficulty visualizing the data input to a computer. Accordingly, Display 1 leads off with the matrix (table) format of the data input to the computer for the analyses of 236 cross-national characteristics discussed with respect to Displays 2-4. Each *row* of the table in Display 1 defines an IBM card with the data for the characteristics punched in it. Because there was such a large number of characteristics, more than one card was needed to complete a row. Thus, for Afghanistan, the first card had data punched for characteristics 1-13, the second card for characteristics 14-26, etc., until all 236 characteristics were punched. Similarly, a second set of cards is punched for the second row, Albania, and a third set for Argentina, and so on until 82 sets of data cards for the 82 nations are completed. Then these sets of cards, with each set representing the data for a particular nation, are stacked behind each other in the order of the nations in the table and fed to the computer along with a program deck of cards that instructs the computer as to the computations to be done on these data.

The actual data punched on the cards according to the format of Display 1 need not be in any particular units. Ratio of agricultural workers to economically active workers, for example, can be in percentages or proportions. Population data can be in millions, thousands, or the full values can be punched. For the type of analysis employed to discern patterns of relationships between these characteristics, the computer is instructed to standardize the data to make them comparable regardless of the units in which they are expressed.

Display 2 gives the flow of computer analyses of the data shown in Display 1. The analysis begins with the data and immediately divides into two parts. The main line of analyses represented by steps 2, 3, 4, and 5 is concerned with data screening and transformations. Step 2 is the determination of the data averages, standard deviations (scatter of values around the average), extreme data values (such as the United States for GNP per capita), and the frequency distributions. By inspection of the results and of a statistic (chi square) that measures the departure of the frequency distributions from the ideal, it was determined what data required transformation to bring them into greater uniformity with the mathematical model (i.e., product moment cor-

Characteristics

Display 1. Matrix input to 236 variable cross-national data analysis.

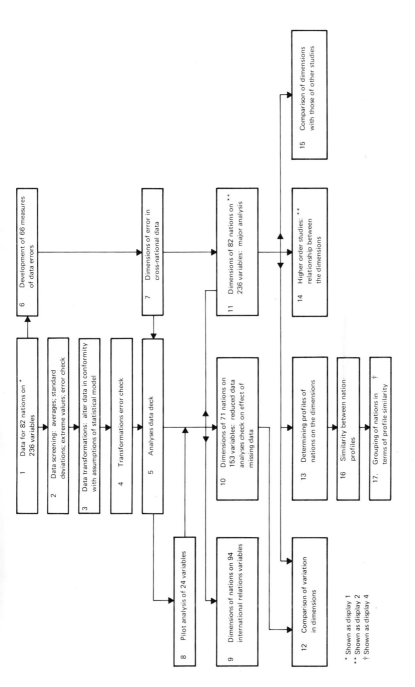

Display 2. Flow diagram of computer analyses of data on 236 cross-national variables.

relation coefficients and factor analysis) to be used in the analysis. The goal of the analysis was to determine general patterns of variation between nations. But a few nations (like the U.S., U.S.S.R., and U.K.) with extremely high values on some variables usually were also high on others. Transformations were therefore necessary to lessen the effect of extreme values on the patterns found and to increase the variation among those nations that would otherwise be lumped together with small values. With correlated extreme values and the highly skew distributions that were found, analysis would yield results that only contrasted the variation between two groups of nations: The U.S., U.S.S.R., and U.K. (and perhaps France) *versus* all other nations. The transformation had the effect of lessening this large, rich nation dominance, and making the patterns of variation among nations more general to all the 82 nations included.

Beside giving information needed for the transformation of the data, step 2 also checked for extreme data collection or punching errors.[8] Since all nations for each variable having extreme values were ranked and listed in the output, inspection of this list enabled us to spot oddities, such as Yugoslavia having the largest national area or Saudi Arabia the third greatest density. By checking such oddities against published data sources we were able to eliminate those errors whose magnitude could distort the analysis.

Step 3 was the computation of the transformations. Although given here as one step, it involved an iteration between the computer and our assessment of the adequacy of the transformation. Data would be transformed, then descriptive statistics on the transformed data would be computed and compared with that on the raw data and with what was desirable. Then the cycle of transformation, descriptive statistics, and comparison would be repeated until the best possible transformation to lessen extreme values and change the data distribution (to normalize it) was found. When the most desirable transformations were thus determined the data were transformed and punched onto a new deck of cards by the computer.

Step 4 was the error check for the previous step. The preparation of the punched transformed data deck of step 3 could have involved clerical error in the input of raw data to the computer, in the specification of the final transformation to be punched, or in the order of the punched transformed data on the cards. A check of the process was made by

---

[8] Although the data had already been punched twice to minimize punching error, some errors were still found during data screening.

calculating descriptive statistics on the punched transformed data using a computer program different from that involved in step 2 or 3. These descriptive statistics were then compared with those of the correct transformation computed at step 3 or, in the case of no transformation, at step 2. In this fashion several clerical errors were found, corrected, and rechecked. The corrected transformed data deck then became the analysis deck at step 5 to be used in subsequent analyses.

Steps 2-5 prepared the data. The branch (and here at work is the branching capability described in the last section) from step 1 to step 6 on the right of the diagram comprised, on the other hand, the development of error tests for the data. Data on nations are contaminated with random and biasing (values systematically over or under reported) errors resulting from unreliable methods of national data collection (e.g., for population statistics), incomplete national coverage (e.g., infant mortality rates based on data from only the major cities of a nation), use of different definitions of the data on a characteristic (e.g., number of radios), official control of the actual values (e.g., exchange rate) or those reported (e.g., number of riots). As shown in detail elsewhere (Rummel, 1967), in order to gauge the effect of error on the analysis of the cross-national data an error substudy represented by steps 6 and 7 was done. Step 6 involved developing for as many of the characteristics as possible an error measure (index) of the magnitude of error in the datum of a nation on a characteristic (e.g., population). Sixty-six such measures were defined and each nation was coded on them.

These measures were analyzed, in step 7, through the computer to determine the major patterns of error in the data and the best six indicators of these patterns were selected. Codings on these indicators of the major kinds of biasing error in the data were then merged with the analysis deck as shown by the arrow in Display 2 from step 7 to step 5. Subsequently included in the analysis of the cross-national data, these indicators made possible a determination of the dimensions of variation among nations that were independent of or related to these error patterns. This knowledge of the role of error in the results thus disciplined our conclusions.

Once the analysis deck at step 5 was completed for all 236 characteristics, a substudy limited to a small number of variables to test out the adequacy of the research design for the larger analysis was desirable. Accordingly, a pilot analysis of 24 conflict characteristics (e.g., number of riots), including two error measures, was done in step 8. Although I mention this here as though it were a minor part of the overall design, step 8 actually turned out to be my Ph. D. dissertation; since the cross-national conflict patterns found in the pilot study are of interest in their own right, the dissertation is published in its entirety elsewhere (Rummel, 1963).[9]

With the experience gained from the pilot analysis of step 8, it was possible to move directly to the analyses. Three major analyses were done. The first, step 9, analyzed those 94 characteristics, out of the 236, describing the foreign relations of a nation, like trade, aid, number of embassies and legations, and tourists. As reported in Rummel (in press), among the several patterns in the foreign affairs of nations delineated, the primary ones are general participation in the international system, foreign conflict, and foreign aid.

The second major analysis, indicated by step 12 in Display 2, attempted to control for the effects of data missing for some of the 82 nations on some of the 236 characteristics. About 17 per cent of the data was missing in total. This amount is sufficient to influence the results. To determine whether, in fact, the results were affected, those nations and characteristics with the most missing data were removed from the analysis deck. This reduced the data to that on 71 nations for 153 characteristics with about 3 per cent missing values. This reduced analysis deck was analyzed similarly to that of the full 236 variable deck and the patterns found were compared with those emerging from the full analysis of step 11. The comparison, shown in step 12, was done through the computer (using Ahmavaara's transformation analysis[10]) and proved that the major patterns found in step 11 are invariant of missing data effects. As a consequence of the analysis of the reduced deck, we can gauge which patterns are general to the 236 characteristics for 82 nations and independent of the effects of 17 per cent missing data. Step 10 is thus another variant of the controls for error, seen in steps 2, 4, 6, and 7, empowered by the speed and capacity of the computer.

The basic analysis for which the data were collected is shown in step 11. The patterns of variation among nations delineated are given in Display 3 and will be discussed below. Steps 9, 10, and 11 again show the potentiality for branching our research designs. The speed of the computer enabled these analyses to be completed in a matter of hours (the full analysis of step 11 took $3^1/_2$ hours on the now primitive IBM 709), the capacity enabled over 200 variables to be analyzed, and a matter of changing one card of instructions (variable format card) to the computer or removing data on selected nations from the analysis deck enabled the branching to be done.

---

[9]For republications of all or part of these results, see Rummel (1965, 1966b) and Tanter (1966).

[10]For a statement and applied example of this mode of comparison, see Ahmavaara (1957).

With a specification of the patterns of variation among nations given by step 11, the analysis could again branch in three directions as shown by steps 13-15 in Display 2. One of these branches, step 15, is yet again another type of error check. The reliability of the results of step 11 were judged by systematic comparison (using Ahmavaara's transformation analysis) with cross-national patterns of variation determined by others (Cattell, 1949; Catell et al., 1952; Catell and Gorsuch, 1965; Berry, 1961; Schnore, 1961; Russett, 1966) who had analyzed different samples of nations for different years on many similar characteristics. These comparisons indicated that the major patterns of variation among nations found in step 11 were reliable when compared against those found by others. In total, the results of all the error checks of steps 2, 4, 6-7, 10, 12, and 15, the transformations of step 3, and the pilot study of step 8 gave us a feel for the nature of our data and the extent to which we could generalize from the results. We thus gained the ability to answer a large number of questions of the type "Would your results be different because of . . . ?" or "What would happen if you . . . ?"

Step 13, the next branch from the primary analysis of step 11, initiated a set of analyses attempting to define the profiles of nations on the patterns found (step 13), measures of the similarity (distances) between nations in terms of their profiles (step 16), and the similarity grouping of nations on their profiles (step 17). The results of the final steps are shown in Display 4 and will be discussed there. The third branch off the results of the 236 variable analysis of step 11 was the studies (step 14) defining the higher order patterns in the data. These patterns are given in the next display. They and the meaning of "higher order" will be discussed in a moment.

Using the DON research design as a basis, I have hoped to show the scope of analysis possible through the computer as well as the error controls and branching operations that are now conceivable. Display 3 shows in particular the results of the 236 variable analysis and the higher order studies. Within the scope of this paper it is not possible to give the results in detail. Display 3 is an attempt to meaningfully condense as much of the findings into one table as possible.[11] Down the left side of the display the different types of attributes of nations are indicated. The attributes (variables) themselves, organized by type (domain), are given in Appendix I. A moderate or high relationship[12] of any one

[11] The primary findings consist of 15 biquartinium oblique factors rotated from the principal axes solution of a product moment 236 variable correlation matrix with unities in the principal diagonal. The 15 factors account for 76.8 per cent of the variance. All positive eigenvalues were extracted.

[12] This is defined as an oblique factor coefficient equal to or greater than an absolute value of 0.60.

specific type of attribute to the primary dimensions (patterns) of cross-national data, given in ellipses is shown by an X in the appropriate column.   For example, an educational type of attribute (namely, pupils per primary teacher) is related to the economic development pattern, the first pattern at the top.   Accordingly, in the row for the educational type characteristic an X is placed in the column under the pattern.   Similarly, the X in the economic development pattern for the international collaboration type of characteristics (behavior) indicates that some of the collaboration of a nation with others is related to its level of economic development.   The lack of an X, such as for military type characteristics for the economic development pattern, means that those types of characteristics are unrelated to the pattern.   Thus, in the case of military characteristics, the magnitude of economic development of a nation does not correlate with its defense budget, either absolutely or relative to GNP, or with the size of its military forces, either absolutely or relative to population.

The primary dimensions across the top are numbered in terms of their rank position in the amount of cross-national variation in the 236 variables related to them.   Thus, economic development, power bases (size), and political democracy are first, second, and third in importance and together account for (can reproduce) about 40 per cent of the variation in the data.

The patterns are named in this way.   The computer indicates through a listing of coefficients what attributes are linked in a distinct pattern of interrelationship and to what degree.   Taking cognizance of the characteristics (variables) included in and excluded from the pattern as well as those characteristics showing the highest relationship to the pattern, a descriptive label is found by the researcher which best reflects or describes the characteristics forming the pattern.   The "economic development" label was therefore given to the first pattern because so many of the highly interrelated variables linked into the pattern, such as GNP per capita, telephones per capita, vehicles per capita, and proportion of agricultural workers, reflect the economic development of a nation.   For the power bases pattern it was found that almost all the basic indicators of a nation's power capability listed and described in international relations texts, such as population, size, area, national income, resources, and political centralization, were linked into the same pattern of interrelationships. This pattern was therefore labeled "power bases," although because of a high relationship of population and area to the pattern it might be also labeled "size."   Where the nature of the variables linked into a pattern did not readily suggest a label, the pattern was named after the atribute most highly related to it.   This was the case for the tenth pattern (high emigrant to population ratio), for example.

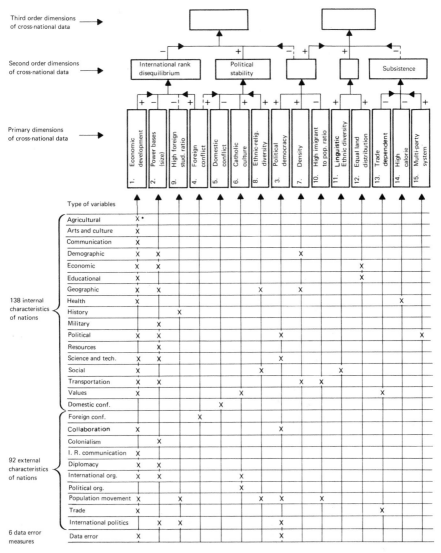

Display 3. Dimensions of variation among nations on 236 cross-national variables.

Although the patterns themselves are distinct, the value of a nation on one pattern, such as economic development, may not be completely unrelated to its value on another pattern, such as foreign conflict. The patterns themselves may be accordingly interrelated in different ways, thus forming into *second order* patterns. In Display 3, the second order patterns (dimensions) of relationships among the primary patterns are shown by arrows drawn from the primary patterns.[13] It can be seen, for example, that economic development, power bases, and foreign conflict form into a second order pattern labeled "international rank disequilibrium." The signs next to the arrows show whether the relationship with the higher order pattern is positive or negative. Thus, for the first second order pattern, nations tending to be high in economic development and low in power capability tend to have more foreign conflict. This is consonant with the rank disequilibrium hypothesis of foreign conflict put forward by Johann Galtung (1964) and this second order pattern was labeled accordingly.

The dotted arrows indicate a small marginal relationship of the primary pattern to the higher order one and those ellipses left blank reflect my inability to think up a satisfactory name. The second order patterns in turn have small interrelationships as shown in Display 3 by the third order patterns (dimensions).

Although the idea of higher order patterns may at first appear strange, the student of politics is accustomed to thinking in terms of them and should, on reflection, have little trouble with the notion here. With regard to the United States Congress, for example, we consider legislative voting on bills to form distinct patterns of voting behavior dependent on whether the bills relate to agricultural, civil rights, welfare, or foreign policy issues. These primary voting patterns themselves are thought to be loosely patterned by the region (South, Middle-West, etc.) of the legislator voting and these second order regional patterns are often considered to be interrelated into one third order pattern: liberal to conservative.

We can hardly cover here the full meaning and implications of the results reflected in Display 3. Suffice to say, the empirical results given there, coming out of half of a day's computer work, test many if not most prevailing theories and hypotheses of international relations and cross-national variation (e.g., correlates of economic development and domestic instability). It is left to the interested student to pose several

---

[13]The higher order patterns were determined by a biquartinium oblique rotation of the principal axis solution of the correlation matrix between the primary oblique factors with unities in the principal diagonal. Factor cutoff was made at eigenvalues greater than unity. Solid arrows in Display 3 represent loadings greater or equal to an absolute value of 0.30. Dotted arrows are those loadings between an absolute value of 0.20 and 0.29.

widely held hypotheses (e.g., a foreign conflict is related to domestic conflict) and to test them against the relationships described in Display 3.

As shown by step 13 of the research design flow diagram given in Display 2, the profile of each nation for each pattern[14] was determined. These profiles describe each nation as to the magnitude of its values across the patterns. Nations also were compared as to their profile similarity[15] and categorized into nine groups of independent profiles.[16] These nine groups are shown in Display 4.

Nations placed in the same group are together because their profiles on the fifteen primary patterns given in Display 3 share more in common with each other than they do with other nations. The coefficient given to the left of each nation measures the correlation of each nation with the group profile. This coefficient can be understood better, perhaps, by squaring it and multiplying by 100. The result is the per cent of variation of a nation's profile common with that of the group. Thus, for Group I, Portugal with a correlation coefficient of 0.50 shares 25 per cent (0.50 squared x 100) of its profile with that of the group. Only nations with group correlations greater than 0.39 are listed. Nations that have unique profiles (that have less than 16 per cent of their profile in common with one of the nine groups) are also shown. Thus, Argentina, France, and Poland, among others, can be seen to have unique profiles, meaning that they have rather odd mixtures of attributes not found elsewhere.

Perhaps one of the more interesting findings from the display is the two member group formed by the U. S. and U. S. S. R. This is an empirical confirmation of the long held suspicion that the U. S. and U. S. S. R. have more in common with each other than does each with any other nation.

Looking at the other groups, one can see some rather startling combinations, as the inclusion of South and North Korea with Netherlands, Belgium, Japan, and West Germany. Such combinations are surprising because we are used to categorizing nations in terms of political systems, economic development, culture, or geographic location. However, these often used grouping categories may not hold up, as is the case here, when

[14] These were the estimated factor scores on the dimensions.

[15] Euclidean distances between nations were computed using their projections, in terms of the estimated factor scores, onto the largest fourteen oblique dimensions. The correlations between the dimensions were also involved in computing the distances.

[16] The distance matrix for nations was directly factored using the principal axis technique and this solution was rotated to a varimax (orthogonal) solution. The distance matrix was first scaled so that distances lay between zero and unity with unity meaning a zero distance. The principal diagonal of the scaled matrix contained all unities. The factor cutoff for the principal axis solution was an eigenvalue of unity.

Groups *

I	II	III	IV	V	VI	VII	VIII	IX
.71 Mexico	.80 Ethiopia	.68 India	.65 Netherlands	.69 Sweden	.71 Switzerland	.63 Costa Rica	.59 Syria	.64 USA
.70 Ecuador	.78 Yemen	.66 Indonesia	.64 Belgium	.65 Norway	.70 Austria	.62 Bolivia	.51 Venezuela	.57 USSR
.69 Honduras	.74 Afghan.	.57 Israel	.58 Japan	.64 N. Zealand	.67 Lebanon	.57 Uruguay	.46 Iraq	
.68 Peru	.73 Albania	.51 Burma	.56 W. Germ.	.59 Australia	.54 Ireland	.52 Chile	.41 Iran	
.67 Guatemala	.71 O. Mongolia	.49 Yugoslavia	.49 S. Korea	.58 Finland	.53 Cambodia	.51 Panama		
.67 Dom. Rep.	.69 Bulgaria	.41 Bolivia	.47 England	.57 Denmark	.48 Turkey	.46 Belgium		
.65 Haiti	.66 S. Arabia	.41 Canada	.44 N. Korea	.49 Greece		.46 Philippines		
.64 Nicaragua	.66 Nepal		.43 Formosa	.48 Libya				
.62 El. Sal.	.62 Rumania		.42 E. Germ.	.40 Liberia				
.61 Brazil	.52 Spain		.42 Italy	.40 Jordan				
.53 Paraguay	.51 Thailand							
.52 Cuba	.49 N. Korea							
.50 Portugal	.48 Paraguay							
.49 Italy	.45 Columbia							
.49 Columbia	.45 Jordan							
.46 Panama	.44 Portugal							
.45 Spain	.41 China							
.40 Ireland								

Nations with no group membership

Argentina
Ceylon
Czechoslovakia
Egypt
France
Hungary
Pakistan
Poland

* These groups are the orthogonally rotated factors of the distances between nations in the space of the largest fourteen dimensions of 236 cross-national variables. Each dimension has equal weight in the results. Only 79 out of the 82 nations involved in the determination of the dimensions could be grouped because of computer program limits.

** Coefficients are the correlation of each nation with the group. The square of this coefficient times 100 gives the per cent of variation of a nation on its characteristics that is in common with the group. These nine groups are independent of each other, i.e., their profiles are uncorrelated.

Display 4. Similarity profile grouping across their major patterns of variation in 236 characteristics.

Group Profile **

I		II		III	
.71	Mexico	.80	Ethiopia	.68	India
.70	Ecuador	.78	Yemen	.66	Indonesia
.69	Honduras	.74	Afghan	.57	Israel
.68	Peru	.73	Albania	.56	U. of S. Africa
.67	Guatemala	.71	O. Mongolia	.51	Burma
.67	Domin. Rep.	.69	Bulgaria	.49	Yugoslavia
.65	Haiti	.66	S. Arabia	.47	Bolivia
.64	Nicaragua	.66	Nepal	.45	Canada

Groups	Central Nation	1. Economic Development	2. Power Bases	3. Political Democracy	4. Foreign Conflict	5. Domestic Conflict	6. Catholic Culture	7. Density	8. Ethnic-relig. Diversity	9. High Foreign Student ratio	10. High Emigrant to Pop. ratio	11. Linguistic-Ethnic Diversity	12. Equal Land Distribution	13. Trade Dependent	14. High Calorie	Short Label
I	Mexico	L*	L/*M	L/*M	L	L/M	H	L/*M	L/M	L/M	L/M	L/M	L/M	M/*H	L/M	Peaceful, poor Catholic nations
II	Ethiopia	L/M	L*	H/*M	L/*M	L*		L/M	L/*M	L/*M	L	L/*M	L/M	L/*M	L/*M	Undeveloped, non-emigrant non-democrat nations
III	India	L				L	L*	L/*M	H/M	L/M	L/M	M				Poor non-Catholic, linguistically & ethnically diverse nations
IV	Netherlands			H*	L*	L	L/*M		M*	L/*M		L/*M	M/*H	M*	M*	Densely populated, internally peaceful nations
V	Sweden	M/*H	L/M	H	L	L	L/M	L/M	L/M	L/M	M/*H	L/*M	L/M	M*	M/*H	Internally peaceful democracies
VI	Switzerland	L/M	L	H	L	L/M	L/M	L/M	M/*H	M/M	L/*M		L/*M	L/M	M/H	Peaceful democracies with low power capability
VII	Costa Rica	L*	L	H		L	H*	L*	M/H							Internally & externally peaceful dem. with low power capability
VIII	Syria	L/M	L			L	L/M	L	L/*M	L	H*	M	H*	H	M/H	Sparsely pop. trade dependent nations with low power cap.
IX	USA	H	H		H	L	L/M	L	M/H	L	L		L	L	M/H	Conflictful economically-developed powers

* For nations only with at least 25% of their variation in common with the group. This is a correlation coefficient of at least .50.

** L = low on dimensions; M = within one standard deviation of the mean; H = high. Blank cells indicate the nations within the group ranged between L and H on the dimension.

Display 5. Descriptions of group profiles.

our basis of categorization is extended to encompass the full range of variation in national attributes. In order to see what profile similarities account for the odd groupings found, Display 5 was prepared.

The major fourteen patterns[17] are given across the top and the distinguishing profile values for each group are displayed. Only when a member of the group shares the same profile values for a pattern is it shown; short labels based on the most distinguishing profile values for a group are given. Thus, because members of Group I are uniformly low in foreign conflict, high in Catholic culture, and low in economic development (for those group members with at least 25 per cent of their profile variation in common with the group), the group is labeled "peaceful, poor Catholic nations." The inclusion of South and North Korea with the Netherlands group can therefore be seen mainly as a consequence of their sharing high population density and little overt domestic conflict. Another apparent anomaly is the categorization of Israel and the Union of South Africa with India and Indonesia in Group III. From the display this can be seen as a result of their all being poor, non-Catholic, linguistically and ethnically diverse.

One of the virtues of Display 5 is that it gives a typology widely grounded in the patterned relationship among the many and diverse internal and external attributes of nations. Such a typology furnishes a set of independent empirical concepts for describing the variation among nations. It indicates the major sources of national variation to be held constant or accounted for in developing a scientific theory of national differences or international behavior and it describes the parameters that should serve as the framework for simulation of international relations.

DISPLAYS 6-15

The following set of displays are selected to demonstrate the kind of computer analysis possible on international relations data that are closer to those with which the policy maker and student traditionally deal. The foreign policy maker is daily confronted with a deluge of bits of apparently unrelated data (facts). The U. S. S. R. threatens Turkey, for example, as Turkey carries on "defensive" military movements against Greece and Cyprus. Simultaneously, the Vietnam and Yemen Wars are going on and military clashes are taking place between Malaysia and Indonesia, and between Israel and her Arab neighbors. Moreover, these events overlayed the daily speckling of international relations with

[17] The loadings of the fifteenth dimension were so low as to be dropped from the determination of the profile grouping of nations.

the boycotts, accusations, diplomatic protests and snubs, attacks on embassies and antiforeign demonstrations, etc. between other nations. The job of the policy maker and student is to discern the patterns — the regularities that exist in these numerous diverse kinds of behavior. A grasp of these patterns gives coherence to discrete events in time and space and enables forecast of where present relations between specific nations are leading. Assessment of current patterns and the anticipation of the course of relations with other nations lies at the basis of foreign policy planning.

The following displays may suggest how the computer can be helpful in this area. They are taken from an analysis of the patterns of conflict behavior between nations and the data are from a coding of all incidents of such conflict behavior reported in *The New York Times* daily edition. Display 6 gives the format of the coding sheet used to collect the data. One conflict act is coded per sheet. These sheets are then punched onto IBM cards according to the card column numbers given at the top of each block in the sheet. "Actor and object" block at the upper left are filled in with the appropriate numerical nation codes. Thus, if the coder reads that Turkey is carrying on military movements with respect to Greece, he codes the "actor" as Turkey and the "object" as Greece; he codes the "date" and other descriptive coding information, and then checks off the block for "warning or defensive act" and the block describing the particular act as "military movements." These data will then be punched into an IBM card that will be filed with other similar collected data. All these data can then be easily sorted, counted, and analyzed through the computer.[18] The code sheet is more fully described in Rummel (1965).

Using the code sheets, foreign conflict data were collected for 1955, frequencies counted, and the totals cast into a data matrix with the format given in Display 7. Each row of this matrix now refers to a directed pair of nations (e.g., Albania's behavior toward Greece) and each column to a specific conflict act. The data in each cell is the frequency of occurrence of the act for the directed pair. For example, if Albania made nine warnings to Greece during 1955, the figure nine would go in the warnings column for Albania → Greece. The punching of this matrix onto IBM cards for analysis proceeded in the same fashion as for the cross-national data of Display 1, except in this case each card referred to data on a directed pair of nations rather than a single nation. The patterns discerned in these data will thus refer to

[18] The kinds of error controls that may be employed for such data are exemplified in Rummel (1963) and Tanter (1966).

FOREIGN CONFLICT DATA CODE SHEET

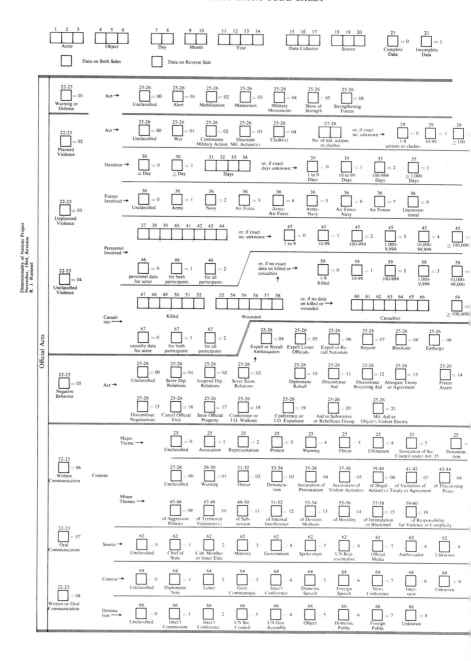

Display 6. Foreign conflict data code sheet
(front side).

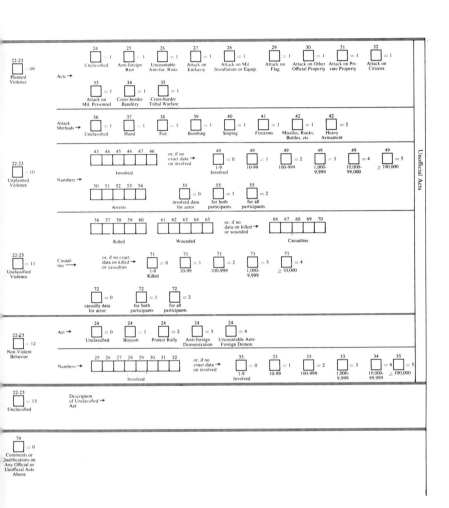

Display 6. (Continued) Foreign conflict data code sheet
(reverse side).

Display 7. Matrix input to sixteen variable raw and transformed dyadic analyses.

between nation behavior rather than to patterns of cross-national behavior as with Display 1. The paired nation format of Display 7 should be kept in mind when assessing the meaning of the subsequent displays.

Display 8 is the flow diagram for the computer runs on the data. The data were analyzed in two ways. First, the matrix of directed pair data shown in Display 7 was analyzed to determine patterns of internation conflict. Secondly, a matrix like that of Display 1 giving the frequency of occurrence of different conflict acts for each nation such as number of threats made by the U. S., U. S. S. R., Egypt, etc. was analyzed to define the patterns of national conflict behavior. The analysis of the directed pair data is called the *dyadic analysis* and that of the nation frequencies is called the *bynation analysis.* The flow diagram parallels that of the 236 variable analysis in some respects. One of the more important departures consisted of the branching at step 2 to two analysis decks, one for the raw data and the other for the transformed. This allowed a comparison to be made of the effect of transformation on the data and gave an answer to the query "Since the raw data represent the way the world really is, aren't you distorting your perception of this world through transforming (i.e., meddling with) the data?"

As shown at steps 7 and 8, a second departure from the 236 variable design was to test alternative data theories: (1) the data reflect the actual distributions of conflict behavior between nations, (2) they are a sample from so-called normal distributions,[19] or (3) that the data are nonadditive.[20] A discussion of the methods by which these tests were done would take us too far afield;[21] they are mentioned to show the extent to which alternative conceptualization can be easily explored through the computer.

[19]This would mean that moderate conflict behavior is the norm between nations while lack of conflict or extremely violent conflicts are rarities.

[20]By nonadditivity is meant here that the scale intervals between units cannot be assumed equal. As a case in point, there may be much more of a conflict jump from nations with no threats between them to those with one than there is from those with five to those with six threats. Yet the scale interval (increment) of one threat is the same in each case. Similarly, the conflict behavior of the nations with no killed between them may be qualitatively different from those with ten killed, and more so than the conflict difference between nations with 3,000 and 3,010 killed.

[21]These tests involved separate factoring and comparison of factors of (1) the tetrachoric correlation coefficients calculated for data alternatively dichotomized at the raw data mean and transformed data mean, of (2) the product moment correlation coefficients of raw and transformed data and of (3) the product moment correlation coefficients of raw data dichotomized into zero and nonzero values.

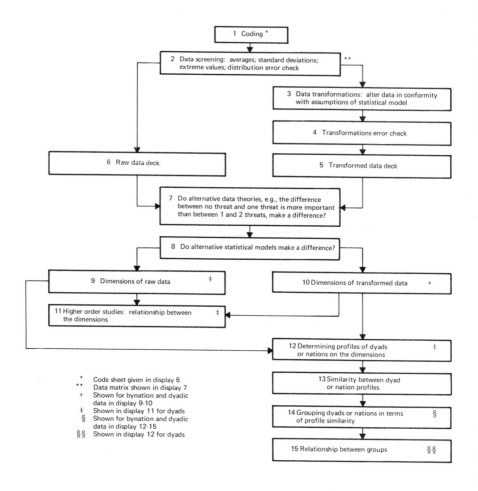

Display 8. Flow diagram of computer runs of data on 1955
foreign conflict for bynation and dyadic analyses.

A final departure from the 236 variable design was to determine, at step 15, the relationship between the groups of nations (dyads in this case) with similar profiles. These will be discussed subsequently.

Display 9 shows the results of analyzing the raw and transformed conflict data decks for the directed pairs of nations.[22] All pairs of nations, 340 in total, manifesting conflict for 1955 are included in the analysis. Down the center of the display are given the sixteen foreign conflict variables formed from frequency counts by code for 2,139 different conflict acts recorded from the NYT.[23] The right side of the display shows the raw data patterns of behavior of dyads (directed pairs of nations) on the variables. The military action pattern (dimension), for example, indicates that the magnitudes of behavior (on the variables) linked into it by arrows generally co-occur for pairs of nations. At a higher level of generality, the second order patterns disclose that the military violence and negative communication patterns are related.

The transformed data results are given on the left side of the display. The data transformations were made to reduce high magnitudes of conflict behavior and to give more weight to the occurrence of conflict, and less to its magnitude. The transformed data results therefore show more of the pattern of conflict behavior *incidence* on the variables than the raw data patterns. The difference can be significant. One may, for instance, find little correlation between the observed magnitude of thunder and that of lightning. Transforming the data as has been done for conflict, however, would show (and as we know, meaningfully) a pattern of incidence in the occurrence of both.[24]

[22]The patterns represent the primary pattern factors of a biquartinium oblique rotation of a principal axis solution. The product moment correlation matrix was factored with squared multiple correlation coefficients in the principal diagonal. The number of factors extracted was based on the number of eigenvalues greater than unity of the correlation matrix with unities in the diagonal. The higher order patterns were similarly determined.

[23]By no means of rationalization can I assume that these data represent a complete census of conflict acts during 1955. They represent the *New York Times* world and the patterns formed in the data described this particular world. Although error controls previously used suggest these patterns mirror those found in reality, the point to be made here is that if we can get such results from one newspaper's data, then consider the importance of a similar analysis on the much more complete data on conflict behavior filed (buried?) in foreign ministries and intelligence agencies.

[24]Perhaps another analogy might be helpful. Consider the plight of a being from another planet trying to make sense of the phenomena he observes on earth. Let him be especially concerned with the relationship between the movement of four wheeled machines (automobiles) and the existence within them of odd looking bipeds (people). Now, one technique he can use is to assess the correlation between the number of bipeds in the machine and the speed of its movement. This would probably yield him a very low correlation and suggest the conclusion (if the alien

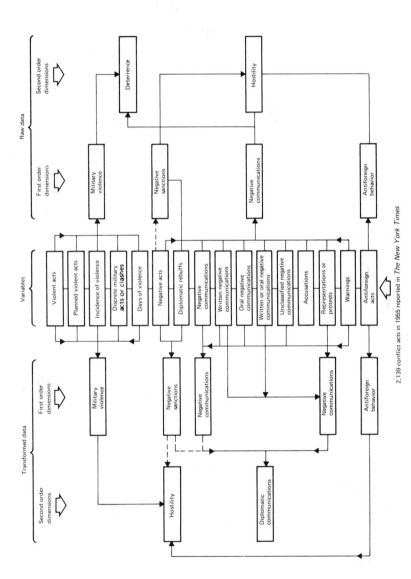

2,139 conflict acts in 1955 reported in *The New York Times*

Display 9. Dyadic conflict dimensions (for 340 dyads).

It may be recalled from the discussion of the results for the 236 characteristics that the label given to a pattern is dependent upon the variables linked into the pattern. The naming of the patterns in Display 9 is assigned on the same basis. The "military violence pattern," for example, is labeled that because it delineates the interrelationship between military acts of violence. The covariation between these acts (as indicated by their forming this common pattern) is distinct from that represented by the other patterns, such as the "negative communication" one.

Note that conflict behavior involves several patterns. Even at the higher order, there are still two patterns of conflict behavior. This implies that conflict behavior *between* nations is not unidimensional — one continuum of behavior — as is often supposed, but maybe two, four, or five dimensional depending on the level of generality and whether magnitudes of behavior (raw data) or incidence of behavior (transformed data) is of concern.

Although the temptation to dwell on these results is great, let us move on to Display 10. This reveals the patterns of behavior on 26 foreign conflict variables for nations rather than for dyads. More variables could be analyzed for nations because of the larger frequency of occurrence of some acts when the total behavior of a nation is considered rather than its behavior towards a particular nation. For example, although a nation may make twenty protests, they may be directed at twenty nations. As a rule of thumb only that behavior occurring for 10 per cent or more nations or dyads was analyzed. This avoided having the results come out overly specific to a few incidents or actors.

Only one of the many interesting aspects of Display 10 will be mentioned before we move on. Note that the multipatterning of conflict behavior of dyads is consistent with the patterns found for the raw bynation data. However, when we transform the bynation data we find at the second order, in contrast to the dyadic analysis, that conflict *is* unidimensional. Even at the level of the primary patterns for the transformed data, the 26 kinds of conflict behavior reduce to two patterns: official conflict behavior and antiforeign (or private) behavior. This is a considerable reduction of information by the computer to a small number of discrete

---

[24] (cont.)
were hasty) that bipeds and the movement of machines were independent. Another approach, however, would be to deal through data transformation with contingency and assess the correlation between the presense or absence of the machines' movement and the existence or nonexistence of bipeds in the machine. His results would show almost a perfect correlation and lead to the correct conclusion that the two are intimately linked.

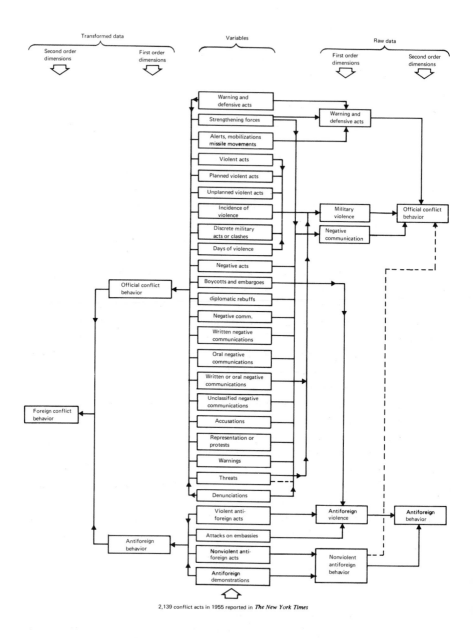

Display 10. Bynation conflict dimensions (for 82 nations).

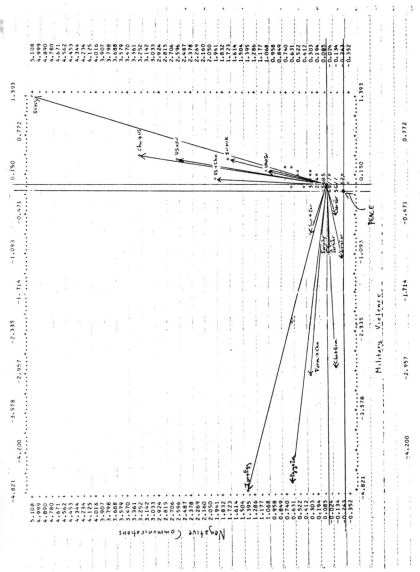

Display 11. Plot of dyads on military violence and
negative communication dimension of raw 1955 data.

empirical concepts by which all the variation in the data can be described. For the transformed data these results mean that nations involved in one kind of *official* conflict behavior, such as protests or negative acts, are usually involved in other kinds of *official* conflict behavior. Involved in *antiforeign* behavior is a distinct but overlapping group of nations. There is, however, as evident from the second order combination of official and antiforeign behavior, a tendency for nations with one kind of conflict behavior to manifest the other. There is thus a conflict *syndrome* for nations that encompasses the range of conflict behavior but not its magnitude (as can be seen by the several patterns arising from the raw data). Moreover, as shown by the dyadic results, general conflict behavior is not uniformly directed at the same nations but is diffused among a number of objects.

Again let us move on. These displays are meant to give you a taste of the fruit of the orchard and not to serve a meal. Display 11 is a computer plot of dyads with the most extreme values on two of the raw dyadic patterns. The plot not only displays another use to which the computer can be put, but it also gives a nice picture of the distribution of pairs of nations on the patterns and graphically demonstrates what is meant by the two patterns being distinct. The dyads high[26] on negative communication (the vertical axis) form a spray that is nonoverlapping and quite separate from the spray of dyads high in military violence.

Display 12 groups by profile similarity on the primary raw data patterns of dyadic conflict behavior. The correlations between the groups is also given and the positive or negative direction of correlation is indicated by a plus or minus sign. Thus, the group of conflict behavior profiles represented by U. S. S. R. → U. S., China → U. S., U. S. → China, and U. S. → U. S. S. R. have only a small inverse (negative) similarity to the behavioral profiles of those dyads of Group IV and no relationship to the profiles of dyads in other groups. "Something unto themselves" would therefore be an applicable description of the conflict behavior patterns of the U. S. S. R. → U. S., U. S. → U. S. S. R., and the other pairs in this group.

The underlying conflict profiles of each group are revealed in Display 13. And the group of dyads headed by the behavior of the U. S. S. R. → U. S. now can be seen to consist of high negative communication and negative sanctions and little military violence.

Displays 14 and 15 give analogous tables for the bynation raw data patterns. Like the grouping of nations on the 236 variable patterns, grouping on the bynation patterns of Display 10 is such that the profiles between groups are unrelated.

[26]The coordinants (scale values) for the two dimensions are factor scores.

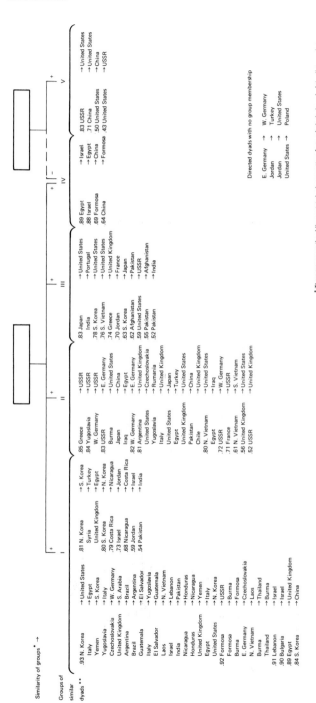

Display 12. Similarity profile grouping of directed dyads data patterns of foreign conflict.

* These groups are the oblique rotated primary pattern factors (principal axes) of the distances between dyads in the space of the raw data dimensions of foreign conflict.

** Only the 75 dyads high on conflict along any one of the violence, negative communication, negative sanctions, or anti-foreign behavior are included. "High" equals a score on a dimension of more than 1.5 standard deviations. The coefficients give the degree of similarity of the dyad's profile to that underlying the group.

Central Dyad	Group	Military Violence	Negative Communication	Negative Sanctions	Antiforeign Behavior
N. Korea → US	I	Some	Some	None	None
Greece → USSR	II	None	None-Some	Some-Many	None
Japan → US	III	None	None-Many	None-Some	Some-Much
Egypt → Israel	IV	Much	Many	Some-Many	None-Some
USSR → US	V	None-Some	Many	Many	None-Much
	VI*	None	Some	None-Some	None

*This group is not shown. It is composed of 258 dyads whose conflict behavior was not significant along any one of the dimensions.

Display 13. Description of group profiles.

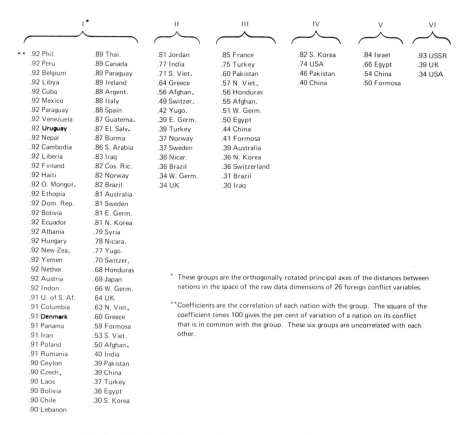

* These groups are the orthogonally rotated principal axes of the distances between nations in the space of the raw data dimensions of 26 foreign conflict variables.

**Coefficients are the correlation of each nation with the group. The square of the coefficient times 100 gives the per cent of variation of a nation on its conflict that is in common with the group. These six groups are uncorrelated with each other.

Display 14. Similarity profile grouping of nations on raw data patterns of foreign conflict behavior.

Group Profiles

Central Nation	Groups	Warning and Defensive Acts	Military Violence	Negative Communication	Antiforeign Violence	Nonviolent Anti-foreign Behavior[1]
Phila.	I	None	None	None	None	None
Jordan	II	None-Some	None-Much	Some-Many	Some-Much	None-Some
France	III	Some-Many	None-Much	None-Many	None-Some	None-Much
S. Korea	IV	None-Many	None-Much	Many	None-Some	Some-Much
Israel	V	Some-Many	Much	Many	None	None-Some
USSR	VI	Some-Many	Some-Much	Many	None-Some	None-Much

Display 15. Description of group profiles.

CONCLUDING REMARKS

The displays that have been discussed were intended to show the kind and of data reduction order discerning value of the computer in studying international relations. Our notions, beliefs, and theories about the behavior of nations are fundamentally based on an intuitive or experimentally derived assessment of cross-national and international patterns. By linking the computer to these patterns in the manner shown here we can connect it to the fundamentals of international politics. With current methodological developments this linkage can take the following forms.

1. The computer can identify patterns in the characteristics and behavior of nations.
2. It can define the crucial characteristics and actions of nations that discriminate between the patterns.
3. It can describe the profile of each nation on these patterns and group nations into distinct groups of similar profiles.
4. It can spot the shift in patterns and in profiles with time.
5. It can determine the crucial indicators related to these shifts in patterns and profiles.
6. It can monitor existing patterns and crucial pattern shift indicators.
7. It can forecast areas of potential conflict and crisis as well as of cooperation and integration and can anticipate shifts in behavioral patterns.

In short, what the computer enables us to do *now* is to build a meteorology-like science of international relations. Much as the meteorologist has developed a knowledge of weather patterns we can define regularities in international relations. Moreover, as he has delineated the crucial weather indicators like temperature, air pressure, and humidity, we can now do the same for international relations (perhaps, and it is a little more than a guess at this point, in terms of threats, mail flows, trade, tourists, and existence and staffing of embassies and legations). And most importantly, as the meterologist can monitor the existing weather and compare this data with his previously acquired knowledge of weather patterns and shifts to forecast the occurrence of storms or pleasant weather, we may also in international relations forecast the occurrence of conflict and cooperation.

The meteorologist deals with large aggregates — with large scale statistical regularity. He is not capable of point predictions of the precise amount of rain to fall on a given field at a particular hour no more than the student of international relations will be able to predict the precise intensity of a conflict in terms of the threats made or the number killed. But like the meteorologist we can now handle national behavior in the aggregate and break it down into its component uniformities.

REFERENCES

1. Ahmavaara, Yrjo. (1957) "On the Unified Factor Theory of Mind," *Annales Akademiae Scientiarum Fennicae,* Serial B, 160 (Helsinki).

2. Alker, Hayward R., Jr. and Bruce M. Russett. (1965) *World Politics in the General Assembly,* New Haven, Conn.: Yale University Press.

3. Banks, Arthur and Robert Textor. (1963) *Cross Policy Survey,* Cambridge, Mass.: M.I.T. Press.

4. Berry, Brian J. L. (1961) "Basic Patterns of Economic Development," in Norton Ginsburg (ed.), Atlas of Economic Development, Chicago: University of Chicago Press, pages 110-119.

5. Cattell, Raymond. (1949) "The Dimensions of Culture Patterns of Factorization of National Characters," *Journal of Abnormal and Social Psychology,* 44, pages 443-469.

6. Cattell, Raymond, H. Bruel, and H. P. Hartman. (1952) "An Attempt at a More Refined Definition of the Cultural Dimensions of Syntality in Modern Nations," *American Sociological Reivew,* 17, pages 408-421.

7. Cattell, Raymond and Richard L. Gorsuch. (1965) "The Definition and Measurement of National Morale and Morality," *The Journal of Social Psychology,* 67, pages 77-96.

8. Deutsch, Karl W., Chester I. Bliss, and Alexander Eckstein. (1962) "Population, Sovereignty, and the Share of Foreign Trade," *Economic Development and Cultural Change,* X, July, pages 353-366.

9. Galtung, Johann. (1964) "A Structured Theory of Aggression," *Journal of Peace Research,* 2, pages 15-38.

10. North, Robert C., Ole R. Holsti, M. George Zaninovich, and Dina A. Zinnes. (1963) *Content Analysis,* Evanston, Illinois: Northwestern University Press.

11. Osgood, Charles E., G. J. Suci, and B. H. Tannenbaum. (1957) *Measurement of Meaning,* Urbana, Illinois: University of Illinois Press.

12. Rummel, R. J. (1965) "A Field Theory of Social Action with Application to Conflict within Nations," *Yearbook of the Society for General Systems,* X, pages 183-211.

13. _____. (1966a) "The Dimensionality of Nations Project," *in* Richard Merritt and Stein Rokkan (eds.), *Comparing Nations,* New Haven, Conn.: Yale University Press, pages 109-129.

14. _____. (1966b) "The Dimensions of Conflict Behavior Within Nations 1946-1959," *Journal of Conflict Resolution,* March, pages 65-73.

15. _____. (in press) "Patterns of Foreign Relations in the Mid-1950's," *Journal of Peace Research,* 4 (title of article is tentative).

16. _____. (1965) "A Foreign Conflict Code Sheet," *World Politics,* December, pages 283-296.

17. Russett, Bruce M. (1968) "Delineating International Regions," *in* J. David Singer (ed.), *Quantitative International Politics.*

18. _____. (1966) "The Yale Political Data Program: Experience and Prospects," *in* Richard Merritt and Stein Rokkan (eds.), *Comparing Nations,* New Haven, Conn.: Yale University Press.

19. Russett, Bruce M. with Hayward R. Alker, Jr., Karl Deutsch, and Harold Lasswell. (1964) *World Handbook of Social and Political Indicators,* New Haven, Conn.: Yale University Press.

20. Schnore, L. F. (1961) "The Statistical Measurement of Urbanization and Economic Development," *Land Economics,* 37, pages 229-245.

21. Stone, Phillip J. and Robert F. Bales, J. Zvi Namenwirth, and Daniel M. Ogilvie. (1962) "The General Inquirer: A Computer System for Content Analysis and Retrieval Based on the Sentence as a Unit of Information," *Behavioral Science,* 7, pages 484-494.

22. Studensky, Paul. (1961) *The Income of Nations,* New York: New York University Press.

23. Tanter, Raymond. (1966) "Dimentions of Conflict Behavior Within and Between Nations, 1958-1960," *Journal of Conflict Resolution,* X, March, pages 41-64.

24. Woytinsky, W. S., and E. S. Woytinsky. (1955) *World Commerce and Government: Trends and Outlook,* New York: Twentieth Century Fund.

APPENDIX I

List of 236 Nation Characteristics
Involved in the Dimensionality of Nations
Project Cross-National Analysis[27]

---

[27]The primary findings consist of 15 biquartinium oblique factors rotated from the principal axes solution of a product moment 236 variable correlation matrix with unities in the principal diagonal. The 15 factors account for 76.8 per cent of the variance. All positive eigenvalues were extracted.

1. *Agricultural Domain*

    1.   agricultural workers / economically active
    2.   agricultural production / gross national product
    3.   agricultural population / population
    4.   (omitted)

2. *Arts and Cultural Domain*

    5.   motion picture attendance / population
    6.   book titles / population
    7.   library book circulation / population

3. *Communications Domain*

    8.   newspaper circulation / population
    9.   newsprint consumption / population
    10.   illiterates / population 10 years of age or older
    11.   telephones / population
    12.   pieces domestic mail / population
    13.   radio receivers / population

4. *Demographic Domain*

    14.   rate of population increase
    15.   population aged 0-15 / population
    16.   population / arable land
    17.   population / national land area
    18.   population
    19.   births / population
    20.   population in cities of at least 20,000 / population
    21.   primary measure[28]

5. *Economic Domain*

    22.   gross national product
    23.   gross national product / population
    24.   fixed capital formation / gross national product
    25.   manufacturing / gross national product
    26.   public administration and defense / gross national product
    27.   (omitted)
    28.   cost of living index
    29.   (omitted)
    29a. national income
    30.   food expenditure / private expenditure
    31.   per cent increase in national income / per cent increase in population
    32.   economically active / population
    33.   unemployed / economically active
    34.   GINI number (area under Lorenze Curve) for land distribution
    35.   per cent population with 50 per cent of land
    36.   Lorenze Curve slope at 95 per cent of land ownership

6. *Education Domain*

    37.   government education expenditures / government expenditure
    38.   primary school pupils / primary school teachers

[28] An index to the number of large cities and their differential population sizes.

39.   primary school pupils / population aged 5 - 14
40.   secondary and college pupils / population

7.   *Geographical Domain*

41.   national areas
42.   arable national land
43.   arable land / total land area
44.   average temperature
45.   average rainfall
46.   coastline length / square root of area

8.   *Health Domain*

47.   infant deaths / live births
48.   population / physicians
49.   proteins / calories
50.   calories consumed minus calories required[29] / calories required
51.   sugar supplies / population
52.   population / hospital beds
53.   life expectancy at birth
54.   deaths by tuberculosis / population
55.   deaths by typhoid / population
56.   deaths by cancer / population
57.   deaths by heart disease / population
58.   deaths by accident / population

9.   *History Domain*

59.   age of country

10.   *Military Domain*

60.   defense expenditure
61.   defense expenditure / government expenditure
62.   military personnel / population
63.   population x energy production
64.   military personnel

11.   *Political Domain*

65.   freedom of opposition
66.   voting system
67.   political centralization
68.   federalist, unitary
69.   tax revenue from income and wealth / total revenue
70.   customs tax revenue / revenue
71.   press censorship
72.   legality of government change
73.   legitimacy of present government
74.   tenure of last two governments
75.   defense expenditure / gross national product
76.   government expenditure / gross national product
77.   government revenue / government expenditure

[29]Which varies according to the young and old in a population, the climate and the employment.

78.   political parties
78a. political development

12. *Resources Domain*

79.   energy resources potentially available
80.   energy resources potentially available / population

13. *Science and Technology Domain*

81.   book titles published in pure science and applied science / book titles
82.   energy consumption
83.   energy consumption / population
84.   electricity generation
85.   energy production / population
86.   energy production
87.   steel production
88.   value of industrial output / industrial workers
89.   students in science and engineering / college students

14. *Social Domain*

90.   religions
91.   membership of largest religion / population
92.   ethnic groups
93.   membership of largest ethnic group / population
94.   languages
95.   membership of largest language group / population
96.   (omitted)
97.   nationalities
98.   native born / population
99.   negroes / population
100. mongolians / population
101. caucasians / population
102. (omitted)
103. dwellings with running water / dwellings
104. divorces / marriages
105. marriages / population
106. industrial workers / population
107. national holidays

15. *Domain Omitted*

16. *Transportation Domain*

108. road length / national land area
109. railroad length per person to population distance
110. railroad length / national land area
111. railroad length
112. railroad freight / railroad length
113. railroad freight / population
114. vehicles / population
115. vehicles
116. air passenger kilometers / population
117. air passenger kilometers
118. seaborne goods / gross national product
119. seaborne goods

17. *Values Domain*

    120.   religious titles published / book titles
    121.   religious holidays
    122.   Buddhists / population
    123.   Roman Catholics / population
    124.   Protestants / population
    125.   Mohammedans / population
    126.   female students / students
    127.   female workers / economically active
    128.   minimum voting age
    129.   monarchy, or not
    130.   communist party membership / population
    131.   students in law / college students
    132.   desire for achievement
    133.   desire for affiliation
    134.   desire for power
    135.   other-directedness

18. *Domestic Conflict Domain*

    136.   assassinations
    137.   general strikes
    138.   guerrilla warfare
    139.   major government crises
    140.   purges
    141.   riots
    142.   revolutions
    143.   demonstrations
    144.   killed in domestic violence

19. *Foreign Conflict Domain*

    145.   antiforeign demonstrations
    146.   negative sanctions
    147.   protests
    148.   countries with which diplomatic relations severed
    149.   ambassadors expelled or recalled
    150.   diplomatic officials of lesser than ambassador's ranks expelled or recalled
    151.   threats
    152.   military action, or not
    153.   wars
    154.   troop movements
    155.   mobilizations
    156.   accusations
    157.   killed in foreign violence

20. *Collaboration Domain*

    158.   (omitted)
    159.   (omitted)
    160.   economic aid received
    161.   economic aid received / (gross national product^2) per cap
    162.   IFC and IBRD subscription / (gross national product^2) per cap

163. balance of official donations
164. balance of official donations / gold stock
165. contributions to technical assistance received / (gross national product^2) per cap
166. contributions to technical assistance
167. technical assistance received / (gross national product^2) per cap
168. technical assistance received
169. treaties
170. military treaties
171. multilateral treaties
172. military treaties / treaties
173. acceptance of jurisdiction of International Court of Justice

21. *Colonialism Domain*

174. possession of colonies
175. national land area / national and colonial land area
176. national population / national and colonial population
177. national and colonial population

22. *IR Communication Domain*

178. foreign mail
179. foreign mail / population
180. foreign mail sent / foreign mail
181. foreign titles translated / book titles

23. *Diplomatic Domain*

182. embassies and legations in other nations
183. embassies and legations from other nations

24. *International Organization Domain*

184. representatives to United Nations
185. IGO (intergovernmental international organizations) of which a member
186. NGO (private international organizations) of which a member
187. International Organization headquarters in nation
188. arts and culture NGO / NGO
189. UN payment delinquencies / UN assessment
190. UN assessment / total UN assessment
191. Engineering technology and science NGO / NGO
192. law NGO / NGO
193. peace and friendship NGO / NGO
194. religion NGO / NGO
195. medicine NGO / NGO
196. education and youth NGO / NGO

25. *International Politics Domain*

197. bloc prominence
198. bloc membership
199. membership in British Commonwealth

    200.   membership in neutral bloc
    201.   trade with Western bloc / trade with Communist block and Western bloc
    202.   US aid received / USSR and US aid received
    203.   US aid received
    204.   English titles translated / foreign titles translated
    205.   Russian titles translated / foreign titles translated
    206.   English titles translated / Russian and English titles translated
    207.   per cent of votes in agreement minus per cent of votes in opposition to US votes in the UN General Assembly
    208.   per cent of votes in agreement minus per cent of votes in opposition to USSR votes in the UN General Assembly

26. *Political Geography Domain*

    209.   nations contiguous to colonies and national territory
    210.   air distance from US
    211.   air distance from USSR
    212.   air distance from US / air distance from USSR and US

27. *Population Movement Domain*

    213.   immigrants
    214.   immigrants / population
    215.   emigrants / population
    216.   immigrants / migrants
    217.   foreign visitors
    218.   foreign visitors population
    219.   UN technical assistance fellowships received
    220.   UN technical assistance fellowship recipients in country
    221.   foreign college students in country
    222.   foreign college students / college students

28. *Trade Domain*

    223.   trade
    224.   exports
    225.   imports / trade
    226.   exports of raw materials / exports
    227.   balance of payments / gold stock
    228.   exports / gross national product
    229.   leading export / exports
    230.   agricultural exports / exports
    231.   agricultural exports / agricultural trade
    232.   import duties / imports
    233.   balance of investments
    234.   balance of investments / gold stock
    235.   trade / gross national product

29. *Data Error Domain*

    236.   gross national product data error measure
    237.   missing data error measure
    238.   population data error measure
    239.   random normal error measure
    240.   Error Dimension I[30] (demographic data type error)
    241.   Error Dimension

[30]Derived from a factor analyses of 66 error measures.

Chapter 9

SIMULATIONS AND WAR GAMES

N. C. Dalkey

According to popular accounts in the press, computers, simulations, and war games have taken over most of the decision making in the Pentagon. You, of course, are fully aware that it is a long way from a study, such as a war game, to any kind of significant decision. Nevertheless, there is a grain of truth in these accounts, and perhaps a small portent for the future, in the sense that the role of computer simulations and war games in military decisions has expanded by a large factor in the past few years; in fact, it has expanded so fast, that we can almost speak of an explosion. It is difficult to get any numbers in this area because of the rapid growth; but I would say that within the past four years something of the order of two to three hundred major simulations have been built in the military area and the results of studies using them have been passed on to the Pentagon. Some kind of simulation has been constructed in practically any field of military interest, research and development, procurement of weapons, deployment and employment of forces. And the activity is moving into more peripheral fields, such as arms control, crisis management, and the like. Therefore, it is important to get some feeling for just how useful simulations are for these kinds of decisions.

There is no question but that the explosion has resulted mainly from the development of high-speed computers. Both simulation and war gaming have a rather modest history, stretching back well over a hundred years. But it wasn't until the high-speed computer became available that this sudden outburst of activity occurred. There is another background reason, which was there all the time, that has also contributed to the popularity of simulation, and it is that simulation is a way of creating a precise, reproducible model in areas where more traditional kinds of analysis don't seem to work. These are primarily areas concerned with complex systems with intricate and nonlinear interactions, which is precisely the kind of situation you have in military conflict.

The rationale of simulation is quite elementary. If you are concerned with a process that is too complex (or too expensive, or too dangerous) to examine directly, a simple way of proceeding is to build a *simulacrum* and study it. (A simulacrum is something that is similar to the process, which is easier — or less expensive, or less dangerous — to examine). This general notion has very wide applicability. The type of similarity can be physical, as for example, in the case of a model ship in a test basin, or a field exercise of an army. As another way of setting up a form of similarity, you can make use of the role-playing capability of human beings, as for example in political and war games where humans play the role of different nations, of major military commands, and the like. But the kind of simulation that I am concerned with in this article, the one for which computers are applicable, is one in which the similarity is not physical, but is of an abstract sort; that is, the simulacrum is a mathematical or logical model.

The distinction between simulations and more traditional types of mathematical analysis is very fuzzy. There is no good definition for the notion of simulation, and it is not worth a lot of effort to construct one. In general, the difference between simulations and mathematical analyses depend on the degree of *structural* similarity between the model and the process described. In a mathematical analysis the description is in terms of a set of equations, whereas in a simulation, although equations may occur, most of the description will be in terms of a list of procedures for carrying out computations — a flow diagram. In the case of a simulation, the process you are concerned with will be, as it were, mirrored in the model. There will be a one-to-one correspondence between the elements of the model and the elements of the process. Rather than computing the solution of a set of equations, a simulation produces a synthetic history of the process. Beginning with a set of initial conditions, the simulation plays through in time the various kinds of events that would occur. For example, in the case of central nuclear war, a simulation might involve tracing through time the behavior of each individual bomber and missile; whereas a mathematical analysis would describe the conflict by relationships between the number of weapons on each side.

In order to get a simulation into a computer, you have to specify a number of things:

1.   Elements
2.   Attributes
3.   Activities
4.   Plans
5.   Time structure

Elements are the basic entities or things that you are concerned with. In the case of central nuclear war, elements would be things like bombers, missiles, bomber fields, missile sites, targets, interceptors, etc. Elements will normally be specified in the form of a list. In addition you have to define the attributes — the properties or characteristics — of the elements. Thus, bombers have a certain range, speed, load-carrying capacity, etc. Attributes can be attached to the list of elements, or introduced by tables. There are two kinds of attributes, those which are fixed throughout the exercise, and those which are variable. Fixed characteristics are such things as the location of an ICBM site, the fact that a bomber is a B-52, etc. Variable characteristics are items such as the operational status of a bomber, the degree of damage sustained by a target, and the like.

Activities define the kinds of events that can occur during the run — such as bombers taking off from airfields, interceptor missiles attacking missiles, bombs detonating on targets, and the like. Activities will usually be expressed as part of the computation sequence and thus will be computer subroutines.

The next item is one for which there is really no good name in the literature. I have called it "Plans," which is appropriate for many military simulations; other cognate notions are policy, doctrine, strategy. In practically any situation that is of interest to the military, the course of the conflict is determined by decisions — either on-the-spot, or in the form of predetermined plans. This is normally covered up in discussions of the formal structure of simulations, which is unfortunate, because in a sense, this is the heart of the enterprise. Usually, what you are interested in as an operations anslyst is not just trying to get a clear picture of how the world behaves, you are really interested in comparing different kinds of plans or policy and selecting a preferred one. If you were concerned with using simulation as a way of mirroring the world, and were describing a military conflict (or even an industrial process), one of the vital things you would have to include is a representation of the decision processes which steer the course of events. That turns out to be a very difficult thing to do, and, and as a matter of fact, in most military simulations it is simply given up as being too difficult. Rather than having a sub-model of the decision process in the model itself, you have a set of plans, a set of specifications of what is to happen, which is sufficiently complete that it will determine the course of events.

There are various ways in which plans can be input. I won't list all of them. One possibility is to draw up a complete schedule of events for each element. For a central nuclear war, you can create a specification of which bombers are to take off, when, where they are to fly, and what targets they are to hit; similar specifications may be given for missiles. Another way is to introduce what can be called *doctrine,* sometimes called *SOP* (standard operating procedure), which is composed of specific little decision rules — not simulations of decision processes, but rules. For example, instead of specifying where each fighter plane is to go, you can call for a certain fighter-bomber ratio. In the case of military conflict, you have a feature which isn't present in most industrial situations and that is you have to specify plans for at least two sides, for yourself and the enemy. If there are several participants in the conflict, you may have to write down plans for more than two sides.

Finally, you have to say something about how time will be handled. Military conflict has a very intricate time structure, and the role of time can be crucial. Because of the pervasive nature of time, it usually is dealt with in the basic structure of the computer program, i.e., in the master routine. There are two general ways in which you can deal with time. One is called the *interval technique* and the other is called the *event technique.* In the interval technique, you divide time into small slices, usually of equal length, and treat all events that occur during one slice as being roughly simultaneous. The simulation proceeds by starting with a set of initial conditions, which, along with the plans, determines what events will occur during the first time period. The outcomes of those events set up the initial conditions for the next time period, and so the simulation proceeds time period by time period.

In the event technique, the simulation proceeds from one event to the next. In order to achieve this, you must set up beforehand a long list of all the potential events that can occur throughout the conflict. This list of events is determined primarily by the plans, and will usually be constructed by a precompute. The list of potential events has to be continually revised as the simulation proceeds because some events may preclude others, or some occurrences may introduce new events which had not been anticipated. For example, if you have a bomber scheduled to drop a bomb on a given target, but the bomber is shot down by an interceptor before it gets there, then you have to scratch that potential bomb drop. On the other hand, the bomber being shot down may introduce a new nonscheduled event, namely, the detonation of the weapons upon crashing.

Both of these ways of handling time have advantages and disadvantages. The interval technique has the rather big advantage of simplicity. It is easier to program and it is much easier to think through than the event approach. The event technique has the advantage that it enables you to chop time up into a much finer grained sequence than is possible with the interval approach. On the other hand, it has the rather big disadvantage that you spend a lot of time editing the list of potential events. It is possible to employ both, and there have been a number of simulations built in which both have been used. The interval technique is used when more or less routine kinds of events are going on — e.g., if bombers are simply flying across the ocean, nothing critical is involved, so they are simply advanced at regular intervals. When the microstructure of time is significant — e.g., when the bombers are being attacked by local defenses — the event technique comes into play.

One other structural feature of simulation is worth mentioning, namely, the way in which chance is handled. In the simulation of military conflicts, the role of chance is of basic importance. A glance at the names of the basic parameters which describe a military conflict make this clear: CEP (circular error probable), abort rate, warhead reliability, probability of damage. They all involve probabilities. In a very real sense, military conflict is saturated with chance.

Again, there are two major ways in which you can approach this aspect of simulations. One is called the *expected value approach* and the other the *Monte Carlo approach*. As applied to military simulations, both of these are slight misnomers. The expected value approach is not a true expected value computation and the Monte Carlo approach is not a true application of Monte Carlo methods. But the names have become so well established that there is no point in insisting on fine distinctions. In the case of the expected value approach, the simulation is essentially a deterministic one, where the probabilities are considered as fractions. So, for example, if there is a group of bombers flying over enemy territory — say ten bombers to make the illustration simple — and they are attacked by fighters, and there is a probability of a half that a bomber will be shot down, then after the event there will be five bombers still flying and five will be presumed to be shot down. In the case of the Monte Carlo approach, when a chance event of this sort comes up, the outcome will be determined by an actual chance (or pseudo-chance) event. The kind of chance mechanism that's normally used is the computation of a pseudo-random number by the computer. For example, with the ten bombers flying over enemy territory and attacked by fighters, the machine would compute a random number for each of the bombers. The random numbers, say, are selected from the interval between zero and one.

Each of these is compared with one-half. If the random number is less than a half, the bomber is presumed to be shot down, if it is greater than a half, you assume it survives. The outcome of that series of chance events might be that all the planes survived, or that none survived. On the average, if you ran the exercise many times, five of the bombers would survive and five be shot down.

As you might presume, both of these approaches have their advantages and disadvantages. The major advantage of the expected value approach is that it is simple. In addition, it does produce an estimate of the expected outcome. The estimate is usually only an approximation, however, and it is generally very difficult to determine how good an approximation.

With the Monte Carlo approach, all you get with one run of the model is a single sample — one data point out of a vast region of possible outcomes. In order to obtain an estimate of the expected outcome, it is necessary to make a number of runs. If you have the time and can afford these replications, you get as an additional bonus some information concerning the dispersion — how far away from the expected the outcome can lie. The expected value model cannot be used to obtain information concerning dispersion. It cannot tell you anything about how wide a range of outcomes you might get. The expected outcome might look very favorable to you, but there may be a nonnegligible probability that outcomes may occur that are very unfavorable. The Monte Carlo model can be used to investigate dispersion — at a cost.

Another advantage of the Monte Carlo approach is that it enables maintainance of a sense of realism in the synthetic history. In an expected value model, probabilistic events concerning single objects suffer a distortion. To continue the previous example, if there is a lone bomber flying over enemy territory, and it is attacked with a probability of fifty per cent of being shot down, in the expected value computation there would result one-half of a bomber shot down, and one-half still flying. This leads to some strange talk, if, for example you have one-half of a bomber being attacked by one-third of a fighter. There are conceptual problems here as well. It is generally assumed that interactions defined for integral values are valid for fractional values as well, but there is little opportunity to confirm this assumption. The Monte Carlo approach does not lead to problems of this sort.

As with the two approaches to time, it is possible to combine expected value and Monte Carlo computations. Most Monte Carlo models, as a matter of fact, include many computations of the expected value type.

The preceding covers most of the basic features of simulation models. For those who like to think in abstract terms about this sort of thing, you can conceive of a simulation as consisting of, first of all, a state description

S. S consists of the list of elements and their attributes. It is clearly a function of time. The activities and plans determine a transformation T on that state description, which produces a state description for a succeeding time; i. e., we have

$$T \cdot S(t) \rightarrow (t + \Delta)$$
$$T = T(t, S, P)$$
$$P = P(P_1, ..., P_n)$$

The transformation T is a function of time, of the state, and of the plans, where you may have plans for several players. It is this complexity of the transformation T that gives simulation its power.

The reason I present this abstract characterization of a simulation is to say something dull but important. We can give a fairly good abstract description of a simulation, but we don't know anything mathematically interesting about this kind of system. Very generally, in the abstract, a simulation resembles the kind of structure that you have in dynamic programming or in stochastic processes. But the kind of theory that has been worked out for these mathematical systems is not applicable to the more complex simulations. In the case of stochastic processes, most of the theory is concerned with asymptotic behavior, or with steady-state behavior. But military conflict is very far from a steady state. In the case of dynamic programming, no one has conceived of doing a dynamic programming computation on anything as complex as a major military conflict, and in addition, dynamic programming with two-sided processes where concurrently two programs are being devised is in a very elementary state. There has been some theoretical work concerning the theory of sampling for Monte Carlo models, but even this work concerns the simpler forms of models.

The first dull but important point, then, is that we don't know very much about the mathematical characteristics of simulations. Point number two is that we are sadly lacking in the theory of military conflict itself. Let me refer to the article in this volume by Cecil Leith. It was pointed out that all of the theory that was necessary in order to make projections of the behavior of the atmosphere was well known before the turn of the century. The equations of motion in liquids and gases were complete; all that was necessary was to obtain the description of the initial conditions and of the earth's surface, and to set up the equations so that they were computable. We do not have anything that is comparable to hydrodynamics in military matters — we do not have a theory of military conflict. The nearest thing we have to a military theory is the simulations now being constructed. There is quite straightforward sense in which a simulation can be called a theory of the process it attempts to describe. But I am sorry to relate, and this is probably well known to you, that attempts to validate simulations as theories are very few and far between in the area of military conflict. There is a widespread misconception to the effect that all the military analyst has to be concerned with is the accuracy of his inputs — that if the input numbers are firm and well grounded, then the results of the simulation will be correct. That is, of course, far from the truth. The inputs can be as accurate as you please, and yet, if the functional relations in the computer routines are incorrect, you can produce nonsense. We are faced with the unpleasant situation illustrated below:

$$I \to S \Rightarrow 0$$
$$?\ \ \ \ ??\ \ ???$$

where this symbolic rebus indicates inputs into a simulation producing outputs. Particularly for simulations which involve decisions for future forces, the inputs — the characteristics of weapons, size of the threat, circumstances of onset of the conflict, and enemy plans — are highly uncertain. I use a question mark to illustrate this uncertainty. In addition, the simulations themselves have even more drastic uncertainties. That merits two question marks. It seems only reasonable that the output should be qualified by three question marks.

The situation is not quite as hopeless as it might seem to be at first sight for two reasons: one of the basic advantages of simulation over most other forms of analysis is that you can break down a complicated phenomenon into a series of elementary or simple phenomena. So, for example, if you have the computer capacity — and the time and patience — you can break down the flight of a bomber into a large number of elementary activities. Now most of these elementary activities can be studied during peacetime— takeoff and landing, refueling, bomb drop, damages from blast, etc. Thus, by segmenting the process, it is possible to use data acquired during peace- time to validate the submodels, but not all of them. There are some aspects of the situation which clearly are dependent upon wartime conditions.

The second point is that there is often no better alternative. Suppose you don't use simulation because of all those question marks, what do you fall back on? Since there is no theory, you have to rely on what is called judgment, experience, intuition, etc., and in a period of rapid obsolescence of experience such as we are going through, there are obvious drawbacks to this recourse. However, if you think of judgment and experience as consisting of a group of assumptions and beliefs, and these can be made precise enough, then you can formulate them in terms of a simulation, and simulation does have the desirable feature that it is an objective, repeatable model. Thus, it is a way of seeing whether your assumptions are consistent and whether the conclusions that you thought followed from them actually do or not. As a logical structure for making assumptions explicit, and for tracing the consequences of assumptions, simulation can introduce a nonnegligible degree of objectivity into analysis.

Of course, to make anything of this point at all, it is necessary to guard against the rabbit-in-the-hat fallacy. It is possible that one or two assumptions will dominate, and, in fact, fix the conclusions. It is not easy to guard against this fallacy. If the simulation is very complex, it may introduce enough noise so that the relationship between assumptions and conclusions is obscured rather than clarified. In this area, the judgment of the analyst is irreplaceable. Although the best of all possible worlds would be one in which there existed well-verified theories, and complete input data, and in which we could hope to derive very solid conclusions, we are not living in that kind of world as far as military analysis goes.

I have not mentioned one of the standard replies to the issue of uncertainties in inputs, namely the possibility of sensitivity analysis. If the inputs are uncertain, but you have a fairly good grasp of the range over which the numbers can vary, then, in principle, you can replicate the computations over the range of variation, and get some feeling concerning the sensitivity of the conclusions to uncertainties. If you are lucky, the conclusions will not be overly sensitive to some of the uncertainties; if you are unlucky, at least you have a basis for qualifying your conclusions. I hesitate to even mention this point because there is more talk about than implementation of sensitivity analysis. The reason is clear — in any sizeable simulation, the number of parameters easily climbs into the thousands, and the space of possibilities becomes too vast to contemplate exploration.

The point concerning sensitivity analysis leads me to my final negative comment about simulation which is that it is generally a fairly slow, cumbersome, and expensive way of conducting an analysis. For computer simulations there is the sequence of designing the model, programming and coding it for the computer, debugging the program, collecting inputs, running cases, analyzing the results. Almost inevitably there are side excursions. After developing the model and running it a few times, it is probable that you will want to make some changes. For even a modest-sized simulation this sequence requires a sizeable investment in time and effort.

There are a number of developments in computer technology which promise to ameliorate some of the problems here. In particular, advances in man-machine interaction, such as graphic input and output, will speed up the process of building and analyzing the results of simulations. Another advance that is already finding application is the development of specific computer languages for simulations. There is quite a list of such languages — Simscript, Militran, Gasp, GPSS — and the number can be expected to increase rapidly. What these languages do is furnish the analyst who is not an expert in designing simulations with a predetermined structure — a skeleton of a simulation, as it were — into which the analyst can fit the specifics of his problem. The languages include convenient ways to specify elements and attributes, ways to define activities, preprogrammed timing structure which will automatically schedule events, and simple ways of prescribing outputs. Most of the present simulation languages tend to overlook the special significance of plans, a drawback that hopefully will be remedied in some future languages.

While the simulation languages are not convenient for all forms of models, for a very large class of simulations they enable a significant shortening of the time for getting the model onto the machine. It is also the case that the languages are of value to the neophyte in designing his model — i.e., the general form of a simulation embedded in the language acts as a conceptual guide for structuring the problem.

The problem of dealing with the vast range of uncertainties can be helped by using what I call a family of models. It is possible to construct models of the same situation at different levels of aggregation, or different levels of abstraction. The same military conflict can be described in great detail, or very simply with most of the detail suppressed. Highly detailed models have the drawback that running more than a few cases is uneconomical; they have the advantage I mentioned earlier that they can resolve the conflict into many elementary activities for which peacetime information is relevant. Small, abstract models have the advantage that many cases can be examined; they have the disadvantage that we do not have a military theory to guide their construction, or substantiate the results. It is possible to take advantage of the good features of both and to ameliorate the drawbacks of both by building not a single model, but a set of models at different levels of aggregation, where the models can be tied together in various ways. A simple form of such a family is the hierarchy illustrated in Figure 1. In this simple hierarchy, the highly aggregated model can be employed to survey a wide range of possible plans, and to conduct sensitivity analyses on the relatively few parameters involved. The intermediate model can be used to check the rough feasibility of those cases that appear interesting from runs of the small model, and to unpack the results for use by the detailed model. The detailed model can then be employed to test the operational feasibility of plans and check the outcomes predicted by the more abstract models. With this kind of scheme, you can begin to think in terms of possibly using the small model to look for optimal or preferred policies and then using the more detailed models to check out these preferred strategies.

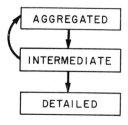

Figure 1

We have built such a family of models at RAND in the central nuclear war area. The aggregated model is a small, two-sided war game that will run on an IBM 7044 in about one-fiftieth of a second. At that speed it is feasible to survey literally hundreds of thousands of simulated nuclear wars. If, on the basis of such a rapid survey, it looks like certain strategic attack plans on our part are interesting, then we have an intermediate model which requires about a tenth of a minute to run, and it is feasible to investigate several hundreds of the more interesting cases at that level. Finally, we have a very detailed model that we almost never run, which requires four hours for a single case; and which can be used for a final proving out.

Considering the rapid advances that are occurring in man-machine interaction, simulation languages, and model structures such as the family of models, it appears fairly certain that the application of simulation to military conflict is going to continue to accelerate over the next several years.

REFERENCES

1.   G. A. Bekey, D. L. Gerlough, "Simulation," Chap. 32 of *Systems Engineering Handbook,* Robert E. Machol, ed., McGraw-Hill, New York, 1965.

2.   N. C. Dalkey, *Families of Models,* The RAND Corporation P-3198, August 1965.

3.   S. H. Hollingdale, ed., *Digital Simulation,* Claud Gill Books Ltd., London, 1966.

4.   E. S. Quade and W. I. Boucher, eds., *The Role of Analysis in Defense Planning,* The RAND Corporation R-439-PR (abridged), August 1965.

5.   R. D. Tocher, "The State of the Art of Simulation — A Survey," *Proceedings of Fourth IFORS Conference,* Boston, 1966, Session H-1.

Chapter 10

NUMERICAL SIMULATION OF THE EARTH'S ATMOSPHERE

Cecil E. Leith

The problem of predicting the behavior of the earth's atmosphere, I suppose, is one of the oldest scientific problems that man has been faced with, because it is such a familiar problem. Aristotle was worried about the question of how to predict the weather, and wrote a book on the subject. It is a problem which, as most of us realize, has not been well solved yet. The behavior of the earth's atmosphere is so complicated that it is very difficult to make any decent predictions as to what is going to happen in a few days' time. It is a subject which technological advances throughout the centuries have always seemed to help in some way or other, and the most recent of the important technological advances which is having something of an impact on this problem of the behavior of the earth's atmosphere is the development of high-speed computers.

An interesting aspect of the behavior of the atmosphere, is that it is really in some ways very simple in detail. It is only as a combination of the whole system that it becomes so complex that it is very hard to predict what is going to happen. What I am saying, is that since the end of the last century the problem of the way the states of the atmosphere should evolve in time has been considered a purely computational problem. During the last century mathematical physicists became well aware of the fundamental laws governing fluid flow and hydrodynamic motions, and it was felt, and is still felt that the atmosphere is, after all, nothing but a very complicated example of hydrodynamics or aerodynamics. In fact, the first effort to make such a calculation of the behavior of the atmosphere by numerical techniques was started by a

215

British mathematical physicist named Richardson in 1911. He did not have access to the computing facilities now available and set this calculation up as a hand calculation. He divided the atmosphere of England and part of Europe into boxes, zoning it or dividing it into a mesh, a familiar technique in calculations of this sort now, and starting with the best information that he had at the particular time on a particular day for values of wind velocity components, temperature and moisture, and so on, he proceeded to carry out a single time step of a calculational cycle to advance all of these quantities to a time three hours later. Three hours later doesn't seem to be much in the way of making a prediction of the behavior of the atmosphere, especially since it took him several years to do it. Evidently, this was to have no immediate application as a technique of weather prediction. The years that he spent doing this were the years of the First World War — he was an ambulance driver at the front and he spent many of his spare hours in carrying out this very tedious hand calculation. He had spent a long time first in programming this and in setting up work sheets and checking techniques, and the like.

The results of this calculation were almost lost in the confusion of the surroundings, but were fortunately recovered, and in fact in 1920 he published a book describing the results of this calculation. It was what we would consider a dismal failure. He predicted a change in surface pressure in three hours which was some 60 times greater than anyone had ever seen in any three-hour period. This, was so discouraging in fact that people stayed away from this activity, especially by hand computational techniques, for a good many years after that. However, the Second World War saw the beginning of the development of high-speed computing techniques, and afterwards, a group at the Institute for Advanced Study at Princeton under the guidance or encouragement of the mathematician, John von Neumann, decided to take another look at the question of whether it would not be possible to compute the flow of the earth's atmosphere and in this way make some effort to predict its behavior.

In the interim since Richardson's failure, people had come to realize what his problem was and what had gone wrong. There were in fact two things which had led to his results. One of them is a problem which is still with us to some extent and is based on the fact that his observations of the conditions in the atmosphere at the starting time in his calculation were not precise. This was because they were based on observations or measurements which have a certain amount of error associated with them. These errors introduced into this initial state of the atmosphere a component of what we would refer to now as noise, corresponding physically to sound waves. The equations which he used permitted these sound waves to exist in his calculation, and they moved so rapidly and violently that they caused destructive effects in his three-hour period. The atmosphere, in fact, doesn't have this particular mode of hydro-dynamic motion present in it to any great extent — except occasionally when a volcano blows up or explosions are set off. Then, only in a very minor way do these sound waves compare to the magnitude of sound which can be induced by errors in the observation of the winds, temperatures, and the like.

The other difficulty was one which is well understood today, but one Richardson was unaware of, and that is that he did not satisfy what we now refer to as a stability condition so far as his choice of time step was concerned. He should have in his case taken a time step of five minutes instead of three hours. However, since he only took one, that probably did not make much difference; it would have been after hundreds of such time steps, perhaps, that the trouble would have shown up, a point he could not have reached at the rate he was able to calculate.

Recognizing both of these difficulties, a new attack was made on this problem in the late 1940's by introducing a rather simplified numerical model of the behavior of the atmosphere, and by making use of newly gained knowledge in the area of numerical techniques. This first simple model was one which described the atmosphere as if it were a two-dimensional sheet of incompressible fluid flowing over the surface of the earth, which did not have vertical structure within it. This was supposed to describe in some sense the average behavior of the atmosphere over the region of the United States. These calculations were remarkably success-ful almost from the very beginning; so successful, in fact, that von Neumann's group felt that there had been a tremendous change in the whole possibility of making weather predictions. True, the predictions they made were only a little bit better than people had been making, but they were a little bit better and they had the feeling that this was just the beginning and that in a few years they would be doing very much better.

More than fifteen years later, numerical techniques are used by weather services around the world for making predictions of the weather. I think we all know that weather prediction ability has not increased remarkably in the past fifteen or twenty years, although there has been a slow and steady improvement. Much of the trouble resides not in the numerical methods but in the original problem that one does not know what the actual state of the atmosphere is at any particular time with sufficient accuracy so that one can predict from this initial condition accurately what is going to happen. The work that has been going on in my laboratory is not in the weather prediction business but in another aspect of this problem. We have been making an attempt, which has been reasonably successful, to set up a numerical model of the atmosphere which can be used to compute for many weeks or months. In addition it should be sufficiently realistic so that no matter what the initial conditions one starts with, after a period of a month or so in atmosphere time, the model will start generating some of the typical behavior that is observed in the real atmosphere. In order to do this we have to take into account many of the long-term influences in the atmosphere (the energy sources and sinks in particular) in considerable detail. It is felt that if we should develop such a model we can use it as a tool for a better under-standing of how the atmosphere itself behaves and perhaps eventually use it as a model for carrying out experiments on such things as the influence on climate of changes in the sea surface temperatures, or other things that might eventually have something to do with control of climate. That, I want to add, is still a long way off.

The procedure that is followed in these models is very much the same that Richardson used, but with more sophisticated numerical techniques. In our model we divide the atmosphere over the whole globe into six layers and into a horizontal mesh, which is five degrees in latitude and longitude; that is, about 300 miles on a side. At these mesh points in this three-dimensional array we define the values of temperature, water vapor, and horizontal wind velocity components as well as given values of surface pressure. This collection of numbers serves to define at a particular time in the calculation the thermodynamic and hydrodynamic state of the atmosphere. The calculational process is simply one of using the equations of conservation of mass, momentum, and water substance to advance all of these quantities ahead by a time step, in our case ten minutes, and then repeat this procedure over and over again for weeks or months of atmosphere time.

One important ratio in connection with this work is the one that tells you how long it takes to compute one day, that is, the time ratio between computer time and atmosphere time. In this case, fortunately, we com-pute some twelve to fifteen times faster than the atmosphere time. I have come to feel that these models, to be more useful perhaps, should be com-puted even faster than that — something like 50 times faster than atmosphere time. This has to do with certain psychological aspects of the person carrying out the calculation; that is, if a calculation takes too long to complete, the person has forgotten what he was trying to calculate or has lost interest in it by the time it is completed.

If we should succeed in getting a reasonably reliable or accurate model of how the atmosphere behaves we will be faced with the problem which has been known for some years, that is, that this tremendous array of numbers which is describing the state of the atmosphere will be evolving in some way which is quite realistic but which will be just as confusing to us in many respects as the behavior of the real atmosphere. There is a serious question of whether with such a complicated model you know any more than you did before.

There are two points in this connection which I might mention; one of them, of course, is that with a model it is possible to carry out experiments to find out what the influence of changes in some parameters are on the behavior of the model atmosphere and thereby try getting some causal relationships between the multitude of things which are influencing the behavior of the atmosphere. The second point is that this could be a very useful prediction device even if we don't understand how it works.

This touches on a rather interesting point in connection with the use of computers for simulating quite complicated physical systems. We see that it is starting to replace what one used to think of as the theory of the behavior of a physical system. A theory of the atmosphere, for example, would be considered a good one if it were seen to have a certain prediction value, and it would also be considered good if it were simple enough so that people sort of understood what was involved in it. In this case we have the prediction value, but we are missing that human understanding. From a purely practical point of view, I suppose, it is the predictive value of a theory which is more useful, even if the understanding is more pleasing to the pride of humans.

But it may be that we are going to be faced in the future with a situation in which we can do things which we don't understand.

This is a complex system, and we have the problem of knowing what is going on in this model. We have had to turn to display techniques which are an effort to exhibit what is happening in some form which is more digestible, perhaps, than the pages and pages of numbers which we would get if we printed out the results of the calculations. There are some 50,000 numbers which are defining the state of the atmosphere in this model at one time; so if we printed out 50,000 numbers at every ten-minute time step we wouldn't really learn anything. So what we have turned to are graphical display techniques, mapping techniques, which are carried out on the computer which is used.

Some examples of the graphical displays that we have developed in connection with this model will show you something about the behavior of the model. Figures 1-3 show some maps which have been made on the computer at a particular time in the course of the calculation. Figure 1 shows a weather map which was started as a completely artificial state of the atmosphere but has been run for 20 or 30 days and is beginning to show some really characteristic behavior. There is a polar projection of the northern hemisphere with the pole at the center and the equator as a circle on the outside. Continent outlines are drawn as well as isotherms at a five-degree interval of sea surface temperature. This is one of the ways we use to define the geography of the continents; these are mid-January conditions, the oceans are relatively warm but the continents are relatively cold; this is winter in the northern hemisphere and this difference in sea surface temperature is the only way in which the model knows where the continents are.

Figure 2 shows a temperature distribution midway up in the atmosphere, as far as pressure is concerned, and also shows a rather smooth wave of about five lobes in it. This is a so-called planetary wave. It is somewhat similar to the appearance of the atmosphere in these midlevels where much of the fine detail that you find at the surface has been smoothed out.

Figure 3 shows the most familiar of meteorological variables — the surface pressure. Maps of this are what are printed in daily newspapers. The dotted contours correspond to low pressure areas. One can see quite clearly the extensive low pressure area in the North Atlantic usually called the Icelandic Low.

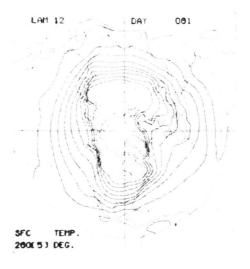

Figure 1

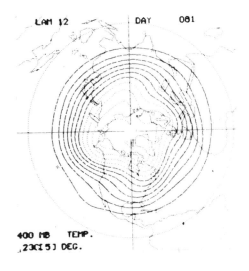

Figure 2

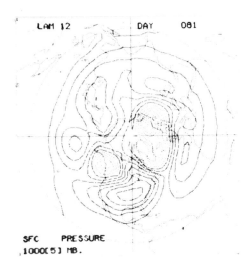

Figure 3

Chapter 11

BURDENS FOR THE DESIGNER OF A COMPUTER SIMULATION OF INTERNATIONAL RELATIONS: THE CASE OF TEMPER[1]

Morton Gorden

INTRODUCTION

This paper is written to share the burdens of computer simulation of international relations in the hope that future work will benefit from a discussion of some of the problems associated with one of the earliest efforts to model international relations in a computer. The author, with the aid of his former associates,[2] has selected six persistent and pervasive problems of the development of the TEMPER computer simulation. The problems are described below as they relate to the TEMPER simulation of international relations. They are cast as burdens for simulators to carry as they interact with the computer. Most of the problems discussed are not unique to computer simulation, but are shared by verbal

[1] The writing of this paper was supported by JWGA/ARPA/NU Project (*Advanced Research Project Agency, SD* 260) on Simulated International Processes of Northwestern University.

[2] The author wishes to thank his co-designers, Dr. Clark C. Abt and James C. Hodder, for their substantial share in developing the thoughts in this paper. Dr. Abt was the primary designer of the model and Mr. Hodder was the primary designer of the simulation. Dr. Gorden was the intermediary translator between model and simulation. This paper was written for Abt Associates, Inc. An abbreviated version was presented at the Conference for Computers and Policy at Livermore Laboratory, University of California, 1966.

theorists as well (29). However, the problems are aggrevated by being present in the environment of a computer and are singled out here for the consideration of verbal analysts who are interested in exploring the computer as an aid to their work. The paper is written for this audience, and familiarity with a computer and its terminology is not necessary. The frame of reference is the TEMPER simulation, briefly summarized below.[3]

Work was begun in 1960 by Dr. Clark C. Abt, at the Raytheon Company, to design a "Strategic Model Simulation of Wars, Weapons, and Arms Controls." Its original purpose was to provide a quantitative description "and hence hopefully an improved qualitative description of the interactions of world powers... in a dynamic structure describing the gross relations among world power blocks" (23). In its scope and size it represented a pioneering effort on untried ground. As the model progressed, it took on the name TEMPER (*T*echnological, *E*conomic, *M*ilitary, *P*olitical *E*valuation *R*outine) and its purpose became more concrete, moving in the direction of research and teaching. However, the original design never called for specifications beyond application for some heuristic function. The model was never designed to "make policy," only to help carry out a broadly conceived heuristic role for policy planners. While its different users and supporters may have imbued the effort with multiple purposes, the model itself has maintained an experimental character. In recent years, an improvement program to make the model more operational has gone on, and the gaming aspect of TEMPER has been highlighted and used in the Industrial College of the Armed Forces.

At the most abstract level of description, TEMPER may be viewed as a list of variables with rules of interaction among them. The variables are given values in the data base, and the rules are carried out to manipulate symbols according to a prespecified design. In addition, there are handling instructions in a program to facilitate the manipulation of operations within the computer. In the formal sense, the TEMPER simulation is a flexible receptacle for many possible international relations (11). However, the present simulation has filled the formal

---

[3]The paper does not try to survey the field of computer simulation in the social sciences, this having been done recently as part of the efforts of both Abt Associates Inc. (3) and the Northwestern Simulated International Processes project (12, 13). Nor does it attempt a discussion of the many issues raised by the computer for social sciences, this having been done by others (6, 7, 10, 14, 21, 22). Nor does it describe and relate the TEMPER simulation to other literature, which has been done elsewhere (1, 11, 2, 4). The paper limits itself to a discussion of selected examples of problems and solutions bearing on the use of a computer to simulate international relations.

structure with substantive content and given the variables specific values.

In scope, TEMPER is global. It has 39 nation groups which aggregate nations into different regional groupings. These nation groups are provided with a resource base and goals describing their preferred values. The nation groups, within the constraints of competing values and cultural and ideological predispositions, try to improve their positions. The goal seeking process operates like a homeostat, seeking to achieve a balance among goals and constraints, in the context of other nation groups which may be competing or cooperating for the same ends.

Nation groups can engage in or threaten to carry out various levels of conflict, escalating or de-escalating according to the situation. The actors can bargain with each other to achieve advantage, either a solitary victory or a mutual advantage. They can alter relative investments of resources to achieve their desired ends. They can seek to enhance their alliances, weaken their enemies, and spread their influence among uncommitted nations.

The rules which govern this variety of behavior are, of necessity, many and complex. Many hundred "if-then" statements must be written to prepare for the different contingencies to be anticipated. To make the interacting web of relations operate with plausibility and enough richness to inspire useful thinking about international relations is an imposing task. TEMPER has had its successes and failures, but the paper's purpose at present is to delineate some of the problems which are likely to be encountered by simulators using similar techniques.

Of course the foremost problem is knowledge about international behavior (27). If we really knew the rules which govern international behavior under the selected series of "if" statements, we should not need a simulation to develop them. However, this problem is not the subject of the paper. Whether or not the simulated rules are true is a separate task. The following six burdens are illustrated with examples which are not examined for their correctness, but which are choosen because they highlight sources of difficulty in the simulation of international relations on a computer.

The difficulties which will be examined deal with the need to be highly selective in the computer environment where time for running the machine and space for machine instructions are limited and costly. Related to this difficulty is the choice of an appropriate level of generalization. A computer simulation should be more than a list of specific case studies flooding the machine and its user and should still operate with statements of general applicability that are not so general as to be trivial or inapplicable to real problems. When the choices of material and the level of generalization are made, the modeled factors must be described in a dynamic environment which accounts for changes among interacting sets of variables. Describing these complex interactions is a burden that is to be carried with attention to clarity and precision. These interacting variables change each other's relative status on quantitative indexes. The quantification of the variables is difficult and leads to still another burden, "tuning" — adjusting the numerical levels so that they interact according to design rather than as artifacts of the formal mathematical structure in which they are embedded. The sixth burden discussed relates to the problem of interdisciplinary communication. The programmer has a different set of constraints than the designer on his capacity to perform, but the designer must carry these burdens if he wants his work to be implemented with fidelity.

Such are the burdens of computer simulation discussed in this paper. They were selected because of their pervasiveness in TEMPER and the likelihood of their presence in other such efforts. The idiosyncratic problems are not reported here for they are not of general interest. While an attempt was made to focus on those problems generally inherent in computer simulation rather than verbal theory, the first two burdens of selectivity and generalization are quite clearly problems for all theorists. The problems are only aggrevated in a computer simulation because the cost of failure is high and immediately demonstrable. The other burdens have much less in common with verbal theory and the more the discussion proceeds, the closer we get to problems closely identified with computer simulation as a technique.

The initial idea for this paper included the thought that something was lost in the translation of verbal theory into mathematical form in preparation for computer programming. It was felt that distortion was introduced into the ideas by expressing them in a program. However, as research and discussions proceeded, the source of difficulties did not seem to lie in the translation from prose to mathematics, but in the burdens which finally came to occupy the attention of the discussions. While the resulting problems are not as linked to the translation from verbal to mathematical symbols as was expected, the familiarity of these problems makes them all the more necessary to solve.

BURDEN ONE: TIME, SPACE AND THE NEED TO BE SELECTIVE

As large as the computer storage is today, and as large as it is likely to be in the near future, there will still not be enough storage space to accept the many instructions which a sizable model of international relations is apt to require. The first TEMPER design fit an available computer but a more complete version had to be moved to a machine twice the size. Future gains in hardware and software will make machines and languages available which will facilitate a far larger number of instructions and therefore reduce the need to be intensely selective of the materials to be simulated, but a global multipurpose model can readily press the financial and physical limits of available space and time (18).

While the technology of processing is rapidly improving to allow faster runs and larger models, the situation will never improve enough to be easy and inexpensive — time and manpower having a substantial absolute cost. Technological advance will make the problem less difficult, but it will not eliminate the need for selectivity. All human intellectual effort requires selectivity. In this burden, computer models are not unique, but the cost of poor selection in a simulation is high both in economic resources and in what is concealed from view.

The larger the model, the more time and money are required to run it on a computer. TEMPER originally required one quarter hour to run its course. As the model expanded, something closer to an hour was required. If we multiply this by the need to do many runs of the simulation for research purposes, it would not be long before the time and money necessary to use the tool would far exceed reasonable limits. Staying within time limits forces selectivity.

A large simulation of international relations can be so complex and concealed from view, that it is difficult to discover what is selected for treatment and what is glossed over briefly or left out entirely. The output of the simulation may not clearly indicate selections which are much more evident when in book form than in a computer program. In a book, as either author or reader, we rarely follow through the complex inter-relationships resulting from our selections, and when we do, the criteria for selection are either stated openly or accessible by inspection. However, in a simulation, the machine grinds through an inexorable and not easily accessible process from input to output. Selection of inputs and interaction structures among variables can have a profound effect which the complexity of both size and interaction patterns is apt to conceal. Examples of some of the unfortunate limitations of having to be selective to avoid financial excesses and excessive complexity can be found in the design of the alliance routine of the TEMPER simulation.

One of the decisions which had to be designed into the TEMPER simulation deals with a specification of the conditions under which an ally will come to the aid of another ally engaged in a conflict. This is a complicated decision in real life, and also complicated in even a simplified computer simulation of reality, because a general statement dealing with as many possible conditions as can be included must be designed to handle a multitude of possible interactions. Clearly, if we take all nations in the TEMPER data base and have them deal with each other in all possible modes, we have an enormous set of possibilities which will quickly exhaust time, resources, and patience. Selections must be made. One selection suggested a division of the nations of the world into three main blocs: West, East, and Neutral. In 1961, when the first version of TEMPER was designed, this oversimplification of the divisions in the world had more justification than it has today.

The three-part division helps to delineate likely areas of interaction, the relevant spheres of influence and concern, and the limits of possible interactions. For example, having defined allies for the United States areas of involvement, we must proceed to determine the conditions under which the United States would aid the ally or refuse support. Considering recent history, it appears that one condition for denial of support of an ally is when he is engaged in conflict with a neutral. When a TEMPER ally is engaged in military conflict with a neutral, the United States is likely to deny assistance. This design arose from consideration of such cases as British and French involvement in Suez, Portuguese operations in Angola, and the Pakistan disputation with India. In all of these conflicts, the usual alliance support was withdrawn because the conflict involved an uncommitted nation. Since some selection had to be made to narrow the range of alternatives, it was felt that this general limiting rule would create only a few violations of real behavior. A general statement was made applying to the behavior of each bloc with the other.

Some time after the design was implemented, a particular game was run in simulation form involving the United States, Cuba, and a Latin American neutral. The Cubans began a campaign against the neutral and the United States came to the aid of the neutral, resulting in difficulty for Cuba. Cuba called on its ally, the Soviet Union, for assistance but the Soviet Union summarily refused.

In the real world, the Soviet decision would have been more complicated. In the simulation, the general decision rule to deny involvement when an ally conflicts with a neutral was a convenient limiting rule. However, when applied to the Soviet Union, with a goal of spreading communism, the decision rule should not apply with equal generality. However, the need to limit space and time in the simulation led to artificial limits of decision making among nations and to sharing decision elements which did not apply in the case of two major powers with differing aims.

The problem posed is not insoluble. Using an expanded decision element, the United States and the Soviet Union could both make reasonable decisions to enhance their particular values. We would at least have to adjust inhibitions on conflict levels with particular parties and add more specific and special purpose decision elements. However, such a design to solve the problem would have meant still one more addition to an already saturated simulation. The designers accepted the limitations which make it impossible to successfully play a specific range of scenarios on the simulation.

Still another set of scenarios which cannot be usefully played involve converting an enemy nation into an ally. TEMPER'S design of three major political blocs facilitates much communication and saves much space and running time, but it denies other capabilities. During the course of a run, it is impossible, except by much infeasible manual intervention, to convince a member of an enemy bloc to come over to a new position. The TEMPER simulation cannot handle the wooing of Poland or Rumania to try to change their basic political loyalty. This design decision was made as a concession to computer considerations, not foreign policy objectives.

While it is true that foreign policy objectives of the early sixties were based on containment rather than the roll back of communism, current relaxation of bloc relations makes the program's loss of such a capability more costly. The TEMPER simulation is bound to be dated whenever the process of international relations must be simulated by artificially adding structural constraints to decision rules.

In a later version of TEMPER, blocs were expanded to include several nation aggregates, but the enormous cost of time and memory storage space required to overcome the structural limitations of bloc communications could not be invested to remove all of the restrictions initially placed in the simulation for practical reasons.

In the last example, the loss of the possibility of wooing opposing bloc members is not perhaps as great as the earlier example of restrictions on Soviet policy, but in both cases the selection of alternatives based on structural requirements rather than intelligent choice limited simulation capabilities that would have been useful to call upon. Flexibility is desirable if the objectives of the simulation cannot be defined readily, and the frequency of different types of international relations change with time. Since simulation, at this stage, can be a research tool which explores open-ended problems, flexibility is necessary. However, flexibility is too costly in terms of time and space and the selections are too readily concealed. Only the model designer or an operator very familiar with the simulation could have discovered that Soviet refusal to help its ally was not due to some plausible explanation, like fear of escalation, but simply a decision rule based on convenience, not communism.

The burden of selecting materials for inclusion within a limited time

and space allocation was to be the designers' in a way that is not unusual in any theory building endeavor. Priorities were established which
allowed selections to be made in terms of the original purposes of the
design of TEMPER. As indicated earlier, the purposes were many and
priorities did not remain fixed throughout the life of the design program.
As priorities shifted and requirements were placed on performance, a
number of goals were sought. However, two substantive simulation
purposes remained throughout: The simulation should demonstrate
that military strategy in the nuclear age had to be made in the context
of multiple factors included in the TEMPER acronym (Technological,
Economic, Military, Political Evaluation Routine); and that international relations with enemies is not necessarily a zero sum game,
in which a gain for one is a loss for the other. While these purposes
may seem limited in retrospect, the strategic debates in this country
during the late fifties and early sixties illustrated that the implications
of these general ideas did not undergo a thorough examination.

For the first major purpose, variables were selected that were particularly salient for the interaction of military strategy and political
values. For example, to avoid failure in performance, arms budgets
had to be set consonant with other demands placed on the economic
system, or these other demands would have to be lessened by political
activity. Thus, a user of the simulation would discover limitations on
military procurement set by demands for consumer goods, unless the
nation were convinced of the threat to its values which necessitated
delayed gratification.

The other major purpose, dramatizing the possibility that the cold
war relations between antagonists could include some cooperative
behavior for mutual advantage, required selections of time and space
which would emphasize bargaining capability for long-term restraint and
control of arms races and short-term conflict management. Even though
these alternatives required an elaborate communications structure with
provisions for biased perceptions, priority was given to this use of space
as part of a conscious set of allocation criteria. The directors of the
simulation applied selectivity by basing criteria for selection in the
purposes of the model.

It should be emphasized that the need to be selective is not limited to
designers of computer programs. Parsimony is appreciated in all forms of
theory building. However, publishers are less likely to throw away super-
fluous pages from a manuscript and audiences less likely to walk out on a
lecture a few minutes too long than a programmer is apt to say that this
part of a model will not fit in the space and time provided. The space and
time limitations in computers make good selection a critical burden. Such

constraints also highlight the need to make the criteria for selection explicit, for the errors of commission and omission are not as evident to the naked eye as with other forms of theorizing.

BURDEN TWO: AN APPROPRIATE LEVEL OF GENERALIZATION

The burdens of intelligent selection to meet the limitations of time and space are related to a second burden, the selection of an appropriate level of generalization. Such a burden is not unique to the design of computer simulations (24, 27), but in computer operations, time and space constraints of a machine forbid special designs for each case. Generalizations applying to many different circumstances become absolutely essential.

One of the important generalizations is the assumption that the differences in structure of different nations' decision making is sufficiently irrelevant to the outcome of decisions made by these nations so that the differences in real-world structures of decision units can be omitted in favor of a common simulated decision logic. This does not mean that the national values are shared; each nation decides to take different action on its own behalf, but there is a shared systematic reasoning process which is assumed not to depend on the nature of the political system in its democratic or totalitarian forms. In simulating nations at this level of generalization, the simulation dispenses with a large number of national differences. This generalization has enormous convenience for the simulator because he does not have to design and program many different types of governmental structures. Other factors are used to account for the difference in national performance.

Still another area of difficulty in selecting the appropriate level of generalization can be found in the example of TEMPER's escalation and de-escalation instructions for the raising or lowering of international conflicts running in the simulation. The decision is immediately recognizable as an exceedingly complex one which for even one simulated conflict will have many case-specific elements. Any generalization that would cover various circumstances is apt to be suspect because there are so many factors in each case. However, a computer simulation does not reconstruct one past event; it builds possible elements for many future events and different possible outcomes. Some general statement must be made.

In TEMPER, there are formulae to compute the cost of escalation, de-escalation and letting the conflict stay at its present level. The formulae are very complex and include multiple factors which are not pertinent in this context. What is pertinent is one of the factors that is left out in TEMPER, but is presumably important in some selected cases.

In the early 1960's, there were illustrative discussions among strategists asking colleagues to choose a level of acceptable losses in human lives during nuclear conflicts of different intensities. After having set the number of human lives one could tolerate losing, the respondents were asked to replace the words "human lives" with "Russians" and "Americans." The answers showed that there were some differences between the value assigned to a human Russian or American life. The next question substituted "Chinese" for "Russian," and there was a dramatic shift in the increased tolerance for the loss of human Chinese life.

These questions were not systematically asked, so the distribution of answers cannot provide any reliable information. However, the conversations suggest that the human cost of escalation varies depending on who the humans are. If we try to make a general statement about the human cost of escalation and tell the TEMPER simulation to de-escalate after some tolerance level has been passed, we must make specific reference in each case to the cultural relations between antagonists which affect their international relations.

No model or simulation can be complete. If it were, it would defeat its own purpose to simplify and manipulate. But the selection of the appropriate level of generalization is a difficult burden which a designer must make and the user understand before the output of a simulation can be applied for specific purposes. In TEMPER, generalizations about the implications of governmental structure for international relations and generalizations about the human cost of escalation are but two areas where outcomes are affected by design decisions that may be relevant to the use of the output of the simulation.

Cognizant of these possible limits, one area of the TEMPER design was expanded to provide for a level of generalization suited to likely usage. In addition to the general statements dictating the possibility of conflict management between two enemies, a set of special rules was established to apply when allied troups were engaged in a conflict. For example, were a nation offered a truce by its antagonist, the offer could not be accepted unless agreed to by allies whose power to decline would be roughly proportionate to their degree of commitment.

When the designers recognized that demands for simulating proxy wars were to be placed on the design, the previous level of generalization dictating outcomes of conflicts was deemed inadequate and these new features were added.

While it is clear that problems of selecting appropriate levels of generalization are not unique to computer simulations, the effects of faulty procedure are more pronounced than in verbal theory formulation. A simulation moves from the starting input conditions to the final output, relating the interacting variable along the way in a complex maze of patterns and feedback relationships. This inter-relatedness suggests that the designers of TEMPER had to be careful not to give fine grain structure and detail to one section of the model, only to have the output grossly handled in another. The desired effects of lowering the level of generalization can be negated by a step glossed over at a higher level of generalization later in the interaction process. The design team solved these problems by using flow charts of the overall design and communicating with each other about the use of output from one section of the model to the other to discern the degree of detail needed to successfully interact. Although never completed on a systematic basis for the entire model, some sensitivity testing was also done to provide a more accurate sense of the power of selected variables to determine outcomes. Verbal communications between programmer and designer and selected sensitivity tests helped to avoid the consequences of uneven levels of generalization in an interacting set of variables.

BURDEN THREE: DESIGNING A DYNAMIC SIMULATION

An added burden on the designer/user of an international simulation is carrying through the relations of variables at different levels of intensity over time. Much of international relations theory is static in its conception. Stress is placed on how a system is likely to act over a large range of circumstances at any given point in time. One of the purposes of a simulation is to check a large number of possibilities during the process of events. As an effort to improve the predictive and explanatory powers of international relations, simulation tries to explore the process of change not dealt with by other techniques. That means that a simulation must describe time rate of change and instruct a machine to handle the relations among variables over a period of time as they change their levels of intensity.

One such case arose in the design of a set of relationships among variables involving the willingness of nations to use force to achieve their ends. In prose we often describe this propensity in terms of how aggressive a nation might be. One of the first steps in going from words to a computer simulation is the expression of this sentiment on a quantitative scale such that each nation is given a numerical value relative to other nations. Each nation is thus given a number from one to ten expressing its relative propensity to use various forms of coercion.

The next step toward making the simulation is to recognize that there will be different situations for the application of forces. For example, even if a country is ordinarily a peace-loving power desirous of settling conflicts by peaceful negotiation, it will be very likely to change when attacked militarily.   Therefore, the simulation has to provide for the acceptance of different modes of behavior based on a change of circumstance.   An instruction was given to raise the level of willingness to use force when a threat became intense.   This instruction was put into mathematical form and programmed.

After a few test runs of the simulation, it was noted that aggressive nations were attacking more peaceful nations and subduing them before the loser could mobilize for a fight.   A design evaluation disclosed that a term had been left out of the equation which would have given a greater rate of change to those nations with a low starting point on the scale so they could more rapidly match the aggressor.   The error was based on the bad habit of thinking through situations without considering the dynamics that take place over time.   The conversion from prose to program failed to take into account the rate of change as it occurred over time.

One of the more difficult burdens is thinking through the likely end product over time in the interacting environment of a computer.   The model, when it is forced into a dynamic environment, must be more specific and comprehensive than our tolerant minds might otherwise allow.   In the example above, an analysis of test runs of the model uncovered the flaw and corrections could be made.

Another more general example of the problems of dealing with a dynamic model is the need to specify the impact of one variable on another at the limits of their interaction. Presumably, there are levels of intensity too low to have any significant impact and levels so high where a saturation effect takes place, such that the addition of one additional unit does not have the same impact as the previous unit (nonlinearities).   The marginal utility of each unit of measurement must be described in a dynamic model and, furthermore, the shape of the curve must be interpreted as a trigger for action on other variables. It might be necessary to act one way or another if a growth curve is or is not responding to "expected" patterns.   Appropriate expectations about the course of change over time are not easy to determine.

Karl Deutsch's comments on integration among European nations imply that its growth can be expected to be linear — following a straight line on a graph (9). The deceleration of European integration is therefore taken as a sign of slow-down in the integration process which bodes ill for future integration.   The designers of TEMPER generally did not assume linearity of development, for they found that many of the curves would exceed scale maximums if not bounded at the high end by a device which recognizes critical thresholds. In most of the growth phenomena under investigation it was assumed that deceleration was a "normal" condition. At some point for example, integration among nations might be expected to taper off because the area for potential integration had been narrowed due to previous success, giving rise to a greater expected difficulty of the next possible unit of growth chosen from a smaller field of possibilities.

While there is no simple solution to the problem of expected rates of change for growth phenomena the TEMPER designers most often relied on the assumption that the dynamic models would have curves with slow starting and finishing rates, with a more steeply ascending slope at the mid-range. This assumption helped the designers to carry the burden of dynamic modeling of variables at different levels of intensity. Of course, the preferred solution to the problem would be to apply the results of empirical research to accommodate the requirement of specifying patterns of change, but such research results are not yet available.

Another solution to dynamic modeling of uncertain relations, but still not the preferred one, is to admit ignorance and rather than replace it with intuitive assumptions, to replace ignorance with a random number expressing the uncertainty about the phenomenon being described (22). This solution was used in TEMPER when the frequency and intensity of determining factors in an interaction pattern was truly unknown, but these factors were known to be significant at different times. For example, in some military engagements where all the factors that were known were calculated and the relative strengths of adversaries still might not result in evidence of a clear victory for either side, a random number was drawn to indicate the role of "chance" phenomena like weather or *esprit*.

The burdens imposed by the design of a dynamic simulation have not been readily solved in TEMPER, in part because there is no ready solution which may be borrowed from verbal theory. Verbal theory often uses words like "too much" or "exceeds the breaking point" or "too much to bear" without specifying these levels for the simulator. The burden is not unique to simulation (15, 20), but once again it is aggrevated by the computer environment which demands an understanding of the dynamics of interaction in order to set the rules for change from one variable state to another.

BURDEN FOUR: QUANTIFICATION OF AGGREGATED CONCEPTS

The conversion from theory in prose to simulation in mathematics entails still another burden for the international relations analyst. It is useful to state the data for the simulation in quantitative terms, which

offer greater manipulability and clarity than "more" or "less." However, in spite of the numerical clarity which quantitative expression gives,
the data are used to measure highly aggregated concepts. In TEMPER there
is a variable called *External Dynamism* which is an aggregated measure
of the vigor with which countries will pursue an influential role in
international affairs.   The problem posed for the analyst is how to
quantify such a highly aggregated concept to be generalizable over
many nations.

The first step is to make the concept more precise. Just because
the concept exists in some six-letter FORTRAN symbol, and has a
numerical value attached to it, it is not any more precise than the ill-
defined meaning assigned by the analyst.   In the clarification step it
becomes evident that vigor in pursuing an international role has different meaning for members of the "wooing" East and West blocs
than for the nations in the Neutral bloc. If a nation is in the wooing
blocs, External Dynamism has to do with willingness to allocate resources abroad, to run deficiences in trade for political purposes, and
to stand firm in conflicting situations. But a Neutral usually expresses
his desire for influence by maintaining his independence.   One of
the first steps was to give instructions that the same word in FORTRAN
had two different references in the English language. This is a switch
from the usual complaint that verbal theorists are confused in their
use of language.   To save storage space, the confusion was tolerated
in computer language as well.

Having specified at least two meanings, both of which aggregate a
great deal of behavior, some numerical index must be found for both
meanings.   The author was once asked to find a research assistant who
could set the data base numbers for 117 nations and send him to a
library for the afternoon. Nowhere will a researcher find a magic lantern
to illumine the dark recesses of a concept like External Dynamism. A
series of numbers which can express the relative standing among nations
on this dimension cannot be found in any source book.

As close as one might practically come to numbers which offer a
relative ranking index is the economic growth rate of nations.   The
activity invested in internal growth is often correlated with international
activity. There are important exceptions: on the high end of the growth
rate scale the cases of post-war Germany and Japan must be considered;
on the low end, Indonesia. There is also an important economic fact
that growth often follows a pattern of tapering off at the high end, and
very successful economies will have smaller rates of growth but will
start with a larger base. Barring these exceptions, for which adjustments
can be made, it was deemed possible to use the economic growth rate as a

fair measure of relative dynamism among the various nations in TEMPER —
even though some errors will be made if the general index is not examined
for exceptions in specific instances.

Given the highly aggregated nature of the concept, no single number or
groups of numbers will accurately appraise individual cases. What is perhaps more important, we must take a long inferential step from the index
to what it is measuring. Surely, such a step puts a burden on the designer
to be cautious and clear about what he is doing. He may well be open to
the charge of specious specificity, in which a concrete and clear number
derived from a "hard" data source is used to measure an imprecise and
vague concept.

For some other cultural and ideological values, it is less useful to
apply indexes from "hard" data than it is directly to express qualitative
judgments in quantitative terms. One of the drawbacks of such a method
is the subjective determination of value by the designer, resulting in an
unreliable data base. To alleviate this difficulty in the data base of
TEMPER, a mail questionnaire was utilized to gather judgments about
the relative positions of the United States and the Soviet Union on a
broad range of ideological and cultural values included in the simulation (11).
The final tally of 149 respondents, selected by reputational and positional
criteria, included roughly four out of ten members from the largest
firms in industry and finance; three out of ten members affiliated
with the American mass communication network; and three out of ten
government members, primarily from the executive branch.

These respondents were asked to rank the Soviet Union and the United
States, relative to each other, on a ten-point scale matching the variables
in the model. The panelists were asked a set of questions dealing with
domestic affairs, international relations, and strategic military considerations.
A stereotyped answer reflecting a belief in polar opposites of the U. S. and
Soviet decision rules was typical when evaluating domestic issues, and the
visions of the panelists were in agreement with each other and the model
designers. However, as the questions probed into international relations
and the values which dictate the use of coercion of one nation by another
were examined, the panelists perceived a similarity of values between the
two major powers, differences arising only over spheres of desired influence. The differences hypothesized by the designers which would have accounted for different behavior regarding the use of nuclear weapons was
also modified by the panelists' insistence that the value of global real es-
tate was different for each power, but there would be no marked difference
of behavior when the prized territories were threatened.

These findings were among those which modified the judgments of the
designers. Values were reset in the data base of the simulation as a

result of the opinions of a large panel of judges representing a broader cross section of opinion than had been previously available.

The burden of the quantification of aggregated concepts was dealt with in TEMPER by indexes for some variables derived from "hard" sources and applied to the "soft" concepts; for other variables by a numerical expression of a qualitative judgment; and for still other variables by solicitation of the opinions of a number of important respondents. In each of these cases some of the more difficult philosophical and substantive problems had to be overcome or be held in abeyance with assumptions until time and resources could permit their solution (5, 16, 19, 25, 26).

BURDEN FIVE: "TUNING" A SIMULATION

A further exploration of the concept of External Dynamism will illustrate another major problem for the quantitative international relations analyst — *tuning.* A quantitative model of international relations must put together numbers from various submodels dealing with many interacting variables. In the case of winning over a Neutral nation, a Neutral nation's decision (whether or not to be independent and refuse to accept the persuasion or pressure of a wooing party) is made in an equation. If a wooing party gives many benefits to a Neutral, the Neutral may well increase his friendship, but lose his independence. The numerator of the equation is representative of the amount of favors, but the divisor is External Dynamism, and if the nation is very desirous of independence (recall this means it has a high growth rate), then the divisor will be large and the favors will be reduced in impact. The number which emerges from this calculation assigns political credits to East or West, depending, in part, on the relative value of one contestant over the other and the rate at which favors are being dispensed. These credits can be used as measures of relative performance.

Behind this relatively simply equation are several numbers coming from different sources in the model and referring to different units of value. These are dollar favors, percentage growth rates (not expressed in dollars because elsewhere they are needed in different units), and political credits. While all these numbers have been checked for relative significance from one nation to another, they have not, until this point, been "tuned" to make sure they are compatible with each other. A large number, uncorrected for the context in which it was first generated, can send an equation off scale and create unrealistic decisions. The reduction of all variables to numbers does not assure that these numbers will have a desirable impact when interacting with others. Tuning is the process of following through the calculations to make sure that decisions are not an artifact of incompatible numbers but a matter of design.

In this tuning process, one has to be careful not to throw away the value of a simulation. Unexpected results of a trial simulation may be the result of bad policy, not numerical artifacts which need to be tuned away. Surprising findings are possible outcomes and should be sought in the evaluation of consequences of actions. However, if improperly tuned numbers go off scale and create "unreal" expectations, it may be difficult to separate a consequence of an act from an artifact of the interacting numbers. Tuning is also designing, and must be done with the same care as selecting the elements of an equation.

As a practical matter, it is impossible to exercise full caution in the tuning process. Every calculation of every major equation would have to be examined for a whole range of issues. If one recalls the problem of dealing with changing relations in a dynamic environment, one can see that it is an enormous task to tune such a model as TEMPER perfectly across the full range of its possibilities. To assure realistic output from all the various data base inputs when they interact is a practical task of large proportions, so large that one time when a variable began to go off scale a programmer did the designer a "favor" by putting an automatic threshold on the variable. When the limit was exceeded, the simulation refused to go above it. This dampened the impact of a faulty design so that the simulation ran on pacified, and only later did the designer realize that the programmer had become a designer by pushing the skeleton back in the closet. Amends had to be made later to avoid arbitrary tuning.

The problems of tuning are closely related to the problems of validation of simulation output. One indication of successful tuning is valid output. It is beyond the scope of this paper to deal with validation, a subject receiving a great deal of treatment in the Simulated International Processes project at Northwestern University, under the direction of Harold Guetzkow (8, 30). However, tuning had to be done by some criteria of reasonableness of output and the designers were given output from different parts of their work to pass judgment on the plausibility of its occurring in the "real" world. During the early phases of development, much of the model was checked out in this fashion, but work is currently going on in the Simulmatics Corporation and Mathematica which will contribute to the validation and criticism of TEMPER in much more depth.

From the early tuning efforts of TEMPER designers, some mistakes were uncovered that showed distortion in some parts of the simulation, causing a nuclear conflict between the Soviet Union and the United

States over an incident in the Arctic. On the basis of the judgment of the design team, such an occurrence was highly unlikely and adjustments were made.

In TEMPER, the basic criterion for tuning was reasonableness of output based on the logic of what was designed into operations, the logic being developed from the experience and studies of the designers. However, history past and future has not and will not necessarily conform to an already known logic. TEMPER has primarily been tuned to meet the canons of known logical consistency. The model is essentially a series of "if-then" statements. These statements can be incorrect from the points of view of logical inconsistency and from empirical data. Primary emphasis has been placed on consistency verification, and tests of "real" world reasonableness were originally applied only to the validating of the tuning operations. The enormous task of empirically validating the hundreds of theories that are stated in TEMPER algorithms can only be accomplished as verbal theory itself moves toward that goal.

BURDEN SIX: SENSITIVITY TO PROGRAMMER PROBLEMS

The experience of programmer tuning mentioned above brings us to a very serious burden which must be carried by the designer. He must understand the constraints which operate on the programmer who implements the designer's idea. The designer must live within these constraints or the progammer will, as described above, unwittingly fall into the role of designer. Instead of implementing what the designer wants, the programmer may implement only what is possible. The designer is faced with the burden of making the desirable possible. He cannot leave it exclusively to the programmer; not because the programmer is by nature a different being from a substantive analyst, but because a programmer operates under rather different constraints from designers. These constraints have to be recognized to take into account what a programmer's probable behavior will be when faced with designer ambitions for a simulation. It is very likely that the programmer will not be able to gratify all of the ambitions of a designer and priorities must be established. For time and computer memory space reasons, and because a project is budgeted with finite dollars and deadlines, unforeseeable programming problems have to be settled on a priority basis and in subtle ways. To avoid missing deadlines by changing the design rather than fulfilling the original design, the designer must share the programmer's burdens.

One of the decision functions in the model which illustrates the fate of an idea under program constraints, can be found in the escalation and de-escalation routine. A cost-effective model was designed for the evaluation of decisions in international relations. The design included several different acts that a nation could carry out, and it provided a basis for comparing the cost and effectiveness of each act, selecting the most cost-effective. A nation could, for example, bargain with the enemy; it could hit the enemy harder than before; it could make a threatening speech; it could do nothing.

All of these acts are evaluated for their cost and effectiveness. Speeches are not very costly, but if one speaks too often without acting, then one gets less and less effectiveness out of verbal behavior — a recognized bluff.

One can bargain. The cost of bargaining is determined by how much one has to give away and how much one gets in return. These costs include many factors, and they are then compared against the other possible choices to see if the bargain should be accepted.

After about a year of many runs of the simulation, it was discovered that the cost-effectiveness model was not implemented in the simulation. The programmer encountered insoluble time and budgetary constraints within the original design, and made some modifications which resulted in selecting only an approximately cost-effective choice over several tries of the simulation. To compare each of the options at one point in time would have meant storing data and logic in a computer that had already been fully loaded. The design simply exceeded possible constraints, and the priority system of the programmer allowed modifications which were not easily recognized by the designer.

This change is an exceedingly serious one and it might well be asked why the difference went undiscovered. The discrepancy was difficult to identify because, over time, the nations would do all the various possible acts, but not for the reasons designed into the simulation. The programmer's definition of cost-effectiveness was sufficiently close to the original intention to conceal what was going on in the machine. At times it was identical, but only after much experience could the patterns of decision be recognized to establish different priorities than those in the designer's ambitions. In the complex maze of interactions, why something was happening was not as easy to determine as the fact that it was happening.

The solution used to minimize discrepancies between the design and the program included much discussion in which a great deal of mutual education was necessary. Both designers and programmers had to learn a great deal about programming and international relations, respectively. Several changes of personnel were required until the proper people were found who could practice each other's art. Several reorganizations were carried out so that specialization of functions did not prevent communications from relating intention to performance.

In spite of the substantial efforts in the direction of discussion and organization, errors did occur. The solution lies in two different directions. First, output displays must be created which give rapid and clear feedback to the designer and a set of facts around which the programmer and designer can orient their communications. Remote access consoles and cathode ray tube output will help a great deal both for the problems of tuning mentioned earlier and for checks on the reliability of the communications between designer and programmer. These hardware improvements can contribute greatly to making the designer sensitive to the programmer's work as he follows it step by step. Likewise, the programmer will find that the designer can give him advice and verification of priorities when the implemented model is readily examinable.

Secondly, the training of graduate students in the social sciences to master the programmer's art will greatly increase the probability of accurate communications and sensitivity to the demands placed on the programmer. In 1961, when TEMPER began, there were very few recruitable people who knew about both the substantive problems of international relations and the workings of a computer program. Happily, the number of available people trained to apply the technology of the computer to international relations is growing. It is expected that these students will make the burdens discussed in this paper somewhat less difficult and more amenable to solution. If designers are more sensitive to programmer constraints, then the process of communication can alleviate the gap between design and program.

SUMMARY AND CONCLUSION

Six of the more pervasive difficulties facing a designer of a computer simulation have been discussed with reference to TEMPER. The burdens of selectivity, generalization, dynamic modeling, quantification, "tuning," and programmer constraints have been examined as sources of problems for a designer. The programming of international relations theory, at least in the case of TEMPER, has resulted in some of these burdens being successfully carried, some only partially dealt with, and others only tolerated.

Many of the problems of computer simulation are shared with verbal theory, especially the problems of selectivity and generalization. This is to be expected, for the TEMPER simulation is an expression of verbal theory (11). Some of the problems are especially associated with computer simulation. Problems of dynamic modeling, quantification, tuning, and programmer constraints are chiefly computer induced. However, at least for the first two, dynamic modeling and quantification, it would be beneficial for verbal theory to face these problems as well. As regards these desirable characteristics, verbal theory is not more virtuous, it is just less explicit about its sins. If much of verbal theory were put to the test of being programmable and theory designers were forced to carry the burdens of a computer simulation, shortcomings would be discovered and connections would thus be improved. The least that can be said for computer simulation is that it focuses attention on some necessary criteria of parsimony, rigor, clarity, and consistency. If the designer is to succeed in giving proper attention to these criteria, he will need the verbal theorist as well. The mutual sharing of these burdens, particularly at the points of overlapping mutual suggestiveness, holds promise to be of benefit to those who try.

ADDENDUM: BURDEN FOR THE USER OF A COMPUTER SIMULATION
FROM THE POINT OF VIEW OF THE DESIGNER

Though the most salient burdens have been discussed, still another problem of simulation of international relations, the problem of the loss of comprehension and control over simulation operations, deeply affects the capacity to use the output of the simulation for decision-making purposes. Any model of the international system will be multivariate with complicated interaction patterns. One of the reasons for simulating international relations on a computer is to handle a system that is too large for an analyst to comprehend as a single entity. Only in the environment of a computer can many of the system implications be worked out and manipulated for the user's purposes. However, there is irony in putting a model into a machine to augment human capability, only then to have the user insist on understanding what he initially gave up as incomprehensible. If one believes something because of hundreds of factors interacting virtually simultaneously, he will be at a loss to justify his beliefs. He must, as in the natural sciences, give up the requirement of understanding the location of every particle in a system in order to make statements about system behavior. This may violate our traditional notions of responsibility in the practice of international relations.

There are analogies in the policy process that make the problem familiar. Operators in the State Department do not have to understand what is going on at all levels of the Department to create an intelligent foreign policy. Scholars do not have to comprehend the workings of a university in order to write a good book. A corporation president does not have to understand the tasks of all lower levels to know that he has a profit or loss. One does not have to know everything. In computer simulation, one gives up knowing about the process in detail to gain knowledge about the system in a larger perspective. The whole is larger than the sum of the parts (16). This is the intellectual "profit" of a simulation.

Whether or not the TEMPER simulation is "profitable," the essential impossibility of a solution to the problem of comprehension requires limits to the application of the simulation. We are unlikely to overcome the problem of comprehension of the enormous complexity which the simulation techniques allow a designer to build into his model. Because we cannot trace through every "why" and justify every step, because control over the model as a unit is not readily accessible, we must necessarily limit its applications. Making decisions with the simulation violates our notions of responsibility. Perhaps the best roles for the designers of simulations is to help make users more knowledgable about their own implicit theories behind their decisions. As a teaching device, as a check on the "if-then" statements of human decision makers, as a stimulant to articulation of "why" for the policy maker — these are the roles which can contribute toward helping men carry their responsibilities. We are not ready to turn over responsibility for men's decisions, as these decisions exist internally to machines, but we can call on machines to help men carry the responsibilities which necessarily lie in their hands.

REFERENCES

1. Abt, C. C., "War Gaming," *International Science and Technology,* 32 (August, 1964), pp. 29-37.

2. Abt, C. C. and M. Gorden, "Report on Project Temper" in Snyder, R. and D. Pruitt, editors, *Reader in International Conflict,* forthcoming.

3. Abt Associates, "A Survey of the State of the Art: Social, Political, and Economic Models and Simulations," Cambridge, Mass.: Abt Associates, November, 1965.

4. Alker, Hayward R. and Ronald D. Brunner, "Simulating International Conflict: A Comparison of Three Approaches," prepared for New England Regional Meeting of the International Studies Association, April 29-30, 1966.

5. Banks, A. S. and R. B. Textor, *A Cross-Polity Survey,* Cambridge, Mass.: M. I. T. Press, 1963.

6. Borko, H., editor, *Computer Applications in the Behavioral Sciences,* Englewood Cliffs, N.J.: Prentice-Hall, 1962.

7. Browing, Rufus P., "Computer Programs as Theories of Political Processes," *Journal of Politics, 24* (August, 1962).

8. Chadwick, R. W., "Theory Development through Simulation," Mimeo, 1966.

9. Deutsch, Karl, *France, Germany and the Western Alliance,* New York: Charles Scribner and Sons, 1966.

10. Feigenbaum, E. A. and J. Feldman, editors, *Computers and Thought,* New York: McGraw Hll, 1963.

11. Gorden, Morton, "International Relations Theory in the TEMPER Simulation," Mimeo, paper delivered at 1965 American Political Science Association Meeting.

12. Geutzkow, H., "Simulation in International Relations" from *Proceedings of the IBM Scientific Computing Symposium on Simulation Models and Gaming,* Thomas J. Watson Research Center, Yorktown Heights, N. Y., 1966.

13. Geutzkow, H. and L. Jensen, "Research Activities on Simulated International Processes," *Background,* 9, No. 4 (February, 1966), pp. 261-274.

14. Howe, F., "The Computer and Foreign Affairs," Occasional paper No. 1, Center for International Systems Research, Washington, D. C., Department of State, 1966.

15. Lazarsfeld, P. F. and M. Rosenberg, *The Language of Social Research,* Glencoe, Ill.: Free Press, 1957, pp. 203-230.

16. Lerner, D., editor, *Parts and Wholes,* Glencoe, Ill.: Free Press, 1963.

17. Lerner, D., editor, *Quantity and Quality,* Glencoe, Ill.: Free Press, 1961.

18. Licklider, J. C. R., *Libraries of the Future,* Cambridge, Mass.: M. I. T. Press, 1965.

19. Merritt, R. L. and S. Rokkan, editors, *Comparing Nations: The Use of Quantitative Data in Cross National Research,* New Haven, Conn.: Yale University Press, 1964.

20. Moore, W. F., *Social Change,* Englewood Cliffs, N.J.: Prentice-Hall, 1963.

21. Naylor, T. H., J. L. Balintfy, D. S. Burdick, and K. Chu, *Computer Simulation Techniques,* New York: John Wiley & Sons, 1966.

22. Pool, I. De Sola, "Simulating Social Systems," *International Science and Technology,* 28 (March, 1964), pp. 62-70.

23. Raytheon Company, Strategic Model Simulation of Wars, Weapons, and Arms Controls, Bedford, Mass.: Raytheon Company, BR-1286, p. 1.

24. Rosenau, J. N., editor, *International Politics and Foreign Policy,* Glencoe, Illinois: Free Press, 1961, p. 141.

25. Rummel, R. J., J. Sawyer, H. Guetzkow, and R. Tanter, *Dimensions of Nations,* 1966.

26. Russett, B. M., H. R. Alker, K. Deutsch, and H. D. Lasswell, *World Handbook of Political and Social Indicators,* New Haven, Conn.: Yale University Press, 1964.

27. Singer, J. D., *Human Behavior and International Politics,* Chicago, Ill.: Rand McNally, 1965, p. 6.

28. Singer, J. D., "The Level of Analysis Problem in International Relations," *World Politics,* XIII (October, 1961), pp. 77-92.

29. Welsh, W. A., "Models in the Social Sciences: A General View," in Golembiewski, R. T., W. A. Welsh, and W. J. Crotty, *A Methodological Primer for Political Scientists,* Chicago: Rand McNally, forthcoming, Chapter 14.

30. Zinnes, D. A., "A Comparison of Hostile Behavior of Decision-Makers in Simulate and Historical Data," *World Politics,* XVIII (April, 1966), pp. 474-502.

Chapter 12

ARTIFICIAL INTELLIGENCE
AND INTERNATIONAL RELATIONS[1]

James R. Slagle

ABSTRACT

This paper describes the general nature and purpose of the heuristic programming approach to *artificial intelligence.* It concludes by mentioning some future applications of heuristic programming to the analysis, teaching, and conduct of international relations.

THE HEURISTIC PROGRAMMING APPROACH
TO ARTIFICIAL INTELLIGENCE

The beginning of this paper describes the general nature and purpose of heuristic programming. We then define and discuss gametrees and conclude with an introduction to the heuristic programs that play games.

1. ARTIFICIAL INTELLIGENCE

A research scientist in artificial intelligence tries to get a machine to behave intelligently. Since the machine is almost always a computer, artificial intelligence is a branch of computer science. A machine that behaves intelligently is said to have artificial intelligence, whereas a person has natural intelligence. *Webster's New Collegiate Dictionary* (1961) gives definitions of intelligence that are adequate for our purposes.

[1]Work performed under the auspices of the U. S. Atomic Energy Commission.

246

A. The power of meeting any situation, especially a novel situation, successfully by proper behavior adjustments.

B. The ability to apprehend interrelationships of presented facts
in such a way as to guide action toward a desired goal.

2. DIGITAL COMPUTERS

Almost all the machines to be discussed are computers. By a computer
is here meant a high-speed, general-purpose, stored-program, electronic
digital computer. A computer consists of a storage unit (for example,
magnetic cores), an arithmetic unit, a control unit, input units (for
example, a card reader), and output units (for example, a card punch).
For a particular problem, such a general-purpose computer receives a
program and data through the input units. A program is a list of detailed
instructions which tells how to solve problems of a certain type. The
data given to the computer are those associated with a particular problem
of that type that the program can handle. The computer puts the program and data into the storage unit. The control unit examines the
instructions one by one and uses the arithmetic units when appropriate.
Temporary results are put into the storage unit. An output unit is used
to communicate final results.

In most applications, computers work as extremely fast and accurate
morons. They can, for example, multiply about a million 12-digit numbers
in one second and perform billions of operations without making a
mistake. They manipulate the given data by obeying their instructions
to the letter.

In some applications, computers simulate (behave like) other systems.
For example, they have been used to simulate the United States economy,
the operation of a particular firm, various networks, and even other computers. The behavior of the computer may be anything from a crude
approximation to a near replica of the system being simulated. It may be
faster or slower than the system being simulated. Here and elsewhere in
this paper, when we say that a computer or program does something,
we mean that the combination of computer and program does that thing.

3. APPROACHES TO ARTIFICIAL INTELLIGENCE

The three approaches that researchers have taken to artificial intelligence are artificial networks, artificial revolution, and heuristic pro-

gramming.   Since this paper is about heuristic programming (the approach preferred by the author), only a word will be said about the other approaches.

A network consists of a large number of simple elements and their interconnections.   An artificial network is either simulated on a computer or real.   Often each element is an artificial neuron (nerve cell). One advantage of this approach is that usually the network is adaptive, that is, it can "learn" from experience.   The researchers who take the artificial-network approach point out that many people think that natural intelligence is based on (natural) neural networks alone.   About the best the artificial networks have done is to "learn" to recognize simple visual and aural patterns.   Thus the performance of the networks is far short of intelligent behavior.   One difficulty with this approach is that there is little prospect of making an artificial network as large as the approximately 10^{12} (million million) nerves in the human brain.   In addition, neural physiologists are far from completely understanding how nerves operate and are interconnected.

In the artificial-evolution approach to artificial intelligence, computer-simulated systems are made to evolve by mutation and selection.   Artificial systems have been made to evolve into systems that can solve very simple equations.   Researchers who take this approach point out that many people think that human intelligence evolved by mutations and natural selection.   One difficulty with this approach is that natural evolution is not completely understood.   Another is that this approach is practical only if artificial evolution can be made to proceed enormously faster than natural evolution.

Heuristic programming is the only approach described in the rest of this paper. A heuristic program is a computer program that uses "educated guessing" to discover the solutions to intellectually difficult problems. A heuristic program is good to the extent that it discovers solutions efficiently.   According to *Webster's New Collegiate Dictionary* (1961), the adjective heuristic means "serving to discover." The word heuristic is related to the word eureka ("I have found it"), which comes from the Greek word *heureka.* Some heuristic programs play checkers, chess, and several card games.   The checker program now beats almost everybody and will, it is expected, soon perform beyond the capability of any human.   Other programs can deduce answers to questions from given facts.   Still others solve calculus and chess problems, or prove theorems in mathematical logic and geometry.   For example, the geometry program can prove the rather difficult theorem that if the segment joining the midpoints of the diagonals of a trapezoid is extended to intersect a side of the trapezoid, it bisects that side.

4. PURPOSES OF HEURISTIC PROGRAMMING

The main purposes of artificial intelligence and therefore of heuristic programming are to understand natural (human) intelligence and to use machine intelligence to acquire knowledge and solve intellectually difficult problems. A researcher having the first purpose is a psychologist. He observes subjects thinking aloud while trying to solve intellectually difficult problems. He constructs a model of such problem-solving in the form of a computer program. He notes how the performance of his program deviates from the performances of his subjects. He observes the subjects further and constructs an improved model. The cycle is repeated over and over. There are two important advantages in embodying a model in a computer program. The model is completely specified, and consequences of the model may be found by simply running the program on a computer.

A researcher having the second purpose is interested in getting intelligent behavior and does not care whether the computer uses methods that people use. He hopes that the computer will eventually solve important, intellectually difficult problems, including problems in economics and the social sciences. In his own researches, the author emphasizes the second purpose of artificial intelligence.

An analogy will clarify the two purposes. Unfortunately, this analogy is somewhat unfair to the psychologists. A flying machine might be constructed by an ornithologist or an airplane designer. The ornithologist wishes to understand the natural (bird's) ability to fly. The airplane designer wishes to use the flying machine for transportation.

To date, which purpose the heuristic programmer emphasizes cannot be easily deduced from the heuristic program itself. This is largely due to the fact that a researcher with the second purpose (machine performance) tends to furnish his machine with methods used by people because people are more intelligent than present-day machines. The future work of researchers is expected to diverge according to their purposes, unless the problem domain itself largely determines the methods needed for their purposes.

5. FUTURE APPLICATIONS TO INTERNATIONAL RELATIONS

The applications mentioned below either are not being made at all or are being made on a much smaller scale than the author envisions. Although nobody knows how long it would take to bring them into being, the author fears that it might take a great deal of effort and a long time. On the other hand, he has no doubt that these applications will eventually be made. The applications discussed are to the analysis, teaching, and conduct of international relations.

The analyst should embody his theory in a heuristic program. As we saw before, embodying a model in a computer program has two important advantages. The model is completely specified, and consequences of the model may be found by simply running the program on a computer. The idea is to make these computer models far more realistic and sophisticated than those produced heretofore. The first stage of analysis would be embodied in programs for international relations, arms control and disarmament, world opinion, etc. International relations may be considered an n-person game in which each nation is a player and can take various actions, evaluate situations, and try to maximize the value from its own point of view. Similarly, arms control and disarmament is an n-person "game" among the United States, the Soviet Union, France, etc. The game theory evolving from heuristic programming is far more relevant to these models than is the game theory based on the game matrix. World opinion is a problem-solving task roughly analogous to what occurs in the geometry and calculus programs. The problem solver, the United States, can take various possible actions, which will lead to situations in which (possibly) different actions are possible, etc. Possible future situations can be roughly evaluated. The problem is to perform an action which leads to the greatest possible expected value. The second stage in analysis for the "games" is to simulate the behavior of the nations other than the United States; the simulation is based on past experience with the actions and reactions of the other nations. A computer model is good to the extent that it predicts what really happens.

Heuristic programming will help in the teaching of international relations in several ways. Once the analysts have produced fairly realistic computer models, the student can participate in the model as player or problem-solver. The student can be taught the content of the model so that he will have a deep understanding of international relations. As a teaching machine, the computer can use the computer model to teach the student the contents of the model and how to solve problems in international relations.

Four of the ways in which heuristic programming will help in the conduct of international relations are listed below in order of increasing sophistication. First, a heuristic program will be written to retrieve information. The program is given almost raw data including defense intelligence reports, counterintelligence reports, photo-reconnaissance data, etc. A credibility (probability of being true) is input with each datum. By retrieving information quickly and accurately from a very large amount of data, the program will greatly aid the person conducting international relations. Second, a heuristic program will deduce answers to questions from the given data. The computer will assign a credibility to each answer. Third, once the analysts have produced fairly realistic computer models, the policy maker can try out his ideas in the model before trying them out in reality. The model tells him what other nations will and might do. In this way, he can make very intelligent policy decisions. Fourth, in the even more distant future a heuristic program will make its own very intelligent policy decisions, perhaps beyond the capability of any human.

BIBLIOGRAPHY

1. George W. Baylor and Herbert Simon, "A Chess Mating Combinations Program," *Proceedings of Spring Joint Computer Conference, Boston, 1966.*

2. Daniel Bobrow, "A Question-Answering System for High School Algebra Word Problems," *Proceedings of Fall Joint Computer Conference, AFIPS, San Francisco, 1964*, p. 591.

3. William S. Cooper, "Fact Retrieval and Deductive Question-Answering Information Retrieval Systems," *J. Assoc. Comp. Mach.* (April 1964) p. 117.

4. Edward A. Feigenbaum and Julian Feldman, eds., *Computers and Thought* (McGraw-Hill, New York, 1963).

5. Herbert Gelernter, J. R. Hansing, and D. W. Loveland, "Empirical Explorations of the Geometry Theorem Machine," *Proceedings of the IRE-AIEE-ACM Joint Computer Conference, San Francisco, May 3-5, 1960*, p. 143. Reprinted in *Computers and Thought* (see Ref. 4).

6. Allen Newell and Herbert Simon, "Empirical Explorations of the Logic Theory Machine," *Proceedings of the Western Joint Computer Conference, 1957*, p. 218. Reprinted in *Computers and Thought* (see Ref. 4).

7. J. A. Robinson, "A Machine Oriented Logic Based on the Resolution Principle," *J. Assoc. Comp. Mach. 12*, No. 1, 23 (1965).

8. James R. Slagle, "A Heuristic Program That Solves Symbolic Integration Problems In Freshman Calculus," *J. Assoc. Comp. Mach. 10*, 507, (1963). Reprinted in *Computers and Thought* (see Ref. 4).

9. James R. Slagle, "A Multipurpose, Theorem-Proving Heuristic Program That Learns," *Information Processing 65* (Proceedings IFIP Congress 1965), Vol. II, 1965.

10. James R. Slagle, "Experiments With A Deductive |Question-Answering Program," *Comm. Assoc. Comp. Mach. 8*, No. 12, 792 (December 1965).

11. Lawrence Wos, D. Carson, and George Robinson, "The Unit Preference Strategy in Theorem Proving," *Proceedings of Fall Joint Computer Conference, AFIPS, San Francisco, 1964*, p. 615.

Chapter 13

THE MONTE CARLO METHOD

Harry Sahlin

The objective of this discussion is to describe the Monte Carlo method without being too abstract. The basic ideas behind the Monte Carlo technique for solving complicated problems are extremely simple. We hope to make the basic concepts stand out clearly without incumbering the discussion with too much mathematics. A brief list of references to the literature on the subject is given at the end of the article for the benefit of those readers who may wish to pursue the subject further.

The name Monte Carlo suggests that the technique has some connection with the laws of chance or probability. Before pursuing this connection, I would like to repeat an amusing story that was created by the comedian Bob Newhart.

The story concerns a man who has read that, according to the theory of probability, if enough monkeys are allowed to play with typewriters for a long enough period of time, they will succeed in producing all the work of Shakespeare. The man decides to put the theory to experimental test, and sets 100 monkeys to work with typewriters. After several weeks of experimentation, the monkeys have produced nothing but nonsense, and the man is about to abandon the experiment, when he notices one of the monkeys beginning to type TO BE OR NOT TO BE THAT IS THE ZEGORNINPLOTZZ.

As an interesting sidelight on this story, it has been observed that nothing would be gained by this means of creating great works like those of Shakespeare, because it would take at least another Shakespeare to separate the good material from the gibberish.

[1]Work performed under the auspices of the U. S. Atomic Energy Commission: AEC Contract No. W-7405-eng-48.

HISTORY

The theory of probability is very old, and nearly everyone is familiar with the simpler problems to which it may be applied, such as the prediction of the results of various coin-flipping or dice-throwing experiments. The technique to which the name Monte Carlo is applied is relatively new. The Monte Carlo technique applies the old theory of probability in a new way, namely, to the solution to physical problems. The Monte Carlo method was introduced in 1944 by John von Neumann (the father of the modern computer) and S. Ulam at Los Alamos Laboratory, as a method for dealing with some of the complex problems connected with the development of the atomic bomb. Important contributions to the development and application of the theory were made by Enrico Fermi, Nicholas Metropolis, Herman Kahn, and others.

As an interesting historical note, Steven Brush of the Lawrence Radiation Laboratory has discovered that Lord Kelvin introduced and applied a method that is essentially the same as the modern Monte Carlo method in a paper entitled "Nineteenth Century Clouds Over the Dynamical Theory of Heat and Light," which was published in 1901. This paper by Lord Kelvin is remarkable in other respects. The clouds he pointed to in this article were the failure of the Michelson and Morley experiment to detect a dependence of the speed of light on the speed of the source, and the inability of the existing theories of statistical mechanics and electromagnetic radiation to explain the observed spectra of black body radiation. The first of Lord Kelvin's clouds required the development of the special theory of relativity (1905), and the second foreshadowed the development of quantum mechanics (1925-26). The physicist David Bohm has commented that Lord Kelvin certainly knew how to pick his small clouds.

The Monte Carlo idea introduced by von Neumann and Ulam is essentially based on the observation that one may devise a game of chance which, when played a sufficient number of times, yields final results that are the same as those that would result from some physical process. Instead of solving the "deterministic" equations governing the physical processes, one obtains an estimate of the behavior of the physical system by playing the "indeterministic" game of chance. The fact that one can obtain the behavior of a system that obeys a physical law by probabilistic means, which we think of as being characterized by the absence of a physical law, seems somewhat disconcerting. The harder one thinks about this "paradox," the foggier the distinction between probabilistic and physical laws becomes. However, we shall see that in practice, it is clear how and why the method works, and we do not need to delve deeply into the distinction or lack of distinction between physical and probabilistic laws.

We wish to emphasize that the Monte Carlo method has no necessary connection with high-speed computers. However, in practice the number of times we must play the game of chance in order to obtain a reasonable estimate of the behavior of a physical system is large enough that one is usually forced to use a computer. It is no accident that the rise of the Monte Carlo technique has paralleled development of high-speed computers, and that the originator of the modern computer concept was also one of the inventors of the Monte Carlo method.

SOME SIMPLE RESULTS OF PROBABILITY THEORY

Before proceeding with a discussion of the Monte Carlo method, it will be helpful to discuss briefly a few aspects of probability theory.

If one flips an "honest" coin, the probability p of getting a head is $\frac{1}{2}$, and the probability of not getting a head, i.e., of getting a tail, is $1-p=\frac{1}{2}$. If coin flipping or some similar process is carried out a large number of times, N, and in the course of N trials n heads result, then $\bar{p} - n/N$ is an experimental estimate of the exact probability p. Probability theory predicts that for N large, the probability $P(\bar{p}-p)$ that $\bar{p}$ (the average value of p) and p differ by a fixed amount $\bar{p} - p$ is given by

$$P(\bar{p}-p) = (2\pi\sigma^2)^{-1/2} \exp(-\frac{1}{2}(\bar{p}-p)^2 /\sigma^2), \qquad (1)$$

where σ^2 is called the dispersion or mean square deviation, and is given by

$$\sigma^2 = \frac{p(1-p)}{N}. \qquad (2)$$

The expression given by Eq. (1) is the mathematical form of what is commonly called the *bell-shaped curve,* or *error distribution function,* or the *Gaussian distribution.* The expression is valid even when p *is not* $\frac{1}{2}$. The form of the curve is shown in Figure 1. The area under the curve is one; necessitated by the fact that the total probability of obtaining all possible differences $\bar{p} - p$ is one. Ninety-five per cent of the area under the curve lies between $\bar{p} - p = 2\sigma$, and $p - p = -2\sigma$. This fact tells us that 95 per cent of the time we carry out the coin-flipping experiment, we will obtain an estimate $\bar{p}$ that differs from the exact value p by no more than 2σ. If we consider values of $\bar{p} - p$ which lie between $\pm\sqrt{10}\,\sigma$, then more than 99.9 per cent of the experimental estimates $\bar{p}$ of p will lie in this interval, and so for practical purposes we may say that the experiment estimate $\bar{p}$ "is certain" to differ from p by no more than $\sqrt{10}\,\sigma$.

Now assume that we wish the maximum difference $\sqrt{10}\,\sigma$ between $\bar{p}$ and p

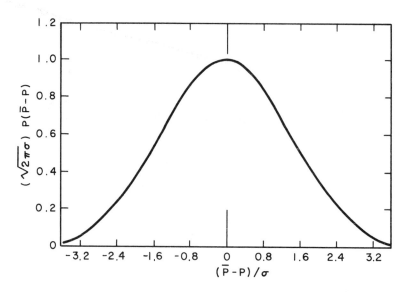

Figure 1. The Gaussian distribution.

to be no greater than some fraction p/m of p. If m is 100 then we are asking that the experimental estimate $\bar{p}$ be within one per cent of the exact result p. By using the expression for σ^2 given by Eq. (2) we may obtain an expression for the number of times N we must flip the coin to obtain the desired accuracy, namely

$$N = 10m^2 \, \frac{(1-p)}{p}. \tag{3}$$

In the case of the coin-flipping experiment, $(1 - p)/p$ is one, and so to obtain an estimate $\bar{p}$ within one per cent of p (i.e., $m = 100$) we require $N = 100{,}000$ flips of the coin. Since it requires about five seconds to slip a coin and record the results, a little over 17 eight-hour days would be required to perform the experiment. We can also see from Eq. (3) that if we are content with an estimate accurate only to ten per cent ($m = 10$), then only 1000 flips of the coin are required, while an accuracy of $\frac{1}{10}$ per cent would require ten million flips of the coin.

It should be mentioned that we have used the known value $p = \frac{1}{2}$ to estimate the number of coin flips required to estimate a number we already know. However, in practice we would not know p but might have some idea that its value is roughly $\frac{1}{2}$. Then the preceding discussion would tell us that roughly 100,000 repetitions of the experiment are required to obtain a "good" experimental estimate of the unknown quantity p.

THE MONTE CARLO METHOD

It is really not necessary to flip a coin in order to estimate the probability of getting a head. The coin-flipping experiment can be replaced by an equivalent experiment. For example, we can construct a dart board that is one foot square, and draw a horizontal line that divides the board into two rectangles of equal area. The top half of this board we could call "heads," and the bottom half of the board "tails." Then we can throw darts at this board and obtain an estimate p by counting the number of darts that land in the top half of the board, and divide this number by the total number, N, of darts thrown. It is, of course, assumed that the darts strike the board "randomly" and that no darts miss the board. The meaning of the term *random* like many basic concepts is intuitively clear but extremely difficult to define precisely. Readers might amuse themselves by trying to provide their own definition of the term.

The dart board that we have used to simulate the flipping of a coin is a simple example of what mathematicians call an abstract sample space. A sample space is simply a "dart board" where different regions correspond to different possible results of a game of chance. If we had wished to simulate the throwing of a die with our dart board, we would have divided it into six regions of equal area, and numbered these regions from one to six.

From the practical point of view, very little has been gained by replacing coin flipping by dart throwing, because both are equally time consuming. However, it is possible to carry out the "dart throwing" mathematically on a high-speed computer, and on the faster computers now in existence, one can "throw a dart" in a little over one-millionth of a second, and complete the entire experiment of 100,000 throws in less than a second. It is now clear why the computer enters the picture. In addition to speed, computers are generally superior to humans at such tedious things as throwing many darts, because they don't get tired and make mistakes, and they can be made to work 24-hour days rather than eight-hour days.[2]

To simulate the dart throwing on a computer one must have a rapid means of generating random numbers whose values lie between zero and

---

[2]We are sometimes inclined to fear computers as a threat to human beings because they are much better than humans at many tasks. However, the machines are at their best when they are employed to do tedious repetitive jobs, and in reality they emancipate people from tedium so that they are free to expend their energy on more creative and satisfying tasks.

one. There are a number of simple means for generating on a computer what are known as *pseudo-random numbers,* where the term *pseudo* is intended to imply that while the numbers are not random in the purest sense, that they are sufficiently random to provide a basis for Monte Carlo computer experiments without causing "significant" distortion of the results obtained through their use.

To carry out the dart-throwing operation on a computer one simply generates a random number that has a value between zero and one. If the number is greater than $\frac{1}{2}$, we record the fact that our mathematical dart has landed in the top half of the board, and if the number is less than $\frac{1}{2}$ we interpret this to mean the dart has failed to land in the top half of the board. This procedure of replacing the flipping of a coin by the throwing of mathematical darts on a computer is a simple illustration of the Monte Carlo technique. Some people would object that we should not call this Monte Carlo, since the game of chance played on the computer simulates another game of chance, coin flipping, rather than a physical process. We shall not concern ourselves with this somewhat academic distinction.

A more interesting game of darts may be devised to estimate the ratio of the circumference of a circle to its diameter. To do this we make a dart board one foot on a side and inscribe a circle of radius $\frac{1}{2}$ foot in this square. The area of this circle is $\pi \left(\frac{1}{2}\right)^2 = \pi/4 \approx 0.78$ square foot, and the area of the dart board is one square foot. The ratio of n, the number of darts that fall inside the circle, to the total number N of darts thrown is an experimental estimate[3] of $\pi/4$, or $4n/N$ is an estimate of π. To play this game on the computer we need to select two random numbers between zero and one for each dart. The first number is used to determine the location of the dart from the left edge of the board, and the second number is used to determine the height of the dart above the bottom edge of the board. After each point is located, the computer determines if the point lies inside or outside the circle; this fact is recorded, and the procedure repeated. In Table 1 several estimates of π obtained by throwing 1000 and 100,000 darts on a computer are shown. Note that the estimates of π based on 100,000 throws tend to be accurate to one more decimal place than those based on 1000 throws.

A slightly more general dart game results if some arbitrary line $y = f(x)$ separates the top of the dart board from the bottom as shown in Figure 2, and we wish to estimate the area of the portion of the board that lies under this line $y = f(x)$ by throwing mathematical darts, as in the previous example, and determining what fraction of the points fall in

[3] A famous problem known as the *Buffon needle problem* is connected with the experimental determination of π and is discussed in the two *Scientific American* articles listed in the bibliography.

Table 1. MONTE CARLO ESTIMATES OF $\pi = 3.1415927\ldots$

Experiment No.	1000 Darts	100,000 Darts
1	3.136	3.13240
2	3.132	3.14760
3	3.182	3.13908
4	3.192	3.14576
5	3.160	3.14124
6	3.140	3.14380
7	3.068	3.13950
8	3.220	3.14040
9	3.228	3.15196
10	3.076	3.14600

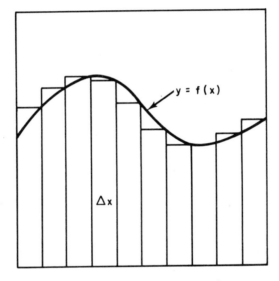

Figure 2. The calculation of the area under a curve.

the region of the dart board below the line. Since the area of the board is one square foot, the fraction n/N that falls below $y = f(x)$ is an estimate of the area under the curve. If this area is about $\frac{1}{2}$, then we know that about 100,000 points are required to get an estimate of the area that is in error by no more than one per cent. There is an easier way to obtain this result. The area under the curve may be approximated[4] by m little rectangles of width Δx as shown in Figure 2. The area of the individual rectangles is easily calculated, and the sum of their areas provide an

[4]The estimate of the area by means of little rectangles is the technique of integral calculus.

estimate of the area under the curve. Note that the rectangles tend to stick above or below the curve by about Δx, and so an upper limit on the error in the estimate of the area under the curve by this method is $[m \, (\Delta x)^2] / 2$, and since $m\Delta x = 1$, the error is about $\Delta x / 2$. If we require this error to be one per cent of the total area of $\frac{1}{2}$, then Δx must be $\frac{1}{100}$, or about 100 rectangles are required to obtain the estimate of the area to the desired accuracy. Thus, estimating the area with little rectangles requires only 100 points, while the Monte Carlo method requires 100,000 points to obtain the same accuracy, and so Monte Carlo is clearly a poor way of obtaining the area under the curve.

If we consider problems similar to that of obtaining the area under the curve in spaces of higher dimensionality, then the virtue of the Monte Carlo technique will become clear.

Consider a cube of edge length one where the top portion of the cube is separated from the bottom portion by some surface $z = f(x,y)$. We wish to obtain an estimate of the volume of the cube that lies under this surface, and we assume that this volume is roughly $\frac{1}{2}$ of the volume of the cube. To obtain the estimate by the Monte Carlo method, we select three random numbers to determine the x, y, and z coordinates of a random point inside the cube, and then determine if the point is above or below the surface. The ratio of the number of points that fall below the surface to the total number of random points selected is then an estimate of the volume of the portion of the cube under the surface. If we want to estimate the volume in a manner analogous to the use we made of little rectangles in the previous case, then we must approximate the volume under the surface by little blocks of length and width Δx. The height of each block will be roughly that of the surface at the location of the block. If we use m little blocks to make the volume estimate, then the error in the estimate will be roughly $m(\Delta x)^3 / 2$, where $m(\Delta x)^2 = 1$, and for one per cent accuracy we would require about 10,000 little blocks. On the other hand, since the volume under the surface is about $\frac{1}{2}$ $\left(p \approx \frac{1}{2} \right)$, the Monte Carlo method would require 100,000 points, as in the previous example, to obtain an estimate accurate to one per cent, and so the Monte Carlo compares more favorably to the method of using little blocks in this case than it did in the one-dimensional example.

It is possible to carry on the reasoning to the determination of a portion of the "volume" of four-, five-, or even 100-dimensional cubes, but it is not possible to visualize such higher dimensional spaces. One finds that as the number of dimensions increases, the number of Monte Carlo points required to obtain an accurate estimate remains at 100,000. However, the estimates based on summing up little volume elements require an increasing number of points so that the Monte Carlo method becomes the most efficient method at about four dimensions, and is the only feasible approach when the number of dimensions of the space is greater than five. This discussion uncovers the feature of the Monte Carlo method that underlies its importance: *the number of samples required is virtually independent of the dimensionality of the space.*

We shall see that many practical problems are equivalent to determining a portion of the volume of a hypercube (a many-dimensional cube) in spaces of several hundred dimensions. The Monte Carlo method is the only existing approach capable of dealing with the more complex multidimensional problems. Even in problems involving only two or three dimensions, the Monte Carlo method is often useful. This is usually the case when the boundary of the region of space being investigated is unpleasantly complicated, resulting in the impotence of both analytical methods and deterministic numerical schemes. For example, the temperature distribution in a right circular cylinder heated by a resistor lying along its axis is amenable to analytic treatment, while the same problem for a corkscrew would defy analytical treatment.

THE IMPORTANCE OF BEING CLEVER

We have indicated that the Monte Carlo method would require the same number of experimental points, to attain a given accuracy, for a problem in a 300-dimensional space as would be required for a similar problem in a one-dimensional space. This fact, however, does not imply that the same amount of computer time is consumed in each case. In the 300-dimensional case, one must select 300 random numbers for each point, and, consequently, the computer time per point goes up at least linearly with the number of dimensions. The mathematical form of the many-dimensional surface that separates the volume of the hypercube into two regions may cause the difficulty of deciding if a Monte Carlo point is "above" or "below" this hypersurface to increase as the square of the numbers of dimensions. Consequently, the computer time per point in a 300-dimensional space could be as much as 90,000 times larger than the time per point for a similar one-dimensional calculation. Thus, if the one-dimensional calculation required one second to do 100,000 points, the 300-dimensional calculation might require 25 hours of computer time for 100,000 points. Since high-speed computer time may cost between $100 and $1000 per hour, there is clearly a strong incentive to devise more clever Monte Carlo schemes that can reduce the computation time by a factor of 10 or 100. In fact, much of the present literature on Monte Carlo techniques is concerned with the problem of reducing computation time by developing more sophisticated applications. Even if cost is not the consideration, large reduction in the computation time is quite desirable. Modern high-speed computers are quite remarkable when their speed at doing arithmetic is compared to that of a human being (the best existing computers can exceed human ability to do calculations by a factor of as much as 300 million), but they are still rather weak tools when compared to the requirements of many interesting problems that one might wish to tackle. Clever Monte Carlo techniques can permit one to tackle problems of otherwise impossible difficulty on existing machines.

To provide a simple example of one means of reducing computational time, we will consider another dart board example. Consider the dart board shown in Figure 3. Instead of wanting to know the area of one of the circles shown in the figure, we assume that we want to know the average score our random dart thrower would obtain if he threw a large number of darts. We shall assume that the 10-, 20-, 30-, 40-, and 50-point regions shown on the figure all have the same area. Then on the average we will expect the same number of darts to land in each region that has a point value of ten or more. The average score would be computed by multiplying the number of darts that fell in each region by the point value of that region, and then dividing the sum of all these values by the total number of darts thrown.

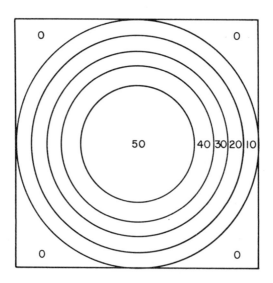

Figure 3. All nonzero point value regions have the same area.

This "Monte Carlo" method of estimating the average score is inefficient because the 50-point region will contribute five times more heavily to the score than the ten-point region, but we have allocated the same number of darts to the ten-point region as we have to the 50-point region. Because the regions of smaller point value contribute less significantly to the score than regions of high point value, it is not necessary to be as accurate in estimating the contribution of the low-point-value regions as in estimating the contribution of the regions of high point value.

In order to be more efficient in obtaining the estimate of the average score, we need a method which directs the darts preferentially toward the regions of greatest importance. One way of doing this is to replace the old dart board by the new dart board shown in Figure 4. The regions of this new board all have the same point value, but the area of the regions has been selected so that the ratio of the areas on the new board is the same as the ratio of the point values of the corresponding regions on the old board. It can be seen that this procedure will cause the most darts to fall in the regions that contribute most significantly to the average score. This example is an illustration of what is known as *importance sampling.* One uses knowledge of the relative importance of various regions to bias the computer game so as to expend computer time on the various regions in proportion to the importance of their respective contribution to the answer.

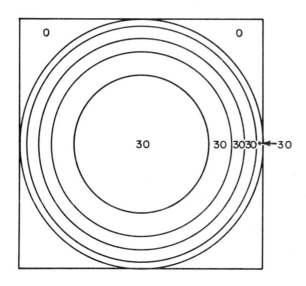

Figure 4. Biased random sampling.

PHYSICS AND MANY-DIMENSIONAL MONTE CARLO

We would now like to indicate why many types of physics problems are equivalent to the determination of the hypervolume of a region in a many-dimensional space. In the book *One Two Three Infinity*, George Gamov discusses what is known as the *random walk problem* by considering a drunkard staggering around a lamp post. The inebriated individual starts at the lamp post and moves in a particular direction a distance L, and then falls down. When he stands up again he moves off in a random direction a distance L, falls again, and so on. Thus, the motion of the drunk consists of a large number of randomly directed path segments of length L. The problem is to determine the probability of finding the man a distance r from the lamp post after he has taken a large number of steps. The answer to this problem is proportional to the expression given by Eq. (1) if $\overline{p} - p$ is replaced by r, and the dispersion σ^2 increases linearly with time.

For simplicity we will assume that there is a sidewalk that runs past the lamp post and we will use the edge of this sidewalk as an x axis, and then consider only the component of the drunkard's motion that is directed along this sidewalk. It can be seen that the component[5] of the drunk's motion between falls that is directed along the sidewalk will range between $+L$ and $-L$.

We wish to consider the mathematical formulation of the problem of predicting the probability that the sidewalk component, or x component, of the drunk's position will have some value x_n after he has executed n straight-line segments of length L. From now on we will refer to these path segments as *steps*. We will let x_0 be his x coordinate before he has taken the first step. If he begins his random walk at the lamp post, then $x_0 = 0$. After the first step, the drunkard's x coordinate may have a number of values which we will designate by the variable x_1. Similarly, x_2 will stand for his possible x coordinate after two steps, x_{3_i} the coordinate after three steps, etc.

We will let $K(x_0, x_1)$ stand for the "one-step probability"[6] that if the man was at x_0 then after one step he would be at x_1. Similarly $K(x_1, x_2)$ will represent the probability that after his second step his x coordinate will have changed from x_1 to x_2, etc. We will assume for simplicity that the possible x coordinate values are discrete. For example, we might specify his position to the nearest sidewalk square.

[5] The component along the sidewalk of the ith path segment of length L will be $L \cos \theta_i$ where θ_i is the angle this path segment makes with sidewalk; all values of θ_i are equally profitable.

[6] $K(x_i, x_{i+1}) \propto L \cos(\theta_{i+1})$

Then if we wish to know the probability $P(x_0, x_2)$ that the man's x coordinate has changed from x_0 to x_2 in two steps, we must multiply $K(x_0, x_1)$ by $K(x_1, x_2)$ and sum over all permissible one-step values x_1.

$$P(x_0, x_2) = \sum_{x_1} K(x_0, x_1) \, K(x_1, x_2)$$

This summation over x adds up the contribution of possible two-step paths between x_0 and x_2. For fixed values of x_0 and x_2, this summation over x is equivalent to determining the area under a curve, where the line $y = f(x)$ in Figure 2 is given by $f(x_1) = K(x_0, x_1) \, K(x_1, x_2)$. We have seen that the Monte Carlo method may be employed to solve such problems.

Similarly, if we want to know $P(x_0, x_3)$, the probability that the man's x coordinate changes from x_0 to x_3 in two steps, we must carry out the double summation

$$P(x_0, x_3) = \sum_{x_1} \sum_{x_2} K(x_0, x_i) \, K(x_1, x_2) \, K(x_2, x_3), \qquad (4)$$

where the sums on x_1 and x_2 add up the contributions of all paths leading in three steps from x_0 to x_3. A graphical representation of the paths leading from x_0 to x_3 is shown in Figure 5. If x_0 and x_3 are held fixed and the points x_1 and x_2 are moved up and down, then all paths linking x_0 and x_3 are generated. The double summation

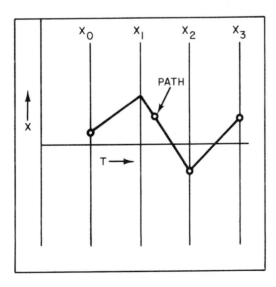

Figure 5. Three-step random walk paths.

involved in the determination of $P(x_0, x_3)$ is equivalent to determining the portion of the volume of a cube that lies under a surface. The equation of the surface $z = f(x_1, x_2)$ is given by the K product in Eq. (4). It can now be seen that the determination of $P(x_0, x_n)$, the probability that the drunkard's x coordinate is x_n after n steps, would be equivalent to the Monte Carlo problem of determining a portion of the volume of a hypercube in an n-dimensional space.

The problem of the motion of a drunk is by no means impractical. Many physical problems have a behavior very similar to that of a man staggering around a lamp post. For example, if a bottle of ammonia is opened at one end of a still room, then about a half an hour will be required before the smell of ammonia is detectable at the other side of the room. This is a little surprising when one realizes that the ammonia molecules move with the speed of a rifle bullet. The reason these fast moving projectiles require so long to cross the room is because they collide many billions of times per second with air molecules. The ammonia molecules suffer a change in direction of motion each time they collide with another molecule, and so their path has the same irregular character as that of a drunk.

The behavior of neutrons in a nuclear reactor also has this random-walk character. The rapidly moving neutrons collide very frequently with atoms of the reactor materials, and once born in fission they diffuse around inside the reactor until they escape, are captured by an atom, or cause the fission of another uranium nucleus.

One might even simulate a "simple" problem in economics by considering a town of 1000 people who initially possess $1000 apiece. Imagine that each person may spend up to $10 a day, and ask what the distribution of wealth is after this economic system has evolved for 100 days. This problem is similar to that of the drunkard, or the ammonia molecule, or the neutron diffusion. The mathematical formulation of all these problems has the same structure. The individual character of a specific problem is contained in the mathematical expression employed for the "one-step probabilities" $K(x_i, x_{i+1})$. The mathematical form of K is determined by the particular physical law that governs a system's one-step behavior. In the case of the 1000-person economic model, $K(x_i, x_{i+1})$ would be an expression determining how an individual will distribute the $10 he spends in a single day among the other members of his community. Physical problems are much simpler than economic problems, because in most cases the physical laws needed to determine K are known. The real difficulty connected with human behavior problems is not deducing results once K is given, but in discovering laws or approximate laws which permit one to obtain an expression of K.

BIASED RANDOM WALK

The random-walk problem of the drunkard that we have considered does not really involve physical laws but only probabilistic laws. This is because we have assumed that when the man stands up after a fall, he is equally likely to move in any direction. We have not considered the possibility that certain physical features of this environment could cause him to move preferentially in one direction. Many random-walk-like problems actually have a mixed nature that involves both probabilistic and physical laws. We want to consider how certain features of the drunkard's environment can be used to illustrate this mixed behavior.

If the wind is blowing in a particular direction, then we would expect the drunkard to move more often with the wind than against the wind. Thus, under the combined influence of alcohol and wind, the steps of the drunkard are no longer completely random. The wind has established a preferred direction. Similarly, if the ground near the lamp post has a shallow valley, then the drunk is likely to be found near the bottom of this depression, because it takes less work to take a step downhill than to take a step uphill. The wind and the topography of the ground are examples of environment factors that introduce a causal component into the drunkard's otherwise random behavior.

Finally we wish to consider how one can be sophisticated in the application of Monte Carlo techniques to problems of a random-walk nature. We have mentioned that if the ground has a depression the drunkard will tend to wander into this depression. If we imagine the rather unlikely situation that the drunkard is wearing stilts, then he can take very long steps. Long steps will tend to carry him quite a bit above the bottom of the depression, and he will be unable to complete many of his steps, because they require too much energy. Thus, big steps will result in many false steps, while smaller steps lead to gradual changes in elevation permitting the drunk to easily find the path of least resistance, and wander to the bottom of the little valley.

If one solves this problem by Monte Carlo simulation, then the random selection of points will have the same consequence as large steps, much computer time will be wasted on regions of little significance, and only a small part of the time will be used to explore the important region near the bottom of the depression in the ground. What is needed is a Monte Carlo scheme that will cause the sampling to concentrate on the important regions; we need to simulate the drunk's ability to "blunder" along the path of least resistance. It can be seen that such a scheme should select a new Monte Carlo point near the previous Monte Carlo point, and allow a small step downhill with a greater probability than a small step uphill.

Such a biased random-walk method has been developed by Metropolis, Rosenbluth, and Teller to deal with problems in statistical mechanics. One problem to which we have applied this method is the determination of the properties of matter in the centers of very dense stars. It is possible to simulate the behavior of systems of many particles by considering only about 100 mathematical particles on the computer. In such a calculation each particle has its own three-dimensional space, and so the study of 100 particles requires a 300-dimensional space. The Monte Carlo investigation of a problem of this type is similar to the random walk of a drunk in a 300-dimensional space. The physical characteristics of the problem create a "valley" in this 300-dimensional space, and the most important contributions to the results come from the bottom of this valley. The Metropolis-Rosenbluth-Teller method forces the computer time to be expended primarily in the region of greatest importance. This form of importance sampling permits a calculation that would require 25 hours of high-speed computer time, if done by less sophisticated methods, to be carried out in an hour or less.

CONCLUSION

We have illustrated the nature of the Monte Carlo method and indicated why being clever in its application is important. In applying the basic laws of Monte Carlo to problems, one should be guided by what might be called the *principle of democratic ignorance.* This principle dictates that any partial knowledge one has of the behavior of the system under study should be used to bias the random sampling so as to favor the selection of Monte Carlo points in the regions that contribute most strongly to the final result. In regions where one has no prior knowledge of relative importance, the sampling should be democratic, i.e., unbiased.

Finally we would like to emphasize that the Monte Carlo technique is a tool for dealing with complex problems, once a quantitative formulation of the problem has been achieved. The primary difficulty in the non-physical sciences is arriving at the problem formulation. One method of problem formulation that might be employed is to use existing knowledge to make an educated guess at the laws governing a system's behavior, and then use the postulated laws to create a mathematical model whose behavior can be investigated by some technique such as the Monte Carlo method. The consequence of the model may then be compared with experience to see if the postulated laws lead to a realistic simulation of the real system. Iterative use of this procedure could lead to the development of increasingly realistic laws. It seems likely to me that computers will ultimately be more important to the behavioral sciences than to the physical sciences. The reason for this belief is my feeling that the inherent complexity of human behavior will make it impossible to develop models that are simple enough to be investigated without a computer and still possess any significant predictive value.

Computers have an extremely important influence on efforts to quantify concepts, an influence that is not often stated. To employ a computer to the solution of any problem, one must state the problem with absolute precision. By being forced to be absolutely explicit about the problem statement, one often reaches a much deeper understanding of the problem. It is possible to gain more from the rigorously disciplined process of posing the problem to the computer than from the numerical answers that are obtained from the calculation.

REFERENCES

1. Lord Kelvin (1901). "Nineteenth Century Clouds Over the Dynamical Theory of Heat and Light," *Phil. Mag* (6) *2*, 1-40.

2. Daniel McCracken (1955), "The Monte Carlo Method," *Scientific American,* May, 1955. A popular introduction to the Monte Carlo method.

3. George Gamov (1947), *One Two Three Infinity,* Viking Press. An enjoyable, and authoritative popular treatment of mathematics and physics. A discussion of the random-walk process is given in this book.

4. Mark Kac (1964), "Probability," *Scientific American,* September, 1964. A popular introduction to probability theory.

5. Herman Kahn (1950), "Random Sampling (Monte Carlo) Techniques in Neutron Attenuation Problems," I and II, *Nucleonics 6,* 27-37 and 60-65. A readable introduction to Monte Carlo methods and variance reducing techniques.

6. *Symposium on Monte Carlo Methods* (1956), edited by Herbert Mayor, John Wiley and Sons. This volume contains a collection of papers presented at a symposium on Monte Carlo methods held at the University of Florida. These papers, and particularly the paper by Herman Kahn, provide an excellent introduction to Monte Carlo techniques. The volume also provides information on the history of the development of the Monte Carlo method as well as an extensive list of references on the Monte Carlo method.

7. Hammersley and Handscomb (1964), *Monte Carlo Methods,* John Wiley and Sons. This book is a concise introduction to the Monte Carlo method and its application to a variety of mathematical and physical problems. The book also contains an extensive list of references on the Monte Carlo method.

8. *Methods in Computational Physics,* Vol. 1 (1963), edited by Berni Alder, Sidney Fernbach, and Manuel Potenberg, Academis Press. This book contains eight extensive articles on the application of Monte Carlo methods to a variety of physical problems.

9. N. Metropolis, A. W. Rosenbluth, M. N. Rosenbluth, A. H. Teller and E. Teller (1953), "Equations of State Calculations by Fast Computing Machines," *J. Chem. Phys. 21,* 1087-1092. This is the fundamental paper on the application of Monte Carlo methods to statistical mechanics.

10. S. G. Brush, H. Sahlin, and E. Teller (1966), "A Monte Carlo Study of One Component Plasma," *J. Chem. Physics 45,* 2102-2118. An application of the Monte Carlo method to the properties of matter at very high density.

11. *The Monte Carlo Method* (1966), edited by U. A. Shreider, translated from Russian by G. J. Tee, Pergamon Press (1966), Russian edition (1962). This recently issued translation of the Russian original, provides a readable discussion

of the Monte Carlo method, and treats a variety of applications. The book contains an extensive bibiliography that includes many Russian references, and text provides interesting information about Russian computers.

Chapter 14

PICTURES, COMPUTERS, AND INPUT-OUTPUT

G. A. Michael

ABSTRACT

Graphic data processing is presented in relation to high speed computation as a powerful input-output technique. An attempt has been made to discuss methods and equipment aspects in terms of the elementary properties of the picture generating devices presently being used. Enough detail is included to permit estimation of the applicability of these methods to various problems.

INTRODUCTION

I have assumed that it is not necessary to belabor the singular importance of vision in conveying data to the brain. This faculty is fundamental to computer graphics, or as we will refer to it in this article, *graphic data processing*. The importance of this method was never really doubted by the first computer users, but it is only in the last five years or so that it has caught the attention of a great many people. The single, most compelling reason for this is the increasing speed of computing devices. That is, the earlier computers were not generally fast enough to do both computing and display control.

Because the role of graphic data processing will thereby take on added significance, let us pause for a moment to review the progress in computer technology. Since 1950 the internal processing speed of computers[1] has risen by a factor of 1000 or so. Memory capacity,

[1] As used in this article, the term computer always means *digital* computer.

in turn, has been increased by a factor of 100. Figure 1 shows this
development and attempts to indicate what we can expect in the

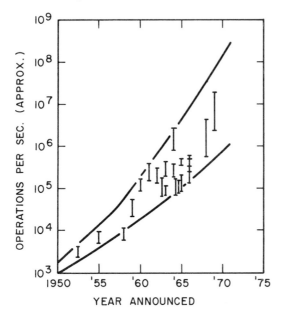

Figure 1. Improvements in computer speed.

future.   The UNIVAC (1953) had a 1000 word memory, took 525
μsec for addition and 2150 μsec for multiplication. Contrast this with
the CDC 6600 (1965)[2] with 131,072 words which adds in about 0.3
μsec and multiplies in about 0.5 μsec.   Beyond the issue of speed,
today's computers also have larger and faster backup storage devices,
such as disks and drums, and a much expanded command repertoire.
While speed and memory have increased, purchase costs have risen
by less than a factor of ten.   This improvement in speed was brought
about by a technology based on solid state physics, and constitutes
one of the most significant advances in computing during the past
fifteen years.
    In contrast to the feverish efforts to improve the computer, very few
improvements have been made to input-output procedures. While we
might choose from among all sorts of flattering definitions for graphics
the most honest one simply says that graphic data processing is fundamentally a very efficient input-output technique in which information
is exchanged between the computer and the user primarily in the form

[2] The times quoted assume optimum utilization of the computer.

of pictures. The measure of efficiency is from the point of view of the user, not the computer, and the idea of a picture is broader than that of a photographic image. It should be noted that not all system designers agree with this point of view, particularly on the issue of efficiency measurement. Thus what follows represents only one point of view.

In any case, when we consider that during the next one or two decades computer speeds may increase by another factor of 1000, we naturally expect that some thought be given to how this increased capacity can best be used.

So far, the idea of structuring results according to user convenience seems sound. Rather than redirect the way people acquire information it seems easier, at least initially, to make the computer conform to people. Thus the rationale for graphics arises out of an immediate need to cope with the enormous flood of data being produced through computation.

There is one other point about graphics and user efficiency worth noting. The optimum utilization of a computer is on a demand basis from the point of view of the user. That is, he wants what he wants when he wants it, and very often even he can't control his own needs. To see this we note that the true symbiosis of man and machine has each doing what each is good at. It is only necessary then, to observe that primarily, the man is providing creativity, albeit randomly, while the computer does the routine, programmable tasks and stores a complete record of the transactions in a retrievable form. Thus, a system will be useful in direct proportion to the degree of cognizant interaction it provides to the user. This, in turn, translates simply into two basic computer requirements: memory and speed, in that order. Given these we can build real systems that will serve large numbers of people on their own terms.

EQUIPMENT

It is not my intention to consider specifically, the kinds of equipment used for graphics but since the cathode ray tube (CRT) is so commonly used for this work, some understanding of its functional properties is necessary. The name, *cathode ray* was first used by W. Hittorf (in 1868) who was studying the phenomena of flourescence in connection with the discharge of electricity in an evacuated glass bottle. W. Crookes showed (1879) that these rays were better thought of as negatively charged particles; he assumed that the particles were negatively charged atoms. Other researchers, H. Hertz (1892), J. Perrin (1895), J. J. Thomson

(1897), succeded in deducing that they were much smaller, and in fact today these particles are called *electrons* and are thought to be one of the several basic entities in the universe. (One of Thomson's collaborators, J. Stoney is credited with the first use of the word, *electron.* Thus while the cathode ray tube is more accurately called an *electron beam tube,* it is rather unlikely that the original name will ever be replaced.

A CRT is usually an elongated high-vacuum tube having a cylindrical section mated to a conical section (Figure 2). The glass base of the cone is called a screen or face plate and is coated on the inside with a compound that emits light when struck by electrons that have been emitted at the other end of the tube. The movement of electrons is defined as electrical current and rather precise methods are available for controlling this current. After the electrons have been ejected from the cathode or gun, they can be accelerated, focused, and deflected. That is to say,

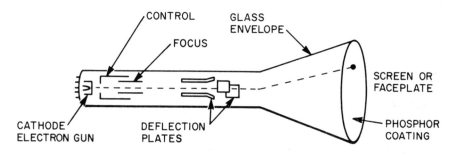

ELECTROSTATIC DEFLECTION

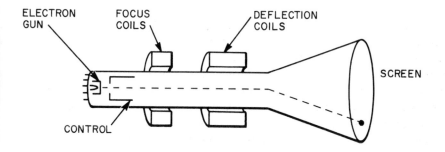

MAGNETIC DEFLECTION

Figure 2. Magnetic deflection.

there are electrical and magnetic equivalents to lenses, prisms, filters, shutters, and so on. In any case, the reason for using a CRT under computer control is that it provides us with the ability to transform electrical signals into light which we can see or photograph. Furthermore, the electron current can be turned on and off and deflected both very rapidly and precisely.

There are two general methods (Figure 2), for controlling the light-producing beam of electrons. The electromagnetic (or magnetic) deflection scheme is ordinarily held to be capable of higher positioning accuracy than the other way. Alternatively magnetic deflection takes longer. Some CRT's use a combination of the two, but whatever the niceties may be, the most significant aspect for our purposes is that we can use this device to build up (so to speak) pictures point by point. With sufficient effort, this process could imitate photography. From the point of view of information content, however, we ordinarily prefer to have small amounts presented rapidly. The method by which a computer-oriented description of a picture is translated into electrical currents and voltages need not concern us. It is enough to know that it can be done. Figure 2a shows some of the functional relationships between the components of a display generator although I do not wish to imply that all of them are always necessary.

Let us go one final step, however, and consider the mechanics of picture generation. When we wish to plot something we also have to say where to plot it. The addressing scheme normally chosen is obtained by assuming that a two-dimensional Cartesian coordinate system is superimposed on the screen of the CRT. In both the horizontal (X) and vertical (Y) directions we can assign integers for each point to which the electron beam may be digitally deflected. Most CRT's provide at least 1024 X and 1024 Y locations, and any X may be associated with any Y value. The conventional way of denoting this is with powers of two since most computers use binary arithmetic. Thus we have $2^{10} \times 2^{10}$ points in the example above. While distances spanned in each direction depend on the screen size, it is most useful for the purposes of graphics to require that they be as equal as possible. The (square) array of points thus obtained is technically called a *lattice*, but *raster* is more commonly used. In any case, two numbers (X and Y) are needed to define a screen address. One number is needed to define the CRT function (point, line, character, etc.). Numbers would also be needed for intensity, for size control, and whatever else there may be. The computer program must pack all these together in the appropriate "display word" format prior to sending them to the display where they will be decoded and acted upon.[3]

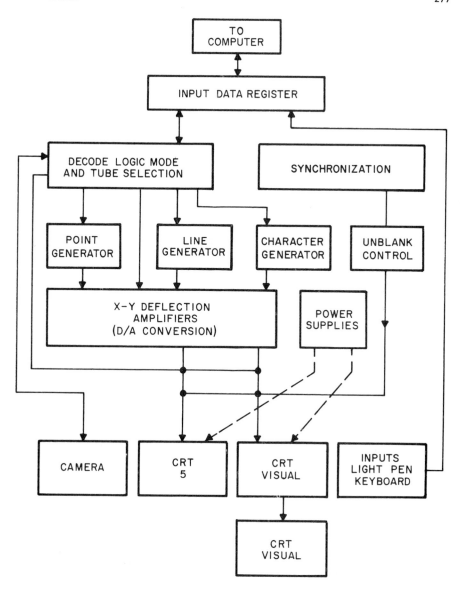

Figure 2A. Display generator block diagram.

<hr>

[3]Whenever possible it is most efficient to make the display word size commensurable with the computer word. Furthermore the chosen positions of the various numbers within the word should be convenient relative to the instruction repertoire of the computer.

There are a variety of ways to interconnect a computer and one display. Indeed such configurations exist at hundreds of installations around the country. Aside from a few special military applications, there are hardly any configurations of multiple display terminals attached to a central computer. By implication it is suggested that this is a major technical problem confronting graphical data processing today. How do we economically provide for a large number of display consoles to be attached to one central computing facility so that they may each function independently and simultaneously? One immediate solution that suggests itself is indicated in Figure 3. That is, we share computer capacity among several remote terminals thereby exploiting the difference in "reaction" times between men and computers. Obviously we also expect that the cost per user is lower for this arrangement.

There are several observations we can make about Figure 3, which are keyed to the circled letters:

At A: Any computer could be used. The display procedures are easier if the computer is "time shared" and has such features as

A1   A large addressable memory,
Floating point arithmetic,
Indexing and indirect addressing,
Bit and byte manipulation,
Buffered input-output and priority interrupt,
A cycle time comparable to display processing time.

B: The buffer memory can be part of the computer's memory. If the memory is associated with the display it still can act like computer memory. The main difference is primarily cost (private buffer memory tends to cost more).

C: Regardless of the memory option, a transmission unit is needed if the display is physically located more than a few hundred feet from the computer. If the buffer memory is physically located at the display terminal, lower bandwidth digital data lines can be used but the transmission time increases.

D: The display generator is functionally that device which receives digital signals, interprets (decodes) them, and produces all the necessary sequential signals, both analog and digital, needed to cycle the CRT or other display devices. For the usual CRT this amounts to generating the inputs to the deflection amplifiers (X and Y), and focus amplifiers, the unblank amplifiers, and so on — all of which control the

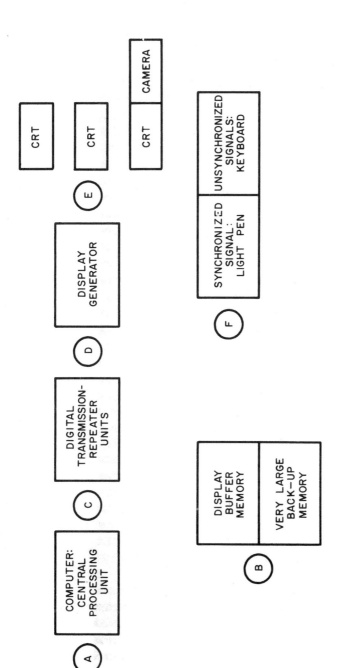

Figure 3. Multiple display — computer interfacing.

electron beam.   Synchronizing pulses are also sent both to the CRT and the transmission unit.

E: The appropriate outputs control the actual display of information on the CRT's. Some independent manual controls such as focus, intensity, light pen sensitivity, and gross raster positioning are often available to the viewer.

F: The light pen signals (see p. 293) are synchronized in the sense that the "name" of the picture part that the light pen sees is "available" to the computer. An active interrupt, or a flag, which can be sampled by the program is set when the light pen sees light. Inputs such as keyboards are unsynchronized in the sense that what is being displayed at the instant that a key is depressed is not necessarily correlated to the key action.

In either case the information is usually returned through the transmission unit (C) or directly to the central control unit of the computer. In some few instances where a private buffer memory is used, light pen hits cause a bit to be set in the appropriate word. Entire strings of characters are also often deposited in the local memory so that the computer, upon receipt of a "message ready" signal, will read the whole message into its own memory for further processing.

We should note one additional point that is more pertinent to microfilm recorders. The problem of interfacing a display device to a computer is logically subordinate to deciding whether to display at all. An alternative is to write a tape in an agreed upon format and subsequently "play it" off-line on the display. Both approaches have advantages some of which are given below, though from a user's point of view it is usually more satisfying to be able to plot *and* watch on-line.

Off-line operation advantages:

1.   The tape record is permanent and can be produced into film at any later time.
2.   Film wastage is minimized since unneeded plots can be skipped over on tape and recovered later if desired.
3.   Picture quality can be higher because the display can be given a "special tune-up" prior to plotting.
4.   Computer time is saved.

On-line operation advantages:

1.   The time needed to plot a picture can be overlapped with other

computer activities. If subsequent copies are needed the film can be duplicated.

2.   The "average" display can accept output faster than standard tape writing takes place.
3.   Very often errors can be caught (by observing the equivalent visual display) and quickly corrected — thereby saving a certain amount of computer time.
4.   The more important time to save is that of people, not machines.
5.   Off-line operation usually ties up a tape unit which is thereby unavailable to computer users.

The standard use of computer controlled microfilm recorders is in the production of flow charts, graphs, listings, engineering drawings, and so on. Some of this film is first mounted on aperture cards, or viewed directly with a variety of microfilm reader-printers. Various techniques have been devised for also marking the film with a machine readable code for automatic filing, sorting, and retrieving. Other applications use the film as an intermediate material on the way to making prints, because no other present output method is as fast, flexible, and inexpensive. At our laboratory, for example, we use nearly 30,000 feet of film per month, and make hard copy from about 85% of it. About 75% of the printing is done one page per frame, but the rest consists of computer generated reports, and many copies are made. The remaining 15% of the microfilm is devoted to motion picture production. A growing number of research centers moreover have begun using their equipment to produce these motion sequences. By and large, the material is drawn from the physical sciences and mathematics although it is by no means limited to these fields. No amount of verbalizing has quite the power to convey information or stimulate our intuition as have motion sequences. Beyond the use of motion it is also possible to employ color and stereoscopic views to add even more content to the filmed output. These techniques become relatively easy to employ by using computer control, but at the same time they require some additional explanation. When we consider motion, it is in context of sensing changes in the position of one body relative to another at particular time-points. For example, a standard motion picture camera photographs the positional relationships every $\frac{1}{12}$ of a second. This time taken as an independent variable, is called *real time*, or *problem time*, as distinguished from the *computer time* necessary to actually do the calculation. Thus a calculational model of, say, galactic evolution might require only a few hours to run on a computer, while the real time implied is several billion years. Again, it might take several hours to calculate the motion of a projectile fired from a gun barrel while the real time is only a few tenths of a second.

Some of the space programs use computers to control the launch procedures in real time. In this case the problem (real) time is roughly the same as the computer time.

Suppose we wanted to make a motion study of a bouncing ball. We might then identify the following picture features:

1. An object or set of objects that are to be moved (or animated).
2. A set of procedures, algorithms or equations that describe each type of motion.
3. Special visual effects, cues, and backgrounds.

Most likely we would use a circle (or sphere) to represent the ball, but we might for the sake of realism want to cause it to deform in a physically correct way as it bounces. From the computer program point of view, a circle is either a large set of points to identify the edge of the ball, or ideally, a set of equations which are used to generate the points. The physical laws that describe the motion of falling bodies are, in this example, precisely the set of procedures that describe the motion of the ball. They simply "say" at a given time where the ball is located relative to some starting point. To these we could add descriptions (again mostly mathematical) of the elastic properties of the ball and the surface on which it is bouncing. The question of special effects has to be answered relative to a particular requirement. *Any* effect that can be described in terms of the elementary computer and display properties can be pictorialized. When modeling physical motions such as a bouncing ball, we are often interested in seeing a "slow motion" representation. The real time interval at which the equations of motion are evaluated controls this type of visual effect.

Again, by changing the "size" of the ball we can give the illusion of motion toward or away from the viewer. A calibrated set of scales will permit an estimate of how high a "real" ball would bounce. The range of possibilities is predominantly limited by the designer's imagination. In programming rapid motions one caution is that they tend to produce a stroboscopic effect if successive positions are too dissimilar. This can be interpreted as setting a practical upper limit on the time interval between successive frames.

PROGRAMMING AND OTHER SYSTEM CONSIDERATIONS

From a user's point of view, we might be more properly interested in a list of elementary abilities that a display generator can have today. It is easy to see that whatever the display produces, must, in the final analysis, be combinations of its elementary functions. I have tabulated these in descending order of importance in Table I. That is, plotting a point seems to be most basic in the sense that lines, arcs, and characteristics can be made with points. All the other features are time savers, although admittedly of great importance. Depending on factors such as frequency of use, execution times and costs, some of these functions will be expressed as computer programs while others can be built into the display generator circuitry. In most cases, the "wired in" functions are chosen on the basis of speed considerations, but these clearly make the equipment more complicated and expensive. A circle generator is an example of a built in function that might be so justified; although when time is not a serious problem, programming methods exist for producing very satisfactory results in almost every case.

As we have seen, a motion picture of a bouncing ball, is basically a sequence of plotted points, lines, film movements, and so on. For user convenience one can combine certain of these elementary functions, into defined or derived functions of functions and do this in a fairly general way. Thus the user need not always think of, say, three connected line segments, but rather call for the "triangle" function. Further, we can link the "triangle" function with others of these higher functions to any desired level. This is one of the properties of the artifice I have called a *glyph*. A glyph is *any* combination of the elementary or higher functions to which is assigned a unique name. There can clearly be combinations of glyphs. We can also assign properties to them such as color, size, rotation and translation rates, and so on. The total description is kept in a nesting of file lists and directories such that the programmer can, with a minimum of bookkeeping distraction, produce graphical presentations and alter them at any depth he desires. The second part of Table I gives some examples of typical properties that glyphs might be useful. An important thing to notice is that such files imply a precise, reproducible description of a picture or an actual thing in a form suited to automatic processing. They are alterable, retrievable, and communicable. Thus, they are clear statements of ideas or procedures in terms of a fixed, known set of primitives. The user guides the kind of processing done with these lists. For example, he may request a visual display or hard copy or he may make modifications to the basic files or generate new subsets from them.

The ease of doing these things depends somewhat on the equipment but more so on the programming design and implementation. As things stand today, this is an area in which there are more questions than answers. We have very few good guidelines and essentially no theory.

Let us consider four typical operations that could be applied to the displayed data. A stereoscopic view can be produced, color marking is often helpful, a perspective mapping can be done, and finally, we can employ texturing. These and many other techniques, separately or in various combinations, are useful because they can improve the realism of the output. But more significantly, they are ways of packing more information into a display.

While the method we use to add color to a picture gives the best and most consistent quality, it is only appropriate to filmed displays. The total picture is organized in the computer as a number of separate picture parts according to the colors that we want the finished picture to have. When these picture parts are plotted, and photographed, each frame of the black and white film contains only those picture parts that are to ultimately appear in one color. We call this procedure *logical color separation.* It is obvious that any reasonable number of separate black and white frames (and therefore hues) could be produced for each final frame of color film. In practice we have used eight separate colors and obtained satisfactory results. The separated picture parts are remerged through the appropriate color filters, onto color film using a "special effects optical reduction step printer." Figure 4 shows this schematically.

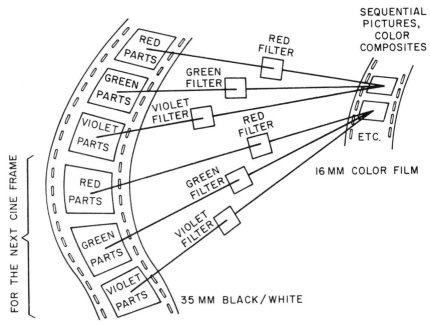

Figure 4. Method of color separation.

The illusion of three-dimensional projections requires that two related views be produced. One view is for the left and the other is for the right eye. It is a simple matter for the computer to generate these views. Stereo viewing is achieved simply by permitting each eye to see only the appropriate view. Both cross polarizing glasses or eye screening give satisfactory results (see Figure 5).

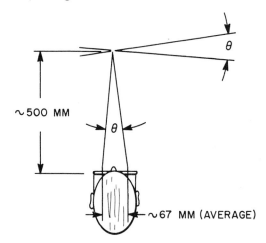

θ IS VARIED ACCORDING TO INDIVIDUAL TASTES

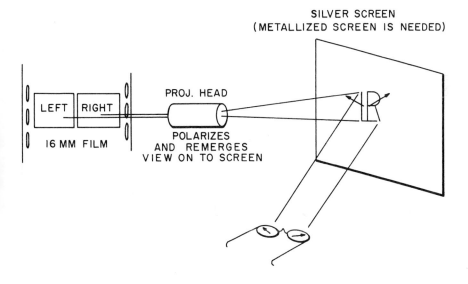

Figure 5. Stereo viewing.

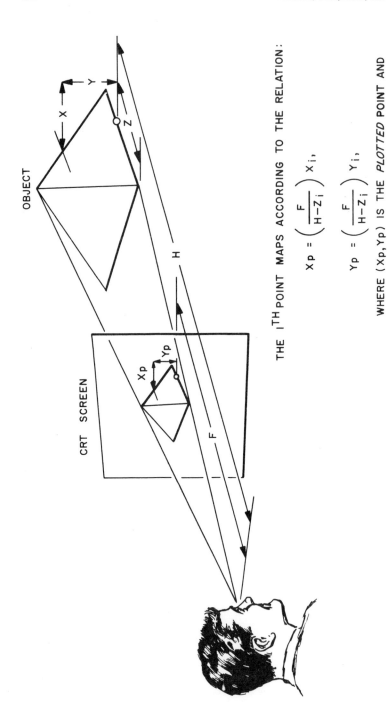

THE i^{TH} POINT MAPS ACCORDING TO THE RELATION:

$$X_p = \left(\frac{F}{H - Z_i} \right) X_i,$$

$$Y_p = \left(\frac{F}{H - Z_i} \right) Y_i,$$

WHERE (X_p, Y_p) IS THE *PLOTTED* POINT AND (X_i, Y_i, Z_i) IS THE *TRUE* COORDINATE OF A POINT ON AN OBJECT.

Figure 6. Perspective relationships.

Very often the illusion of depth can be adequately conveyed by displaying a perspective view. Figure 6 is a schematic showing the interrelationships between the viewer's eyes, the CRT screen (film plane), and the viewed object. In this formalism each (three-dimensional) point is suitably projected into the viewing plane. The various parameters can take on any desired values and personal preferences tend to vary from person to person. Again there are other methods of producing a perspective view.

The fourth operation, texturing or shading is useful to make the surfaces of an object visible. A planar solid is made visible in space by showing the lines of intersection of the defining planes. This, obviously, is not very useful if the surfaces are not planar. Sometimes surfaces are regular enough so that they can be made visible by rulings — that is, by drawing a number of parallel lines from one edge to another or by crosshatching as we often do on a spherical surface. Another method which is somewhat more time consuming, is to randomly "spatter" dots on the surfaces. If the CRT has enough resolution, then controlling the number of dots per unit area will approximate the optical density variations obtained by ordinary photography. In many cases, the spatter method has to be used with stereo in order to see the desired spatial distribution of spots. Figures 7 through 10 show examples of these various methods. The figures are given in stereo format to provide a basis for deciding when it is appropriate.

When we display solid three-dimensional objects, the degree of realism often depends on "hiding" those edges not now visible to the viewer. The general problem of hiding edges is not fully solved for arbitrary surfaces but a number of particular solutions have been published. The main limitation with most of these is the large amount of computing needed to decide what can and what cannot be seen. For most applications it is not now possible to sustain a moving, hidden-line display for real time viewing. Although this is not a serious limitation, the problem itself is a challenging one.

These and any other techniques that come to mind are of value only to the extent that they convey useful information to the viewer that would be more difficult to obtain in other ways. The fact that they tend to produce visually striking results is accepted as a bonus and perhaps even as a stimulus. But the first importance has to be attached to the technical information content.

With the exception of color filming[4] most of what we've discussed so

---

[4]Several display devices for producing visual color pictures are commercially available, but so far not with "vivid" color output nor with the overall resolution that most users say they want.

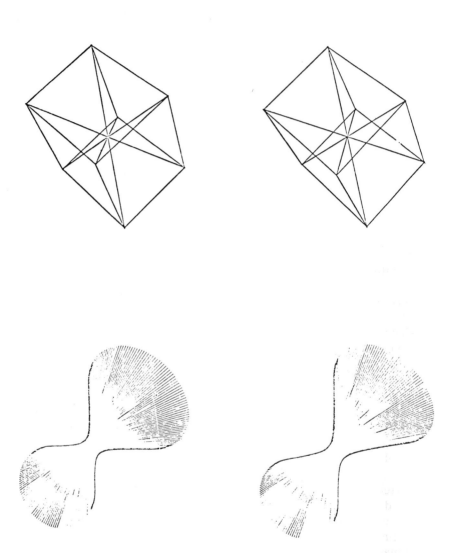

Figure 7

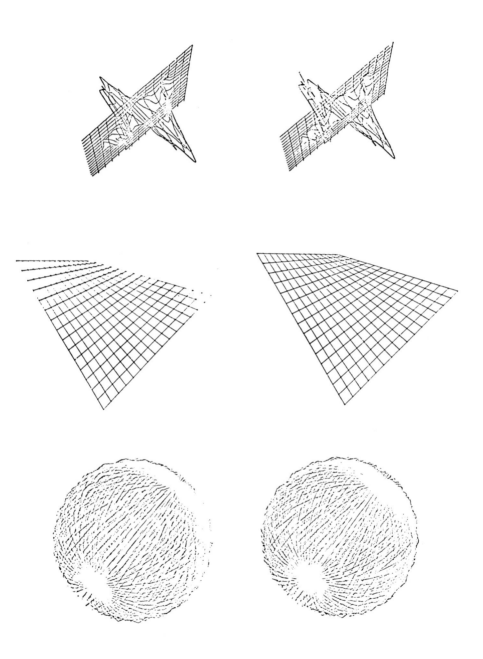

Figure 8

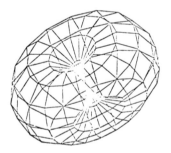
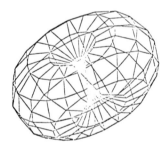

Figure 9

Figure 10

far has been more or less applicable to the general topic of graphics. We will want to consider briefly the activity known as "on-line man-machine interaction" and finally the question of graphical input devices. Let me, however, explicitly point out that through language development we are striving to unite the various facets of graphic data processing. Thus, with the exception of the advance film function, all of Table I applies to on-line viewing.

The human visual faculty is an extremely sensitive "data channel." Not enough is known yet about the relationships between it and the brain but if "very good visual data" is badly presented in part, the average viewer tends to reject the entire picture. For most people, a flickering picture is generally bad. For some, a lack of contrast is an annoying factor. In general, it is a matter of individual taste as to what is acceptable and what is not. The usual procedure is to provide a few manual adjustments to control such things as picture size, focus, and brightness. Some consoles can even be tilted to suit individual tastes.

Beyond reducing the number of things to be displayed, a user cannot directly do very much to solve the problem of flicker. Most people do not like it although some of the early radar display operators often found that flicker actually helped them to notice new "blips" quicker. The rate of flicker is a function of the time needed to display the entire picture once. Other factors also having some influence are the type of phosphor used, the brightness and contrast of the picture parts, the level of background illumination, and the sensitivity of the viewer's eyes. The average persistence time for human vision is usually given as $\frac{1}{40}$ second. This means simply that in order for our eyes to see some point of light on the CRT as a constant intensity source it must be refreshed at least once every $\frac{1}{30}$ to $\frac{1}{60}$ second. Some phosphors have such short decay times that the illusion of constant brightness depends mostly on the persistence of vision.[5]

There are numerous ways to refresh a display. The most elementary method simply requires the recomputation and (unbuffered) retransmission of each picture part so many times per second. That portion of computer time used this way is obviously not available for other processing. Recomputation may be needed because the display list is too big to fit in the computer's memory. If enough computer memory is available, the usual procedure is to reserve a portion for the display lists which then can be buffered out to the visual console while the computer proceeds with other tasks. All new or large computers have as a standard

[5] For example, the P-24 phosphor which emits strongly in the blue portion of the visible spectrum, has a decay time of about 20 microseconds. Refresh cycles as low as 35/second could be used with the P-24 phosphor but the flicker is then obvious though not necessarily annoying. (Most manufacturers recommend a refresh rate of 50-60 per second.)

feature, the ability to start an input/output process that can then proceed more or less independently from central processor control. The idea of a buffered display list then evolves naturally.

As we have seen, most display devices can be equipped with their own "personal" memory. The computer then simply transfers the list to that memory and starts the display running. Whichever memory is used the display generator processes the list, command by command, into visual picture parts. Points, line, and characters are the "raw materials" but simple nonplotting actions are also useful. The last entry in a list might mean, for example, "start the list at the beginning if (say) $\frac{1}{60}$ second has gone by since the last time the list was started. If $\frac{1}{60}$ second has not elapsed, wait until it has and then start up again." The idea of waiting is mainly to provide for a uniform brightness that is independent of the shortness of the list. Again, Table I contains suggestions of what could be in the list.

No discussion of man-machine consoles would be complete without some mention of the various input devices that have come to be associated with CRT use. Thus while we attach great value to the visual presentation, it is often equally important to be able to conveniently and quickly interact with the computing process. There are several types of input devices that are commonly associated with this activity. An ordinary typewriter suitably connected to the computer is one example. Keyboards, arrays of toggle switches, pushbuttons, and tuning knobs are others.

By program we can assign various special functions to any key or button. Striking the "R" key on a typewriter for instance, ordinarily causes an "R" to be typed. The program, however, might be made to "change the perspective" of the image on the CRT when the "R" key is activated. As with any programmable device, how such things are used depends on the programmer, and their great ability derives precisely from the fact that they are programmable. At one instant we can be using the keyboard to type in a new program, and immediately thereafter use it to move an image around on the CRT screen.

Another kind of input device is epitomized by the so-called "light-pen" (or pencil). As such it is a hand-held thing that can sense the presence of a *brightening* spot of light when held at or near the CRT screen, and so signal the computer. The existence of the signal can be correlated with the display list to deduce (by program) which particular item was being displayed at the instant that the light pen "hit" was encountered. This is an example of a synchronous input. In other words, it is possible for the computer program to find out where and at what, the user is pointing, and inferentially, what he wants to do. We can distinguish two programmed styles of using the light pen. First, we may wish to *follow* or track the light pen as the user moves it around on the screen thereby drawing lines or paths. Second we may wish to *designate* or activate a new procedure or mark some particular picture part. For example, a common procedure is to program a series of bright points at, say, the lower portion of the screen.   These can be treated as programmable push buttons.   By selectively touching these buttons with the light pen the user can tell his program what he wishes to be done. Some common functions include "buttons" to control enlarging (zooming), rotating, erasing, and tracking.

Still other devices that provide functions similar to those of the light pen are available. Both the "joy-stick" and the "track-ball" are used to control the position of a hardware generated cursor that is displayed along with computer generated images.   The Rand tablet-stylus is approximately like a digital version of the light pen except that the sensing is not done at the CRT screen.   This article would be unduly lengthened if each of these input devices were discussed separately. Table II gives a more complete list of display associated input devices along with references to more detailed information.

In some sense the light pen is the simplest and the most general or flexible input device. Even so it is often found necessary to supplement its abilities with one or more push buttons. One limitation is that it cannot be used to designate a place where no image is being displayed. That is, in order to know where the light pen is, the computer must "see" it. On the other hand, devices such as the track-ball "volunteer" their position coordinates. The trouble is that the procedure for correlating this position with the display list often becomes more complicated because the input is not synchronized with the display list. It is not clear at this point which of the various schemes is most useful. Obviously any decision relating to how much and what sorts of input devices a graphics terminal should have, is best made in the light of the anticipated uses. In fact, the "best" things probably are not invented yet.

GRAPHIC INPUT

So far in this article we have ignored the question of how the original data is supplied to the computer. It may be that graphic methods are indeed the best way to interact with a computer, but without data such a decision has no foundation. Most data is not in digital form when we first decide to use it. Hence the material, be it photographs, drawings, or even lists of numbers, must first be digitized in order to feed it into the computer. Some applications require only a trivial amount of digital data and can therefore be serviced by ordinary computer input devices such as card or tape readers. In some cases we can get data in through a keyboard or with a light pen. There are, however, huge sets of potential data from sources that are completely outside of any computer environment. In order to be used these must somehow be gotten into a form that the computer can handle. This fact may be obvious but very often it seems to have been overlooked. Establishing a data bank is not easy. For example, modern sciences such as high energy physics annually produce millions of photographs which often represent the only record of experiments, tests, and observations. Up to six or seven years ago, most of this digitizing was done by hand. Since then, several types of machines and programs have been developed that attempt to automatically read (digitize) graphic material directly under computer control. In addition to these, there is also a variety of alphanumeric character reading machines for special applications. For the moment, I would like to concentrate mostly on the general purpose graphical input devices. We will require only enough description to see what limitations there may be in their use.

Basically these machines consist of a light source, appropriate optical components, a way to hold and transport the graphical record, and certain other parts to detect and measure the amount of light remaining after "interaction" with the source document. Figure 11 shows the functional relationships involved. There are two general ways to use light as an information probe — that is, to see. If the information appears on a transparent material such as film, the light is transmitted through it, while if the record is opaque, reflected light is used. After transmission (or reflection), the light contains information about the object being digitized.

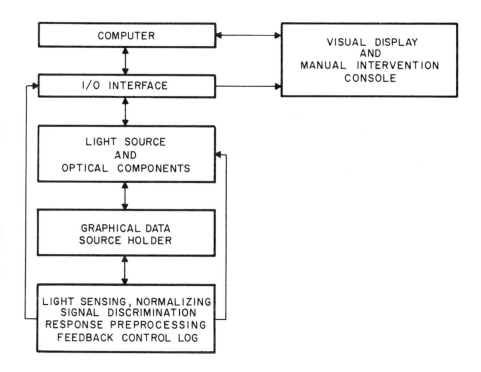

Figure 11. Graphical input device functional relationships.

The newer reading devices use a computer-controlled CRT as a light source, particularly if the input documents are transparent. There are two types of information we can obtain from any pictorial record. Qualitatively, we might wish to know what is in the picture, and this operation is called *scanning.* Shape, for example, is a qualitative item. Quantitatively, certain of the images will be selected for *measuring.* Position, distance, and photographic density measurements are examples of quantitative data. Of the two, scanning (that is, pattern recognition) is far more difficult to express as an automatic procedure.

In operation, the computer program tells the CRT to display a point of light at some designated location (X, Y). The lenses image this spot on the (film) sample. The amount of light that passes through the (transparent) film, for example, depends on the clearness or blackness (photographic density) at that point. Whatever does get through is converted into an electrical signal by a photosensing device. This may then be compared with a suitable reference signal obtained by sampling the (unattenuated) CRT light. The comparisons are used to make the measurements independent of light source variations and for other control functions. Finally, some (or all) of the results are presented to the computer for appropriate use by the program. Figures 12A and B show schematically the design of typical film readers for transparent and opaque materials.

By repeated interrogation the digitizing program builds up various kinds of elementary "facts" about the input data. For example, we might be trying to deduce an ordered set of coordinates (x, y) that give the mid-point locus of some curved trace on the film. Or we might wish to find all the places where the photographic density is greater than some given value. There are some applications in which the (x, y) coordinates were precisely the total data needed from the graphic record. Frequently, however, these elementary facts serve only as input for a pattern recognition program, in which we are more interested in the logical orderings or sequences of the sets of facts than we are in each fact individually.

When the graphic data is opaque the method outlined in Figure 12C is preferred. In this case, the light source does not have to be under computer control but the light sensing part must be. We can regard this device as logically equivalent to a television camera. The principle difference in our design is that tiny elements or portions of the visible scene are interrogated in the order that the computer program chooses while the "TV" camera is built to sequentially scan line by line. In general the recently developed camera design is potentially more adaptable than a film reader. Merely by using the appropriate lenses it can look like anything from a microscope to a telescope.

The characteristics of the several different machines now in existence are summarized in Table III. We should not, however, conclude that a single machine having these properties could or should be built. Because the digitizing procedure is under computer control we could reasonably expect it to be dramatically faster than a human reader. Unfortunately

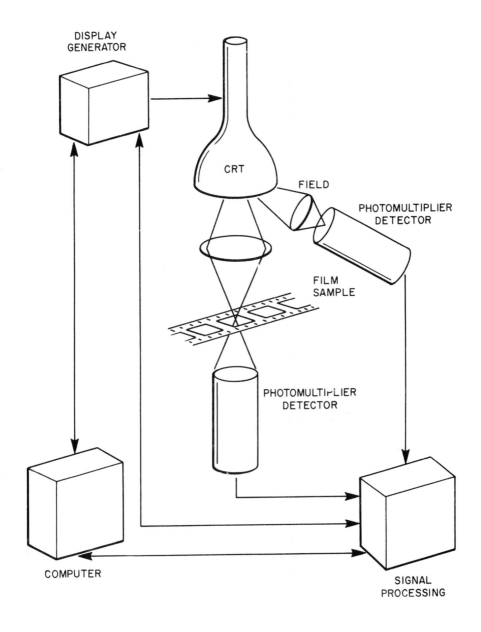

Figure 12A. Eyeball — film reader.

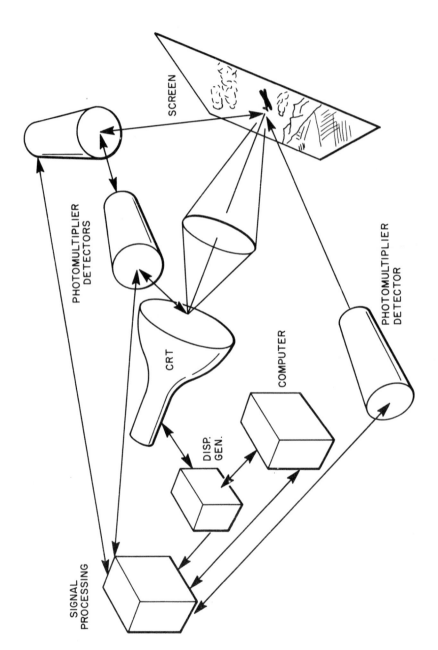

Figure 12B. The opaque reader.

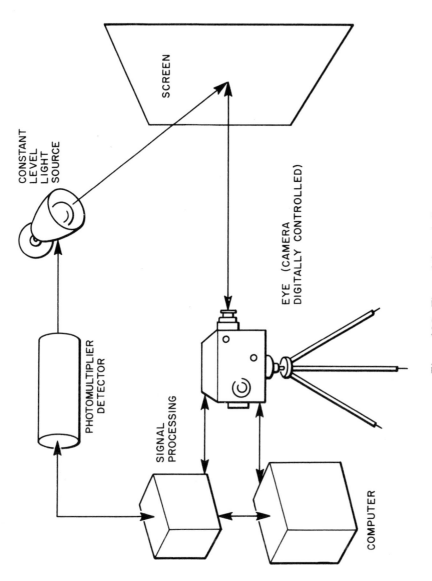

Figure 12C. The mobile eyeball.

this is usually not the case, primarily because humans are better than computers as general pattern recognizers. However, human readers make nonsystematic errors whose rate depends on things like inexperience, fatigue, and emotions. So we would like to use graphical input devices not only to handle large volumes of input data but also to minimize subjective biasing. The chief obstacle in the way of full utilization of graphic input devices is the difficulty of programming them. Or, putting it another way, practically any of these machines has capabilities that have not yet been fully exhausted by programming.

It is easy to see, especially in the case of a CRT light source, that the graphic input document becomes an array of tiny picture elements exactly corresponding to the raster points mentioned earlier. Furthermore, in general, only one of two values can be associated with each point. Hence the successful use of these devices implies that we somehow must ask the right questions. The first problem then becomes one of deciding which points belong to the information we seek, given that we are limited in what we can ask.

The important point to emphasize is that the answers we get depend totally on the questions we ask especially as these relate to the fundamental characteristics or properties of the information (light) probe. For (a somewhat strained) example, suppose a picture contains among other things, a round uniformly black blob. We cannot tell if it is hard or soft, spherical or flat because we have no way of asking such questions. We could however, decide if it was really circular. It seems to me that a broader truth is involved here. We ordinarily know things *only* in terms of their interactions with the particular measuring device we use.

Even though it is somewhat of an oversimplification, we might suspect that one basic task for pattern recognition is the production of computer-compatible descriptions of the objects we wish to identify. That is, how *do* we describe what something "looks" like to a computer? (When we look at something we "recognize" it primarily by the amount of agreement between our mental image of it and our "memory" of things similar to it.) We can either prepare these "property lists" or better yet make the computer build its own lists. Of course this begs the question a bit. As far as I know, there is no suitable theory of perception or cognition that we can draw upon. Similarly, there is no concise set of heuristic procedures that can be made into a general computer program. One thing being done at present is to write codes that work for very limited applications. Another approach is to let the computer do the digitizing but arrange for a human to do the pattern recognizing through a graphic terminal.

In general the digitizing will contain extraneous information which degrades the data. Dirt becomes noise and so do scratches. As far as the program is concerned, anything about the graphic document that is *not* the data *currently* being extracted is noise. Thus intermittent component failures show up as noise, as do scratches, dust, low contrast images, and so on. If two or more of the objects being examined touch or overlap they act as sources of noise for each other. The recognition procedures must be capable of deciding that some particular array of spots is an 'E' even if it is smudged or touching a neighboring character. Noise not only complicates the problem but to many people it is *the* problem.

Quite often, a certain amount of noise filtering can be safely applied to the data as it is produced by the reading machine, but to be acceptable, the pattern recognition scheme must at least be able to correctly function with noisy data. In addition it must be independent of data conditions like size, position, orientation, and perspective variations. That is, recognition of an object, depends on the object and not the apparent size, or where it is on the film or the direction it is facing. Finally a practical solution must be expressible in a comparatively small number of steps, must require a finite amount of time and memory for execution and must be iterative. That is, reapplication of the algorithm should improve the results.

Despite the scope and number of difficulties confronting workers in the field of pattern recognition, it would be erroneous to conclude that little or no progress is being made. Quite the opposite is true. In the area of character recognition there are at present several commercially available machines to choose from depending on the number of restrictions placed on the size of the front and document format. Similarly, a few general purpose designs are also on the market for research and production applications and more are coming. One such machine has now been in operation about four years. To date it has digitized oscilloscope traces at a rate of about one million pictures per year, becoming in the process a simple example of a research project that successfully evolved into a production application. So while not wanting to minimize the difficulties in this field, we can expect eventually some measure of success.

THE FUTURE

We have considered some current aspects of graphic data processing as an input-output technique and by intention we have restricted the context to that of equipment presently available. What about future developments in this field? The overall goal of research activities such as graphics is to develop things that are useful in the production sense to a large number of people. I have suggested that at least on the basis of costs, present equipment is not yet ready for a general production role. Thus one future goal clearly is the development of low cost display terminals, suitable memory and computing devices. However, it may be closer to the truth to observe that when a particular need is pressing enough, we suddenly find that we can afford the costs. As we have already seen the combination of increasing computer speeds and more sophisticated applications creates such a need.

It is not as easy to say when a programming package is acceptable for production use, but if past experience is any indication the users will be very quick and liberal with their evaluation of the system. In any case, a future goal is to apply the knowledge gained in research to production applications.

Another aspect of the future in which costs are less influential is the improvement of display features. Despite its fantastic versatility, the CRT imposes certain restrictions on picture composition and speeds. There are requirements for such things as larger, brighter screens, high quality color toning, real three-dimensional imaging and three-dimensional human interaction devices. In working on these applications all sorts of components and methods are being tested and the sheer diversity of the effort more or less guarantees that there will be "something for everybody."

I have consciously resisted the inclination to speculate about any particular directions that might be pursued. Instead it seems more appropriate to conclude with the following small anecdote: some fifteen years ago the UNIVAC was presented to all who would listen as the world's first commercially available stored program digital computer. At the time, so we are told, someone who presumably had the right to make statements like this, estimated that the total market for such large computers would not be more than six. Before we smile too tolerantly, it might be useful to also recall that a nontrivial number of "top decision makers" believed the statement.

Table Ia

Elementary Function	Speed Range	Remarks
Plot a point	1-50 μ sec	
Advance film	3-200 msec	Cameras are pulse operated, sprocketed, or claw pull down and pin registered
Draw a line	1-1000 μ sec	The "best" line generators have the writing rate independent of line length
Change the beam position	1-50 μ sec	To position the beam at the beginning of a line
Display a character	1-1000 μ sec	
Change brightness	–	
Change image size	–	
Change image aspect ratio	–	
Change effective raster size	–	

Table Ib

Function	Remarks
TURN	three-axis rotation
PAN, ZOOM-MOOZ	three-axis translation
PERSPECTIVE-PROJECTIVE	geometric transformations
STEREO	two-views
BLINK	attention direction
SHADE	optical density variations; texturing
COLOR	associate a color with the image (parts)
PHOTO	take a picture
MOVIE	take a sequence of pictures
NAME	associate a name with the image (list)
ATTACH	join line segments
CONNECT	special glyph linking
DRAW	follow the light pen
SMOOTH	apply a relaxation operator to the data
MODIFY	same change to a display list
DIMENSION	assign lengths (areas, volumes, masses)
ERASE	remove the image (parts)
WRITE	prepare for text

Table II. GRAPHICS TERMINAL INPUT DEVICES

Type	Remarks
Typewriter Keyboard	Most useful for entry of alphanumerics.
Track Ball Joy Stick S. R. I. Mouse	Control a visible (either hardware or program generated) cursor on the CRT screen (see ref. 7).
Push Buttons Foot Pedals Toggle Switches	Procedural Controls — usually a one-bit signal; often in conjunction with some other input device (e.g., light pen). (See ref. 7).
Analog to Digital Converters (manually controlled), Potentiometers, Shaft-Angle Encoders	Very useful for on-line input of quantities whose values are related to some qualitative aspect of the graphical diaplay: That is, for the cases where the precise digital value is less important than some given interrelationship.
Rand Tablet-Stylus Voltage Sensing Pencil Light Pen	(See refs. 4 & 5). (See ref. 24).

Table III. SUMMARY OF GRAPHIC INPUT DEVICE CHARACTERISTICS

CRT Addressability and	$2^{14} \times 2^{15}$ ($2^{15} \times 2^{15}$ is coming)
Raster Size	5" and 7" tube
Document Format	Any film or paper size (solid objects require the camera method)
Measurement Accuracies	Measurements accurate to 2-5 μ over 9 inch square
Optical Density Range	Up to 100 levels in the range 0 to 3. With a density increment of 0.05.
Speeds	Depend on the required signal-to-noise ratio on the film density range. Two-level digitizing in 10-15 μ sec/pt.

REFERENCES and Additional Reading

Reports:

1.   A. Cecil and G. Michael, *DD80 Programmers' Manual,* Lawrence Radiation Internal Laboratory Report (updated), 9 (1966).

2.   R. K. Cralle, *A Language for Making Movies on a Computer.* Talk presented at Annual Meeting of the American Association of Physics Teachers, New York, 1 (1966).

3.   D. Engelbart, *Augmenting Human Intellect: A Conceptual Framework,* Stanford Research Institute Report, Project 3578, 10 (1962).

4.   D. Fink, *Television Engineering Handbook,* McGraw-Hill, Inc., New York, 1957.

5.   L. Gales and G. Michael, *A Computer Controlled Film Reader with Manual Supervision Features,* Lawrence Radiation Laboratory, UCRL-70010, 6 (1966).

6.   G. Michael, *A Survey of Graphical Input Devices,* UCRL Rept. (in preparation), 11 (1966).

7.   G. Michael, *A Survey of Graphic Data Processing Equipment for Computers,* UCRL-70195, 11 (1966).

8.   L. G. Roberts, "Machine Perception of Three-Dimensional Solids," in *Optical and Electro-Optical Information Processing,* M. I. T. Press, Cambridge, Mass. (1965).

9.   J. Soller, M. Starr, G. Valley, *Cathode Ray Tube Displays,* McGraw-Hill, Inc., New York (1948) (Dover Edition — reissue) (1965).

10.   I. Sutherland, *Sketchpad: A Man-Machine Graphical Communication System* (Thesis) M. I. T., Cambridge, Mass., I (1963).

11.   A. van Dam, *A Survey of Pictorial Data Processing Techniques and Equipments,* AD 626-155, Defense Documentation Center 8 (1965).

12.   E. E. Zajac, "Computer-Made Perspective Movies as a Scientific and Communication Tool," *Comm. ACM,* pp. 169-170, 7 (1964).

13.   *A Laboratory for the Study of Graphical Man-Machine Communication,* a series of papers by members of the staff of General Motors Research Laboratories, Proceedings — Fall Joint Computer Conference, San Francisco (1964).

14.   R. Siders et al., *Computer Graphics,* American Management Association, New York (1966).

15.   H. H. Poole, *Fundamentals of Display Systems,* Spartan Books, Washington, D. C. (1966).

16.   *Journal of the Society fof Information Display,* v. 3, n. 3 (May/June, 1966).

Chapter 15

THE TRANSITION TOWARD
MORE SOPHISTICATED PROCEDURES

Harold D. Lasswell[1]

In this discussion I hope to join you in facing the issues that arise in moving from where we are now to where we want to go. In many decision-making situations, we are now a long way from the deliberate, well-balanced use of the systematic devices of data gathering, storage, and retrieval that best serve the ends of policy clarification, strategic invention, and evaluation. The essential recommendation is that we introduce into conventional practice a set of more disciplined modes of conducting the policy process. I shall use a label — decision seminars — to refer to the bundle of suggestions outlined here.

If we are to elicit the motivations that transform current decision practice toward the ultimate incorporation and mastery of sophisticated techniques, it will be necessary to show that more systematic procedures fit "common sense." Common sense is the name for what experienced men of decision congratulate themselves for having acquired and exercised through the years.

One difficulty with common sense is that what is sensible is less commonly agreed to than might be supposed. Some of its reputation appears to depend on its elusive, even ambiguous, unpinned-down quality. If we are to manage a smooth passage from the traditional to the disciplined, traditionalists must become interested in discovering their own assumptions, hence in becoming more systematic. For this purpose the idea of a decision seminar offers a specific program. As we

[1]For more detail consult: Lasswell, *The Future of Political Science*. New York: Atherton Press, 1963; and Lasswell, "The Policy Sciences of Development" (review), *World Politics*, XVII (January 1965), 286-309.

shall see, decision seminar technique is an integration of well-known components. Decision seminars are *contextual* and *problem-oriented.*

To say that the approach is contextual means that it is continually concerned with the relationship of whole and part. The decision process itself is a series of subjective and behavioral events through time. Further it is oriented toward a larger sequence of decision and postdecision effects through time. Hence the relevant context emphasizes the past, present, and future pattern of events whose interactions affect one another. In world politics the context is global-wide; and in coming years will pass well beyond the surface of our globe. One aim of the seminar procedure is to keep an up-to-date image of the whole at the common focus of attention and to cultivate the practice of deliberately weaving back and forth between images of the whole and of each particular part.

To say that decision seminars include a technique of problem-solving means that they are explicitly designed to further the performance of the five intellectual tasks that are inseparable from any problem, and especially from policy questions in the world political process. I do not, of course, insist on the labels to be used here in naming the tasks. Each of us may have favorite equivalents for each of them. I refer to the five operations with the following words: goal, trend, condition, projection, alternative.

To clarify goals is to specify the overriding aims of policy in the total context.   What kind of world are we attempting to bring into being? Are we concerned with the dignity of man, or with the privileges of a single caste — racial or other?

To describe trend is to explore the flow of past and recent events for the purpose of discovering to what extent the movement in different parts of the globe has been toward or away from the postulated goal.

The analysis of conditioning factors is intended to explain the trends. What combinations of factors account for trends toward or away from preferred outcomes?

The projection of future developments is the attempt to forecast the shape of things to come, assuming that any policy change initiated by the decision seminar has no significant impact on the course of events. Will the present or future conflicts probably escalate into full-scale nuclear warfare?   Will totalitarian regimes gradually decentralize, demilitarize, democratize?

The consideration of policy alternatives calls for the specification of detailed objectives for the immediate and mid-range future; the invention and evaluation of risk, cost, and benefit; and the selection of recommended policy under contingent circumstances.

A third characteristic of decision seminar technique is that it is a *continuing, though intermittent, interaction among a small group of relatively constant membership* — for example, an advisory board of specialists on a particular region who meet regularly, and who follow the agenda appropriate to contextual problem-solving. Another example is a committee of specialists who follow the activities of a selected organization, such as the Supreme Court or the Security Council. As we shall see, continuity is important if the group is to become deeply acquainted with the characteristic predispositions, including distortions, of the members.

A further feature of decision seminar technique is the *systematic use of audio-visual devices.* I am talking about charts, maps, models, and related means of supplying a supplementary brain. Decision seminars meet in a setting that includes old as well as new selective presentations of the total process. Why do we put so much emphasis on audio-visual means of portraying goal, trend, condition, projection, and alternative? Partly because so many valuable participants in decision-making have dramatizing imaginations. They are at their best when they can stay close to envisaging individuals and groups in active interaction. They are not enamoured of numbers or of analytic abstractions. They are at their best in deliberations that encourage contextuality by a varied repertory of means, and where an immediate sense of time, space, and figure is retained.

The seminar room provides an inclusive image of the whole, an image that undergoes gradual modification as a by-product of interaction in the seminar. Every session can produce some change in the audio-visual environment. At one meeting, for instance, a member may introduce charts, maps, or films intended to provide a projection of future Soviet-China-U. S. relations. When some of these materials are added to the collection on seminar walls in subsequent meetings, the members will be stimulated to recall the discussion, hence to operate critically, though within a definite frame of reference. The same point applies cumulatively as seminar members introduce and deposit materials concerning trends, analyses of conditioning factors, overriding goals, or policy alternatives.

The results obtained by the most sophisticated procedures as they are introduced can be reported, summarized, and retained for continuing reassessment in the seminar. Programming is the critical operation in the management of computers, and the results of past simulations, for instance, can be retained to assist in sharpening the judgment of seminar members in future program-making.

Prior to the introduction of computer results a decision seminar can confront itself with the challenge of explicitness. What goal events do I (we) prefer? On the grounds of what data do I assert that trends are more or less favorable in the last few days, weeks, months, or years? Or that rising middle class elements are giving political support to international cooperation (or not)? Or that France will fail (or succeed) in recovering through diplomacy the power that it lost when the Empire collapsed? Or that a policy drive to win mass support for "exchange of youth" programs will strengthen the peace keeping role of the U. N.?

If decision seminar deliberations are recorded and analyzed by technically advanced procedures, it will be possible to contribute to our understanding of policy processes, and also to the insight of participants into their own predispositions. Even without recordings of the private deliberations of the Supreme Court, it is possible to demonstrate many of the factors that influence the judgment of the Court. It can be shown, for example, that some members of the tribunal almost invariably support the claims put forward in the name of labor or of civil rights. I do not deny that predictions of this kind are of some use to the bar in improving strategy for the manipulation of the Court, or in adding weight to scholarly interpretations of trends and conditioning factors. But this is not the same as bringing the role of each participant to his attention as a regular feedback from a procedure to which he has agreed, and which is only known to others to the extent that he chooses to disclose results. A decision seminar can engage qualified specialists to analyze the record in order to bring to their focus of attention data concerning their interactions in the seminar and their estimates of external events.

Concerning interactions in the seminar: Participants are not necessarily aware of predispositions that may be obvious to colleagues, such as a tendency to be over- or under-impressed with the credibility of statements from military sources.

Concerning outside events: Some participants are somewhat unrealistic in forecasting the immediate or mid-range future because of personality characteristics that predispose them toward pessimism or optimism, or toward cyclical fluctuations in outlook. If these participants are exposed to feedback, they may modify themselves; in any case, the strength of the predisposition (or its defense mechanism) will be more obvious.

Since in human affairs our critical instruments are people, not machines, the decision seminar technique is a procedure for "people-calibration," not simply "thing-calibration." The focus is on the total context of external as well as internal events; hence the continuing appraisal of what is "out there" and what is "in here" can be carried forward with optimal expectations of allocating appropriate weights to both dimensions. After the first meeting of a decision seminar, for instance, a regular agenda feature is the obtaining of explanations from the members of why they made correct or incorrect forecasts of events that have since transpired.

Not the least instructive feature of a decision seminar is the experience of thinking explicitly about inclusive models of world social process, and of the interplay of values and institutions with one another. My colleagues and I find it convenient to think of the social process as "*man* striving to maximize (optimalize) *values* (preferred events) through *institutions* using *resources*." We use a short list of key terms for the value-institution categories.

Power is the giving and receiving of support, as in votes and fights. The institutions specializing in the shaping and sharing of power are commonly called government, law, and politics.

Enlightenment is the giving or receiving of information about the social or physical context. Institutions include mass media and research agencies.

Wealth is the giving or receiving of claims to the use of resources. Economic institutions specialize in production, distribution, investment, consumption.

Well-being is the giving or receiving of claims to safety, health, and comfort. It includes institutions that conserve or destroy life.

Skill is the giving or receiving of opportunity to acquire excellence in vocational, professional, or artistic operations. Educational institutions are mainly specialized in skill transmission.

Affection is the giving or receiving of love, friendship, or loyalty. We think of the family and friendship institutions in this connection.

Respect is the giving or receiving of recognition. The institutions of social class and caste belong here.

Rectitude is the giving or receiving of characterizations in terms of responsible or nonresponsible conduct. Ethical and religious institutions specialize in this value.

It is relatively easy to obtain trend and other data for PEWBSARD, which is the curious term we have coined to serve the recall function, since the intellectual division of labor is approximately organized along these lines. *P*ower is studied by political scientists and students of the law. *E*nlightenment attracts specialists on mass media and the sociology of science. *W*ealth occupies economists; well-*b*eing occupies specialists on public health; *s*kill engages educational specialists in the occupations, professions, and the arts; *a*ffection mobilizes experts on family and kinship; *r*espect engages sociologists and anthropologists; rectitu*d*e implicates scholars and scientists who deal with morals, religion and criminality.

Decision seminars include so many familiar elements that the conception may be confused with many other procedures. For example, a major industry has a chart room; however, it is used, not as a genuine decision seminar, but as a public relations device to make a quick impression on members of the board of directors or shareholders who are exposed to glib interpretations of the visual material.

The introduction of an occasional map or model is routine in almost all modern committees or seminars. However, these are not decision seminars, partly because the exhibits are not cumulative or systematic; partly because they are not woven into the evaluation of policy objectives and strategies that may be under consideration. A general staff war room or the Commander-in-Chief's situation room are not necessarily employed to encourage the continual evaluation of the context as it relates to all features of the social process. There may be no systematic reminders of the interplay of power and economics, of power and the media of communication, of power and the well-being level of the total population; of power and the acquisition or deterioration of skill levels, of power and the decline or consolidation of nuclear family units, of power and the attrition of castes, or of power and the spread of alienation or acceptance of civic responsibility among youth.

Decision seminars are approximated where planners and their advisors consider the probable repercussions of locating embassies or military missions, installations and personnel, in or near big cities or middle-sized towns; or loaning a billion dollars to modernize a traditional society. Those who deal with a program of change in a small community (as at Vicos, in Peru) can inaugurate a prototype that may be transferred to hundreds or thousands of small communities. The planners can and sometimes do employ a decision seminar technique to assist them in thinking through the probable results of initiating a change in one value-institution sector. Unavoidably, all sectors of society are presently affected, and the contextual approach recommended here can accustom a decision group to adopting systematic categories of thought and engaging in a systematic agenda of thinking.

As indicated before, one fixture on the agenda of each meeting can be the presentation of composite estimates of the future, followed by attempts to account for accurate or inaccurate past predictions. The specific procedures can be adapted to the purposes of the group. For example, a self-selected body of Wall Street economists was organized several years ago to meet regularly for the exchange of information and judgment. To some extent the participants are keenly competitive with one another. They prepared in advance estimates of how the stock market would fluctuate. The composite result might be presented by a secretary for discussion. The forecasts were filed as part of a personal file entirely under the control of each individual. He might, however, authorize the secretary to send a certified copy of the file to a prospective employer if he felt especially proud of his record.

This allusion to competitiveness is a reminder of some of the factors that must be overcome in introducing the full decision seminar technique. Because of mutual rivalry and hostility it will be necessary to move toward the seminar procedure at points in the institutional system where professional standards are high and the capacity for objectivity concerning the self as a flow of events among events is best developed. Perhaps a strategic spot is at advanced training institutions, or in connection with panels of experts who are devoted to specific countries.

In some spots in our complex governmental and social order we are accustomed to role playing — to gaming — as an acceptable technique of training and planning. Note that decision seminars are flexible enough to include sessions or reports of subsessions devoted to gaming. But the various adaptations of military, diplomatic, and other forms of game technique are not substitutes for decision seminars. Seminars are oriented toward the entire relevant context; and performance cannot ultimately be assessed by currently living umpires. Only the march of future history will settle yesterday's uncertainties. Unlike gaming technique — which is a valuable training and policy-inventing device — the decision seminar does not cultivate expertness in anticipating the response of the current corps of umpires.

Perhaps it is worth emphasizing how the problem-solving emphasis prepares the way for five kinds of models to serve intellectual purposes; also, how the consideration of any one model stimulates the use of all other kinds. Start with a goal model: it would, I suggest, include movement by consent toward a world in which collective policing would be sufficient to prevent significant violence. Furthermore, the preferred future pattern would come about by consent. If such a goal model is to be most useful, it must stimulate policy models that show what combination of factors, manipulated by what strategies, can thinkably culminate as desired. What scientific interdependencies shall we accept? This carries us directly to the current stock of scientific models and findings; if these are unsatisfactory, research policy is likely to be affected. In estimating the strategic moves most appropriate to the emerging situation, our attention will be directed toward the adequacy of trend and distribution data, since we must have dependable maps of contemporary demands, expectations, identities, and resources if we are to make trustworthy projections.

The decision seminar technique is obviously well-adapted to discovering the assumptions on the basis of which experienced decision makers rely. Consider, for example, a discussion of the future of De Gaulle. Who expects him to resign? Under what circumstances? What past situations are interpreted as exhibiting the importance of factors in De Gaulle's personality that would result in resignation under identifiable circumstances? If our decision analysts examine the recorded discussion, it will be feasible to contribute explicit propositions to guide inquiry into trends and conditions, and in this way to aid in the transition to more disciplined, systematic approaches to the decision process and to the world political process itself.

I have refrained from introducing many of the conceptions that will no doubt prove helpful in comprehensive models of the social and political process. Let me say in passing that the social process model can be usefully extended to include: *participants, perspectives, situations* (organized, unorganized), *base values* (available assets), *strategies* (for example, diplomatic, military, economic, informational), *outcomes, effects* (value accumulation, enjoyment). In the analysis of power outcomes we distinguish seven components of a total decision system: *intelligence, promotion, prescription, invocation, application, termination, appraisal.*

Our decision makers and analysts are in the midst of the most rapid transformation in history of the intellectual tools at their command. If the transition is to be realistic as well as accelerated it is important to make full use of the common sense that comes of experience, and to move toward more disciplined ways of matching our hunches with our procedures for reality testing.

Chapter 16

AN EDUCATIONAL
EXPERIMENT

Jeffrey S. Milstein and Davis B. Bobrow

The papers which make up the previous chapters are indicative of two major developments since World War II. The first is the advent of computers. The second is the increased effort (and progress) to develop empirical, scientific approaches to international relations. This trend in international relations may or may not produce findings with the elegance and power of the natural sciences. It is clear that it does produce increasingly unambiguous classifications of parts of the international system, rules for arriving at conclusions about international relations, and an enlarged capacity to make the sort of cumulative progress in understanding which leaves future researchers and administrators with a better grasp of problems and roads to solutions. Computers did not initiate this intellectual development in international relations, but they have provided a powerful catalyst and capability for it.

The two developments noted above have directly involved only a very small portion of international relations analysts, educators, and administrators. This state of affairs is dysfunctional both from the point of view of the diffusion of new ideas and tools and that of focusing innovation on significant concerns of a general intellectual community. Remedies to this lack of communication and influence must involve not only contact, but also a meaningful exchange of information about problems, needs, attitudes, skills, goals, and even values. This sort of an exchange is an educational process.

This chapter attempts to evaluate the educational results of a two-week experiment involving computers and international relations. The experiment was an Institute on "Computers and the Policy-Making Community,"

supported by the Atomic Energy Commission and the Carnegie Endowment for International Peace, which was held at the Lawrence Radiation
Laboratory, Livermore, California, in April 1966. The evaluation we will
report consists of an analysis of questionnaires filled out by the participants
before and after the Institute.

I. THE INSTITUTE

It seems useful to summarize the subjects which received attention in
the program, many of which are presented in preceding chapters. The
Institute activities were organized in three blocks: (1) lectures devoted
to the nature of computers and their capabilities as indicated by natural
science applications; (2) a series of small discussion group meetings with
a computer scientist to discuss problems of particular concern to the
participants and to supplement the first program unit; and (3) lectures
devoted to the rationale for, problems with, and rewards from computer
applications to international relations problems. The first block of
lectures is represented by the papers of Fernbach, Wyman, Krider,
Howerton, Leith, Slagle, Sahlin, and Michael; the second block of lectures
(part 3), by the papers of Bobrow, Holsti, Rummel, Dalkey, Gorden,
Lasswell and the remarks of Carter, Churchman, Pool and Gerard in
Appendix A. Presentations not in this volume were given by Kenneth
Janda on information retrieval (Janda, 1967), Alan Manne on the
simulation of a developing economy, and Karl Deutsch on international
relations data bases. In addition to the oral presentations, each participant
was given a number of articles suggested by the lecturers (see Schwartz,
1966, pp. 11-12) and three germane volumes (Greenberger, 1962; Borko,
1962; and Feigenbaum and Feldman, 1963).

Of the 33 participants in a "student" role at the institute, eighteen
were relatively senior and high-level government officials drawn from
the Department of State, the Central Intelligence Agency, the Defense
Intelligence Agency, and the Arms Control and Disarmament Agency.
The rest of the participants consisted of young and mid-career university
teachers and researchers, and senior officials and analysts from such
organizations as the United Nations and the Foreign Policy Association.
We will say more about their relevant characteristics when we turn to
the evaluation data. At this point, we can note that the composition of
the group reflected the intentions of the Institute planners not only to
cross the gaps between computer users and nonusers, but also to establish
a forum for relatively sustained and cooperative exploration by policy-
oriented international relations experts and academics of a common set

of technical questions. In this sense, the Institute was trying to be educational in several ways.

II. EVALUATION METHODS

In order to better evaluate the effects of the Institute program, we asked the participants to answer on a voluntary and anonymous basis questionnaires distributed on the first and the next to last days of the Institute. The questions dealt with the participants' attitudes, plans, information, past behavior, and expectations or conclusions about various aspects of the program, about the use of computers, and about approaches to the analysis, teaching, and management of international relations. We used before and after questionnaires to clarify the extent and nature of change in the participants' attitudes, plans, expectations, and information about the applications of computers and scientific approaches to international relations.

The questionnaires sought to realize the benefits of open-ended questions, which gave the participants more freedom of expression, and of scaled, fixed-response questions, which gave us data susceptible to more powerful and precise analytic techniques. The scaled items were primarily of two kinds. The first tried to measure the extent to which participants felt that the Institute served a variety of scientific information exchange functions (Menzel, 1958; Menzel, 1966). The functions were: answering specific questions arising in one's work; acquiring a knowledge of what is being carried on, where, and by whom: acquiring scientific knowledge one might otherwise not have learned in good time; providing opportunities to find out details of the work of others; informing others of one's own work and problems related to it; discussing broad scientific topics of general interest to one's work group; making new contacts with scientists and administrators in different relationships to national policy; and acquiring new skills. We asked the participants to rate each of the three parts of this program as contributing to each of these functions not at all, a little, in large measure, or to a great extent.

The second type of scaled response question applied the semantic differential device (Osgood, Suci, Tannenbaum, 1957) to three important types of computer application to international relations. These were information retrieval, quantitative analysis of data, and simulation. The participants were asked to place each of these families of applications on +3 to -3 scales connecting ten pairs of polar descriptive terms. The descriptive pairs were:

1. relevant to my work . . . not relevant to my work;
2. useful for me to know . . . not useful for me to know;
3. feasible for my work . . . infeasible for my work;
4. desirable in my work . . . undesirable in my work;
5. revolutionize my work . . . not revolutionize my work;
6. alter my work . . . not alter my work;
7. simple to use in my work . . . difficult to use in my work;
8. important for my work . . . unimportant for my work;
9. adequate for use in my work . . . inadequate for use in my work;
10. reliable and valid for use in my work . . . unreliable and invalid for use in my work.

In addition, we collected information on the following attributes of the participants filling out each questionnaire: percentage of time spent in teaching, research and analysis, and administration; focus of attention on alternative classes of problems (military, political, economic, cultural, or management); major field of academic study; U. S. government or not U. S. government employee; and age. We received 26 completed forms for each of the questionnaires and the personal attribute data indicate that the participants who did respond were reasonably representative of the group as a whole.

III. FINDINGS[1]

We can now turn to what we learned about the opinions of the participants with regard to computers and international relations and the change in opinions between the beginning and the end of the institute. We shall report and discuss three groups of findings: (1) opinions at the beginning and the end of the institute; (2) the relationships between a number of germane opinions both at the beginning and the end of the institute; and (3) explicit expectations about and reactions to the institute and their implications for future education in computer applications to international relations. Before we turn to these subjects, it seems useful to emphasize that the primary purpose of the institute

[1]The authors wish to extend their deep appreciation to those who helped in the evaluation effort. In particular, Professor William J. Paisley, of the Communication Department, Stanford University, provided invaluable help with his advice, loan of analytic computer programs, and gift of computer time to run our data through these programs; Jane Milstein helped to code the data and criticize our interpretations of it. Of course, the cooperation of the institute participants in filling out our questionnaires was essential.

planners was to diffuse a view of computers as useful assistants with promising applications if one engaged in careful problem definition and evaluated the results with sceptical awareness of the assumptions and data on which they were based.

OPINIONS BEFORE AND AFTER THE INSTITUTE

We used the 26 questionnaires completed at the beginning and the 26 completed at the end of the Institute. The identifying information on the returned forms indicates that the respondents were representative of the group in terms of background and general organizational affiliation (i.e., government or nongovernment). We limit the analysis here to aggregated percentages with the result that the important attribute of the data is its general pattern and not any particular percentage.

We find a striking change in the capabilities which are seen as necessary for the international relations professional to "use computers effectively."

Table I. USER CAPABILITIES

Respondent Mentioned	Before (%)	After (%)
Training in quantification techniques	31	77
Training in operationalization of social science concepts (measurable and observable variables)	19	62

The participants as a group revised their perspectives on necessary user capabilities in favor of training in quantification techniques and in the statement of social science analytic concepts in measurable and observable terms (See Table I).

This trend was accompanied by a clear increase in the perceived current usefulness of computers for long range studies in international relations. In the second questionnaire, 100% of the respondents felt that computers are now useful for this purpose; in the first, only 85% expressed that opinion. The percentage which attributed current usefulness when immediate results are desired increased from 62% in the first questionnaire to 89% in the second.

In order to see the more specific opinion changes and continuities which underlie these general views, let us turn to appraisals of three broad classes of computer applications (simulation, information retrieval, and data analysis) made at the beginning and at the end of the Institute. In contrast to the first part of this section, we are now looking for "turnover," that is, the extent to which respondents reversed the direction of their responses after being exposed to the Institute program. Accordingly, the relevant data are not all the completed questionnaires from our two information requests. Instead we use 21 pairs of before-and-after questionnaires whose common origin we have inferred from personal identifying data and the handwriting of the anonymous respondents. Personal data indicate that these 21 pairs are reasonably representative in terms of group characteristics.

What we have done is to: (1) compare answers to identical questions on the pre- and post-Institute surveys; and (2) combine the answers into two categories which we label "positive" (on the plus side of the original seven-point scale) and "negative" (zero and minus answers on the original seven-point scale). We can observe the effects of the institute by noting significant changes in one direction or another.[2]

Simulation appraisals before and after the Institute are shown in Table II. At both times, a large majority of the participants thought that, in relation to their work, simulation was relevant, useful, feasible, desirable, altering, difficult, and important. The respondents were relatively evenly split with regard to whether or not simulation had revolutionary implications for their work and was adequate, reliable, and valid. In only two instances do the appraisal changes even approach directional significance. We note a marked negative shift with regard to the reliability and validity of simulation and increased recognition of its difficulty.

[2] Our research hypothesis is that the probability that any respondent will change his attitude in the positive (e.g., more useful direction) is greater than the probability that he will change it in the negative direction; the null hypothesis is that the probabilities are equal. We chose the binomial test which is appropriate for evaluating the effectiveness of the Institute as an "experimental treatment." Also, the test fits our data characteristics of small expected frequencies in the cells indicating change, before-after measures, and dichotomized nominal classes. Our null hypothesis of equal probability of change in the positive or negative directions is compatible with the binomial test (Siegel, 1956, pp. 36-40, 63-67). Because of the small N of respondents and our equal probability null hypotheses, we have used the "Table of Probabilities Associated with Values as Small as Observed Values of X in the Binomial Test" to locate the probabilities associated with the smaller of the two change scores in our turnover tables (Siegel, 1956, p. 250). We chose a significance level of 0.10 which leads us to reject our null hypothesis of equal probability whenever the probability associated with the smallest change cell in our tables is equal to or less than 0.10. That is, whenever the probability is not greater than the significance level of 0.10, we conclude that the institute had a statistically significant effect in producing attitude change in one of our two possible directions.

Table II. ATTITUDES TOWARDS SIMULATION (frequency of response)

Pre-Institute expectations	Post-Institute Conclusions		P
	Negative	Positive	
Relevant to my work			
Negative	1	2	> 0.188
Positive	1	16	
Useful for me to know			
Negative	0	1	> 0.188
Positive	1	18	
Feasible for my work			
Negative	1	2	> 0.500
Positive	2	15	
Desirable in my work			
Negative	1	3	> 0.188
Positive	1	15	
Revolutionize my work			
Negative	7	3	0.500
Positive	2	8	
Alter my work			
Negative	3	3	0.500
Positive	2	12	
Simple to use in my work			
Negative (difficult)	12	1	0.109
Positive (simple)	5	2	
Important for my work			
Negative	1	3	0.500
Positive	2	14	
Adequate for use in my work			
Negative	6	2	0.145
Positive	6	5	
Reliable and valid for use in my work			
Negative	6	3	0.113
Positive	8	3	

The data in Table III show that both before and after the Institute, a large majority of participants thought that *information retrieval* applications

Table III. ATTITUDES TOWARDS INFORMATION RETRIEVAL
(frequency of response)

Pre-Institute expectations	Post-Institute Conclusions		
	Negative	Positive	*P*
Relevant to my work			
Negative	2	0	>0.5
Positive	1	18	
Useful for me to know			
Negative	0	1	>0.188
Positive	1	19	
Feasible for my work			
Negative	1	1	>0.188
Positive	1	18	
Desirable in my work			
Negative	0	2	0.500
Positive	3	16	
Revolutionize my work			
Negative	5	6	0.377
Positive	4	6	
Alter my work			
Negative	3	2	0.344
Positive	4	12	
Simple to use in my work			
Negative (difficult)	9	4	0.637
Positive (simple)	4	4	
Important for my work			
Negative	1	1	>0.188
Positive	2	17	
Adequate for use in my work			
Negative	7	0	*0.062
Positive	4	9	
Reliable and valid for use in my work			
Negative	4	1	*0.035
Positive	7	9	

*Significant change in one direction

were relevant, useful, feasible, desirable, altering, difficult, and important. Opinion was rather evenly divided on whether or not this family of computer applications would revolutionize the work of the participants. After the Institute, the participants shifted significantly toward seeing retrieval as less than adequate, reliable, and valid for their work.

Before and after views on *data analysis* are compared in Table IV. We see that the large majority perceives this family of applications as relevant, useful, feasible, desirable, altering, difficult, and important. There is no consensus on the revolutionary potential of data analysis. The only significant shift in opinion is toward viewing data analysis as more difficult.

In sum, the set of before-after turnover calculations reported in Tables II, III, and IV indicates that the Institute participants recognized positive rewards from computer applications to international relations, but were moved to a greater emphasis on the role of the user in securing these rewards.

Intuitively, one can see how the findings to this point leave the behavioral outcome in question. That is, the participants may want to use computers more than before, but the requirements for effective use may discourage them enough to decrease their employment of computer applications. Obviously, a strong answer to the question of which possible effect will dominate requires data on the behavior of the participants sometime after the Institute. We do not have such information.

What we do have is their opinions about what they planned to do involving computers as of the end of the Institute and some indications of how this compares with their plans at the beginning. Two complementary bits of data merit our attention: first, the increased percentage of the group (from 0% to 42%) using or planning to explore using all three types of computer applications (simulation, information retrieval, data analysis); and, second, the response from 88% of those completing the second questionnaire that they planned to make more use of computers as a "result" of the Institute. We suggest that the impact of heightened expectations about rewards from computer applications outweighed that of learning more about the requirements and limitations of some current computer applications.

RELATIONSHIPS BETWEEN OPINIONS BEFORE AND AFTER THE INSTITUTE

Up to this point, we have made no attempt to see what opinions are in some patterned association with others. In this section we will look at the

Table IV.   ATTITUDES TOWARDS DATA ANALYSIS
(frequency of response)

Pre-Institute Expectations	Post-Institute Conclusions		P
	Negative	Positive	
Relevant to my work			
Negative	1	1	> 0.5
Positive	0	19	
Useful for me to know			
Negative	0	1	> 0.5
Positive	0	20	
Feasible for my work			
Negative	0	2	> 0.5
Positive	2	17	
Desirable in my work			
Negative	2	3	> 0.128
Positive	0	16	
Revolutionizing my work			
Negative	8	3	0.500
Positive	2	8	
Altering my work			
Negative	4	1	> 0.188
Positive	1	15	
Simple to use in my work			
Negative (difficult)	12	0	*0.06
Positive (simple)	4	5	
Important for my work			
Negative	1	1	> 0.188
Positive	2	17	
Adequate for use in my work			
Negative	6	3	0.656
Positive	3	8	
Reliable and valid for use in my work			
Negative	4	4	*0.500
Positive	3	10	

*Significant change in one direction

relationships between the opinions held by the participants in two ways: first, we report the results of a factor analysis of each set of questionnaires (before and after) in order to gain some understanding of how the participants clustered their opinions before and after the Institute; second, we report the results of a series of cross-tabulations designed to find out to what extent appraisals of any one of our families of computer applications depend on appraisals of another.

For our factor analyses, we selected all those questions whose responses met the criteria for applications of this method (i.e., response scales were strictly ordinal and there were less than 20% no answers). We submitted these data to an orthogonal rotation procedure to discover the organization of participant opinion. In both the results for the pre- and the post-Institute questionnaires the factor structure was highly fragmentary, i.e., there were numerous factors. We will only report and discuss the most important.[3]

When the reader looks at these data, he will note that we have grouped the variables (rows) in the matrices into three classes: (A) opinions about computer and international relations techniques and approaches; (B) opinions about the usefulness of the program; and (C) respondent characteristics. As abbreviated in Tables V and VI, "AM program" refers to the lectures on computer technology and natural science applications; "PM," to the lectures on social science applications.

Table V presents the most important factors found in the pre-Institute questionnaires. The table contains four factors which may be thought of as distinct dimensions. If we look for those rows with the highest numbers in each "F" column, we can readily summarize the main content of each factor and arrive at the labels in the table. We in essence have factors which primarily involve: (1) opinions about simulation; (2) opinions about data analysis; (3) opinions about information retrieval; and (4) opinions about the usefulness of the sessions as an information exchange forum. The similarity of signs in each of the first three factors (F-I, F-II, and F-III) suggests that we have a relatively homogeneously positive or negative appraisal of a particular family of applications. Opinions about data analysis do not seem to depend on those about information retrieval and vice-versa. Opinions about simulation are moderately indicative of opinions about data analysis and information retrieval. It is important to note the relative absence of a patterned connection between attitudes toward computer applications and our other two sets of variables — program appraisals and respondent characteristics.

[3]To select major factors for discussion, we used the arbitrary rule that the sum of squares over variables must be greater than 4.0.

Table V. ORTHOGONALLY ROTATED FACTOR MATRIX, PRE-
INSTITUTE QUESTIONNAIRE (60 items)

Variables	F-I Simulation	F-II[a] Data analysis	F-III[a] Information retrieval	F-IV[a] Information exchange
Sum of squares	10.777	6.915	4.529	4.102
A: Immediate approach to IR problems				
Long-range approach to IR problems				
Quantification and formal and testable modeling				374
IR defies quantification, formal and testable modeling				
Quantification and modeling distorts IR problems				
Quantitative analysis relevant	417	778*		
Quantitative analysis useful		901**		
Quantitative analysis feasible	364	822*		
Quantitative analysis desirable		853*		
Quantitative analysis revolutionizing own work	350		-309	345
Quantitative analysis altering work	524*	434		
Quantitative analysis simple to use in work	303	532*		
Quantitative analysis important in own work	460	780*		

Table V. Cont. ORTHOGONALLY ROTATED FACTOR MATRIX, PRE-
INSTITUTE QUESTIONNAIRE (60 items)

Variables	F-I Simulation	F-II[a] Data analysis	F-III[a] Information retrieval	F-IV[a] Information exchange
A: Quantitative analysis adequate for use in own work	559*	651*		
Quantitative analysis reliable and valid for use		803*		
Information retrieval relevant			482	350
Information retrieval useful			817**	
Information retrieval feasible	409		734*	
Information retrieval desirable		356	774*	
Information retrieval revolutionizing own work	313		318	497
Information retrieval altering work	316		427	423
Information retrieval simple to use in work	316			
Information retrieval important in own work	554*	444	495	
Information retrieval adequate for use in own work	738*		332	
Information retrieval reliable and valid for use	637*	422	359	
Simulation relevant	941**			
Simulation useful	587*			

Table V. Cont.   ORTHOGONALLY ROTATED FACTOR MATRIX, PRE-INSTITUTE QUESTIONNAIRE (60 items)

Variables	F-I Simulation	F-II[a] Data analysis	F-III[a] Information retrieval	F-IV[a] Information exchange
A: Simulation feasible	898*			
Simulation desirable	887*			
Simulation revolutionizing own work	793*			
Simulation altering work	914*			
Simulation simple to use in work				
Simulation important in own work	909*			
Simulation adequate for use in own work	749*			
Simulation reliable and valid for use in own work	859*			
IR training in quantification techniques				
IR training in operationalization of concepts				
B: AM program: answers specific questions in own work				572*
AM: knowledge of what is being done	425			
AM: scientific knowledge			408	
AM: learn details of work of others	363			

Table V. Cont.   ORTHOGONALLY ROTATED FACTOR MATRIX, PRE-INSTITUTE QUESTIONNAIRE (60 items)

Variables	F-I Simulation	F-II[a] Data analysis	F-III[a] Information retrieval	F-IV[a] Information exchange
B: AM: inform others of own work and problems				944**
AM: obtain useful advice and criticism of own work				865*
AM: discuss scientific topics of general interest				
AM: new contacts				
AM: new skills acquired	393	361	318	
PM: program answers specific questions in own work				
PM: knowledge of what is being done				399
PM: scientific knowledge			694*	
PM: learn details of work of others				
PM: inform others of own work and problems				602*
PM: obtain useful advice and criticism of own work				476†
PM: discuss scientific topics of general interest				
PM: new contacts				
PM: new skills acquired				

Table V. Cont.   ORTHOGONALLY ROTATED FACTOR MATRIX, PRE-
INSTITUTE QUESTIONNAIRE (60 items)

Variables	F-I Simulation	F-II[a] Data analysis	F-III[a] Information retrieval	F-IV[a] Information exchange
C: Attitude of co-workers and supervisors to computers				
Percentage of time in research/analysis				
Percentage of time in administration				
Government or non-government affiliation				
Age				

blanks = factor loadings < 0.30.
 * = factor loadings $\geqslant 0.50$.
 ** = single item most correlated with factor.
 A: = responses of attitudes towards techniques and approaches.
 B: = responses about usefulness of presentations.
 C: = personal, job, or affiliation attribute.
 † = decimals omitted from all loadings.
 a = signs reversed.

Let us see to what extent a similar set of opinion clusters emerges from the post-Institute questionnaires. Table VI presents the relevant data. In the post-institute matrix, we find six major factors. If we again scan the columns we can summarize the content of each: (1) future usefulness of computer applications and appraisals of data analysis; (2) simulation; (3) information retrieval; (4) usefulness of the lectures and small group discussions for acquiring scientific knowledge and new skills; (5) usefulness of discussion groups for participant's work problems and general interests; and (6) usefulness of the program for new contacts with scientists and administrators in different relationships to national policy. When we compare Tables V and VI, we first notice the basic similarity in the nature of the first three factors each centered on a different family of applications. We also notice the tendency of opinions about applications to be on different factors than opinions about the program. However, two differences also merit mention. First, it seems that by the end of the

Table VI. ORTHOGONALLY ROTATED FACTOR, MATRIX, POST-
INSTITUTE QUESTIONNAIRE (88 items)

Variables	F-I Computer applications and data analysis	F-II Simulation	F-III Information retrieval	F-IV Uses of groups: knowledge and skill	F-IV Uses of groups: information for own work	F-VI New contacts
	11.089	9.249	8.020	7.158	4.766	4.752
A: Present usefulness of information retrieval for immediate approach to IR		311	428	300		
Present usefulness of data processing for immediate approach to IR	309		458			
Present usefulness of simulation for immediate approach to IR						
Present usefulness of information retrieval for long-range approach to IR			564*			
Present usefulness of data processing for long-range approach to IR	621*					
Present usefulness of simulation for long-range approach to IR		368				
Future use of information retrieval for immediate approach to IR	739*					317
Future use of data processing for immediate approach to IR	742*					

Table VI. Cont.   ORTHOGONALLY ROTATED FACTOR, MATRIX, POST-
INSTITUTE QUESTIONNAIRE (88 items)

Variables	F-I Computer applications and data analysis	F-II Simulation	F-III Information retrieval	F-IV Uses of groups: knowledge and skill	F-IV Uses of groups: information for own work	F-VI New contacts
A: Future use of simulation for immediate approach to IR	523*	405				
Future use of information retrieval for long-range approach to IR	844*					
Future use of data processing for long-range approach to IR	935**					
Future use of simulation for long-range approach to IR	839*					
Quantification and formal and testable modeling						
IR defies quantification, formal and testable modeling				462		
Quantification and modeling distorts IR problems						
Quantitative analysis relevant	734*				398	
Quantitative analysis useful	789*					
Quantitative analysis feasible	764*					
Quantitative analysis desirable	730*		337		332	
Quantitative analysis revolutionizing own work	762*					

Table VI. Cont. ORTHOGONALLY ROTATED FACTOR MATRIX, POST-INSTITUTE QUESTIONNAIRE (88 items)

Variables	F-I Computer applications and data analysis	F-II Simulation	F-III Information retrieval	F-IV Uses of groups: knowledge and skill	F-IV Uses of groups: information for own work	F-VI New contacts
A: Quantitative analysis altering work	751*	394				
Quantitative analysis simple to use in work	438				403	
Quantitative analysis important in own work	753*	431				
Quantitative analysis adequate for use in own work	377					-444
Quantitative analysis reliable and valid for use	496					
Information retrieval relevant	368		785*			
Information retrieval useful			792*			
Information retrieval feasible			748*			
Information retrieval desirable			858**			
Information retrieval revolutionizing own work			812*			
Information retrieval altering work			679*			
Information retrieval simple to use in work		336				
Information retrieval important in own work			847*			
Information retrieval adequate for use in own work		371				

Table VI. Cont. ORTHOGONALLY ROTATED FACTOR MATRIX, POST-INSTITUTE QUESTIONNAIRE (88 items)

Variables	F-I Computer applications and data analysis	F-II Simulation	F-III Information retrieval	F-IV Uses of groups: knowledge and skill	F-IV Uses of groups: information for own work	F-VI New contacts
A: Information retrieval reliable and valid for use			318		351	
Simulation relevant		876*				
Simulation useful		824*				
Simulation feasible		920**				
Simulation desirable	310	891*				
Simulation revolutionizing own work		723*	341			
Simulation altering work		892*				
Simulation simple to use in work		396			493	
Simulation important in own work		887*				
Simulation adequate for use in own work		667*				
Simulation reliable and valid for use in own work		717*				
Attitude change, machine capacities						315
IR training in quantification techniques	357					
IR training in operationalization, research design	409					
B: AM: program answers specific questions in own work				471	461	391
AM: knowledge of what is being done				338		460

Table VI. Cont. ORTHOGONALLY ROTATED FACTOR, MATRIX, POST-INSTITUTE QUESTIONNAIRE (88 items)

Variables	F-I Computer applications and data analysis	F-II Simu-lation	F-III Infor-mation re-trieval	F-IV Uses of groups: knowl-edge and skill	F-IV Uses of groups: information for own work	F-VI New contacts
B: AM: scientific knowledge			307	842*		
AM: details of work of others				414		
AM: inform others of own work and problems						358
AM: obtain useful advice and criticism of own work						
AM: discuss scientific topics of general interest						343
AM: new contacts						797*
AM: new skills acquired				808*		
Group: answers specific questions in own work					879*	
Group: knowledge of what is being done				613*		
Group: scientific knowledge				905**		
Group: details of work of others				325		
Group: inform others of own work and problems				413		
Group: obtain useful advice and criticism of own work					748*	
Group: discuss scientific topics of general interest	306			397	695*	

Table VI. Cont. ORTHOGONALLY ROTATED FACTOR MATRIX, POST-INSTITUTE QUESTIONNAIRE (88 items)

Variables	F-I Computer applications and data analysis	F-II Simulation	F-III Information retrieval	F-IV Uses of groups: knowledge and skill	F-IV Uses of groups: information for own work	F-VI New contacts
B: Group: new contacts	337	313		697*		
Group: new skills acquired				769*	414	
PM: program answers specific questions in own work		304				
PM: knowledge of what is being done			459			430
PM: scientific knowledge			335	417		
PM: details of work of others						
PM: inform others of own work and problems						
PM: obtain useful advice and criticism of own work						
PM: discuss scientific topics of general interest					309	445
PM: new contacts						895**
PM: new skills acquired				818*		
Changes in conference to learn more of value						
C: Difficulty of morning speeches	−477					
Difficulty of afternoon/evening speeches						
Attitude of co-workers and superiors to computers		367				

Table VI. Cont. ORTHOGONALLY ROTATED FACTOR MATRIX, POST-INSTITUTE QUESTIONNAIRE (88 items)

Variables	F-I Computer applications and data analysis	F-II Simulation	F-III Information retrieval	F-IV Uses of groups: knowledge and skill	F-IV Uses of groups: information for own work	F-VI New contacts
C: Degree of change in plans about using computers				322		
Degree of satisfaction expected from planned use			402	337	461	
Articles read during institute (number)						
Percentage of time in teaching			-390		411	-600*
Percentage of time in research/analysis						
Percentage of time in administration			352			337†
Government, non-government affiliation			-411[b]			-544*[b]
Age	-336[c]					325[d]

Blanks = factor loadings <0.30.

   * = factor loadings ≥0.50.

  ** = single item most correlated with factor.

  A: = responses of attitudes towards techniques and approaches.

  B: = responses about usefulness of presentations.

  C: = personal, job, or affiliation attribute.

  † = decimals omitted from all loadings.

  a = signs reversed.

  b = negative value indicates tendency towards government affiliation on this factor.

  c = negative value indicates tendency towards younger respondents (<35 years).

  d = positive value indicates tendency towards older respondents (≥36 years).

Institute the degree of optimism about future computer applications of any of our three kinds was strongly dependent on the extent to which the respondent positively appraised data analysis, and vice-versa. That is, his position on one or the other of these sets of opinions was quite a good indicator of his position on the other. Second, in contrast to Table V, Table VI contains a number of cases where respondent attribute characteristics seem strongly tied to opinions about computer applications and the program.[4]

This tie deserves special attention because when we find a strong, patterned relationship between respondent characteristics and other opinions we have a useful handle on who will think what, and a clue to some of the reasons for his opinions. On the post-Institute questionnaire, we find that:

— Respondents who had less difficulty with the computer science lectures had more positive attitudes toward future computer applications and data analysis (F-I).
— Those who expected the attitude of their co-workers and superiors to be favorable towards the use of computers in their work tended to have more positive opinions about simulation (F-II).
— Those who expected their future use of computers to be satisfactory tended to have more positive conclusions about information retrieval and the informational usefulness of the program (F-III, F-IV, F-V).
— Those who planned to use computers more in their work felt more positively about the imparting of scientific knowledge and new skills (F-IV).
— Those who spent less time in teaching and more in administration tended to have more positive views on information retrieval applications and the usefulness of the Institute for new contacts (F-III, F—VI). Not surprisingly, this pattern also tended to characterize government participants (F-III, F-VI).
— Those who spent more of their time in teaching were particularly likely to see the discussion groups as useful (F-V).
— The younger participants (under 36) had more positive attitudes toward future computer applications and toward data analysis (F-I).
— Finally, the older participants were particularly likely to see the Institute as useful in the making of new contacts (F-VI).

The importance of factors dealing with a particular family of applications in both the pre- and post-Institute data led us to explore further the relationships between participants' opinions about the different ap-

[4]It is interesting to note that at the beginning of the Institute (Table V), respondents whose superiors and co-workers had *less* favorable attitudes toward using computers had *more* favorable expectations about information retrieval and vice-versa.

plications. As the prose in Tables II, III, and IV indicates, there were numerous appraisals of each family of applications. We wanted to reduce these to a general stance for each participant and then indicate to what extent his stance toward, for example, information retrieval, was related in a statistically significant way to his stance toward, in our case, simulation and toward data analysis. Do appraisals of computer applications to international relations rest on some general orientation or are they relatively unique to each class of applications?[5]

At the beginning of the Institute, the respondent's appraisals of information retrieval are not statistically significant guides to his appraisals of data analysis and vice-versa. The same lack of relationship occurs with regard to information retrieval and simulation. We do find a statistically significant congruence between appraisals of simulation and of data analysis, i.e., a relationship in the direction predicted at a significance level equal to 0.05. The data for this statistically significant relationship are given in Table VII. At the end of the Institute we find no statistically significant relationships. The respondents had apparently come to differentiate between families of computer applications to a striking extent and to form their appraisals accordingly.

---

[5] To arrive at the general stance, we summed the scores of each respondent on the ten appraisal scales for each family of applications. We then recategorized the respondents on the basis of whether they were above or below the same cutting point on each summary scale which represents the same categorization of the original seven-point scales into "positive" and "negative" responses. We then cross-tabulated the recoded responses to test the research hypothesis that there is a systematic congruence in the respondents' appraisals of the different applications. The null hypothesis was that there is not, i.e., that irrespective of their appraisals of one technique, the respondents are equally likely to have positive or negative appraisals of another technique. We applied for this purpose the Fisher Test (using significance levels) for testing the statistical significance of an observed set of values in a 2×2 contingency table. Because of the small number of cases under consideration, we used the Finney Critical Values adaptation of this test. A table of critical values of specified cells in our contingency tables for various levels of significance constitutes the sampling distribution (Siegel, 1956, pp. 96-101, 256-270), i.e., the probability of the occurrence under the null hypothesis of a value as extreme as or more extreme than the particular value of the test statistic in the table of critical values (Siegel, 1956, p. 11). We chose a significance level of 0.05 which leads us to reject the null hypothesis if we obtain a significance level less than 0.05. The region of rejection of our tests is one-tailed since the research hypothesis predicted the direction of the differences. To make this test, we used the "Table of Critical Values of D (or C) in the Fisher Test" (Siegel, 1956, pp. 256-270).

Table VII. APPRAISALS OF DATA ANALYSIS AND OF
                SIMULATION (before)

	Data Analysis		
Simulation	Negative	Positive	*P*
Negative	7	3	
			0.05
Positive	3	10	

REACTIONS TO THE INSTITUTE PROGRAM

We have reported before and after opinion data the comparison of which indicates some of the effects of the Institute on participant thinking about computers and international relations. In this section, we plan to complement the previous findings with evaluative information of two kinds. The first deals with appraisals of elements of the Institute program (as contrasted with its topic); the second presents an impressionistic picture in the participants' own words of the implications of their two-week experience.

It is gratifyingly clear that the participants felt that the educational experiment was worthwhile. All who answered the second questionnaire recommended that the Institute be repeated in the future. It also seems clear that the participants were engaged in the learning experience and fully capable of handling rather complex treatments of computer applications to international relations. On their involvement, 62% read during the two weeks more than 10 of the suggested supplementary articles and 96% read more than 5, in addition to attending a very full schedule of meetings. In terms of comprehension of material on the level of that presented in this book, the international applications lectures posed no particular problem although the computer science and natural science applications lectures did. The relevant data are given in Table VIII.

We also sought from the participants their expectations and appraisals of the Institute as an instance of scientific communication. We asked them to indicate for each of nine communication functions to what extent different parts of the Institute program were useful. They were asked to make these appraisals of the two series of lectures on both the pre- and post-Institute questionnaires, and of the discussion groups on the latter form only. In Table IX, we report that percentage of respondents

Table VIII. COMPREHENSION OF LECTURES

	Very/Extremely Difficult (%)	Not at All Difficult (%)
Computer/natural science	54	0
International relations	8	50

who appraised the program element in question on the upper two points (very useful or quite useful) of a four-point scale (the other points being a little useful and not at all useful). As with the percentage entries in Table VIII, the reader should attend to general patterns rather than to specific figures.

Each row in the table contains appraisals of the extent to which program elements were expected to or did fulfill the function stated in the left-hand column. When we scan Table IX, the following general conclusions emerge. First, on balance, the lecture portion of the program (columns A-F and H) met group expectations as a scientific communication experience. Second, the lectures were clearly found to be more useful than the small group discussions. Third, expectations were higher for rewards of a general rather than a focused, personally specific nature. Fourth, in those areas where the great majority of the respondents expected considerable usefulness, expectations were met. Fifth, both before and after scores were significantly lowered by appraisals of personal opportunity communication functions (raise specific questions, inform others of your work, get advice on your work, acquire new skills).

Parenthetically, we computed turnover tables for appraisals of the program just as we did for appraisals of computer applications to international relations. We have not presented this set of calculations because in only one case did they locate a statistically significant shift in a particular direction. The exception was a significant turnover in the direction of finding the international relations lectures less useful than expected for acquiring new skills. The data are shown in Table X.

These findings suggest, first, that the Institute was in general appropriate to its participants' expectations and successful in meeting those of the majority. They also suggest that the relatively poor small group performance and the low level of personal usefulness are complementary problems subject to a common resolution. Specifically, in future exercises of computer applications to international relations for a similar professional group, it may be wise to use the small group periods

Table IX. APPRAISALS OF THE INSTITUTE PROGRAM

Very/Quite Useful for	A Before	B After	C Direction of Change	D Before	E After	F Direction of Change	G After	H Before	After	Direction of Change
	Computer/Natural Science (%)			International Relations (%)			Discussion Groups (%)	Lecture Appraisal Averages (%)		
Answers to specific questions that arise in your work	35	27	–	40	39	–	27	38	33	–
Knowledge of what is being done	70	85	+	85	88	+	27	80	87	+
Scientific knowledge otherwise not learned early enough	73	58	–	65	62	–	42	69	60	–
Opportunity to learn details of work of others	72	62	–	77	85	+	27	74	74	
Opportunity to inform others of your work and related problems	19	31	+	31	15	–	23	25	23	–
Opportunity to obtain useful advise and criticism of your work	22	12	–	39	15	–	27	31	14	–
Opportunity to discuss broad scientific topics of general interest to you	42	44	+	65	65		19	54	55	+
New contacts scientists/administrators in different relationships to national policy	73	73		77	87	+	46	75	80	+
Acquisition of new skills	58	46	–	54	27	–	32	56	37	–
Average	53	49	–	59	54	–	30	56	51	–

Table X. USEFULNESS OF AFTERNOON/EVENING
PRESENTATIONS FOR ACQUIRING NEW SKILLS

	Post-Institute Conclusions		
Pre-Institute Expectations	Less Useful	More Useful	*P*
Less	9	0	0.008
More	7	5	

for presentations by participants and individual discussions of their work and problems instead of for group tutorials which are led by skilled programmers for randomly selected participants.

To conclude our evaluation, it seems useful to listen primarily to the participants themselves. Accordingly, we will draw on the answers to three of the open-ended questions in the post-Institute form.

1. "During the past two weeks of the Institute, in what ways, if any, have your attitudes towards the use of computers in your work changed?"

   — "I feel more at home with the vocabulary. I know a great deal more about what is possible as compared with what is glibly talked about but not available."

   — "More realistic — less optimistic. Still enthused, but with much better idea of obstacles between my work and computer application to it."

   — "Come to accept a greater willingness to try experimentation in pattern recognition and simulation."

   — "Hopes have become higher. Would like to get collaborators, research assistance, and other support."

   — "Possibilities enlarged, but I didn't have to be sold."

   — "General reinforcement of an already high state of enthusiasm."

   — "I am even more sceptical about them than when I arrived."

2. "As a result of this Institute, what kinds of research or administrative uses of computers do you now plan to explore, if any?"

   — "Tendency to increase number and scope of programs in anticipation of more rapid computational techniques (currently available but unknown to me) and memory storage."

— "Continue exploration of data processing uses; improve information retrieval uses."

— "Simulation if possible."

— "Approximately the same as without the Institute, but presumably much better informed."

3.   "What would you say has been the most important aspect of this Institute for you? Why has it been important to you?"

— "Interaction between academics and government policy/research types. The contacts will be useful for me; and I gained a greater appreciation of the practical problems facing them in their work. The informal interaction gave us time to discuss points of common interest."

— "Interaction between government and academic or quasi-academic viewpoints. This does not obtain so well or work so freely in usual contact with regular academic consultants, who principally accept your assumptions and help you get on with your job as you define it. Interaction of viewpoints much freer and wider ranging in this context."

— "It was a revelation of the capacity and current application of computers in the social science field. I feel that it afforded me an opportunity to acquire knowledge and provided food for thought that otherwise, I would likely not have acquired. I should be more valuable to the Department beyond my present assignment."

— "I got a feeling for the computer and its applications. I think I am in better shape to talk to my students about their work, for some of which the computer may be relevant. This is why I came, and I am glad I did . . ."

Taken together with the data presented earlier, the quotations suggest that the Institute performed two types of educational functions. On the one hand, the formal presentations provided in a systematic way balanced information about computers, how they are, and can be, applied to international relations, and what the international relations user must contribute to the application. On the other hand, informal contact and interaction among the participants from diverse career lines — government and nongovernment, academic and nonacademic, administration and research and teaching — gave many of the participants an enriched perspective on their own and others' work and problems.

In sum, the Computers and the Policy-Making Community Institute fulfilled these two major functions to a sufficient extent to give us confidence on two points. First, institutes which bring together men of diverse backgrounds to learn about a common tool can lead to better understanding of mutual problems in international relations analysis, teaching, and management. Second, such institutes can further the use of computer tools and modern concepts, theories and methods for treating international relations problems.

REFERENCES

Borko, Harold (ed.). *Computer Applications in the Behavioral Sciences.* Englewood Cliffs, N. J.: Prentice-Hall, Inc., 1962.

Feigenbaum, Edward A. and Julian Feldman (eds.). *Computers and Thought.* New York: McGraw-Hill Book Co., 1963.

Greenberger, Martin (ed.). *Computers and the World of the Future.* Cambridge: M. I. T. Press, 1962.

Janda, Kenneth. *Information Retrieval: Applications in Political Science.* Indianapolis: Bobbs-Merrill, Inc., 1967.

Menzel, Herbert. *The Flow of Information Among Scientists: Problems, Opportunities and Research Questions.* Bureau of Applied Social Research, Columbia University, 1958, mimeo. (Available as Technical Report 144390 PB from the Clearinghouse, Dept. of Commerce, Springfield, Va.)

Menzel, Herbert. "Scientific Communication: Five Themes from Social Science Research, " *American Psychologist,* 21 (November, 1966), 999-1004.

Osgood, Charles E., George J. Suci, and Percy H. Tannenbaum. *The Measurement of Meaning.* Urbana: University of Illinois Press, 1957.

Schwartz, Judah L. *Computers and the Policy-Making Community: A Final Report.* Lawrence Radiation Laboratory, University of California, UCRL-14887, 1966.

Siegel, Sidney. *Nonparametric Statistics for the Behavioral Sciences.* New York: McGraw-Hill Book Co., 1956.

Appendix A

THE SOCIAL UTILITY
OF COMPUTERS

A Panel Discussion
Summarized by
Jeffrey S. Milstein[1]

This panel discussion was held on April 8, 1966, in Berkeley, California, as a part of the "Computers and the Policy-Making Community Institute." The panelists were Dr. Launor Carter of Systems Development Corporation (SDC), Dr. C. West Churchman of the Center of Management Sciences at the University of California, Dr. Ithiel de Sola Pool of the Department of Political Science at the Massachusetts Institute of Technology, Dr. R. W. Gerard of the University of California at Irvine, and the chairman of the panel, Dr. Harold Borko of Systems Development Corporation.

Each of the panelists spoke on the general subject of the problems and opportunities computer development will pose for the future conduct, research, management, and teaching of international relations. Following the presentations of the first four panelists, the chairman of the panel took questions directed to the panel from participants in the Institute.

Dr. Carter spoke first on *The Capabilities of Data Processing.* His talk, which was especially concerned with data processing in management, covered time-sharing, data bases, present capabilities, examples of ongoing operations, libraries, and how data base handling helps administrators.

On the implications of *time-sharing* over the next three to five years, Dr. Carter began by pointing out that there are different sized time-

---

[1] At the request of the editors, Mr. Milstein has prepared this summary from notes taken during the panel discussion.

sharing computer systems. Small systems like JOHNIAC and SAINT cover many classes of activities. Medium sized systems like the IBM 360/40 could have time-sharing capable of handling large data bases with good peripheral equipment. It is the large time-sharing systems such as the IBM 360/67 and the CDC 6600, however, which administrators will use. These large systems have the following characteristics which are of advantage to the people using them: First, they allow many users at the computer at one time; second, they have remote on-line display, which is most useful since it allows all users to have access to a common data base; third, they allow the user to use the programming language which he has worked with in the past; and fourth, each user has control over the program which serves his own need, which he can use himself, and which allows him to manipulate the data base in his own individual way.

Dr. Carter pointed out that there are three types of *data base:* those which have an explicit format, those which have no format, and those which are textual and in a natural language. The first are easily handled, the second must be directly entered, and the third have the ability to search but are not really adequate for all information retrieval purposes, because there is not yet a good semantic and meaning analysis by computer. One can still use natural language bases, however, by first editing the data base oneself for those things which are relevant for one's own purposes. Nonetheless, one must still be willing to put up with some error in using natural language data bases. One example of a natural language base is the SDC "proto-syntax" procedure for retrieving information from the *Golden Book Encyclopedia,* e.g., "How do earthworms breed?"

Dr. Carter went on to give examples of *present capabilities* in data processing. One example is the large computerized file of Department of Defense research project description forms now at SDC. The Advanced Research Project Agency can now query this file from remote consoles about the content of any on-going research project which they are sponsoring. Another example is that natural language text can be searched for uncategorized information. Systems are now available which will do a natural language search. The output of these systems is not perfect, but can be useful when surveyed critically. The Los Angeles Police Department, for example, has now digitalized descriptions of crimes made by the policeman on the beat, such as robbery reports. These reports are not indexed, but can be queried by typed questions in natural language. One can get back the full text or the abstract of the report in two to three minutes from the 6000-item file. The output is then judged for its relevance.

Dr. Carter next discussed how *libraries* can use data processing. In the 1962 report by Gil King on automating the Library of Congress, it was stated that it would cost from 60 to 75 million dollars to put the total bibliographic apparatus of the Library into digital form. The Library contains some 43 million items which, incidentally, could be put into digital form so small that these items literally could orbit the earth as a satellite and be queried by telecommunications from any place they passed over! The decision has been made to digitalize the Library, and proposals for doing this are now being evaluated. This task is expected to take five years. The reasons for this deliberate pace are that the process cannot disrupt present Library of Congress services, such as its card catalogues, during the transition to digitalized form and that the innovators want to be successful in this attempt. For if this project failed, other libraries would probably not attempt it.

Other libraries are being considered for automation, and Project INTREX is concerned with automating the M.I.T. technical libraries. Another project that can be applied by libraries is SDC's BOLD (bibliographic on-line display). This allows the user to search, by means of a tree-structure, through large bibliographic data bases (e.g., abstracts of government contract reports) on a cathode-ray tube or a teletype remote console, and call up interesting items for a print-out of a hard copy.

Dr. Carter then spoke of computer *aids for administrative decision-making* that involve more complex tasks than computation. He first pointed out that there are problems of protecting personal files, especially secret ones, when they are stored in some type of computer memory device. Safeguards can be taken, however, for protection of these files. He pointed out the advantage for administrative decision-making of having at one's fingertips access to a large data base on the operations of the entire organization. One can even dictate letters to computers, having them teletyped to the recipient and also placed in a permanent computer file. He warned, however, that administrators must be careful of the kinds of choice they make in this area.

Dr. Carter concluded by summarizing the technical and administrative considerations involved in a computer operation costing about $15 per hour per console and being used two shifts per day. If one is only an occasional user, he would profit by using time-sharing. But if he has many jobs, he would find it less expensive to process them in batches. Administrators, however, must require programmers and systems programmers to fit the computers to the *administrator's* needs, and to make machine efficiency, albeit important, a secondary consideration.

Dr. Churchman was the next speaker. His topic was *Implications of Computers for Economic Planning and Management.* The focus of this talk was on the relationship between information and the way that it is used in policy-making. Dr. Churchman began by saying that science is not simply built out of blocks of information. Scientific *theory* is the attempt to order information in a specific way. Similarly, a *decision* is not simply built of information. One *starts* with the *world* and the information it presents, and then orders this information according to his notions of what the world is like. One's decisions are, and must be, informed by this theorizing. One cannot let information alone dictate his decisions.

Dr. Churchman then spoke about three needs (i.e., deficiencies) of the decision-maker and three *technological developments* related to these needs. The first need of this decision-maker is for *information.* Electronic data processing can afford him ready access to banks of data when they are needed, especially when these data exist in an explicit format. The second deficiency of the decision-maker is *policy rigidity.* Inflexibility imposes constraints and frustrations at all levels in an organization. Using electronic data processing, managers are able to explore more policy alternatives than otherwise, to estimate probable consequences of alternative decisions by means of linear programming and simulation, and to evaluate public responses to alternative consequences. In these two ways, then, electronic data processing supports more rational decision-making.

The third deficiency of the decision-maker is one-sidedness or *bias.* Electronic data processing cannot help, but even exacerbates this deficiency, for a data bank is stupid. A biased decision-maker has an idea — a theory — as to why he wants some information, e.g., to support a policy already decided upon, and goes out and collects for his data bank information which supports that theory. The computer can work only with the data that is fed into it (hopefully, accurate, reliable data), and cannot tell the decision-maker what *other information* there is that is not stored in the computer that is relevant to his decision, or ask him *why* he wants to know the information he has requested. Every user should be aware of this bias problem. There is no hardware solution to it; indeed, large computer systems will facilitate bias, resulting in misuses of information and nonoptimal decision consequences. Exaggeration of bias is just one unanticipated problem of electronic data processing. Users of electronic data processing should be constantly on the lookout for other unanticipated problems associated with the use of computers in policy-making.

Dr. Pool was the next panelist to speak. His topic was *Implications of Computers for Data Analysis and Political Planning.* He opened by specifying three general tasks posed by policy-workers and three general techniques used to perform these tasks. First, policy-makers need to locate specific *facts* in a mass of information. *Information retrieval* is the technique to use for this. Second, at a higher level in policy-making they may want to know what the *significance* of some fact is. *Pattern recognition* is the general process used to determine significance. Third, one may wish to make a *prediction* of what is going to happen. *Simulation* is a useful technique for prediction.

Dr. Pool then went on to discuss the kinds of technology that are used by policy-workers. These are, in decreasing order of the amount of use: speech, writing (about 4,000 years old), telephone and telegraph (about 100 years old), typewriter, archives (about 2,000 years old), text reproduction (e.g., printing, mimeographing, Xerography), and the computer. That the policy-worker has become increasingly dependent upon assistants with technological advance is evident when one observes that a policy-worker himself uses speech, writing, and the telephone; only a moderately trained assistant does his typing; he or his assistant can reproduce text; a professional staff of assistants is needed to make effective use of his archives; and a person with a high level of professional competence is needed to use the computer, since user languages are not yet at the level where all can use them.

One of the important objectives of a policy-worker is to use the technology available to him to predict the future. Dr. Pool observed that we all try to predict the future all the time. Our problem is to predict accurately. Simulation is one promising computer technique for prediction. In using simulation to predict, one takes a given body of data, changes one variable, and asks what changes in the system of all other variables occur? Unfortunately, transformation rules in the social sciences are not very satisfactory, especially for multivariate systems. The rules are generally vague and not explicit, and carrying out the transformation rules is laborious. To minimize the difficulties in transformation the researcher making a prediction must make explicit what his implicit rules of transformation (sometimes called "intuition") are, and then seek to carry out those rules rigorously. Fields such as weapons effects or elections are most amenable to this approach.

The purpose of this prediction procedure would generally be to define determining conditions, and draw logical consequences from them about alternative situations, using the explicit rules of transformation. For example, with a hypothetical scenario one can come up with some fairly good predictions about the 1972 elections, given demographic, economic, political and other relevant data of 1966. The success of the predictions, however, is dependent upon accurate data, explicit rules of transformation, and a well-defined problem. Experimental research using these procedures is now being done in business, gaming, and international relations simulations. The predictions, however, are not yet good enough for present policy use.

Dr. Gerard was the final panelist to speak. His topic was *Computers and a New Education.* Dr. Gerard began with the statement that human intelligence, the source of new technologies, can use those technologies in an autocatalytic way to improve human education, and thus improve human intelligence itself. Humans, like computers, can do only what they are trained to do. However, organisms do respond to the richness of their environment. Human beings, because of the needs imposed by their environment, were forced to develop new technologies, including computers. Throughout biological evolution, response time of organisms has tended to shorten, while the range of responses has tended to widen. This is evident in the evolution of RNA and DNA to single-cellular organisms to multicellular organisms with nervous systems having larger and better circuits of control.

In the process of biosocial evolution, there has been a progression from the invention of symbols, to the organization of symbols into languages, to the development of tested organized language that is science, to the invention of aides to invention itself, e.g., computers. Dr. Gerard explained that we sometimes lose perspective concerning this process of increasingly more complex symbolic invention. He related the story of the three baseball umpires who were discussing how they went about their job of calling balls and strikes. The first umpire said, "Well, I call 'em as I *see* 'em." Seeing his chance to be one up, the second umpire said, "Ha! I call 'em as they are!" The third umpire, wise in the ways of the world and of science said, "Well, *they ain't anything* until I call 'em!" (This story is also relevant to Dr. Churchman's previous discussion of the relationship between fact and theory in science and in decision-making.)

From his background in neurophysiology, Dr. Gerard described the evolution of the brain and its relationship to the improvement of education. He noted that in biological evolution, the receptors of distant stimuli (sight) and the cerebral hemispheres developed as olfactory and audial stimuli inputs increased. In humans, the brain developed quickly as a result of the demands of the use of tools. Similarly, in the individual, nervous processing develops as the amount of stimuli increases; and in rats, the cortex of the brain thickens as their experience increases. Stimulus deprivation, on the other hand, leads to a decreased processing ability of the nervous system.

Dr. Gerard defines *learning* as the alteration of behavioral responses by experience, and *education* as the societal control of learning. Effective teaching can be increased by computer-assisted learning (CAL), since the use of computers in education will allow the presentation of structured experience. Using computers in education will force teachers to explicate their assumptions and procedures, and subject these to test. In the future, it will be possible for a computer to act as a tutor for the individual learner. This computer-tutor could have a data bank which could include all recorded intellectual history (which in a hundred years, could all be put into a form which computers could handle).

In effect, the learner would carry on a dialogue with the data. His computer-tutor, moreover, would be up to date, would learn the best ways of teaching, would learn the ways and patterns in which each individual student learns, would give immediate personal attention to the student, would have infinite patience, and would make possible mass education which allowed individual advancement in response to the rate at which the individual student learned. Obviously, the use of computers in education in this way would vastly change the educational process, having an even greater effect, perhaps, than printing. The distinct boundary between school and nonschool would be gone; there would be no admission or graduation.

Formal education in its present form has existed for only about the last 200 to 500 years. Education has changed and can change. The effects of computer-assisted learning would be far-ranging, and would include an estimated 15 billion dollar saving per year in the United States due to a three-year shortening in the length of *time* (but not learning) of each individual's education. It would, in addition, bring the best educational resources to the underprivileged people of this country and of the world.

SELECTED QUESTIONS ASKED OF THE PANEL

(*To Dr. Churchman*):   Is history an insufficient basis for decision-making? Is decision-making not the outcome of history plus values?

(*Dr. Churchman*):   Will more history do us any good? One must determine whether decision-making allows the use of an old model or requires an entirely new approach to a given system. The use of more history can lead one to think he is improving, while he remains locked in a bad system.

In practice, the information that is collected is that which is easiest to obtain. This can lead one to make a precise and optimal solution to the wrong problem, simply because of one's bias.

(*Dr. Gerard*): When a species cannot change with the environment, it will die off. Generalized forms are the only ones which survive in changed environments.

(*To Dr. Churchman*): Can computers be used to monitor, discover, and reduce error in on-going processes?

(*Dr. Churchman*): It is not easy to see how to break out of old patterns of behavior. A system should be designed to give a manager alternatives.

(*To Dr. Churchman*): Can top administrators use electronic data processing to get more information about the internal workings of their organization than they could otherwise? Could computer systems help, for example, to overcome information suppression by middle management?

(*Dr. Churchman*): Most organizational operations are suboptimal solutions from the point of view of the organization as a whole because elements within the organization seek to satisfy their own goals. We really do not know yet how to make a whole system optimal. No matter how large and complex our analytic models of organizations are, they still do not solve the problem of bias. In fact, management is tending to become less democratic in its decision-making. One way of combating bias in organizations is through fostering open controversy within them.

(*To Dr. Pool*): What will happen in terms of democratic control in governmental organizations and institutions with the advent of computers? Is a totalitarian organization able to make better use of computers?

(*Dr. Pool*): Computers in organizations make possible both an increase in the ability of top managers to make rational decisions (by giving them information about the whole organization), and increased autonomy and decentralization by providing the people at the action levels lower in the organization the information relevant to their actions. The actual effect of computers on middle management is still to be determined.

(*To Dr. Pool*): What relative power in society at large and especially within the government is given to those who have computers over those who do not? Is not this problem especially acute during a transitional state when computers are not generally available?

(*Dr. Pool*):   To answer this question, we can use the relevant analogy of the telephone. The telephone is used by us all, and this requires that there be a large organization to operate the telephone system. This organization, however, affects our individual lives very little. Computers will be used by everyone, too, eventually, although in the transitional state it is true that those who do use them effectively have a relative advantage over those who do not.

(*To Dr. Pool*):   How adequate is the theory used in simulating elections?

(*Dr. Pool*):   It is very elementary theory, very elementary transformation rules. It is our best guess, informed by common sense, and tested by empirical research.

(*To Dr. Pool*):   Do we have enough law-like propositions currently in international relations to justify the use of computers?

(*Dr. Pool*):   In everything but the simple report of a current fact from a data base, we use hypothetical rules of transformation to make inferences about the world and draw implications from facts. The objective is to do this better than it is now being done, and computers are one approach to doing this.

GLOSSARY OF
COMPUTER TERMS

This working glossary is not a comprehensive dictionary, nor do these definitions enjoy the status of industry-accepted standards. Usage in the computer field is subject to regional variations and modification in response to changes in equipment. However, these definitions should provide the reader with a key to the technical terminology in the field.

ACCURACY: freedom from error; the degree of exactness with which a quantity is known or observed (as contrasted with "precision," which is the degree of exactness with which a quantity is stated).

ACOUSTICAL DELAY LINE: a storage device in which acoustical pulses representing binary information are transmitted by means of elastic deformation of the delay line medium (quartz crystal, mercury, or magnetostrictive material); transmission through the medium delays a pulse, permitting circulation of a pulse train by connecting (through an amplifier and signal gate) the delay line output to its input.

ADDER: device (circuitry) producing the sum of two or more numbers delivered to it. *See* half adder *and* full adder.

ADDRESS: a label, usually numerical, that identifies a location in a storage or memory device.

ADDRESS LOGIC: the body of expressions defining the relationships and operations involved, by which a given computer keeps track of the addresses in which needed operands and subsequent instructions are to be found.

ALGORITHMS: procedures used by individuals or machines to solve problems by trying all possible alternatives. Algorithms necessarily lead to a solution, if one is possible, even though this solution may take years to accomplish. *See* heuristics.

ANALOG: a physical, mechanical, or electrical model (used for computation by analogous representation) corresponding in some respect to the original object or concept, with or upon which measurements or calculations are to be performed.

ANALOG COMPUTER: a computer using physically measurable variables (e.g., voltage, angular rotation, length) for calculating.

ANALYTIC ENGINE: a mechanical computing device designed by Charles Babbage (1792–1871); included provision for iterative loops and program transfers; never constructed.

"AND" GATE OR "AND" CIRCUIT: a circuit presenting an output if and only if every input is properly energized; performs the function of the logical "and." *See* "or" gate.

ARITHMETIC INSTRUCTION: a machine word or set of characters directing a computer to perform an arithmetic operation.

ARITHMETIC UNIT: that part of a computer performing arithmetic and logical operations.

AUTOMATIC PROGRAMING: any technique for equipping a computer to accept programs in languages other than machine language and to convert such programs automatically into machine language instructions. *See* compiler.

B

BAND: a group of recording tracks on a magnetic drum or disc.

BASE: any digit or number on which a number system is based (in the decimal system, ten; in the binary number system, two, etc.); the radix.

BINARY: involving two (digits, states, etc.).

BINARY-CODED DECIMAL (BCD): systems of representing decimal numbers as combinations of (usually) four binary digits (bits).

BINARY NUMBER SYSTEM: number system containing only two digits, based on powers of 2.

BIQUINARY: involving two and five; a system of notation representing a mixed base but utilizing binary digits.

BIT: binary digit; a one (1) or a zero (0), or the electrical, mechanical magnetic, or chemical representation of either in an automatic computer.

BLOCK: a group of machine words considered or transferred as a unit.

BOOLEAN ALGEBRA: a system of symbolic logic; an algebra of classes, propositions, on-off circuit elements, etc., associated by operators "and," "or," "not," "except," "if—then," etc.

BUFFER: device or technique for matching (usually) rate of information flow among computer system elements.

C

CATHODE RAY TUBE: a vacuum tube in which electrons emitted by a hot cathode are formed into a narrow beam or pencil and accelerated at high velocity toward a specially prepared screen which fluoresces at the point where the electrons strike; provides visual display of electronic signal information; can be used as a computer storage device. *See* electrostatic storage.

CHANNEL: a path along which information flows. In storage that is serial by character and parallel by bit (e.g., a magnetic tape or drum in some coded-decimal computers), a channel comprises several parallel tracks. In a circulating storage, a channel is one recirculating path containing a fixed number of words stored serially by word.

CHARACTER: any symbol, such as a number or a letter, or its machine representation that may be stored by, or used in, computer operations.

CIRCULATING MEMORY or REGISTER: a circuit in which a pulse train can be stored by circulation in a loop; volatile (information is lost when power is removed).

CLOCK: a primary source (pulse generator) for synchronizing signals in a computer; a reference pulse occurring at a specified rate, for synchronizing circuit operations in a digital computer.

CODE: a system for representing information and rules for representation; to prepare a set of instructions in computer language for a specific computer.

CODING: the act of preparing in code a list of instructions for successive computer operations required to solve a specific problem.

COMMAND: any coded representation to which computer circuits respond by executing a logical or arithmetic operation; also called the operation part of an instruction.

COMPILER: a program equipping the computer, for which it was designed, to accept programs in a problem-oriented language and to transform them into machine language instructions.

COMPUTER: any machine capable of performing numerical and logical manipulations; an automatic computer is one which performs sequences of operations on the basis of wired or initially stored instructions. *See also* analog computer, digital computer, *and* special-purpose computer.

COMPUTER-ORIENTED LANGUAGE: a language that conveniently expresses the operations of a particular computer or a class of computers. *See* machine language *and* problem-oriented language.

CONDITIONAL BRANCH, JUMP, or TRANSFER: an instruction specifying the condition under which the machine should deviate from the principal order of instruction execution in order to branch into an alternate order.

CONTINUOUS FUNCTION COMPUTER: analog computer; a computer forming required outputs on the basis of continuous input functions, as contrasted to digital computers, which require and operate on discrete digits.

CONTROL UNIT: that portion of the hardware of an automatic digital computer which directs the sequence of operations, interprets the coded instructions, and initiates the proper signals to the computer circuits to execute the instructions.

CORE MEMORY: a device for storage of information in a computer, each bit being stored as magnetic orientation of a ferromagnetic toroid. *See* magnetic core storage.

COUNTER: a circuit or device that can be incremented or decremented or reset to zero.

CYBERNETICS: studies comparing the performance of the nervous systems of man and animals to the control and communications functions of information-handling machines.

D

DATA WORD: an ordered set of characters which has at least one meaning and is stored and transferred by the computer circuits as a unit.

DEBUG: to isolate and remove malfunctions from a computer or mistakes from a program.

DECODE: to convert data from machine form into readable characters; to ascertain the intended meaning of the individual characters or group of characters in the pseudo-coded program.

DELAY LINE: device for producing a time delay of a signal. *See* acoustical delay line.

DELAY-LINE STORAGE: storage or memory device that consists of a delay line and the means for regenerating and reinserting information into the delay line.

DESTRUCTIVE READOUT: method of detecting the condition (generally binary) of a device used for information storage in an automatic computer, detection destroys the information.

DIFFERENCE ENGINE: a mechanical digital computer designed by Charles Babbage (1792–1871).

DIFFERENTIAL ANALYZER: an analog computer designed and used primarily for solving or "analyzing" differential equations.

DIGITAL: the quality of using numbers expressed in digits and in a scale of notation.

DIGITAL COMPUTER: a computer that performs mathematical operations with information, numerical or otherwise, represented in digital form.

DRUM MEMORY: a storage device in which information is stored in tracks and bands on the magnetic surface of a (usually) rotating drum. *See* magnetic drum.

DYNAMIC MEMORY or STORAGE: storage in which information circulates and is not randomly accessible, as in acoustic delay lines, magnetic drum, and circulating registers.

E

ELECTROMAGNETIC COMPUTER: a computer using relays, and electrical and mechanical devices, as the Mark I (Automatic Sequence Controlled Calculator).

ELECTRONIC COMPUTER: a computer which operates mainly by means of electronic devices (devices dealing with the motion, emission and behavior of currents of the electrons, particularly in vacuum tubes, gas or phototubes, and special conductors or semiconductors).

ELECTROSTATIC STORAGE: techniques and devices storing information as static (but changeable) charges, as on the screen of a cathode ray tube.

EXECUTE: phase of instruction processing in which the specified operation is performed on data obtained in fetch phase.

EXECUTIVE PROGRAM: a routine designed to process and to control other routines.

F

FEEDBACK: transmission of a fraction of the output of a machine, system, or process to the input, to which the fraction is added or subtracted. This procedure can result in self-correction and control of the process.

FETCH: phase of instruction processing during which required data are obtained for manipulation (and, sometimes, next instruction is transferred from storage to the instruction register).

FIXED POINT NOTATION: a system of representing all quantities (in a given computer or mode of computer operation) by the same number of digits, with the location of the radix point fixed. *See also* floating point notation.

FLOATING POINT NOTATION: a system of representing all quantities (in a given computer or mode of computer operation) by a fractional mantissa and an exponent to which the base is raised to determine the actual radix point location. *See also* fixed point notation.

FORTRAN: problem-oriented (mathematical) language and compilers for IBM 700-series computers; term coined from *formula translation*.

FOUR-ADDRESS INSTRUCTION: instruction specifying the operation and the addresses of four memory locations (in which may be stored three operands and the next instruction).

FLYBALL GOVERNOR: a mechanical speed control device based on the principle of centrifugal force, used in a wide variety of engines.

FULL ADDER: circuit accepting signals representing two digits to be added plus a signal representing a digit carried from next lower order stage, and producing full binary sum and carried digit. *See* half adder.

G

GATE: a circuit, the output of which is energized when and only when certain combinations of pulses appear at the input(s).

GENERAL-PURPOSE COMPUTER: a computer designed to solve a wide variety of problems whose exact nature may *not* be known before the machine is designed; contrasted with "special-purpose computer."

GENERATOR PROGRAM: program equipping a computer to generate machine language coding of programs written in a symbolic or problem-oriented language.

H

HALF ADDER: a circuit having two input channels and producing binary sum (and carried digit) outputs; does not accept carried digit from lower order stage. *See* full adder.

HARMONIC ANALYZER: a device for measuring the amplitude and phase of the various harmonic components of a periodic function.

HEURISTICS: techniques by means of which the individual (or machine) can be equipped to solve problems. If the heuristics are applicable, they will provide a short cut to the goal. However, heuristic methods cannot guarantee a solution and may lead to a blind alley. *See* algorithms.

HOLLERITH CODE: a system of punching holes in cards, to represent numerals and characters, for machine sorting and transfer of information into automatic computers; devised by Dr. H. Hollerith of the U.S. Census Bureau, *ca.* 1900.

I

INDEX REGISTER: a storage location used to retain numbers (increments) for modifying addresses; may be provided with automatic counting capability.

INHIBITOR CIRCUIT: a gate producing an output unless a given input (combination of input signals) appears; one whose output condition (produced by a particular input combination) inhibits subsequent signal transfer.

INPUT: information transferred into a circuit or device.

INPUT UNIT: the unit which takes into the computing system information from outside the system.

INSTRUCTION: a set of characters which defines an operation, together with one or more addresses (or no address), and which, as a unit, causes the computer to operate accordingly on the indicated operands.

INSTRUCTION CODE: an artificial language that expresses or describes instructions for a digital computer.

INTERNAL STORAGE: storage facilities forming an integral physical part of the computer and directly controlled by the computer; the total storage directly accessible to the computer.

J

JACQUARD TECHNIQUE: a technique devised by M. Jacquard to control, by means of punched cards, the pattern produced on a loom.

JUMP: an instruction which conditionally or unconditionally transfers or branches to the storage address specified. *See* transfer instruction.

L

LOGIC: generally, the science that deals with the principles and criteria of validity in thought and demonstration; specifically, the basic principles and applications of truth tables, the relations of propositions, the interconnection of on-off circuit elements, etc.; used to describe operation of a computer.

LOGICAL DESIGN: the symbolic statements describing design (interconnections) of computer circuits to produce required operation.

LOGICAL NET: circuitry interconnected to perform logical operations ("and," "or," and "not").

LOGIC OF MECHANISM (also MATHEMATICAL LOGIC): *See* logic.

M

MACHINE LANGUAGE: a vocabulary of "words" meaningful to a computer; strings of binary digits acceptable to and manipulatable by machine circuits; pulse trains setting and resetting computer circuits.

MAGNETIC CORE STORAGE: storage of binary information as magnetic orientation of a small ring of ferromagnetic material called a core; one core used for each bit in a register; random access to any addressable register; commonly, a single device stores between 8000 and 32,000 words.

MAGNETIC DISC STORAGE: storage of information on one or more discs having magnetizable surfaces and which rotate (on a common shaft); data accessible serially by bit on a single track or bit-parallel on several tracks (a band); commonly, a single device stores millions of words.

MAGNETIC DRUM: a rapidly rotating cylinder whose surface is coated with a magnetic material, on which information may be stored as discretely magnetized areas; registers arranged serially in tracks or in bands; commonly, a single device stores between 8000 and 250,000 words.

MAGNETIC READ-WRITE HEAD: a device for detecting (reading), recording, and erasing information in a magnetic storage medium; usually, a small electromagnet.

MAGNETIC TAPE: tape made of paper, metal, or plastic, coated or impregnated with magnetic material on which information may be stored as discretely magnetized areas.

MAGNETIC (THIN) FILM MEMORY: storage technique based on magnetic orientation of miniature deposits of ferromagnetic material on glass; characterized by extremly short access time (0.3 microsecond); commonly, a single device currently stores 128 words.

MARGINAL CHECKING: a system of testing circuits in a computer by varying certain operating parameters to detect tendencies toward malfunctions.

MATHEMATICAL MODEL: facsimile in mathematical terms; a body of mathematical statements describing a process, parameters, and their relationships to one another and to environments; useful for rigorously studying complex relationships, particularly with a computer.

MATRIX: in computer circuitry, a rectangular array forming a logical network of elements; usually functions as an encoder or a decoder.

MEMORY or STORAGE: any device into which units of information can be copied, which will hold this information and from which the information can be obtained at a later time.

MEMORY ACCESS TIME: a measure of time to communicate with a storage device; the time interval between the instant at which information is called for from storage and the instant at which delivery is completed, i.e., the read time. *See* access, speed of.

MODEL: a facsimile capturing the essence of one or more characteristics of the original, may be mathematical, physical, conceptual, etc. *See* mathematical model.

MULTIPLY TIME: the period in which a computer can perform a multiplication.

N

NAPIER'S BONES: a set of sticks or rods facilitating multiplication; arranged vertically on each stick are the products of one digit and each of ten digits of the decimal system.

NONVOLATILE MEMORY: any storage medium that retains information in the absence of power; e.g., magnetic tapes, drums, or cores.

O

OCTAL NUMBER SYSTEM (also OCTAL NOTATION): the scale of notation having the base 8; convenient in dealing with binary numbers because a group of three binary digits (beginning in digit position adjacent to the radix point) can be "read" as an octal digit (000 = 0; 001 = 1; 010 = 2; 011 = 3; 100 = 4; 101 = 5; 110 = 6; and 111 = 7).

OFF-LINE: equipment whose operation, while part of a computer system, is not under direct control of the computer; tasks performed by such equipment as in conversion of information on tape into card decks, etc. *See also* on-line.

ONE-ADDRESS (also SINGLE-ADDRESS) INSTRUCTION: an instruction consisting of an operation and exactly one address.

ONE-AND-ONE-HALF-ADDRESS INSTRUCTION: instruction specifying operation, address of one operand, and address of next instruction.

ON-LINE: equipment whose operation is under direct control of the computer; tasks performed under direct computer control. *See also* off-line.

OPERAND: a quantity entering into or arising from an operation.

OPERATION: the part of an instruction that usually designates the kind of task to be performed, but not the location of the operands. *See also* instruction code.

"OR" GATE OR "OR" CIRCUIT: a gate or circuit having the property that it produces an output when any (acceptable) input is available. *See* "and" gate.

OUTPUT: information transferred out of a circuit or device.

OUTPUT UNIT: the unit which delivers information outside the computer in a usable form.

P

PARALLEL COMPUTER: a computer in which all bits, or characters, or words are essentially equally accessible for manipulation; or in which arithmetic is performed on all digits in parallel (rather than serially on digits of successively higher powers).

PARITY: a method for increasing the code representation (pulse pattern) of a character handled by and stored in a computer in a manner that facilitates checking the accuracy of character transfers and, in some cases, correcting errors created during transfer.

PROBLEM ANALYSIS: in computer programing, precisely formulating a problem, defining the scope of investigation, stating hypotheses, and establishing statistical techniques.

PROBLEM-ORIENTED LANGUAGE: an artificial language (vocabulary and rules) conveniently expressing relationships of a particular problem or class of problems and the solution method. *See also* symbolic language, computer-oriented language, *and* machine language.

PROGRAM: a set of instructions arranged in proper sequence to cause a computer to perform a desired set of operations.

PROGRAM COUNTER (also SEQUENCE REGISTER): a device in which is recorded the name or number of the storage location of the instruction to be executed following that in process.

PROGRAMING: the procedures contributing to development of a set of instructions for computer solution of a problem; includes problem analysis, program design, coding, and testing.

PUNCHED CARDS: (80- or 90-column) a card of constant size and shape designed for punching holes in meaningful patterns; can be used for storing data, and can be handled mechanically. The punched holes are usually sensed electrically by wire brushes, mechanically by metal fingers, or photo-electrically by photocells.

PUNCHED PAPER TAPE: paper or plastic tape perforated in character groups (cells) along length; for introducing information into and for output from an automatic computing system.

R

RANDOM ACCESS: storage characteristic in which the time required to access the next position from which information is to be obtained is in no way dependent on the position last accessed.

READ: to sense the information contained in patterns of holes punched into cards or tape, or of magnetized areas on discs, drums, and tapes, etc. *See also* write.

REAL-TIME OPERATION: operation in which an event is controlled by information generated by the event. The finite time involved in processing may be compensated by extrapolating and cyclically correcting as the conditions being measured change.

REGISTER: a device that stores information, often one subset (such as a word) of the total information in a digital computer. *See also* storage.

ROUTINE (also PROGRAM or SUBPROGRAM): a set of coded instructions arranged in proper sequence to direct a computer to perform a desired operation or series of operations.

S

SAGE: acronym standing for Semi-Automatic Ground Environment; a comprehensive electronic data processing system used in air defense.

SEQUENCE REGISTER: register containing name or number of location in which is stored the next instruction to be executed. In a one-address machine, this is a counter incremented by one as the present instruction is fetched for execution. Branch instructions can change the contents of the register if the test specified for branching is passed.

SERIAL COMPUTER: a computer which reads out of or writes into storage one bit at a time, performing arithmetic serially on successively higher power positions in numbers.

SERVOMECHANISM: a system, usually combining electronic, electric, and mechanical elements, in which feedback is used to maintain constant performance of the system.

SIMULATION: representation of necessary elements of some object, phenomena, system, or environment facilitating control and study (often by or involving an automatic computer).

SIMULATOR: a computer or model which represents a system or phenomenon and which mirrors or maps the effects of various changes in the original, enabling the researcher to study, analyze, and understand the original by means of the behavior of the model; specifically, a program enabling one computer to simulate another—e.g., to permit design of operational programs for a computer not yet constructed.

SINGLE-ADDRESS INSTRUCTION: *See* one-address instruction.

SOLID-STATE COMPUTER: a computer which uses the magnetic, electric, and other properties of solid materials—e.g., magnetic cores, transistors, magnetic amplifiers, crystal diodes—as opposed to vacuum or gaseous devices as tubes.

SPECIAL-PURPOSE COMPUTER: a computer designed to solve a restricted class of problems—for example, aiming a large telescope in an astronomical observatory, controlling petroleum processing in an oil refinery, navigating an aircraft.

STATIC STORAGE: storage in which information is fixed in space, as a flip-flop or magnetic core.

STORAGE (also MEMORY or STORE): any device used to store information. *See* memory, magnetic disc storage, ultrasonic delay line, drum memory, magnetic core storage, magnetic film memory.

STORAGE CAPACITY: the amount of information that the principal internal storage, or memory, device of a computer can retain; often measured in the number of words that can be retained, given the number of digits and the base of the standard word; customarily expressed in *bits* when comparisons among devices are made.

SUBROUTINE: a subunit of a routine; a short or repeated sequence of instructions; often written in relative or symbolic coding even when the routine to which it belongs is not.

SYMBOLIC LANGUAGE: (in computers) a special language convenient for the programer in preparing computer instructions; converted (one-to-one) by the assembly program into machine language. *See also* problem-oriented language *and* machine language.

T

THREE-ADDRESS INSTRUCTION: an instruction that includes an operation and specifies the location of three registers: two operands and a location for the result of the operation; or two operands and the location of the next instruction; or one operand, the location for the result, and the location of the next instruction.

TIME-SHARING: technique allowing execution of two or more functions essentially at the same time, by allocating (in rotation, for instance) small divisions of the total time for the performance of each function.

TRANSFER INSTRUCTION: a set of characters interpreted by a computer as a direction to "transfer" or branch or jump to a specified location; also a direction to transfer (blocks of) data between memory and external storage.

TRANSLATOR PROGRAM: equips a computer to accept a program *not* in machine language and transform it into the machine language used by it or by another computer.

TWO-ADDRESS INSTRUCTION: an instruction specifying an operation and the location of two registers.

U

ULTRASONIC DELAY LINE: a device capable of transmitting retarded sound pulses, the transmission of which is accomplished by wave patterns of elastic deformation. *See* acoustic delay line.

V

VOLATILE MEMORY: storage in which information vanishes when power is removed, as in mercury delay-line memory, electrostatic storage tubes.

W

WIRE MATRIX PRINTER: an output mechanism which prints by transferring an image corresponding to the pattern of wires energized in a matrix (usually 5 wires in horizontal and 7 in vertical dimensions; one matrix per character in a line, often 120 per line).

WORD FORMAT: the specified arrangement of digits, characters, fields, lines, etc. in a meaningful coded set.

WRITE: to introduce information, usually into some form of storage. *See also* read.

Glossary prepared by Louise Schultz. Appeared first in *Computer Applications in the Behavioral Sciences,* edited by Harold Borko. ©1962 by System Development Corporation, Santa Monica, California.

INDEX

Abacus, the, 20, 21
Abt, Clark C., 222, 223
Adams, J. B., 121
Addition, 46–50
Aiken, H. H., 23
Aiker, Hayward, 157
ALGOL, 32, 67
Allen, L. F., 144
Allport, G. W., 128
Almond, G. A., 117
Alphabetic characters,
        recognition of, 61–62
American Illustrated, 124
Analog computer, 21–22
AND blocks, 35, 39, 40, 42, 48
Angell, R. C., 130
Annual Register of World Events, The, 155
Aronson, E., 132
Artificial intelligence, 246–252
    future applications to, 249–251
    heuristic programming, approach
        to, 246–251
Assembly language, 32, 62–64
Atomic Energy Commission, 316
Authorship, disputed, 134–135

Babbage, Charles, 22–23, 25
Banks, Arthur, 159
Batch monitors, 69
Batlin, R., 120
Bauer, R. A., 135
Bell-shaped curve, 255
Bell Telephone System, 73
Berelson, B. 119, 128, 136, 138, 146
Berry, Brian J. L., 169
Biased random walk, 267–268
Binary adder, 35
Bisco, Ralph L., 5, 9
Black Boy (Wright), 113
Bliss, Chester I., 159

Blocks, logic 35–55
    AND, 35, 39, 40, 42, 48
    DELAY, 35
    NOT, 35, 39
    OR, 35, 39, 40
Blumberg, N. B., 120
Blumenstock, Dorothy, 123
Bobrow, Davis B., 316
BOLD, 349
Boolean algebra, 39
Borko, Harold, 316
Branching, 161
Breed, W., 120
Brewer, T. L., 141
Brody, R. A., 125
Broom, L., 120
Brown, W. B., 117, 124
Browning, Rufus P., 16
Bruner, J. S., 124
Brush, Steven, 254
Buffon needle problem, 258
Bynation analysis, 181

Calculators, 21
Carnegie Endowment for
        International Peace, 316
Carstenson, F. W., 139
Carter, Launor, 316, 347–349
Carter, R. E., Jr., 120
Cathode ray tubes (CRT),
        28, 31, 274–280, 292–294
Cattell, Raymond, 169
CDC 6800, 348
Center for Management Sciences, 347
Change, 8–9
Churchman, C. West, 316, 347,
        349–350, 353–354
COBOL, 32, 67–69
Colby, Kenneth Mark, 11
Color separation, logical, 284
Combinatorial logic, 35–39
Common sense, 307–308
Communication:
    assessing responses to, 136–137
    auditing content against standards,
        122–123
    basic elements of, 115
    describing patterns of, 125

Communication (cont.):
effects of, 135–137
trends in content of, 117–119
Compiler languages, 32, 64-65
Complexity, 7-8
Computer time, 281
Computers:
analog, 21-22
as autonomous social forces, 2
Babbage, 22-23, 25
classified by cost, 33-34
content analysis, 137-146
general implications of, 145-146
General Inquirer system, 139-144
word count programs, 138-139
glossary of terms, 356-367
history of, 20-23
in international relations, 1-19
abundant information, 9-10
change, 8-9
complexity, 7-8
correct descriptions, 4
data analysis, 14-15
desirability, 12
feasibility, 10-11
information management, 13-14
intellectual efficiency, 6-7
misuse of data, 11-12
modeling, 15-16
organization of the volume, 16-17
powerful explanations, 4-5
simulation, 15-16
skills, 12-13
valid predictions, 5-6
value optimizations, 6
organization, 23-24
as personal threats, 2
social utility of, 347-355
speed, 34
words, kinds of in use, 26
Content analysis, 111-153
antecedents of messages, 126-135
communication, effects of, 135-137
computer, 137-146
general implications of, 145-146
General Inquirer system, 139-144
word count programs, 138-139
defined, 112

Content analysis (cont.):
documents, characteristics
of, 115-125
generality, 112
objectivity, 112
research designs, 115
system, 112
when to use, 112-114
Control Data Corporation, 33
Correlation matrix, 159
Counting, 20-21
notations used, 21
Crookes, W., 274
Culture, 131-133

Dalkey, N. C., 316
Danielson, W. A., 121
Data:
analysis, 14-15, 142-144, 323-324
comparison, 159
dependencies, 159
interdependencies, 160
preparation, 142
processing, graphic, 272-306
equipment, 274-282
future considerations, 301-302
input, 294-301
programming, 282-294
retrieval, 73
screening, 158-159
three types of, 348
De Charms, R., 113, 133
De Grazia, S., 128
Deadline Data on World Affairs, 155
Decisions seminars, 308-314
Decker, J. B., 139
Decoding, 44-45
Definition statements, 64
DELAY blocks, 35
DELAY box, 39-43
Delayed J-K flip-flop, 35
Democratic ignorance, principle of, 268
Demographic Yearbook, 154
Descriptions, correct, 4
Descriptors, 76
Deutsch, Karl W., 159, 233
Dibble, V. K., 113

Dictionaries, 138-142
Diebold, John, 9, 14
Dimensionality of Nations Project
    (DON), 158, 162
Direct table program, 143
Directions of International Trade, 154
Disks, 30-31
Document(s):
    characteristics of:
        analyzing style, 125
        auditing communication
            content, 122-123
        patterns of communication, 125
        persuasion techniques, 123-125
        relating attributes of sources,
            119-122
        trends in communication
            content, 117-119
    retrieval, 73-74
    from a single source, 117
    of two or more sources, 117
Douring, Karin, 124
Drums, 30-31
Dyadic analysis, 181
Dynamism, external, 235, 237

Earth's atmosphere, simulation
    of, 215-221
Eckert, J. P., 23
Eckstein, Alexander, 159
Ellison, J. W., 135
ENIAC, 23
Error distribution function, 255
Event technique, 206
Expected value approach, 207
Explanations, powerful, 4-5
External dynamism, 235, 237

Facts on File, 155
Feasibility, 10-11
Federalist Papers, The, 134
Feigenbaum, Edward A., 316
Feldman, Julian, 316
Fermi, Enrico, 254
Fernback, S., 316

Flip-flop, 39-42
    J-K, 48
    delayed, 35
    R-S, 40
    registers, 44, 50
Floating-point representation, 27
FORTRAN, 32, 65-66, 69, 235
Foster, H. S., 136
Friedman, G. A., 132, 133

Gamov, George, 264
Garver, R. A., 124
Gate, 35
Gaussian distribution, 255-256
General Inquirer system, 139-144
Generalization, 112
    in international relations
        simulation, 230-232
Generator, timing, 35, 51
George, A. L., 127, 128
Gerard, R. W., 316, 347, 352-353
Gerbner, G., 119, 120
Glaser, William A., 5
Glossary of terms, 356-367
Glyph, 283
Gorden, Morton, 316
Gorsuch, Richard L., 169
Graphic data processing, 272-306
    equipment, 274-282
    future considerations, 301-302
    input, 294-301
    programming, 282-294
Greenberger, Martin, 316
Gruenberger, Fred J., 2-3
Guetzkow, Harold, 158, 238
Gullahorn, Jeanne E., 15
Gullahorn, John T., 15

Hamilton, Alexander, 134
Hand counter, 21
Harway, N. I., 139
Hertz, H., 274
Heuristic programming approach to
    artificial intelligence, 246-251
Hittorf, W., 274
Hodder, James C., 222

Hollerith, H., 27
Holsti, O. R., 113, 114, 117, 130, 131, 141, 142, 316
Hopmann, P. T., 113, 141
Howerton, W., 316
Hunt, E. B., 144

IBM cards, 145-146
IBM Corporation, 23, 65
IBM 360, 25, 33, 156
IBM 360/40, 348
IBM 360/67, 348
IBM 650, 156
IBM 709, 156
IBM 1401, 33, 76
IBM 7030, 76
IBM 7044, 213
IBM 7070, 33
IBM 7080, 33
IBM 7090, 33
IBM 7094, 28, 33, 156
Iker, H. P., 139
Importance sampling, 263
Income of Nations (Studensky), 155
Indexes:
    author, 78
    multicoordinate, 76, 78
Individual traits, 128-131
Industrial College of the Armed
        Forces, 223
Information:
    abundant, 9-10
    defined, 71
    flow of, 136
    management, 13-14
    retrieval, 71-80, 322
        applications, 77-80
    system, 71
Inkeles, A., 113, 137
Input, graphic, 294-301
Input-output instructions, 27-28
Intellectual efficiency, 6-7
Intelligence:
    artificial, in international relations,
        246-252
        future applications to, 249-251

Intelligence, artificial in interna-
        tional relations (cont.) :
    heuristic programming approach
        to, 246-251
    defined, 246-247
    political, 127-128
International relations, 1-19
    artificial intelligence in, 246-252
        future applications to, 249-251
        heuristic programming approach
            to, 246-251
    computers in, 1-19
        abundant information, 9-10
        change, 8-9
        complexity, 7-8
        correct descriptions, 4
        data analysis, 14-15
        desirability, 12
        feasibility, 10-11
        information management, 13-14
        intellectual efficiency, 6-7
        misuse of data, 11-12
        modeling, 15-16
        organization of the volume, 16-17
        powerful explanations, 4-5
        simulation, 15-16
        skills, 12-13
        valid predictions, 5-6
        value optimizations, 6
    educational experiment in, 315-346
        evaluation methods, 317-318
        opinions before and after,
            319-340
        reactions to the program, 340-345
    objectives, 4-7
    patterns, 154-202
        applications, 162-191
        list of characteristics, 196-202
        research revolution, 154-158
        role of the computer, 158-162
    simulation of, 222-243
        the designer, 242-243
        designing a dynamic, 232-234
        level of generalization, 230-232
        programmer problems, 239-241
        quantification of aggregated
            concepts, 234-237
        selectiveness, 225-230
        space, 225-230

Intelligence, simulation of (cont.) :
   time, 225-230
   tuning, 237-239
Interval technique, 206
Interviews, 81-109

Jackson, H. A., 139
Jacquard, Joseph Marie, 22, 27
Jaffray, George, 2-3
Janda, Kenneth, 316
J-K flip-flop, 48
  delayed, 35
JOHNIAC, 348
Jones, R. R., 121
Joyce, James, 135

Kahn, Herman, 254
Kaplan, A., 146
Kayser, J., 121
Kelvin, Lord, 254
King, Gil, 349
Klapper, J., 135
Klein, M. W., 113, 120
Knepprath, H. E., 125
Knight, Kenneth E., 2
Kobre, S., 113, 120
Krider, Leroy, 316
Kuo Mo Jo, 143
KWIC index, 74

Langevin, R. A., 144
Languages, 32-33, 56-70, 212, 235
  ALGOL, 32, 67
  alphabetic character recognition, 61-62
  assembly, 32, 62-64
  COBOL, 32, 67-69
  compilers, 32, 64-65
  control routines, 69-70
  FORTRAN, 32, 65-66, 69, 235
  machine, 32
  problem preparation, 56-61
  specialized, 70
LARC, 25, 26
Lasswell, H. D., 114, 115, 117-118, 119,
   123, 127, 138, 316
Latch, 39

Lattice, 275
Lawrence Radiation Laboratory, 25,
   254, 316
Lazarsfeld, P. F., 120
Lee, Robert S., 2
Legal evidence, 133-134
Leites, N. D., 119
Leith, Cecil, 316
Lerner, D., 117-118
Lewin, H. S., 112, 122, 123, 133
Libraries, 348-349
Library of Congress, 349
Logic, 35-55
  addition, 46-50
  boxes, 35
  combinatorial, 35-39
  delay, 39-43 45
  primitives, 35
  system, 50-55
  use of, 10-13
Logic blocks, 35-55
  AND, 35, 39, 40, 42, 48
  DELAY, 35
  NOT, 35, 39
  OR, 35, 39, 40
Logical color separation, 284
Los Alamos Laboratory, 254

Maccoby, N., 113, 120
Madison, James, 134
Magnetic core, 28
Magnetic core storage, 30-31
Magnetic tapes, 29-30
Manne, Alan, 316
Markham, J. W., 120
Massachusetts Institute of
   Technology, 2, 347, 349
Matthews, B. C., 122
Mauchly, J. W., 23
McClelland, D. C., 113, 131, 132, 133
McEvoy, J., 121
McGranahan, D. V., 132, 133
Measurement of Meaning (Osgood), 155
Memory, 23-31
  defined, 25
  location, 26
  speed, 29

Menzel, Herbert, 317
Merton, R. K., 125
Messages:
  antecedents of, 126-135
    culture, 131-133
    disputed authorship, 134-135
    legal evidence, 133-134
    military intelligence, 127-128
    political intelligence, 127-128
    traits of individuals, 128-131
  attributes of, 115, 119-122
Metropolis, Nicholas, 254
Michael, G. A., 316
Michaelson, A. A., 254
Military intelligence, 127-128
Miller, George, A., 14
Miller, John A., 2
Milstein, Jane, 318
Modeling, 15-16
Moeller, G. H., 113, 133
Monte Carlo method, 207-209, 253-271
  advantages of, 208
  biased random walk, 267-268
  history of, 254-255
  many-dimensional, 264-267
  results of probability theory,
    255-256
Morley, E. W., 254
Morton, A. Q., 134-135
Mosteller, F., 113
Multicoordinate index, 76, 78

Namenwirth, J. Z., 117
National profile delineation, 154-202
  applications, 162-191
  list of characteristics, 196-202
  research revolution, 154-158
  role of the computer, 158-162
National Science Foundation, 162
Neisser, Ulric, 2
Nelson, C. J., 117
New York Times, The, 177
"Nineteenth Century Clouds Over the
    Dynamical Theory of Heat
    and Light" (Kelvin), 254
Nixon, R. B., 121
North, R. C., 126, 130, 131

Northwestern Simulated International
    Processes Project, 158
Northwestern University, 238
NOT blocks, 35, 39
Numbers:
  misuse of, 11-12
  pseudo-random, 258

Objectivity, 112
One two three Infinity (Gamov), 264
OR blocks, 35, 39, 40
Osgood, Charles E., 126, 140, 155, 317
Output tapes, 31-32
Owens, M., 144

Paisley, William J., 114, 318
Parrish, S. M., 139
Pascal, Blaise, 21
Pauline Epistles, 134-135
Peace Research Institute, 157
Pelley, William Dudley, 133
Perrin, J., 274
Persuasion, techniques of, 124-125
Peterson, R. L., 141
PEWBSARD, 311
Platt, John, 7
Political intelligence, 127-128
Political research, content analysis in,
    111-153
    antecedents of messages, 126-135
    communication, effects of, 135-137
    computer, 137-146
    documents, characteristics of, 115-125
    generality, 112
    objectivity, 112
    research designs, 115
    system, 112
    when to use, 112-114
Pool, Ithiel de Sola, 6, 16, 117-118, 119,
    126, 128, 316, 347, 350-352,
    354-355
Portrait of the Artist as a Young Man
    (Joyce), 135
Predictions, valid, 5-6
Probability theory, 255-256
Problem time, 281

Programming:
    graphic data processing, 282-284
    simulation in international
        relations, 239-241
Project INTREX, 349
Protho, J. W., 112, 117, 136
Pseudo-operations, 64
Pseudo-random numbers, 258

RAND Corporation, 213
Random, 257
Random walk, biased, 267-268
Raster, 276
Raytheon Company, 223
Real time, 281
Reece, Shirley, 120
Reference retrieval, 73, 74
Register, 35, 44
    flip-flop, 44, 50
Revolution and Development of Inter-
    national Relations (RADIR),
    118
Richardson, O. W., 216, 217
R-S flip-flop, 40
Rummel, R. J., 316
Runion, H. L., 125
Russell, J. T., 117
Russett, Bruce M., 155, 157, 158, 169

Sahlin, Harry, 316
SAINT, 348
Sampling:
    biased random, 263
    importance, 263
Scanning, 296
Schneidman, E. S., 129
Schnore, L. F., 169
Schramm, W., 121
Scientific American, 258
Sebald, H., 112, 122, 133
Sebeok, T. A., 139
Selectivity in international relations
    simulation, 225-230
Serial machine, 34
Shift operation, 27

Simulacrum, 204
Simulation, 15-16, 160, 203-214, 320-321
    chance in, 207
    of the Earth's atmosphere, 215-221
    getting into a computer, 204-205
    and international relations, 222-234
        the designer, 242-243
        designing a dynamic, 232-234
        level of generalization, 230-232
        programmer problems, 239-241
        quantification of aggregated
            concepts, 234-237
        selectiveness, 225-230
        space, 225-230
        time, 225-230
        tuning, 237-239
    mathematical characteristics of, 209
    rationale, 204
Simulmatics Corporation, 238
Slagle, James, 316
Slide rules, 21
Smith, M. S., 140
Social utility of computers, 347-355
Space in international relations
    simulation, 225-230
Speed, J. G., 122
Stanford Studies in Conflict and
    Integration, 157-158
Starkweather, J. A., 139
Statements, misuse of, 11-12
Statistical Yearbook, The, 154
Stempel, G. H., 120
Stolz, W. S., 139
Stone, Phillip J., 139, 140, 142, 155
Studensky, Paul, 155
Style, analyzing, 125
Suci, George J., 317
System, 50-55, 112
Systems Development Corporation,
    347, 349

Tannenbaum, Percy H., 317
Tape(s):
    drive, 30
    magnetic, 29-30
    output, 31-32

Tape (s) (cont.) :
  putting information on, 31
  reels, 30
TEMPER computer simulation, 222-243
  the designer, 242-243
  designing a dynamic, 232-234
  level of generalization, 230-232
  programmer problems, 239-241
  quantification of aggregated
      concepts, 234-237
  selectiveness, 225-230
  space, 225-230
  time, 225-230
  tuning, 237-239
Textor, Robert, 159
Theme codes, 142-143
Thomson, J. J., 274
Time:
  computer, 281
  in international relations simulation,
      225-230
  problem, 281
  real, 281
Timing generator, 35, 51
Traits of individuals, 128-131
Tuning in international relations
      simulation, 237-239

Ulam, S., 254
Ulysses (Joyce), 135
Unconditional transfer, 26
United Nations Yearbook, 155
UNIVAC, 23, 24, 26, 28, 34, 302
University of California, 347
University of Hawaii, 158
University of Michigan, 157
USSR, 124

Vacuum tubes, 24, 29
Value optimizations, 6
Von Neumann, John, 216, 254

Wallace, D. L., 113
War games, 203-214
Wayne, I., 132, 133
Weinland, R. G., 141
White, R. K., 113, 124
Whiting, A. S., 114
Wilcox, W., 121
Willoughby, W. F., 121
Word count programs, 138-139
Word of information, 25
Words:
  address of, 26
  cluster of, 142
  definition of, 58
  kinds of, 26
World Commerce and Government:
      Trends and Outlook
      (Woytinsky and Woytinsky), 155
World Handbook of Political and Social
      Indicators (Russett), 155
Worldmark Encyclopedia of Nations, 155
Woytinsky, E. S., 155
Woytinsky, W. S., 155
Wright, Q., 117
Wright, Richard, 113
Wyman, Robert H., Jr., 316

Yakobson, S., 119
Yale Political Data Program, 158
Yale University, 157
Yearbook of International Organizations,
      155
Yearbook of National Account
      Statistics, 154
Yule, G. U., 114

Zaininovich, M. G., 131
Zeps, V. J., 139
Zero, 21
  invention of, 20
Zinnes, Dina A., 130

54833   JX
                                         1291
                                         C56

COMPUTERS AND THE POLICY-
    MAKING COMMUNITY.